Experience JESUS in the GOSPEL of LUKE

Dennis McCallum

Cover design by Taylor Hicks

New Paradigm Publishing

NEW PARADIGM

Contents

EXPERIENCE JESUS IN THE GOSPEL OF LUKE

Introduction to Luke

Lying in third position in our canon the of New Testament is the majestic book of Luke. It's the largest book in the New Testament by word count, and contains some of our most treasured accounts of Jesus found nowhere else.

Luke's Prologue

Luke includes an introduction to his book containing important information.

> Inasmuch as many have undertaken to compile an account of the things accomplished among us, just as they were handed down to us by those who from the beginning were eyewitnesses and servants of the word, it seemed fitting for me as well, having investigated everything carefully from the beginning, to write it out for you in consecutive order, most excellent Theophilus; so that you may know the exact truth about the things you have been taught. (Luke 1:1-4)

First we notice that this introduction ties in directly to the introduction to the book of Acts. Both are addressed to the same man, "Most excellent Theophilus," and in Acts he refers to "the first account I composed," which he said was about the life of Jesus. Luke and Acts both are written in elegant Greek, clearly from the same hand.

The title "most excellent" suggests the recipient was an upper-class Greek or Roman. Many readers are intrigued by the suggestion that Theophilus could have been Paul's attorney for his trial before Caesar in about AD 62. That proposition makes total sense when studying Acts. It's less evident in Luke, but still there. For example, Luke carefully explains why Herod killed John the Baptist—not for any crime, but because of a frivolous, drunken act of lust. He is the most careful gospel writer to stress that Pilate believed Jesus was innocent, and only executed him because of crowd pressure. And we will see several other examples of narratives that would serve this purpose.

Theophilus could have been a wealthy believer who sponsored the writing of Luke-Acts and paid for all expenses including the labor to produce the manuscript.

Luke was definitely written before Acts, because in his introduction to Acts, he refers to "my earlier account" about Jesus. That means Luke was written before AD 62 when Acts was completed. Those scholars who try to date Luke to AD 90 or later are mostly naturalistic theologians who have no category for Jesus knowing the future. He predicted the destruction of Jerusalem and the temple in chapter 21. Therefore, liberal interpreters reason, the book must have been written later than AD 70 when those events occurred.

The apostle Paul traveled with Luke and was his close friend. We have excellent reasons to think that Paul and Luke worked together to write the book of Acts. And, because Acts and Luke are directly linked, we can safely assume that Paul also worked with Luke to write this book.

Paul is the apostolic authority for the book of Luke. But Paul was not a witness of Jesus' life. If he had ever met Jesus before his own conversion he certainly would have mentioned that. Instead, he got his information from direct visions of Jesus, and from others who were eyewitnesses.

The early church fathers all agreed that "Luke the physician" (Colossians

4:14) was the author. They never suggested any other author. We accept that the author is Luke, and he was being overseen by the apostle Paul.[1]

Luke's Sources—Not Oral Tradition

Everyone agrees that Luke had at hand a copy of the gospel of Mark. Eighty-eight percent of Mark is also found in Luke. Some believe he had another written source called the "Q document." Q source material is found in both Luke and Matthew, but not in Mark. It's possible that such a source existed, but also it's clear that Luke had additional sources. Substantial material is found only in Luke.

Many scholars say Luke's other sources were oral traditions passed down for decades. But that's not what Luke says. He says, "Many have undertaken to compile an account of the things accomplished among us" (1:1). This statement means that Luke knew of many *written* accounts. The expression, "to compile an account," is not referring to oral tradition. Instead, the early believers probably had dozens of short written accounts of things Jesus said, or did. The word "many" here could hardly refer to only three or four sources.

The most likely repository for most of these documents would have been the homes of believers living in Jerusalem. They had the means, the opportunity, and the motive to get things written down quickly after Jesus' ascension, when memories were fresh. They would be debriefing those "who from the beginning were eyewitnesses" of Jesus' life just as Luke says.

The fact that the accounts "were handed down to us" could simply mean that the first believers wrote accounts that the church in Jerusalem collected and took care of. Without doubt they also made additional copies so other groups could read them. Luke says he studied these, and he found accounts no other gospel writer found.

Luke's partner in writing the book—the apostle Paul—had been collecting accounts of Jesus' teachings and actions for decades. We see him referring to materials he has been given in the book of 1 Corinthians in chapter 7, 11, and 15.

1. For a more detailed coverage of evidence for Luke as the author, see my discussion in Dennis McCallum, *Experiencing The Book of Acts*, (Columbus, OH: New Paradigm Publishing, 2023), 12-15.

Mary

An excellent example of such a unique source used only by Luke is Luke 1-3. The source is apparently none other than Mary, Jesus' mother, possibly passed down through a family member. Consider the following accounts and ask yourself who would know this story? Who could be a source for each account?

Account	Who Could Be the Source?
John the Baptist foretold to Zechariah by an angel inside the temple (1:5-25).	Only Zechariah was there for this event. Afterward he couldn't talk, so it's highly likely that he wrote the story down if only to explain what happed to his colleagues and Elizabeth, his wife. Zechariah, as a priest, would definitely have been educated in writing and reading (see v. 63 where he wrote a note giving John's name). Both Zechariah and Elizabeth were elderly, so they were long gone before Jesus' ministry, beginning when he was over thirty years old. After his encounter with the angel, when Mary came to visit, he probably gave her that document or a copy of it. After all, both Zechariah and his wife, Elizabeth were "advanced in years," so they were not suitable to be the custodians of the account that Luke used fifty years later.
Jesus' birth foretold by the angel Gabriel (1:26-38).	Only Mary was there when the angel came. Mary didn't write down her own account, because women weren't taught to read or write. She certainly told Joseph at some point. But Joseph apparently died young, so only Mary would be able to relay this story to the early Christians. It's probable that during her three-month stay with them, she told her story to Zechariah and Elizabeth and had Zechariah write it down. Then, she took a copy home with her. Only these three (and later Joseph) knew how important such a document would be.
Mary visits Elizabeth for three months (1:39-45).	Again, only Mary, Zechariah, and Elizabeth were there. This could have been where much of Luke's first chapter was written.
"The Magnificat"[2] or "Song of Mary" (1:46-56).	Mary clearly composed her song of praise, but how did Luke get a written account of it? She probably composed it during the three-month stay with Elizabeth. Then, it would be natural for Zechariah to write it down and send her home with a copy.

2. The "Magnificat," so named by the Roman church after the key word in the Latin translation of the first line of Mary's prayer of praise.

Account	Who Could Be the Source?
John the Baptist is born (1:57-66).	Only Elizabeth, Mary, and Zechariah were witnesses to this event. Others who may have been there were long gone by the time Luke wrote his gospel. So, like the earlier events, Zechariah probably wrote it out, even though he now had his voice back.
Zechariah's Prophecy (1:67-80).	His utterance was said to be prophecy (v. 67), and we know how much ancient Jews valued prophecy—especially when no prophet had spoken in Israel for 400 years! The same players were there when Zechariah broke out in this lengthy word of prophecy. Again, Zechariah must have written it down later. Knowing the importance of Mary's baby, he would have given it to her or made her a copy.
Jesus' birth in Bethlehem (2:1-20).	Nobody could have given us the story of Jesus' birth other than Mary and Joseph. They must have had it committed to writing later, perhaps by one of their literate sons, or perhaps one of Jesus' disciples.
Jesus presented at the temple, and Simeon and Anna prophecy over him (2:21-38).	Only Mary and Joseph witnessed this. It must have been written down some time before Luke's "many accounts," maybe by one of their sons. Or did she recount it while the early believers were waiting in the upper room before Pentecost, and they wrote it down?
Visit to Jerusalem where 12-year-old Jesus amazes the rabbis (2:41-52).	Once again, Mary and Joseph were the witnesses, and Joseph must have passed away before the next events recorded in the Gospels because he disappears from the narrative.
Return to Nazareth (2:39-40).	Finally, the return to Nazareth and the general comments about his childhood must come from Mary.[3]

Mary was one of the most awesome women who ever lived! We know she was at the cross when Jesus died (John 19:25). So she was no doubt still there days later in the upper room where the believers were waiting for the Holy Spirit. Can anyone doubt that the early believers would want to know and capture Mary's experiences? Of course they would! And they would have captured it in writing. The idea that they would wait decades to write down Mary's account is, I think, absurd. Luke says many people had written accounts.

3. See a fascinating analysis of Gospel sources in Richard Bauckham, *Jesus and the Eyewitnesses: The Gospels as Eyewitness Testimony*, (Grand Rapids MI: Eerdmans, 2008). He argues that the morphology of the texts strongly suggests eyewitness accounts rather than decades long oral transmission.

Conceivably, Jesus, who could both read and write (4:16-20; John 8:6), might have written this section as his mother recounted it. But that's unlikely, because it seems clear Jesus avoided writing, no doubt because he knew that anything he wrote would be venerated and worshiped.

Careful study of Paul's chronology and the writing of Acts clearly place the writing of Luke during Paul's two-year imprisonment at Caesarea in the late 50s. Jerusalem was nearby. Luke would have had ample chances to go up to Jerusalem to examine the "many" texts and do interviews with the "eyewitness and servants of the word" (v. 2).

Peter and James

We also see good evidence in Acts that Luke and his partner, Paul, talked to Peter and James. Long swathes of Acts come exclusively from Peter's point of view. These passages speak of things only Peter could know, like his inner thoughts, or encounters with God that nobody else witnessed. So when reading from Peter's point of view, that probably came from Peter. Nobody but Peter had access to this material. He could have passed his stories to someone else, but he could just as easily have talked to Luke and/or Paul.[4]

Paul probably talked to James as well—the top leader of the Jerusalem church and Jesus' half-brother. He could have been the source for some of the material in the first three chapters, sharing material he got from his mother, Mary, and probably in writing.

Luke could have received it directly from Mary if she was still alive (she would have been over seventy-five years old). It's more likely that James and Jude had kept the written accounts from their mother.

We know Paul spent fifteen days with Peter and James early in his spiritual life (Galatians 1:18-19). He naturally would have been pumping Peter and James for stories about Jesus and the things he taught. He either could have memorized what he heard, or more likely, took notes. This fifteen-day meeting was twenty years earlier than the writing of Luke (around AD 37). He may have met Mary during this visit. She would have only been in her fifties then, and we know she was still alive only three or four years earlier, when Jesus rose from the dead.

4. See evidence that Peter was a direct source for Acts in McCallum, *Experiencing the Book of Acts*, 147ff.

It's also possible that Peter and James showed Paul written accounts from Mary's family. Again, he could have either made copies or committed them to memory. Paul would have carefully preserved whatever he had and later made the accounts available to churches he planted. And he would make any text he had available to Luke for their joint project—writing Luke-Acts.

Date of Writing

At the end of the book of Acts, Luke wrote,

> And he [Paul] stayed two full years in his own rented quarters and was welcoming all who came to him, preaching the kingdom of God and teaching concerning the Lord Jesus Christ with all openness, unhindered. (Acts 28:30-31)

Wait. That's it? It leaves the reader hanging in midair. What happened then? He doesn't say because this was end of the book and he had to deliver the manuscript, for whatever reason. In fact, Paul was hanging by a string, facing life or death at his upcoming trial before Caesar. And Luke doesn't even tell us what the verdict was, though we later learn he was acquitted.

Following the chronology of Paul's life, we can confidentially place the ending of these two years at about AD 62 or 63. Since Luke referred to his "previous book" in the introduction to Acts, we know that Luke was already written before the book of Acts.

Before the two years Luke mentions at the end of Acts, Paul was in prison for another two years, and spent half a year journeying from Judea to Rome. Luke was written during this period. Paul's first two-year imprisonment was at Caesarea, on the coast of Judea. He was allowed to bed down in Herod's palace there and to have friends (like Luke) visit. What would a man of action like Paul do for two long years of house arrest? Not nothing. We can safely assume that he and his partner, Luke, compiled the book of Luke during this period. The best date for completion of Luke is AD 59 or 60.

Liberal scholarship assigns Luke to a date either from AD 80-90, AD 100-110, or well into the second century. We will not take up their case, which is purely subjective and unconvincing. We have no good reason to deny the dates Luke and Acts give for themselves.

The Big Picture

The subject of Luke's sources is fascinating and important. Why? Because commentators, including believing scholars, often refer to Luke's "creative style," suggesting he's like a fiction writer. They claim Luke "puts an account in the mouth" of so-and-so. Many commentators think Luke made up speeches, stories, or songs (like Mary's Magnificat) based on his estimate of what they would have said. They portray Luke as more a work of literature than a recounting of history. To back up such claims, they add the claim that Luke's material was based on oral tradition passed down for decades. Then writers like Luke took the oral material, reshuffled it and added to it for the finished product.

Such theories undermine the historicity and authority of Luke and Acts. It's important to see that no such constructs are necessary or warranted. We can see where Luke could get his material, and that his introduction with its claims of eye-witness authority turn out to be entirely plausible. Luke and Paul were in perfect position to collect and combine these written and verbal sources. We will consider Luke's sources at multiple points as we go through his book.

1

In the Fullness of Time

Luke 1:1-25

For 400 years the people of God waited to hear from the prophets, but the silence was deafening. God certainly acted powerfully at times, like during the Maccabean revolt, but no prophet had come since the last prophets in the Old Testament. On that, orthodox Jews were in agreement.[1] That's why even though Jews wrote books during this period, none of them were considered Scripture.

Why did God wait so long to proceed with his plan of redemption? We have no evidence for what some rabbis and Essenes claimed—that the silence was punishment for the Jews' sin. The Bible says that of some earlier times, but never of this inter-testamental period.

The Apostle Paul later wrote, "But when the fullness of time had come, God sent forth his Son, born of woman, born under the law, to redeem those who were under the law" (Galatians 4:4-5). God was deliberately waiting. We're not sure why, but we see several possibilities.

1. Jewish scholar, Flavius Josephus reflected this view and said it was a consensus. Josephus, *Against Apion*, 1:41. A fringe group called the Essenes thought one of their leaders was a prophet, but nobody agreed with them.

Possible Reasons for Waiting

We can see at least six likely factors that may have led God to leave four hundred years of prophetic silence between the Old and New Testament.

1. The Bible has an ingenious built-in system of self-authentication. This involved prophets first foretelling near-term events that came true during their lifetime. That demonstrated that they were prophets, according to Moses' test for prophets in Deuteronomy 18:21-22. Then, those same prophets also predicted distant events, including scores of prophecies fulfilled in the New Testament. Jesus, John the Baptist and the apostles all referred to these frequently as evidence that Jesus was the true Messiah of God.

   These long-term predictions become more amazing because of the long gap in time between when the prophets made the predictions and when they were fulfilled by the New Testament. During these centuries, the Old Testament books were copied and distributed widely. That made it impossible to claim that the documents could have been altered by Christians to fit later events. Most people have heard of the Dead Sea Scrolls that were written long before Jesus came.

2. By the time of Jesus, the Romans controlled the whole Mediterranean basin. They had also created a network of quality roads spanning the entire empire. Under the *pax Romana*, or "peace of Rome," people were free to walk or ride far and wide throughout the empire. This was never possible before. Earlier, people walking from one country to another would be challenged and blocked, possibly imprisoned as spies. Bandits and pirates also infested pathways and waterways earlier, but most had been wiped out under Rome. This worked out well for the rapid spread of the gospel.

3. The Jews resented being under Roman rule, and that made the meager for the coming of a savior, but more in the political sense. That's not what they got with Jesus.

4. After Alexander the Great conquered most of the eastern Mediterranean, the Greek language had spread widely as a trade language. It wasn't the formal Greek of the philosophers, but a *koine*, or common street level Greek. It was much easier to read and write. This is the Greek of the New Testament. As a result, people were able

to communicate with foreigners at a better level than ever before. This is similar to the way English has become the language of the internet, and people all over the world want to learn some English.

5. Another favorable development was the completion and dissemination of the Greek version of the Old Testament, known as the *Septuagint*. This version was readable to most literate people, because Greek was so widely known. Such widespread availability of God's word simply was not the case when the Jews limited the Bible to Hebrew—a language spoken only by trained Jewish rabbis. Not even most Jews could read Hebrew.
6. Also, the prevailing Greek and Roman religions included a mythology that many found ridiculous. The Greco-Roman gods were more like over-grown humans, including all the failings, foolishness, and evil seen in humanity. Historians have shown that many in Roman culture only tipped their hats to the gods and didn't really believe. Already, before Jesus, tens of thousands of Greco-Roman Gentiles were attending Jewish synagogues, because they sensed that biblical monotheism had the real answers. Many of these so-called "God fearers" later became very receptive to Jesus' gospel.

Click! The Forerunner

Then, like a big stopwatch standing idle, the cosmic thumb of God pressed the top button, and the clock began ticking again.

The first to hear from God was a priest named Zechariah:

> In the days of Herod, king of Judea, there was a priest named Zechariah, of the division of Abijah; and he had a wife from the daughters of Aaron, and her name was Elizabeth. (Luke 1:5)

Immediately Luke's concern for history and precision is evident. The date is during Herod the Great's reign. Since Jesus was born six months after John the Baptist and Herod died in the spring of 4 BC, this event must have been in early 5 or late 6 BC (remember, dates go downward in the BC period).

Luke names Zechariah but also has to say that he came from "the division of Abijah," one of the 24 branches of the Levitical priests

(1 Chronicles 24:10). He also names Elizabeth, but adds that she was from Aaron's family.

This addition of relatively unimportant but very specific detail is typical of Luke's style. Where did he get these details, writing more than sixty years after the event? Again, a written source is most likely. It was probably taken down by Zechariah, the fully literate priest, and preserved by Mary and her family. No other source would have access to this information.

God was choosing the people who would become parents, specifying the names of their sons, and selecting the time of their birth. These all show God stipulating how salvation would come. That's in perfect harmony with the Old Testament. For instance, in the Tabernacle God specified how people could come to him in exacting detail. Readers are sometimes surprised that God felt it necessary to spell out even the decorations, the exact number of supports, the materials used, all the measurements, etc. Why?

By spelling out such detail, God was sending a message of grace. He was saying, "You can come to me, but I will specify how." Any human innovation or creativity in the building or operation of the Tabernacle would suggest that humans can decide how we will approach God. But grace must be sovereign. It doesn't help; it does all. And that's what we see in the births of Jesus and John.

Zechariah and Elizabeth

Both Zechariah and Elizabeth are said to be righteous in God's eyes, keeping the laws and teachings of the Old Testament (v. 6). And they were childless and "advanced in years" (v. 7). God selected this family to reawaken his plan for the world.

Elizabeth was childless and now old, so she had to deal with a disappointment much greater in their culture than it would be in ours. People often wrongly viewed infertility as a sign of God's displeasure. The same thing still happens today, even though we now know most of the physical causes of infertility.

Attributing a medical misfortune to God's doing is the same mistake Job's friends made when they attributed his suffering to God's anger and

Job's sin. In fact, it was Job's righteousness that brought Satan's wrath upon him. God was so angry at their know-nothing presumption that he refused to speak to them, and made them pray through Job instead (Job 42:7-9).

We don't know how Elizabeth handled her own infertility, but you can tell she felt disgraced, and she was full of joy when the vision came to her: "This is the way the Lord has dealt with me in the days when He looked with favor upon me, to take away my disgrace among men" (v. 25).

God chose Zechariah and Elizabeth for this groundbreaking mission—to bear and raise the forerunner of the Messiah. God sent the angel, Gabriel, to bring the good news in answer to Zechariah's prayer (v. 13). This happened while Zechariah was in the temple offering incense. He was almost bowled over by the glorious being in front of him. The angel stood to the right of the alter of incense, not the left or in front. You can tell this is an eyewitness account from the detail.

Gabriel is one of only two angels named in Scripture. The other is Michael, said to be the national angel for Israel and an "archangel" (Jude 9). Gabriel may have been an archangel also, but he is never called that in the Bible. The claim that he was an archangel was in the Apocryphal book *Enoch*. He is clearly of very high rank because he "stands in the presence of God" (v. 19). He shows up in Daniel 8:16 to interpret Daniel's dream. He also gave Daniel the prophecy of the seventy weeks (Daniel 9:21-27). It's likely he is also the unnamed angel in Daniel 7:16 and 10:5. Gabriel seems to appear in connection with God's plan and movements in history. He's a revealer of changes to come.

Gabriel's Message

After settling Zechariah down, the angel spoke:

> "Do not be afraid, Zechariah, for your petition has been heard, and your wife Elizabeth will bear you a son, and you will give him the name John. You will have joy and gladness, and many will rejoice at his birth. For he will be great in the sight of the Lord; and he will drink no wine or liquor, and he will be filled with the Holy Spirit while yet in his mother's womb." (vs. 13-15)

The angel doesn't ask if Zechariah is on board, he simply announces what's going to happen. Of course God would never pick someone who was unwilling, and he knew the future. In fact, God's election is based on foreknowledge according to 1 Peter 1:1-2. As in earlier cases when God caused an infertile woman to have a child, the impossible pregnancy showed that God was acting. This would be a supernatural birth, and everyone in the town would know that.

Gabriel says the coming child will be a *forerunner*. Kings, generals, and other notables who wanted attention would send runners ahead of their chariot or horse formation to cry out in the city that they were coming. People would turn out and line the streets to catch a glimpse of the emperor or other famous person. So John would be sensitizing people to the coming of the Messiah.

For some reason, John was to never drink alcohol. No such restriction was attached to his parallel great one, Jesus (e.g. Matthew 11:18-19). It sounds similar to a Nazarite vow, but says nothing about his hair. Nazarites never cut their hair, so that's surprising.

Probably a better suggestion is that John's abstinence was linked to the way Old Testament priests abstained from alcohol when doing temple service (Leviticus 10:9). That would suggest John had a priestly role, and he was after all, of priestly descent. Priests represent people to God, but they also represent God to the people through their teaching work (e.g. Leviticus 10:11, "You must teach the Israelites all the decrees that the Lord has given them through Moses.")

Being filled with the Holy Spirit while in his mother's womb must be quite extraordinary, or the angel would have had no reason to mention it. It was probably unprecedented.

The verse is important for another reason—even though having the Spirit before birth is extraordinary; the fact that it's possible at all shows that babies are human and spiritual before their birth. Whether that happens at conception or later, we don't know. But this verse and others teach that abortion should never happen unless absolutely necessary.

Elijah?

Gabriel went on:

> "And he will turn many of the sons of Israel back to the Lord their God. It is he who will go as a forerunner before him in the spirit and power of Elijah, to turn the hearts of the parents to their children, and the disobedient to the attitude of the righteous, so as to make ready a people prepared for the Lord." (vs. 16-17)

Here Gabriel ties the coming child more closely to the Old Testament with an allusion to Malachi 4:5-6:

> "Behold, I am going to send you Elijah the prophet before the coming of the great and terrible day of the Lord. He will restore the hearts of the fathers to their children and the hearts of the children to their fathers, so that I will not come and smite the land with a curse."

This well-known prophecy, given four hundred years before Jesus, is the basis for the Jewish belief that the prophet Elijah is going to return someday. To this day orthodox Jewish homes keep a chair empty at Passover and leave the door ajar because, according to the rabbis, Elijah will come to the home of a righteous Jewish family during Passover. So they have a welcome ready, complete with a table setting and a glass of wine.[2]

At the time Malachi wrote this, Elijah had been gone for four hundred years. Remember, according to the Old Testament, Elijah never actually died. He was taken up into heaven on a chariot of fire (2 Kings 2:11). So Malachi's prophecy, spoken hundreds of years after Elijah's exit, didn't entail reincarnation. Rather, Elijah will apparently return in his own body. This precursor to the coming of the Messiah was well known even to children at the time, and still is today.

It's important to note the date Malachi gives for the fulfillment: "Before the coming of the great and terrible day of the Lord" (Malachi 4:5). That refers to Jesus' second coming and the day of judgment.

Notice Gabriel makes the connection directly to Malachi when he says, "And he will go on before the Lord, in the spirit and power of Elijah" (v. 17). He doesn't say the baby *is* Elijah; only that he comes "in the spirit

2. Rabbi Or Rose, "Elijah the Prophet and the Passover Seder: Intergenerational Questions and Connections," *Seventy Faces of Torah* (blog), April 14, 2020, https://hebrewcollege.edu/blog/elijah-the-prophet-the-passover-seder-intergenerational-questions-connections/.

and power of Elijah." This intriguing interplay between John the Baptist and Elijah will come up later in our story with powerful implications. For now, we simply note that John was not Elijah, but he was *like* Elijah.

"To make ready a people prepared for the Lord," seems to be describing widespread repentance. That's what John preached. Although this period of Jewish history after the completion of the Old Testament was not characterized by idol worship and flagrant immorality like earlier, a new false teaching had arisen that left worshippers feeling self-righteous and contemptuous toward outsiders. Their belief that they were already keeping God's law was an absolute barrier to receiving God's grace. That's why John needed to prepare the land with his call to repent, which entailed admitting their sin.

Zechariah's Doubt

The next part of their conversation is quite funny, but not at the time.

> Zechariah said to the angel, "How will I know this for certain? For I am an old man and my wife is advanced in years." (v. 18)

This is not that far out. We all have had the experience of doubting God's word. Or we might have said, "Yeah, I remember when you did that, but I haven't seen much recently."

Gabriel was not amused.

> The angel answered and said to him, "I am Gabriel, who stands in the presence of God, and I have been sent to speak to you and to bring you this good news." (v. 19)

So having an angel stand right in front of you—an angel that just scared the bejeepers out of you—isn't enough? Our unbelief must baffle the righteous angels who have never experienced unbelief. Instead of jumping up and down and running in circles cheering, Zechariah is coming back with good old-fashioned unbelief! Gabriel is sort of like, "Okay, I'll give you a sign."

> "And behold, you shall be silent and unable to speak until the day when these things take place, because you did not believe my words, which will be fulfilled in their proper time." (v. 20)

He clarified that God's plan would go forward regardless of Zechariah's unbelief. I'm sure Gabriel had a frown on his face and was shaking his head as he returned to his place next to God.

When Zechariah came out of the temple, unable to speak he had to use hand motions to communicate. The people somehow correctly realized he had seen a vision. Somehow he relayed the message to Elizabeth, who also became pregnant on cue.

> After these days Elizabeth his wife became pregnant, and she kept herself in seclusion for five months, saying, "This is the way the Lord has dealt with me in the days when He looked with favor upon me, to take away my disgrace among men." (vs. 24-25)

Why did she go into seclusion? Maybe she worried that if she claimed to be pregnant as an elderly woman (even though she wasn't showing), people would think she was crazy? Maybe she was worried about false hope and disappointment? Pregnancies failed to go to term far more often in ancient times. Or did she just want to be alone with God? Maybe she didn't want people making a fuss over her? We don't know. But she was back in time for Mary's upcoming visit.

The Big Picture

Knifing into history with decisive choices and plans, God sprang into action. He moved through obscure people in an unnamed town somewhere in Judea. That obscurity matches his pattern with Jesus. Only a few months would pass before he launched the next phase—the incarnation and Jesus' virgin birth. This is not what people expected. The Messiah was coming as promised, but completely different than anyone imagined.

The day God broke his silence, most people in country heard nothing. They saw nothing. It was a typical day tilling the fields or sewing with thread. Yet, a sequence of events had been launched that would lead to the rescue of the human race. So often, we don't know what God is doing until after he does it. That points to the need for reverent faith in waiting on God.

2

Mary
Luke 1:26-80

Gabriel Again

Six months later, God sent his messenger to one of his people in the small town of Nazareth in the northern part of the country. She was a teenage girl of perhaps 14 or 15 years of age—the typical age for betrothal at that time.[1]

> In the sixth month of Elizabeth's pregnancy, God sent the angel Gabriel to Nazareth, a village in Galilee, to a virgin named Mary. She was engaged to be married to a man named Joseph, a descendant of King David. Gabriel appeared to her and said, "Greetings, favored woman![2] The Lord is with you!"[3]

1. Maybe even younger, down to 12 years old. Men married later, usually in their twenties. "Weddings, Marriage & Divorce," *The Roman Empire in the First Century,* 2006, https://www.pbs.org/empires/romans/empire/weddings.html.
2. Catholic interpreters take this description "favored one" to read "full of favor" meaning that she can confer favor to others. But that has nothing to do with this context. It should be understood to mean Mary was receiving favor, not bestowing it.
3. In the KJV, Gabriel says, "the Lord is with you," but adds, "blessed are you among women." Modern versions correctly leave the last phrase out. It is only found in western texts and is omitted in Siniaticus and Vatacannus, two of our best manuscripts. There is no good reason why these earliest and best manuscripts would omit the words if they were present. Rather, this is dittography, where the phrase was copied from verse 42 where the words were actually spoken by Elizabeth. Bruce Metzger, *A Textual Commentary on the Greek New Testament* (New York: United Bible Societies, 1971), 129.

> Confused and disturbed, Mary tried to think what the angel could mean. "Don't be afraid, Mary," the angel told her, "for you have found favor with God! (1:26-30 NLT)

Notice the narrative includes not only the dialogue, but Mary's inner state of mind. It describes her confusion, her mind racing. Gabriel went on to declare what was about to happen:

> "You will conceive and give birth to a son, and you will name him Jesus. He will be very great and will be called the Son of the Most High. The Lord God will give him the throne of his ancestor David. And he will reign over Israel forever; his Kingdom will never end!" (vs. 31-33 NLT)

Here in a few sentences, Gabriel announced the most incredible and extreme claim found in the Bible. Not just that a virgin would have a baby, but that he would be "called the Son of the Most High." It's the incarnation—God putting on flesh and becoming a man.

Just think about it. Almighty God becoming a baby? We know he set aside the use of his divine attributes when he "emptied himself" (Philippians 2:6-8). That's why he had to learn and grow like other humans. Luke says, "Jesus kept increasing in wisdom and stature, and in favor with God and men" (2:52). He wasn't omniscient, he had to learn. When did he realize who he was? We know he knew by the time he was 12 years old (2:49), probably much earlier. He must have learned to talk like other babies.

> Mary asked the angel, "But how can this happen? I am a virgin." (v. 34 NLT)

Unlike Zechariah's request for a sign, Mary is just confused. Is Gabriel saying this is going to happen later, after she and Joseph are married? He explains:

> "The Holy Spirit will come upon you, and the power of the Most High will overshadow you. So the baby to be born will be holy, and he will be called the Son of God."(v. 35 NLT)

Although the language is mysterious, it's clear that this is going to be creation *ex nihilo*—out of nothing. God is going to create the male's DNA contribution—not a big task for the one who spoke the universe into existence. The female part comes from Mary. Jesus is going to be a unique being; partly from a human donor and partly directly from God. His soul or spirit would come from God as well. Thinking about the incarnation can really make your head spin.

Then too, Gabriel puts Mary's encounter into the larger context of God's operations in the world:

> "What's more, your relative Elizabeth has become pregnant in her old age! People used to say she was barren, but she has conceived a son and is now in her sixth month. For the word of God will never fail." (vs. 36-37 NLT)

Can you imagine the shock and confusion Mary must have felt? "Wait . . . I'm only fifteen . . . I'm getting married . . . Nobody's going to believe this. . . ." All true.

Somehow, her deep-seated trust in God prevailed. All the questions, all the confusion come down to the last line: "For the word of God will never fail." She knew she either believed that or she didn't. She ended the encounter with an amazing response:

> And Mary said, "Behold, the bondslave of the Lord; may it be done to me according to your word." And the angel departed from her. (v. 38)

She offered herself and her body to God, like what Paul would later call a "living sacrifice" (Romans 12:1). She knew following God's will in this case would result in pain and suffering. In fact, she had no idea how bad the suffering would be. How many mothers have to watch their son tortured and killed before their eyes?

Calculating the cost of following God's will is pointless. You soon realize that all the hypothetical questions add up to one thing: you either trust him or you don't. This teenage Hebrew girl is an astonishing example of courageous faith.

Although she paid a horrific price for accepting her place in God's plan, how do you suppose she feels about it today? The pain is behind her, and she lives in glory with her son. She ended up playing one of the most important roles of any human.

Although we don't have the story recounted, we can safely assume that Mary was reunited with Jesus after his resurrection. She was probably one of the Mary's that went to the tomb Sunday morning, and we know Jesus also appeared to her other son, James. So there's little chance that they didn't spend time together before his ascension.

If it wasn't for Luke, we wouldn't have this account of Gabriel and Mary. Matthew records an announcement to Joseph that must have been given weeks or even months later. Mark and John jump directly to the ministry of John the Baptist.

Why a Virgin Birth?

Why did God choose to bring forth his Messiah via a virgin birth? We don't have a full explanation on this intriguing question, but we can glean a few points.

- First, if Joseph was Jesus' true father, Jesus would be purely human, no different than other people. The incarnation matches the picture of Jesus being human and divine.
- Also, in the first cryptic prophecy uttered by God himself in the Garden of Eden, he warned the serpent,

  "And I will put enmity
  Between you and the woman,
  And between your seed and her seed;
  He shall bruise you on the head,
  And you shall bruise him on the heel." (Genesis 3:15)

  A bruise to the heel would be a painful wound. But a bruise to the head would be fatal. It sounds like Eve's offspring, or seed, will do damage to the serpent. But why does he refer to the woman's seed in the singular? And why is it "he" instead of "they"?

  This is the first hint of a virgin birth. The woman's seed is Jesus. It's too late to prevent the damage done by the lying serpent, but the seed of woman will get the last word. Jesus fulfilled this prophecy as the God-man.

- When Paul teaches about how humans got their fallen nature, he always says it's through Adam, never Eve (e.g. Romans 5:18; 1 Corinthians 15:45). That's curious, considering that she was the first to eat of the forbidden fruit. For some reason, transmission of the sin nature is through the male. Is it because God gave his directions to Adam before Eve existed? Are there rules at work here that we don't know? Whatever the reason, we know Jesus had no sin nature, because Paul says God "sent his own Son in the likeness of sinful flesh" (Romans 8:3). So, if Jesus had a sinful flesh, Paul wouldn't have said "likeness of sinful flesh." And we know he had no human father.

Isaiah had predicted "Therefore the Lord Himself will give you a sign: Behold, a virgin will be with child and bear a son, and she will call His name Immanuel. the coming of a child named Immanuel ("God with us") (Isaiah 7:14). Liberal interpreters, eager to show that the Bible is not supernatural, argue that Isaiah's word *almah* for "virgin," isn't a prediction of the virgin birth because that word could mean maiden. But The meaning of *parthenos* (virgin) in Matthew is not in doubt.[4]

Journey to Elizabeth

People in Nazareth didn't know Mary was pregnant yet. She wouldn't have been showing, and it's doubtful she was in any hurry to make her pregnancy known to skeptical town folk. Even Joseph may not have known until later. Matthew says, "She was found to be with child by the Holy Spirit." The language suggests this was when she could conceal it no longer—after her three-month trip to see Elizabeth.

It would be natural to put off breaking the news that she knew nobody would believe. She at least must have told her parents or given them some reason to allow her to travel to Elizabeth's house.

Maybe she wanted to get away to adjust to the new reality in quiet before God. Gabriel had told her about her relative, Elizabeth, having a supernatural child, so it makes sense she would turn to Elizabeth as an older, stabilizing voice. Elizabeth was sort of a team mate in accomplishing God's plan. Maybe Elizabeth could answer the questions flowing through Mary's head?

A few days later Mary hurried to the hill country of Judea, to

4. Of course *almah* can mean virgin. Careful study of the historical context for Isaiah's prophecy indicates that the sign was not given to those standing there (because Ahaz refused the sign) but to the whole "house of David."

> the town where Zechariah lived. She entered the house and greeted Elizabeth. (vs. 39-40 NLT)

The expression literally is "in these days" which is more ambiguous than "a few days later." It's not clear how long it took her to decide to flee to Elizabeth. The journey was substantial for a single young lady—from seventy to over a hundred miles to reach the area around Jerusalem.

She had to navigate around Samaria, which was unsafe for Jews. That's why most Jewish travelers took the indirect route either down the valley of the Jordan River or down the coastal plane to reach Judea. Modern depictions show Mary later riding a donkey to Bethlehem, and that's possible. She might have ridden one here too. She may also have attached herself to a group already traveling south.

Arrival

> At the sound of Mary's greeting, Elizabeth's child leaped within her, and Elizabeth was filled with the Holy Spirit. Elizabeth gave a glad cry and exclaimed to Mary, "God has blessed you above all women, and your child is blessed. Why am I so honored, that the mother of my Lord should visit me? When I heard your greeting, the baby in my womb jumped for joy. You are blessed because you believed that the Lord would do what he said." (vs. 41-45 NLT)

Both Elizabeth and Zechariah knew the messianic era was at hand because their miracle baby was to prepare his way. Without any doubt, Zechariah had used writing and a reader to relay to his wife what Gabriel said (vs. 60, 63). But Gabriel didn't say anything to Zechariah about Mary according to our text. It must have been the direct action of the Spirit on both baby and mom. This must have been like Old Testament prophets saying, "The Spirit of the Lord came upon me."

Mary's Song of Praise

Next, Luke cites a detailed source recounting a poem created by Mary. As we saw earlier, she wouldn't have been able to write it down, so someone else did that, and we know a fully literate priest was in the house at the time—Zechariah. There's no reason to think this poem with Hebrew characteristics and allusions to Old Testament verses just spontaneously came to Mary's lips. Rather, it was probably composed and modified over a period of time.

And Mary said:

> "My soul glorifies the Lord
> and my spirit rejoices in God my Savior." (vs. 46-47 NIV)

Notice the Hebraic couplets. Instead of rhyming words, the Hebrews rhyme ideas. This is synonymous parallelism, where the writer states it one way, and then states the same, or nearly the same idea a different way.

Notice Mary says she had to be saved. That flies in the face of the Catholic doctrine of the "immaculate conception." Under that teaching, Mary was born without sin and didn't need to be forgiven.

> "For he has been mindful
> of the humble state of his servant.
> From now on all generations will call me blessed,
> for the Mighty One has done great things for me—
> holy is his name." (vs. 48-49 NIV)

She's been meditating on what's going on, and realizing at a deeper level the enormity of what God is doing through her. She is clearly baffled at why God would select such a nobody as her for such an important role.

> "His mercy extends to those who fear him,
> from generation to generation.
> He has performed mighty deeds with his arm;
> he has scattered those who are proud in their inmost thoughts.
> He has brought down rulers from their thrones
> but has lifted up the humble.
> He has filled the hungry with good things
> but has sent the rich away empty." (vs. 50-53 NIV)

Mary sees the broad sweep of history revealed in the Old Testament. Here too is reversal theology. The proud, the powerful, the rich go away with nothing. The poor and the humble receive God's blessing and they become the agents of his plan in every generation. Reversal theology is a big theme in Luke, but well represented in the other gospel books as well. The biggest proponent of reversal theology was Jesus (e.g. Matthew 11:25-26). It highlights the potential for revolution in the gospel.

> "He has helped his servant Israel,
> remembering to be merciful
> to Abraham and his descendants forever,
> just as he promised our ancestors." (vs. 54-55 NIV)

Mary, like all believing Jews of her day, knew that God's dealings with them were based on covenant promises. God had declared to Abraham that in his seed every nation on earth would be blessed (Genesis 12:3). The reference to God's servant Israel comes right out of Isaiah 44:21 and 49:3, where God's servant is Israel but also Jesus. How much did Mary know about the connection between the Messiah and Isaiah's servant songs?

Mary's lovely poem of praise is a marker for God's pivot to a new and unprecedented move—his own personal invasion of human history through a humble nobody—a girl from a little-known town. She and her elderly relative and friend sat together with Zechariah, pondering and adjusting to the great events at hand. We read that, "Mary stayed with Elizabeth for about three months and then returned home" (v. 56). By then, John, later known as the Baptist, had been born.

John Arrives

> When it was time for Elizabeth to have her baby, she gave birth to a son. Her neighbors and relatives heard that the Lord had shown her great mercy, and they shared her joy. (vs. 57-58 NIV)

This makes it sound like at least some of the neighbors and relatives only discovered Elizabeth was pregnant at the time of the birth. We saw earlier that she kept herself in seclusion for five months. But she must have stayed inside most of the time even after that.

Imagine the shock and astonishment the people in this village must have felt seeing an elderly, barren woman have a baby! This was a time in which people weren't resistant to the idea of the supernatural like today. This amazing event could only mean God was acting in miraculous power.

Every one of them would be watching the child to see what would happen next. Luke confirms, "The neighbors were all filled with awe, and throughout the hill country of Judea people were talking about all these things. Everyone who heard this wondered about it, asking, 'What then is this child going to be?' For the Lord's hand was with him" (vs. 65-66).

The Naming

Zechariah didn't regain his voice when John was born. Instead,

> On the eighth day they came to circumcise the child, and they were going to name him after his father Zechariah, but his mother spoke up and said, "No! He is to be called John." They said to her, "There is no one among your relatives who has that name." (vs. 59-61 NIV)

Apparently they didn't believe her. They wanted to hear it from Zechariah:

> Then they made signs to his father, to find out what he would like to name the child. He asked for a writing tablet, and to everyone's astonishment he wrote, "His name is John." Immediately his mouth was opened and his tongue was loosed, and he began to speak, praising God. (vs. 62-64 NIV)

How happy he must have been, not only having the baby, but ending his time of discipline! No more asking for signs now.

Zechariah's Prophecy

Then "Zechariah was filled with the Holy Spirit and prophesied" (v. 67).

This utterance was not just from Zechariah, but from the Holy Spirit. Like the prophets of old, the Spirit came upon him.

> "Praise be to the Lord, the God of Israel,
> because he has come to his people and redeemed them.
> He has raised up a horn of salvation for us
> in the house of his servant David
> (as he said through his holy prophets of long ago),
> salvation from our enemies
> and from the hand of all who hate us—
> to show mercy to our ancestors
> and to remember his holy covenant—
> the oath he swore to our father Abraham:

to rescue us from the hand of our enemies,
and to enable us to serve him without fear
in holiness and righteousness before him all our days."
(vs. 68-75 NIV)

The main point in this prophetic prayer is that Zechariah understands who is coming in Jesus. He ties the coming directly to the Davidic covenant given in 2 Samuel 7. He names his mission: "salvation." But he says the salvation is from their enemies, not from their sins. We now know that the salvation from Israel's enemies is part of Jesus' mission, but will come in the future. Nobody knew at this time that the Messiah would come twice.

He ties the coming one directly to what "he said through his holy prophets." So the coming of John and Jesus takes its place in God's carefully laid plan of the ages. That includes the unique self-validating effect predictive prophecy has by describing the future before it happens.

And he links Jesus' coming to the Abrahamic covenant, just like Mary had earlier. It's "the oath he swore to our father Abraham." This refers to the oath-swearing ceremony described in Genesis 15. God had Abraham divide animals in half and lay them out so a pathway passed between them.

Normally both parties of a covenant oath would link arms and walk down that path, as if to say, "May God do to me like these animals if I break this oath." The unusual part in Genesis is that only God, appearing as a flaming torch, passed between the animals while Abraham watched. It was a way of signifying that the Abrahamic Covenant was unconditional—God would keep the agreement.

Finally:

"And you, my child,
will be called a prophet of the Most High;
for you will go on before the Lord
to prepare the way for him,
to give his people the knowledge of salvation
through the forgiveness of their sins,
because of the tender mercy of our God,
by which the rising sun will come to us from heaven

to shine on those living in darkness,
and in the shadow of death,
to guide our feet into the path of peace." (vs. 76-79 NIV)

Here Zechariah referred to the coming one who makes straight the ways of the Lord, referring to Malachi 3:1. That would also be how John later described himself, and how Jesus described him (Matthew 11:10, 14; Mark 1:2; Luke 7:27).

In this section he brings in the other crucial task for Messiah: "To give his people the knowledge of salvation through the forgiveness of their sins." It still doesn't mean Zechariah knew about the cross. He merely attributes the forgiveness to "the mercy of our God."

Finally, he speaks of Jesus' enlightening mission as the supreme revelation of God. The sunlight scatters the darkness and death holding humanity in its grip.

The Big Picture

Luke concludes, "And the child continued to grow and to become strong in spirit, and he lived in the deserts until the day of his public appearance to Israel" (v. 80). John the Baptist has been born. This is the man Jesus called, "more than a prophet" (Matthew 11:9). He also said, "Among those born of women there has not arisen *anyone* greater than John the Baptist" (Matthew 11:11). That's quite a statement when you think of all the heroes of faith recounted in the Bible.

John was born into a life of hard duty. He lived in the deserts, eating locusts and honey (Matthew 3:4). He lived under threats and suspicion from the religious leaders, and he ended up in prison and finally executed. Knowing what we do now, if Jesus asked for volunteers to fill the role of John the Baptist, he wouldn't get many hands raised. Yet his greatness will be celebrated long into eternity future.

3

Jesus!
Luke 2

His Birth

Luke launches into Jesus' birth narrative with characteristic concern for historical precision:

> Now in those days a decree went out from Caesar Augustus, that a census be taken of all the inhabited earth. This was the first census taken while Quirinius was governor of Syria. (2:1-2)

Matthew 2:1 and Luke 1:5 say that Jesus' birth was in the time of King Herod the Great. Shortly before the death of Herod, Josephus says there was an eclipse of the Moon.[1] This is Josephus' only mention of an eclipse, so he wasn't fanciful like other ancient authors who sometimes referred to non-existent eclipses. Through astronomical calculations we find that a lunar eclipse did occur in this area on March 13, 4 BC. No lunar or solar eclipse was visible in either 3 or 2 BC. So Jesus was born before March 13, 4 BC.

We have no record of this census from secular Roman sources, but our records are quite fragmentary. Early church fathers, Justin Martyr and

1. Josephus, *Antiquities*, 17.167.

Tertullian both claimed that this census could be verified in the archives in Rome. Those archives were later destroyed, but the fact that these contemporaries appealed to them implies they existed at the time. Hoehner reports on records from Egypt indicating that a census was taken there approximately every 14 years, and that a census had been taken shortly after 20 BC.[2] So this would land in the 6 to 4 BC range.

Luke adds, "This was the first census taken while Quirinius was governor of Syria." Quirinius is known to us from Roman history. Prior to 6 BC he was fighting a war in Macedonia. He also served a term as governor of Syria starting in AD 6. We don't know where he was from 6 to 4 BC, but Tacitus makes a passing mention of his being "in the east." Syria would be considered an eastern province. He may have served two terms there.

Or, another reading is possible. The Greek word for "first" (proto) can also be translated "before." So the verse could be translated, "This was the census that took place before Quirinius was governor of Syria." That would make sense because Quirinius also oversaw a census. "This was before that one," would be Luke's message.[3] The later census is probably the one mentioned in Acts 5:37.

We conclude that Jesus was born between 6 and early 4 BC. Additional chronological notices show up later in Jesus' life, and we'll deal with those as they come up.

Luke continues:

> All returned to their own ancestral towns to register for this census. And because Joseph was a descendant of King David, he had to go to Bethlehem in Judea, David's ancient home. He traveled there from the village of Nazareth in Galilee. He took with him Mary, to whom he was engaged, who was now expecting a child. And while they were there, the time came for her baby to be born. She gave birth to her firstborn son. She wrapped him snugly in strips of cloth and laid him in a manger, because there was no lodging available for them. (vs. 3-7 NLT)

2. Harold W. Hoehner, *Chronological Aspects of the Life of Christ* (Grand Rapids MI: Zondervan Academic, 1978). Adolf Deissmann, *Light from the Ancient East*, 4th ed., trans. by Lionel R. M. Strachen (New York, Harper & Brothers, 1927), 270-71. Luke's use of the present tense means that Augustus was commanding in an ongoing way—e.g. province by province.

3. Bruce agreed with this view. F. F. Bruce, *New Testament History* (London: Doubleday, 1969), 32 n1.

Such a cozy, warm nativity scene! All the animals gathered around . . . the nice little manger that looks like a crib . . . everyone on their knees, and light radiating out from the baby.

> The cattle are lowing
> The baby awakes.
> But little Lord Jesus
> No crying he makes . . .

For $78 you can get a lighted plastic nativity scene for your front yard.

But this romanticized picture is far from the truth. In fact, Jesus' birth is a stark and even horrifying picture of suffering and misery. Anyone who has worked on a farm knows barns with livestock stink to high heaven. Most farmers wear boots when working in a barn with its excrement- and urine-spattered ground. How would you like to lay down in this setting to give birth to your baby?

The manger was not a quaint crib, but an unsanitary feed trough soaked in smelly livestock saliva that leaves a black scum. How would you like to lay your baby into that mess? Maybe there was some straw, maybe they had a cloth. This birth was probably during fall or winter, so it was chilly. They wrapped him in strips of cloth—no cute teddy bear jammies for this baby.

The inn was full. The people inside had no idea what was happening in the barn on the edge of town. It's tempting to see it as a picture of our world—preoccupied with our lives, oblivious to what God is doing. One would think they could have found some space for a woman in labor.

Jesus' life started out in obscurity, hardship, and filth, just like the rest of his life. This is not a normal king. He comes from a nowhere town, with nobody parents, under suspicion of illegitimacy, and instead of laying on satin sheets in a palace, he lies in a dirty feed trough in a stinky barn!

The Shepherds

Appearances can be misleading. God decided to lighten the drab scene with some celebration:

> That night there were shepherds staying in the fields nearby, guarding their flocks of sheep. Suddenly, an angel of the Lord

> appeared among them, and the radiance of the Lord's glory surrounded them. They were terrified, but the angel reassured them. "Don't be afraid!" he said. "I bring you good news that will bring great joy to all people. The Savior—yes, the Messiah, the Lord—has been born today in Bethlehem, the city of David! And you will recognize him by this sign: You will find a baby wrapped snugly in strips of cloth, lying in a manger." (vs. 8-12 NLT)

An angel! These mighty beings were so majestic that seeing one often caused people to collapse (e.g. Daniel 10:8-9). The word for angel is broad in scope. It just means messenger, and could refer to a number of different creatures (e.g. seraphim, cherubim, archangels, world rulers, etc.).

Bethlehem was known as the city of David because King David was born there. Hundreds of years earlier the prophet Micah had predicted:

> "But as for you, Bethlehem Ephrathah, too little to be among the clans of Judah. from you one will go forth for me to be ruler in Israel. His goings forth are from long ago, from the days of eternity." (Micah 5:2)

You can see the ruler's pre-existence from eternity past. This passage on the birth of the Messiah was well-known to rabbis in Jesus' day. Matthew recounts how Herod asked the scribes where the Messiah would be born, and they promptly quoted this passage (Matthew 2:6). Of course, they also expected the Messiah figure to fulfill the next part of Micah's prophecy: "At that time He will be great to the ends of the earth. This one will be our peace" (Micah 5:4-5).But that part was for later. Unfortunately, this interview with the scribes led to Herod's brutal slaughter of children under the age of two in Bethlehem.

Then:

> And suddenly there appeared with the angel a multitude of the heavenly host praising God and saying," Glory to God in the highest, and on earth peace among men with whom he is pleased." (vs. 13-14)

What a dazzling sight! Across the sky, supernatural beings crying out. Or were they on the ground? Maybe dancing? What a contrast between humanity's oblivious outlook and the view from heaven. Apparently they do this every time someone receives Christ (15:7). Did others see this spectacle? Or was this a vision granted only to the shepherds?

The last line could mean that God is pleased by the human race. Or, it could mean that they are declaring peace only to those people with whom he is pleased—i.e. believers. It can be read either way. Probably the latter is right.

Not surprisingly, "When the angels had returned to heaven, the shepherds said to each other, 'Let's go to Bethlehem! Let's see this thing that has happened'"(v. 15). They probably had no difficulty finding him in such a small village. Archeologists' estimates of Bethlehem's population at this time range from 300 to 600.

So God had arranged to have some honor shown to baby Jesus after all. After seeing the baby, the shepherds spread the word to everyone they knew, and the gospel was off and running.

Here we have another story that comes from Mary. Although she wasn't there to see the angels, this is what the shepherds would have told her and Joseph when they found the barn. And we have her description of her own state of mind: "Mary kept all these things in her heart and thought about them often" (v. 19). No one but Mary and Joseph were in a position to preserve this story.

Childhood

Luke doesn't include some of the events Matthew recounted like the visit of the wise men, Herod's slaughter of the innocents, and Joseph and Mary's flight into Egypt to avoid Herod.

We don't know why Luke didn't include these. He may not have been shown them. Or, as in every case, historical authors have to decide what to include and what to skip over. No historian records everything.

Jesus' Circumcision

Luke has some unique accounts of his own. First comes Jesus' circumcision and presentation as the firstborn. On the night of the first Passover in Moses' day, God declared that in the future all firstborns in Israel would be consecrated, or set apart, to God. "You must present all firstborn sons and firstborn male animals to the Lord, for they belong to him" (Exodus 13:12).

This was a way to remind people of the night the firstborns of Egypt were slain by the angel of death, but the Children of Israel were passed over because of the blood of a lamb (Exodus 12). Then, God explains, "You must buy back every firstborn son" (Exodus 13:13).

So, as observant Jews, Mary and Joseph took their baby to the temple and paid the offering prescribed. They offered "either a pair of turtledoves or two young pigeons" (v. 24), which was the offering for poor people. Better off people had to offer a year-old lamb.

Simeon

On the way to give their offering, they ran into an elderly believer named Simeon. Luke explains:

> He was righteous and devout and was eagerly waiting for the Messiah to come and rescue Israel. The Holy Spirit was upon him and had revealed to him that he would not die until he had seen the Lord's Messiah. That day the Spirit led him to the Temple. So when Mary and Joseph came to present the baby Jesus to the Lord as the law required, Simeon was there. He took the child in his arms and praised God, saying,
>
> "Sovereign Lord, now let your servant die in peace,
> as you have promised.
> I have seen your salvation,
> which you have prepared for all people.
> He is a light to reveal God to the nations,
> and he is the glory of your people Israel!" (vs. 25-32 NLT)

Through the Spirit, Simeon was enabled to recognize Jesus for who he was. Because of his time in history this old man wasn't in the thick of battle like the apostle Paul would be. But his closeness to God is amazing. He has God talking to him and making special promises. He's a true friend of God.

He seems to have exceptional insight as well. At this time, rabbinic opinion was that the Messiah would be a powerful ruler who would overcome his enemies by force. They didn't see him as a suffering servant. But

Simeon knew better. He alludes to Isaiah 49:6 where God says to the anonymous servant,

> "It is too small a thing that you should be my Servant to raise up the tribes of Jacob and to restore the preserved ones of Israel; I will also make you a light of the nations so that my salvation may reach to the end of the earth." (Isaiah 49:6)

Even though Isaiah calls the servant "my servant Israel" in verse 3, you can see here in verse 6 that he has the servant raising "up the tribes of Jacob." So the Servant must be someone other than the children of Israel. Simeon must have picked up on this shift. Or he could be alluding to other passages promising salvation to the nations, like Is. 9:2; 51:4 or 60:1-3. The idea that Messiah would bring truth to the whole world was clear enough in Old Testament prophecy.

Simeon handed the baby back and blessed Mary and Joseph. Then he said to Mary,

> "This child is destined to cause many in Israel to fall, and many others to rise. He has been sent as a sign from God, but many will oppose him. As a result, the deepest thoughts of many hearts will be revealed. And a sword will pierce your very soul." (vs. 34-35 NLT)

So the news wasn't all good. Here was a warning to Mary that she would suffer, like having a sword pierce her soul. Also, he warned her that Jesus' path would be full of opponents. Simeon was referring to the polarizing impact Jesus had wherever he went.

This story about Simeon could again only come from Mary. No one but her and Joseph was there.

Anna

Then another elderly believer named Anna recognized Jesus:

> Anna, a prophet, was also there in the Temple. She was the daughter of Phanuel from the tribe of Asher, and she was very old. Her husband died when they had been married only seven years. Then she lived as a widow to the age of eighty-four. She never left the Temple but stayed there day and night, worshiping God with fasting and prayer. (vs. 36-37 NLT)

All this detail must have come out in the conversation between Anna, Mary, and Joseph. This event occurred in 5-4 BC, so no other witness or source would be possible. It must have been written down near the time it happened, before it could be streamlined by elimination of unnecessary details. They learned her age, her father's name, his tribe, and the history of his death.

> She came along just as Simeon was talking with Mary and Joseph, and she began praising God. She talked about the child to everyone who had been waiting expectantly for God to rescue Jerusalem. (v. 38 NLT)

This would have been an exciting encouragement for the faithful remnant who knew the Messiah was due to appear. How did Mary know that Anna was talking Jesus up? They probably had a stream of excited people looking them up and asking to see the baby. They heard about him from Anna.

Return to Nazareth

Luke says, "When Jesus' parents had fulfilled all the requirements of the law of the Lord, they returned home to Nazareth in Galilee" (v. 39). Wait. Matthew says they fled to Egypt for some time, waiting for Herod to die. Critics declare this as a plain contradiction between Matthew and Luke.

In fact, there is no contradiction. As we saw earlier, this is a case of selectivity on the part of the author. Both Matthew and Luke include material not found in the other account. That's typical of eye-witness accounts. The flight to Egypt must have occurred between the story about Anna and the statement in verse 39 saying they went home to Nazareth.

Luke may have felt the flight to Egypt was not relevant to his goals. Maybe he didn't have space. The important point is that Luke's account neither denies nor affirms the flight to Egypt, so there can't be a contradiction.

Likewise, Matthew omitted the story of the shepherds. Why? Either because he didn't have access to that account, or because he chose to omit it. John makes that clear in his gospel: "The disciples saw Jesus do many other miraculous signs in addition to the ones recorded in this book" (John 20:30). And, "Jesus also did many other things. If they were all written down, I suppose the whole world could not contain the books that would be written" (John 21:25). That's reason enough to be selective.

Passover

Luke has another story found nowhere else. It looks like this one comes from Mary as well:

> Every year Jesus' parents went to Jerusalem for the Passover festival. When Jesus was twelve years old, they attended the festival as usual. After the celebration was over, they started home to Nazareth, but Jesus stayed behind in Jerusalem. His parents didn't miss him at first, because they assumed he was among the other travelers. But when he didn't show up that evening, they started looking for him among their relatives and friends.(vs. 41-44 NLT)

This is hard for modern people to imagine. They took off and walked for hours without noticing their son wasn't with them? We wouldn't think about leaving for a trip without seeing each of our kids strapped into their place and buckled. It's hard to imagine losing track of your twelve-year-old, at least for very long.

First, consider that this would have been a chaotic throng of neighbors, friends and family from Nazareth. These in turn were part of a larger throng of thousands descending from Jerusalem to the Jordan Valley. The text explains, "they assumed he was among the other travelers," that is, with his friends from Nazareth.[4]

Also, in this ancient setting, they had less to worry about. So many of the worries modern people have would never cross their minds—their child being kidnapped, being run down by a car, being attacked by a gang, or by some bullies. In village life, things were much safer. Kids knew their neighbors and the parents knew each other as well. Kids were safe running around the village and playing with whoever they wanted. This

4. Norval Geldenhuys points out that we know of cases where traveling communities had the women and youngest children in the front of the caravan, sometimes in carts. The men and older kids would follow behind. If that happened here, Mary could have thought Jesus was back with Joseph. Joseph might have thought he was ahead with Mary. Only at night when they stopped to camp by family did they discover he was missing. Norval Geldenhuys, *Luke,* New International Commentary on the New Testament (Grand Rapids, MI: Eerdmans, 1977), 126-127.

would have been even truer when traveling in caravan. It turned out they had become separated much earlier, on the temple mount.

By this time, Mary and Joseph also had several other children to care for. Jesus had four brothers and at least two sisters, all younger than him (Matthew 13:55-56). They probably felt like Jesus was responsible enough to take care of himself. So we can imagine how the problem started.

Three days later?

But now comes the shocking part, "*Three days later . . .* !"

> When they couldn't find him, they went back to Jerusalem to search for him there. Three days later they finally discovered him in the Temple, sitting among the religious teachers, listening to them and asking questions. All who heard him were amazed at his understanding and his answers.
>
> His parents didn't know what to think. "Son," his mother said to him, "why have you done this to us? Your father and I have been frantic, searching for you everywhere."
>
> "But why did you need to search?" he asked. "Didn't you know that I must be in my Father's house?"(vs. 45-48 NLT)

How is this possible? Jesus didn't realize the trauma his parents would feel? Where was he at night? How can we explain this?

First, ancient counting practice often included any part of a day, week, or year as the whole. Hebrew days also began and ended at sundown. So if Jesus got separated from his parents before sundown and they found him even one day later after sundown, they could describe it as three days, even though it was a little a bit over 24 hours.

It still leaves Jesus spending at least one night alone in Jerusalem. Was he searching for his parents but unable to find them? If so, when he couldn't find them, did he get tired and lie down somewhere on the temple mount to sleep? Temperatures are very moderate at this time and place.

If he didn't know where his parents were, the most common-sense move was to stay near the place where he last saw them, on the assumption that they would retrace their steps and find him. If he ran out looking for his parents without knowing where they were, it would only make it more likely that they would miss each other in the crowd.

While waiting, he went into the courts where the rabbis were teaching and debating, and began asking questions. He wasn't in the temple as some pictures show. Only priests went inside during their temple service. These talks were outside in various areas on the immense temple mount—about the size of thirty football fields. This huge public area had thousands of people moving about every day, especially during festivals like on this occasion. Jesus probably never left the mount. His parents left, assuming he was with them.

When his parents finally found him, they were not only relieved, but also surprised that he was talking with the rabbis. This could be the occasion for him to ask the rhetorical question about being in his Father's house. If so, he would not be expressing surprise at their being upset over losing him. He was suggesting they shouldn't have been surprised that he was interacting with the rabbis, or that he was near the temple where they last saw him.

Viewed this way, the whole story holds together.

So this wasn't a case of Jesus jumping the gun on his ministry and ignoring his family in favor of some early interaction with the rabbis. Rather, it would have been a case of them getting separated, and him assuming they would go back and look for him in the area around the temple—the last place he remembered seeing them. In the meanwhile, he was listening to the rabbis and asking them questions.

Of course we're speculating, but this scenario is at least compatible with what we know of Jesus later.

The situation was certainly confusing enough to result in what we read next: "But they didn't understand what he meant" (v. 41). Rearing the son of God was all new ground for Mary and Joseph. They probably felt like they just had to accept some strange things like this story.

Already Jesus' affinity with and comprehension of Scripture was far beyond what one would expect in a twelve-year-old, as the rabbis observed. But by asking and answering questions, Jesus appeared in this story, not as a teacher (as the apocryphal writings represent Him), but as a pupil.

Back to Nazareth

After this story, we read, "Then he returned to Nazareth with them and was obedient to them. And his mother stored all these things in her heart"(v. 51). Mary once again finishes the story with her own state of mind. The whole story was told through her eyes. She may have been guarding against the impression that Jesus was disobedient or heedless of his parents.

And at last we read, "And Jesus kept increasing in wisdom and stature, and in favor with God and men" (v. 52). This is an important statement, because it shows that Jesus' growth was gradual, and in many ways like other kids. That means he didn't have recourse to his omniscience or other divine attributes. If he had, there would be no progress—an omniscient God doesn't progress or learn new things.

Although Jesus could have accessed his divine power and omniscience, that wasn't his mission. Rather, "It was necessary for him to be made in every respect like us, his brothers and sisters, so that he could be our merciful and faithful High Priest before God. Then he could offer a sacrifice that would take away the sins of the people" (Hebrews 2:17 NLT).

For reasons we don't fully understand, in order for Jesus to be our high priest, he had to live as a human. The author of Hebrews explains further, "Every high priest taken from among men is appointed on behalf of men in things pertaining to God, in order to offer both gifts and sacrifices for sins" (Hebrews 5:1). The rules governing how atonement works dictate that there be a fully human intercessor, or priest. His name is Jesus.

The Big Picture

As the town of Bethlehem slept, the ground was shifting under their feet, but nobody noticed. It would be decades before sizeable numbers of people realized what was going on. During those years Jesus would grow up in the setting of village life. The only thing that seems clear is that he didn't make much of an impression to the neighbors. They seem surprised at his claims when he later preached to them (Luke 4). None of his disciples came from Nazareth.

At twelve, Jesus clearly knew who he was, and what he was to do. Then twenty years go by. Every year was just as long as the one before it. This was a huge wait. At synagogue, he wasn't telling anyone who he was or what he was going to do.

We know he underwent the loss of his earthly father, Joseph, during these years. Joseph was a godly man, and probably a good father. This added to Jesus' suffering. We don't know if Jesus discussed his mission and identity at home, but we know his brothers did not believe in him (John 7:5).

Keeping mostly silent was surely a difficult trial for Jesus. Have you ever had to keep a secret so important that it burns in your chest? The desire to tell people what was going on must have been agonizing. But we have no hint of him living any way other than a normal young man. The Gnostic gospels and other Pseudepigrapha (documents with a false claim of authorship) advance all manner of miracle stories, heroizing young Jesus, but none of them are true. They all originated more than a hundred years after Jesus.

Jesus wouldn't step forward until John the Baptist had come to make his way.

4

John Steps Forward

Luke 3:1-22

Luke sets the stage with his usual load of details:

> Now in the fifteenth year of the reign of Tiberius Caesar, when Pontius Pilate was governor of Judea, and Herod was tetrarch of Galilee, and his brother Philip was tetrarch of the region of Ituraea and Trachonitis, and Lysanias was tetrarch of Abilene, in the high priesthood of Annas and Caiaphas, the word of God came to John, the son of Zechariah, in the wilderness. (3:1-2)

Each of these names are markers for fixing the date. Unlike today, when most of the world uses the Gregorian calendar and the BC/AD dividing point, ancient writers used the reigns of various emperors, governors, and lesser officials to specify a narrow span of time. When those spans are overlaid, they narrow the period in question to a single year or two.

Here Luke names six reigns of different rulers:

Tiberius Caesar

Tiberius was emperor of the Roman Empire from the death of Augustus Caesar. His first year lasted from August, AD 14 until April AD 15. That means Tiberius' fifteenth year would be late AD 28 or early 29. This is the most exact date Luke gives us for the beginning of John the Baptist's ministry.

Some argue that John's ministry could date from Tiberius' "co-regency" where he reigned along with Augustus for two years. That would push the date back two years earlier. But as Hoehner explains, "There is no evidence, either from historical documents or coins, for [dating from the co-regency]—whereas there is abundant evidence that Tiberius reckoned his first year after the death of Augustus."[1] This favors the AD 28 or 29 date.

Pontius Pilate

Pilate was Procurator of Judea from AD 26–36.[2] So that fits.

Herod Antipas

This is the son of evil Herod the Great who tried to kill Jesus at his birth. He ruled as tetrarch (ruler of a quarter) over Galilee and Perea from 4 BC until AD 39.[3] Luke correctly identifies him as Tetrarch, not as a king. He never held that title. This is the Herod who would eventually kill John the Baptist.

Philip

He was another son of Herod the great by his fifth wife, Cleopatra of Jerusalem (no relation to the famous Cleopatra). He was half-brother to Antipas and ruled the northeast segment of his father's realm from 4 BC to AD 34.[4]

Lysanias (the Younger)

Josephus refers to a Lysanias who ruled over Abilene, to the north of Philip's territory. That Lysanias was probably the father of this one in Luke. Scholars used to claim that this was an historical error on the part of Luke. But now two inscriptions have been found proving that in about 36 BC one Lysanias ruled over Abilene as king. So this is a case

1. Hoehner, *Chronological Aspects*, 31-32.
2. Josephus, *Antiquities*, 18.4.2.
3. Josephus, *Antiquities*, 18.7.1-2.
4. Josephus, *Antiquities*, 18.4.6.

where Luke knew more than modern historians. His exact dates cannot be determined today.

The High Priesthood of Annas and Caiaphas

Annas was high priest from AD 6 to 15. At that point he was removed from the high priesthood by the Romans, but he continued to rule through and with his son-in-law, Caiaphas, from AD18 to 37. These two were front and center in condemning Jesus.

When you overlay all these spans of time, only AD 28 or 29 satisfy all of the specs for the beginning of John the Baptist's ministry. This becomes important when trying to date the beginning of Jesus' ministry shortly after John's. The best date for Jesus beginning his ministry is AD 29.

It's also important for refuting those readers who view Luke's book as fiction written in the middle of the second century. Why would a writer from that period include a passage like this? And how would they gain the knowledge to do so? Luke is history, not fiction. Here, Luke has rooted the flow of events firmly into the history of the area in question.

The Word of God Comes

John the Baptist lived an eccentric and austere life, along the lines followed by some Old Testament prophets like Elijah. He dressed like Elijah, too. John's diet was made up of "locusts and wild honey" (Mark 1:6). It's desert food. Prophets sometimes went out to the desert to have dealings with God. Jesus would do the same thing, but not as long as John.

At the specified time,

> The word of God came to John, the son of Zechariah, in the wilderness. And he came into all the district around the Jordan, preaching a baptism of repentance for the forgiveness of sins. (v. 2-3)

Baptism was not new with John. Jews had long been practicing baptism as a cleansing for Gentiles who wanted to convert to Judaism.[5] As

5. Almost all of our information on Jewish baptismal practices come from sources later than Jesus, like the *Mishnah* and the *Talmud*. However, these practices originated much earlier, during the inter-testamental period. Numbers 19:7 prescribes washings for the priests before offering sacrifice (also other washings in Leviticus 13-14). Since proselytes had to offer an offering, it made sense

Gentiles were considered unclean, a washing in water signified that they were discarding the filth of Gentile living, and it made them clean enough to offer their initiatory sacrifice at the temple.

So John wasn't original, but he was revolutionary. He wasn't baptizing Gentiles, but Jews. John's revolution attacked the central assumption of rabbinic Judaism—that observant Jews were righteous. That belief was not only untrue, but also created a complete block to receiving the grace of God. Who needs grace and forgiveness when you're already righteous?

John's message was that you—a Jew—also needed to repent and be washed, because you're not righteous, but sinful. To "Prepare the way for the Lord's coming" (v. 4), he "was preaching a baptism of repentance for the forgiveness of sins" (v. 3). To accept John's baptism, people had to "repent;" a word that means a change of mind or a change of heart. In this case, Jews must turn away from the view that they were already righteous; admit their sin, and their need for forgiveness.[6]

John was also preaching in the power of the Holy Spirit and many thousands were hearing and believing what he said. Luke speaks of "the crowds who were going out to be baptized" (v. 7). Mark says, "All the country of Judea was going out to him, and all the people of Jerusalem" (Mark 1:5). Years later, even after he was dead, cynical Pharisees admitted that "all regard John as a prophet" (Matthew 21:26). Even Josephus, decades later, wrote of people's love and admiration for John.[7]

Some scholars have argued that John got his teaching from the Jewish sect called *Essenes*. This fringe group also expected a coming messiah and they practiced baptism. However, the similarity is superficial, and not really a valid parallel. The *Essenes* practiced baptism as a regular, ongoing washing sometimes done several times a day. It was not associated mainly with conversion but with ongoing purity. So it was nothing like John's baptism.

---

that they must be washed first.

6. The NLT consistently translates the word "repent" as "repent of your sins." (See v. 8). The inserted words are not original and are not a good translation. The word "repent" is *metanoia*, from a combination of *meta* meaning change, and the word *nous* meaning "mind." It means a change of mind or a change of heart, not a decision not to sin, as implied by the NLT translation.

7. Josephus, *Antiquities*, 18.5.2. Josephus recounts how people believed Herod lost a battle as punishment for killing the righteous John. He doesn't seem to know about the details of John's death at the hand of Herod and his blood-thirsty wife and stepdaughter, who demanded his head on a platter (Mark 6:17-28). This story must have come from an inside source in Herod's palace. We will see that Luke and Mark had such a source.

John lived in the wilderness and spoke from a position outside normal culture. Jews of that period would admire his strict life of abstinence. They would have seen it as evidence that he was a holy man.

We never hear of John performing any miracles. When he came out of the wilderness, he was probably traveling from south of the Dead Sea north to the Jordan valley. There, he had a constant supply of waist-deep water in the Jordan river. This was not true for most of Judea. In a land where streams and rivers run dry most of the year, the Jordan continues to flow.

John's Mission in Isaiah

The core of his message was that he was here to "make ready the way of the Lord" (v. 4). John correctly said his citation was from Isaiah, and we find it in Isaiah 40:3-5. Those who deny the deity of Christ must be embarrassed when discovering that "the Lord" here in Isaiah is *Yahweh*, the name of God only. John later clarified that "the Lord" here was also Jesus.

The last line of his citation says, "And then all people will see the salvation sent from God" (v. 6). Here John prophesied that the new covenant would spread out to the whole world, instead of hunkering down in Israel.

Example Interactions

Next Luke gives us some more examples of how John preached.

The Leadership

Luke recounts:

> When the crowds came to John for baptism, he said, "You brood of snakes! Who warned you to flee the coming wrath? Prove by the way you live that you have repented of your sins and turned to God." (vs. 7-8 NLT)

Matthew is more specific in recounting this statement. He explains, "When he saw many of the Pharisees and Sadducees coming for baptism, he said to them, 'You brood of vipers . . .'" (Matthew 3:7). That makes sense. No doubt they were part of a larger crowd, but here were the preachers of the religious view John had come to challenge. He publicly denounced them before the crowd, drawing their lasting ire. He made clear that God places no value on showy actions intended to fake spirituality. Only real, humble faith that bears fruit matters to God.

Against Ethnic Salvation

John also rejected the widespread belief that Jews were automatically saved:

> "Don't just say to each other, 'We're safe, for we are descendants of Abraham.' That means nothing, for I tell you, God can create children of Abraham from these very stones.'" (v. 8 NLT)

The view that Jews automatically inherit salvation is never taught in the Old Testament. Israel's choosing was not a choice to go to heaven, but a call to a mission so that "In you all the families of the earth will be blessed" (Genesis 12:3). So the view that being Jewish was sufficient to gain God's favor was a false teaching. Genesis reveals the real basis for Abraham's acceptance in 15:6: "Then he [Abram] believed in the Lord; and He reckoned it to him as righteousness." Faith, not ethnicity, has always been God's requirement for salvation.

The Dividing Line

John preached a polarizing message that predicted only two possible fates:

> Even now the ax of God's judgment is poised, ready to sever the roots of the trees. Yes, every tree that does not produce good fruit will be chopped down and thrown into the fire." (v. 9 NLT)

According to the previous verse, bearing good fruit is evidence that one's repentance is real. God will expose fake followers and destroy them unless they repent.

Ethics and Good Works

For those who were sincere, John taught what a godly life looked like.

> The crowds asked, "What should we do?"

> John replied, "If you have two shirts, give one to the poor. If you have food, share it with those who are hungry." (vs. 10-11 NLT)

Here, John's message is moderate and in line with both Old and New Testament ethical teaching. Sharing with those in need is basic sacrificial love.

And Tax Collectors

Tax collectors in this setting were nothing like the tax collectors at the IRS. We pay taxes so the government can carry out services beneficial to us. Highways, police, schools, defense, and airports cost money, and it comes from taxes.

These men were not collecting taxes for the Jews' benefit. They were collecting for the military occupiers of Judea, the Romans. The money went into the coffers of the Roman rich, and helped to pay for the very army that was oppressing the Jews. These collectors were traitors and collaborators, collecting from their own people and giving it to their enemies.

That brings us back to John the Baptist. We read,

> Even corrupt tax collectors came to be baptized and asked, "Teacher, what should we do?"
>
> He replied, "Collect no more taxes than the government requires." (vs. 12-13 NLT)

That's again, very moderate, not extreme at all. It would hardly satisfy the hardliners in Israel. He didn't even call on them to leave tax collecting.

Soldiers

Even some Roman soldiers showed up.

> "What should we do?" asked some soldiers. John replied, "Don't extort money or make false accusations. And be content with your pay." (v. 14 NLT)

That is amazingly moderate! Soldiers were able to get payoffs through threats, or false accusations. John called for nothing more than avoiding such unethical self-enrichment.

So this brief profile reveals that John was severe when speaking to those who he believed were faking it, or who considered themselves righteous. But he was moderate and reasonable when dealing with people who were sincerely seeking for God.

These incidents give us a feel for John's ethical teaching. But the core of his teaching was what we saw earlier—humble repentance and conversion.

John's Place in God's Plan

Luke says,

> Everyone was expecting the Messiah to come soon, and they were eager to know whether John might be the Messiah. (v. 15 NLT)

Why were they expecting the Messiah soon? Because Daniel, the Old Testament prophet, had predicted he would come around this time. People weren't able to exactly calculate the year, like we can today, but they knew it was the general time as Luke says. Josephus says about Daniel:

> The books which he wrote and left behind are still read by us even now, and we are convinced by them that Daniel spoke with God, for he was not only wont to prophesy future things, as did the other prophets, but he also fixed the time at which these would come to pass.[8]

Josephus is correct that no prophet specifies the date for the fulfillment of any prophecy in the Old Testament except Daniel. In Daniel 9 he specified the number of years that would elapse from a decree to rebuild Jerusalem until the coming of the Messiah. It comes out to AD 33.

At this point, the Gospel of John gives us extra detail:

> This is the testimony of John, when the Jews sent to him priests and Levites from Jerusalem to ask him, "Who are you?"
>
> And he confessed and did not deny, but confessed, "I am not the Christ."
>
> They asked him, "What then? Are you Elijah?"

8. Josephus, *Antiquities*, 10.266-67.

> And he said, "I am not."
>
> "Are you the Prophet?"
>
> And he answered, "No."
>
> Then they said to him, "Who are you, so that we may give an answer to those who sent us? What do you say about yourself?"
>
> He said, "I am a voice of one crying in the wilderness, 'Make straight the way of the Lord.'"(John 1:19-23)

You can see that he identified himself with Isaiah's crier. He specifically denied that he is the Messiah, Elijah, or "the prophet." "The prophet" refers to Moses' statement in Deuteronomy 18:15 that God would one day send a prophet like him. The rabbis had come to believe that this prophet was the Messiah, and according to Peter, they were right (Acts 3:22).

One Is Coming

After these denials, they pressed him further. He said:

> "I baptize you with water; but someone is coming soon who is greater than I am—so much greater that I'm not even worthy to be his slave and untie the straps of his sandals. He will baptize you with the Holy Spirit and with fire. He is ready to separate the chaff from the wheat with his winnowing fork. Then he will clean up the threshing area, gathering the wheat into his barn but burning the chaff with never-ending fire." (vs. 16-17 NLT)

This response puts the focus on the coming one. John clearly sees his own role can only be understood in that light. When the Messiah comes, he will baptize with the Holy Spirit and with fire. The picture that follows explains what these baptisms are.

He has a "winnowing fork," which is a wooden pitchfork. The farmer lets his grain stalks dry out until they're crumbly. Then, he lays the sheaves on a wooden platform called a "threshing floor." The platform is ideally situated on top of a hill to catch the wind. Next, the farmer threshes the grain, meaning he beats it with a stick, walks on it, or has a farm animal pull a round weight over it. The grain comes loose from the crumbling pods.

Finally, on a breezy day, the farmer takes his winnowing fork, digs into the pile, and throws the mixture up into the air. The wind blows the light chaff away, but the dense grain kernels fall back onto the threshing floor. A few repetitions of this and all the chaff is gone from the floor. At this point he has "cleaned his threshing floor." The chaff now lies on the ground around the platform. The farmer gathers up the worthless chaff and sets it on fire. The grain he gathers, bags it up, and takes it to the barn.

So it's a message of polarization. John isn't authorized to separate believers from unbelievers. But the coming one will have that authority.[9]

Herod

Just like Elijah of old, John's mission included denouncing a wicked ruler, Herod Antipas, and his evil wife.

> John also publicly criticized Herod Antipas, the ruler of Galilee, for marrying Herodias, his brother's wife, and for many other wrongs he had done. So Herod put John in prison, adding this sin to his many others. (vs. 19-20 NLT)

Herodias left her husband, Philip, for Herod. So it was adultery at the least. She was also apparently his niece.[10] It turned out that John would never get out of this imprisonment. His ministry didn't last very long. Jesus' and John's ministries overlapped, but only by a year or so. That, plus a few months before Jesus' baptism, is the extent of his short, very powerful, but sad, ministry.

Jesus' Baptism

Sometime during AD 29 Jesus showed up calling on John to baptize him. Luke's account is very short:

---

9. Some interpreters mistakenly argue that the baptism of fire refers to the tongues of fire that came onto the disciples on the day of Pentecost. That is word association interpretation. Instead, context—here the image of cleaning the threshing floor—is the first factor in interpretation. The fire clearly stands for hell.

10. D. A. Carson, *Matthew,* in *The Expositor's Bible Commentary with the New International Version*, vol. 8 (Grand Rapids, MI: Zondervan, 1984), 338.

> One day when the crowds were being baptized, Jesus himself was baptized. As he was praying, the heavens opened, and the Holy Spirit, in bodily form, descended on him like a dove. And a voice from heaven said, "You are my dearly loved Son, and you bring me great joy." (vs. 21-22 NLT)

This is a clear example where Luke has not arranged his accounts in chronological order. This baptism had to precede the earlier account of John being arrested, because John was the baptizer (Mark 1:9).

Matthew adds the dialog they had. When Jesus came, John felt uncomfortable baptizing him:

> But John tried to talk him out of it. "I am the one who needs to be baptized by you," he said, "so why are you coming to me?"
>
> But Jesus said, "It should be done, for we must carry out all that God requires." So John agreed to baptize him. (Matthew 3:14-15)

Jesus and John were related, as we saw earlier. They may have been second cousins. John seems to know him on sight, suggesting they had spent time. But John didn't know Jesus was the Messiah (see below). His reluctance to baptize him was apparently because of Jesus' reputation for righteous living. Or perhaps if he did spend time with Jesus, he was impressed by the character and spirituality he saw.

Why Baptism?

That raises the question, why was Jesus being baptized, when John's baptism was for repentance and forgiveness of sin? We don't have a definite answer, but Jesus himself says it was something "God requires." The more complete reading is in the NASB: "In this way it is fitting for us to fulfill all righteousness." That seems to suggest that this baptism has something to do with the fullness of God's plan. Four specific reasons are possible.

1. First, by being baptized by John, Jesus was identifying himself with the people of God, the righteous remnant in Israel.
2. At the same time, he was identifying himself with John's ministry, suggesting continuity from John to himself.

3. Every legitimate king in Judah since Saul and David had been anointed by a prophet. Here, we see the last Old Testament style prophet anointing the last Davidic king.
4. 4. Finally, John was waiting for this event without knowing it. One of John's disciples, the apostle John, recounts what John later said of Jesus:

   "I did not recognize him as the Messiah, but I have been baptizing with water so that he might be revealed to Israel.... I saw the Holy Spirit descending like a dove from heaven and resting upon him. I didn't know he was the one, but when God sent me to baptize with water, he told me, 'The one on whom you see the Spirit descend and rest is the one who will baptize with the Holy Spirit.' I saw this happen to Jesus, so I testify that he is the Chosen One of God."(John 1:31-34)

So not until after his baptism did John realize that his own cousin was the Messiah! His mom and dad knew, but they either didn't tell him, or he was a kid at the time, and didn't get it. Or, they may have died before he reached an age where he could understand. After all, they were both "advanced in years." Jesus, for his part, was actively keeping it a secret. But from this point onward, Jesus began to selectively reveal who he was. God's voice from heaven must have left a lasting impression with this crowd.

But most of the time Jesus continued pushing for secrecy.[11] He wanted to reveal himself to those who would believe, but he was always sensitive to the danger of inciting the government too soon. His well-known statement, "My hour has not yet come," fully explains his efforts to keep his identity quiet until later. At the end, on Palm Sunday, things changed. When called on to hush those calling him Messiah he said, "I tell you, if these become silent, the stones will cry out!" (Luke 19:40). By then, his hour was at hand.

The Big Picture

John the Baptist strode from the desert into the history of God's program of rescue for the human race. Why did he spend years in the desert?

11. Jesus constantly told people who saw him perform miracles or recognized him for other reasons to tell no one. For example, Matthew 8:4, 9:30, 12:16, 16:20, 17:9; Mark 1:34, 3:12, 5:43, 7:36, 8:30; Luke 4:41, 5:14, 9:21, 9:36; John 7:3–4.

Were his parents dead, and him an orphan? That actually seems likely. So here is another aspect of his life of suffering. No doubt he was also communing with God in preparation for his ministry.

His short ministry was remembered by all, and even as late as Josephus (writing sixty years later) people were still talking about him.[12]

He was arrested by Herod Antipas and languished in prison for the last year or two of his life. Then, during a drunken feast, Herod's niece danced for the party in a way that "pleased" him so much that he swore he would give her whatever she wanted if she danced again.

Her macabre answer was unexpected. "Having been prompted by her mother [Herod's adulterous wife], she said, 'Give me here on a platter the head of John the Baptist'" (Matthew 14:8). Although reluctant, Herod didn't want his guests to see him break his vow, so he had John beheaded and put his head on a platter. His servants presented the prize to the evil women.

So John gave his life playing his part in God's plan to rescue humans. To the world, his life was a miserable failure. But Jesus said "Truly I say to you, among those born of women there has not arisen anyone greater than John the Baptist" (Matthew 11:11).

Meanwhile, Jesus burst on the scene with a spectacular display of God's favor. The Spirit descended, "like a dove." Was it light in the shape of a dove? The voice from heaven prevented any incorrect interpretation.

Word must have spread like lightning. Everyone standing there would have immediately gone home and told the story to everyone he or she knew. Expectations must have soared. But Jesus didn't follow up this spectacular event with more demonstrations. Instead, he quietly walked out into the desert.

12. Josephus, *Antiquities*, 18.5.2.

5

Mysterious Family Records

Luke 3:23-38

Luke says that when Jesus began his ministry he was "about thirty years of age" (Luke 3:23). That statement makes it clear that Luke didn't know Jesus' exact age. Jesus was born in late 5 or early 4 BC, as we saw earlier. We can also determine that he died in AD 33, and that his ministry lasted three and a half years. That means he began his ministry in late AD 28 or early 29.

At that time it seems he would have been 33 (e.g. 5 [BC] + [AD] 28 = 33 [years old]). But he actually would have been 32, because there is no "0 year." The year 1 BC ended one day, and the next day was AD 1. That's why students of chronology have to add or subtract one year, depending on whether they are adding or subtracting across the AD/BC divide. So Luke was correct: Jesus was about thirty when he began his ministry.

The Ancestors

Luke now gives us a detailed list of Jesus' ancestors reaching all the way back to Adam! The genealogies in the Bible are important because they trace the pathway of God's unfolding plan. They are not for measuring time, because they deliberately leave out some ancestors.[1]

They also disclose prophetic boundaries. For example, out of the whole human race, only one family—Abraham's—was chosen to bring forth the Messiah (Genesis 12:3). Then, out of Jacob's twelve sons, only those from the tribe of Judah were qualified to reign as kings (Genesis 49:10).

Later, God narrowed it down to one family out of the thousands of families in the tribe of Judah—the family of King David (Is. 9:6-7). And even more specifically, it would be the throne of the house of David. So out of the thousands of descendants following David over hundreds of years, only royal sons were qualified to be in the line of the Messiah.

Of course, a child has no control over what family he is born into, so this is an example of prophecy that was not under the control of the ones prophesied, and therefore could not be faked.

Matthew's Genealogy

Matthew gives a genealogy that reflects this sequence of kings, showing that Jesus was descended from the royal line of David through his son, Solomon. But a problem arises. At one point near the end of the Old Testament period, God pronounced a curse on the next to last Davidic king:

> Is this man [Jeconiah] a despised, shattered jar? Or is he an undesirable vessel? Why have he and his descendants been hurled out And cast into a land that they had not known? O land, land, land, Thus says the Lord, "Write this man down childless, A man who will not prosper in his days; For no man of his descendants will prosper Sitting on the throne of David Or ruling again in Judah." (Jeremiah 22:28-30 emphasis added)[2]

The problem is that Jesus was one of Jeconiah's descendants! Matthew

1. Matthew declared after giving his genealogy, "So all the generations from Abraham to David are fourteen generations; from David to the deportation to Babylon, fourteen generations; and from the deportation to Babylon to the Messiah, fourteen generations" (Matthew 1:17). This arrangement was to benefit memory when kids could count on their fingers as they recited the list. The actual list contains a number of generations Matthew leaves out.
2. The final king, Zedekiah, was Jeconiah's uncle, so he wasn't a descendent of Jeconiah either.

has him right there in Matthew 1:11-12. That means, according to Jeremiah, Jesus was not qualified to sit on the throne of David!

Contradiction with Luke's Genealogy

And that's not the only problem. If we compare Matthew's and Luke's genealogies, we find major differences:

Matthew 1	**Luke 3**
Jesus	Jesus
Joseph	Joseph
Jacob	Eli
Matthan	Matthat
Eleazar	Levi
Eliud	Melchi
Achim	Jannai
Zadok	Joseph

And so on. None of the names between Joseph and David match! Luke says Jesus descended from David's son, Nathan (v. 31). But Matthew says he descended through a different son, Solomon (Matthew 1:6). Earlier than David they agree with each other, but here is a plain contradiction.

The solution comes in a careful reading of Luke 3:23 and following. Notice the language is different when it comes to Joseph:

> [Jesus] as was supposed, the son of Joseph, the son of Eli, the son of Matthat, the son of Levi, the son of Melchi, the son of Jannai, the son of Joseph. . . . (vs. 23-24)

Scholars suggest that the implied reading of Luke adds the words in brackets: "Jesus as was supposed, the son of Joseph [but really] the son of Eli. . . ."[3] That's right. Joseph wasn't Jesus' blood father. He was Jesus' *adoptive* father. Under this reading, Eli is Mary's father. He was the true, blood grandfather of Jesus' humanity. Unfortunately, women

3. For example, Norval Geldenhuys, Walter Liefeld, and F. F. Bruce hold this view. Some other explanations have been advanced. For instance, some argue that one or more men listed in Luke's list were part of a "levirate marriage," where a husband dies, and his widow marries his brother to raise up children that preserve his name and inheritance (Deuteronomy 25:5–10). This could lead to different fathers being listed for the same son. But no compelling scenario can be shown. One place where a levirate marriage could fit in is at the point where Shealtiel and Zerubbabel show up in both genealogies.

were usually left out of ancient genealogies, so the record keeper went to the first male.

Matthew's list goes through the royal line of Davidic kings, beginning with king David and king Solomon. That's correct because of the promise God made to David, that his throne, through Solomon, would be eternal. But Jeconiah was one of those kings, and God promised none of his descendants would sit on David's throne. It looks like God created an insoluble dilemma.

But Luke's list shows that Joseph was only Jesus' *adoptive* father. And under Jewish law, adopted sons had the same inheritance rights as natural sons. So even though Jesus is a Davidic king, he is not a descendant of Jeconiah.[4]

That leads to an amazing and unexpected solution to the apparent contradiction in Old Testament prophecy. Jesus' credentials were that he was:

- a true blood descendant of Abraham
- a true blood descendant of Jacob
- a true blood descendant of Judah
- a true blood descendant of David
- and he was not a descendant of Jeconiah.
- Therefore, he was qualified to inherit the throne through his adoptive father.

Luke, who consistently speaks from Mary's point of view, gives us Mary's genealogy. Matthew, who consistently speaks from Joseph's point of view, gives us Joseph's list. Together, they meet all the requirements in Old Testament prophecy.

The Sources?

Where did this information come from? For both genealogies, two sources are possible.

4. The Jews didn't keep track of David's line during and after the exile. There were kings during the inter-testamental period, but they were from the tribe of Levi. So although the Jews of Jesus' day couldn't say who the Davidic inheritor of the throne was, God knew. The heir at this time was apparently Joseph.

One source was the public record, where Levites collected and updated genealogies. The many storerooms around the temple housed these records. Josephus, for instance, reproduced his genealogy which he says he got from public records.[5] Family lines were more important then, especially if you were a Levite like Josephus, or in the royal line of David, like Joseph. It's also reasonable that, knowing who Jesus was, his parents would have paid to have their genealogy updated when they presented Jesus at the temple. All of these public records were destroyed in AD 70 when the temple was burned and looted.

In addition to records at the temple, families had their own records of ancestors. These were often written down, but also used to teach children to recite their lineage. Thus, Mary may have had her ancestry record kept at home. The temple's record would more likely be Joseph's as head of the family.

Matthew's Additions

In an unusual move, Matthew included the names of four women in his list in Matthew 1. They were included because in each case they confronted and contradicted the prevailing view that God only works through righteous people. The four are:

1. "Judah was the father of Perez and Zerah by Tamar" (v. 3). This refers to the disgraceful incident where one of the patriarchs, Judah, committed incest with his daughter in law, Tamar, after she disguised herself as a prostitute. She became pregnant, but when Judah went into a self-righteous fit, trying to kill her, she was able to prove to all the elders that Judah himself was the father! Her son of incest ended up in the line leading to Jesus.
2. "Salmon was the father of Boaz by Rahab" (v. 5). Rahab was a prostitute by trade, and a Gentile from the city of Jericho. She would have been viewed as scum by the self-righteous leaders Matthew opposed. But she saved the Jewish spies and ended up in the line of the Messiah.
3. "Boaz was the father of Obed by Ruth" (v. 5). Ruth was from the hated nation of Moab. They worshipped Chemosh, a blood-thirsty

5. He says in his autobiography, "Thus have I set down the genealogy of my family as I have found it described in the public records." Josephus, *The Life of Flavius Josephus*, i.

idol who demanded human sacrifice. But she was converted and ended up in the line of the Messiah.

4. "David was the father of Solomon by Bathsheba who had been the wife of Uriah" (v, 6). Bathsheba was married to another man—Uriah, one of David's most faithful servants. When David lusted for her, he took her and they slept together. When she got pregnant and they were about to be caught, David decided to lie by saying it was Uriah's child. When that that didn't work, David had him murdered. This is one of the most horrific sins recorded of any follower of God. But Bathsheba's son, Solomon, ended up as king and progenitor of Jesus.

The lesson is clear. God uses common, sinful people in pursuit of his plan.

The Big Picture

Centuries before Jesus, people and events described in the Old Testament were coming and going without any clear picture of where it was all headed. Every synagogue in the first century had their own copy of most or all of these Old Testament books. They called the collection the *Tanakh*.

The books of the *Tanakh* contained a contradiction as to who could be the Messiah, as we saw. Then, when Jesus came, the seemingly insoluble dilemma—that Messiah would be in the royal line of David, but that he could not be a descendant of Jeconiah—was suddenly solved by a virgin birth!

In Jesus' genealogy we have a miraculous confirmation of the reliability of God's word. This is one of multiple points of authenticating prophetic evidence we will encounter as we journey through Luke. We have unquestionable evidence that all the books in the Old Testament were written long before Jesus was born. And it's so implausible that ancient prophets could have somehow rigged their writings to come true. There's only one explanation: God's knowledge of the future. And the objective of these amazing predictions was Jesus.

6

Jesus Confronts His Enemy

Luke 4:1-13

Jesus was now ready to begin his ministry. But before going to the people, he went to face his enemy:

> Then Jesus, full of the Holy Spirit, returned from the Jordan River. He was led by the Spirit in the wilderness, where he was tempted by the devil for forty days. Jesus ate nothing all that time and became very hungry. (4:1-2 NLT)

Moses said, "When I went up to the mountain to receive the tablets of stone, the tablets of the covenant which the Lord had made with you, then I remained on the mountain forty days and nights; I neither ate bread nor drank water" (Deuteronomy 9:9). Doing without water that long would be impossible apart from divine sustenance. But the point is that Jesus and Moses both went early in their ministries on a forty day fast.

We see no claim that Jesus went without water. When it comes to food, however, we know of people in our own day who have fasted longer than forty days, so this is not unrealistic. We also know that Jesus lived as a man. He set aside the use of his divine attributes. That must be the case, because God cannot be tempted (James 1:13). The word for tempting (especially when in the passive, like here) also means to put someone to the test.

Grant Osborn correctly observes, "It is common for critical scholars to label this account a midrashic legend, but that is a worldview problem, not a literary conclusion."[1] Disbelief in a real Satan shreds the Bible's entire message from the Garden of Eden to the end of Revelation. Every act of God must be understood in light of the cosmic struggle so clearly taught in both Old and New Testaments.

Bread

The disciples weren't with Jesus during this episode, so he must have selected these three attacks to recount later, probably because they were typical of the whole struggle.

> Then the devil said to him, "If you are the Son of God, tell this stone to become a loaf of bread."
>
> But Jesus told him, "No! The Scriptures say, 'People do not live by bread alone.'" (vs. 3-4 NLT)

Why does the Evil One say, "If you are the son of God?" He just heard God declare that Jesus was his son in 3:22. He must have known who Jesus was or he wouldn't be chasing him around in the wilderness. He already tried to kill Jesus using Herod. Yet, it might have been confusing. Why wasn't Jesus manifesting his divine power? Why was he acting like a normal man?

We see no evidence that Satan had much knowledge of what was going on. In this encounter, he was either confused about Jesus' nature, or he was baiting Jesus to step outside of God's will in order to prove himself.

The suggestion that he make stones into bread seems innocuous enough. But the Holy Spirit was leading Jesus in the wilderness (v. 1) and Jesus was always sensitive to God's leading. He never went outside of that leading, as he said, "The Son can do nothing of himself, unless it is something he sees the Father doing; for whatever the Father does, these things the son also does in like manner" (John 5:19; see also John 5:36; 8:28; 38; 15:10). Jesus was always careful to avoid autonomy (self-rule).

1. Grant Osborne, *Luke Verse by Verse*, (Bellingham, WA, Lexham Press. Kindle Edition, 2018), 109.

Jesus was hungry; desperately hungry. What's wrong with using his miracle working power to generate some food? Jesus' answer from Deuteronomy 8 teaches on the need to depend on God to provide for our needs. The full verse says:

> "He humbled you and let you be hungry, and fed you with manna which you did not know, nor did your fathers know, that He might make you understand that man does not live by bread alone, but man lives by everything that proceeds out of the mouth of the Lord." (Deuteronomy 8:3)

This verse highlights two alternatives: trusting God to provide for our needs, or striving to meet our own needs. Self-sufficiency is related to pride, and is a sin. This sin lay at the base of Satan's first attack on humans in the Garden. The suggestion that God might be holding you down, and maybe you need to make your own way, is Satan's bread and butter. He thinks anyone who follows God is selling him or herself short and missing out on the fullness of life.

Jesus said exactly the opposite. "The thief comes only to steal and kill and destroy; I came that they may have life, and have it abundantly" (John 10:10). Who will we believe?

Jesus was not confused on the issue. He pointed directly to a passage that refers to "that which comes out of the mouth of God." It's a reference to the well-taught truth that God's word is his provision for our spiritual growth and health.[2]

The World System

After failing in his first attack, the Evil One tried something else:

> Then the devil took him up and revealed to him all the kingdoms of the world in a moment of time. "I will give you the glory of these kingdoms and authority over them," the devil said, "because they are mine to give to anyone I please. I will give it all to you if you will worship me."
>
> Jesus replied, "The Scriptures say, 'You must worship the Lord your God and serve only him.'" (vs. 5-8 NLT)

2. Consider 1 Peter 2:2. See also Psalm 1, 119; Isaiah 55:10-11; John 8:31-32, 15:7, 17:17; Acts 20:32; Romans 10:17, 15:4; Ephesians 6:17; Colossians 1:6, 3:16; 1 Corinthians 3:1-3; 2 Timothy 2:15, 3:16-17; Hebrews 5:11-14.

Wait. Satan owns the world and all its kingdoms? Yes! At least at that time he did. You notice Jesus doesn't challenge his claim, suggesting it was true. Jesus later called Satan "the ruler of this world" and "the prince of this world" (John 12:31; 14:30; 16:11). It wasn't until the cross that this legal ownership was wrested from his grasp (John 12:31, "Now judgment is upon this world; now the ruler of this world will be cast out").

Surprisingly, this is the first time in Scripture that we learn that Satan owns the world, but it is confirmed throughout the New Testament (e.g. James 4:4; 1 John 2:15; 5:19). God originally gave sovereignty over the planet to humans (Genesis 1:28). But apparently when Adam and Eve followed Satan and fell away from God's leadership, they forfeited that position.

Jesus had come, in part, to reverse that scenario and take possession of the world for himself and his adopted co-heirs—the people of God. As a result, the angels sing, "The kingdom of the world has become the kingdom of our Lord and of His Christ; and He will reign forever and ever" (Revelation 11:15).

Paul adds, "The Spirit Himself testifies with our spirit that we are children of God, and if children, heirs also, heirs of God and fellow heirs with Christ" (Romans 8:16-17).

Thanks to Jesus' work, Satan no longer owns the world, but the problem is that he isn't acknowledging the transfer. Instead, he fights to protect his empire against incursions from believers. Each person won over to faith is one less slave for Satan. He ends up in the lake of fire.

So when Satan offered to give Jesus the world and all its glory, he was offering something that would soon belong to Jesus anyway. And he had one nasty condition. The word here for "worship" means to bow down. Jesus bowing before his enemy; that wasn't going to happen. "He replied, 'The Scriptures say, "You must worship the Lord your God and serve only him"'" (v. 8). He was quoting Deuteronomy 6:13.

"In an instant" probably means that this temptation came as a vision.

Most commentators think Satan was trying to get Jesus to circumvent the cross.[3] I will argue that Satan didn't know Jesus was planning to die on

3. Walter Liefeld is typical: "The devil tried to prevent Christ's voluntary death for our sins, the implication of this second temptation was that accepting an immediate kingdom would avoid the Cross." Walter Liefeld, *Luke* in *The Expositor's Bible Commentary*, vol. 8 (Grand Rapids, MI: Zondervan), 864.

the cross. He believed the same thing others did—that the Messiah had come, not to die, but to rule. In fact, Satan was so oblivious to God's true plan that he weighed in himself, helping to bring about Jesus' crucifixion (John 13:2). Too late, he realized his error (1 Corinthians 2:8). The fact that he made Jesus this offer suggests he knew little about Jesus.

Leap!

> Then the devil took him to Jerusalem, to the highest point of the Temple, and said, "If you are the Son of God, jump off! For the Scriptures say, 'He will order his angels to protect and guard you. And they will hold you up with their hands so you won't even hurt your foot on a stone.'" (vs. 9-11 NLT)

Now we see Satan quoting Scripture. The passage he cited in Psalm 91 is a psalm rejoicing in God's protection. It doesn't apply only to the Messiah, but to all believers. Was Satan challenging Jesus' faith? Did he trust God enough to leap off this tower risking death? Yes, probably. And that makes this passage important in defining what true biblical faith is. Faith is not creating bizarre situations by launching ourselves out irrationally and expecting God to clean up the mess.

True faith is based on biblical promises. When God makes a promise, he will keep his word. Psalm 91's promises are addressed to "those who dwell in the shelter of the Most High." And to those who say, "My God, in whom I trust!" (vs. 1-2). Trusting God includes trusting his direction for your life. Leaping from the temple hardly fits that description. Setting my own direction and expecting God to make it come out well amounts to me doing the leading. God is reduced to my fix it guy.

Why leap from the temple instead of one of the many cliffs in that mountainous desert? Probably because it was the most crowded area in the region. Thousands would see Jesus sailing off the spire only to be kept from hitting the ground. That would be a sensational publicity stunt. It's also similar to the previous call to take the furtherance of his ministry into his own hands—a temptation felt by all who serve God.

The dark base underlying this temptation is the suggestion that Jesus must make successful ministry happen. He needs to pressure God. But putting God in the position where he must act because of one's reckless actions is really an effort to manipulate God. That's why Jesus responded, "The Scriptures also say, 'You must not test the Lord your God'" (v. 12).

Jesus' citation of Deuteronomy 6:16 is a call for the kind of reverence people should have toward God—not trying to lead God or tell him what to do, but quietly and patiently waiting on him to show us the way step by step. And we can expect God to show us a path that is reasonable and in accord with his word (unlike this unhinged suggestion of jumping off the temple).

A More Opportune Time

Finally we read, "When the devil had finished every temptation, he left him until an opportune time." (v. 13). Satan only throws a limited number and types of temptations. His predictability probably grows out of his knowledge of human nature and the psychology of sin. He sees no reason to change approaches because the ones he uses are so effective. Knowing how he works and how he thinks should be a distinct advantage for serving believers (2 Corinthians 2:11).

In this passage, Jesus deflected and refuted each of the enemy's attacks. The result? Satan faded away. Jesus gained strength, as Luke adds, "Jesus returned to Galilee in the power of the Spirit" (v. 14). Each time we win out over temptation and Satan's lies, we become more able to meet his attacks in the future. Likewise, succumbing to his suggestions makes it harder to resist him next time.

And there will always be a next time. Verse 13 ends with the ominous phrase, "until an opportune time." Satan is relentless, tireless, and knows how to build on earlier encounters.

The First and Last Adam

1 Corinthians 15:45 says, "The first man Adam became a living being; the last Adam, a life-giving spirit." Adam turned away from following God and was instantly changed. Instead of enjoying an open and free relationship with God and his new wife, he seems tortured. Trying to sew fig leaves to cover his genitals, hiding from God under a bush, lying about his shame, and blaming his wife—these actions signal a horrible dark shift in his nature. And he passed that nature down to all his descendants.

Jesus came to form a new humanity, no longer alienated from God. Adam is the type, and Jesus is the antitype. It's interesting to compare and contrast their experience when attacked by Satan.

Contrast

- Adam was with his wife, in full strength and perfectly healthy. Jesus was alone and isolated. At the end of a forty-day fast, he was weak and hungry.
- Adam was tempted in a lush, beautiful garden where his needs were all met. Jesus faced Satan in a stark, hot, and dry desert.
- Adam's temptation was to do something obviously wrong—God had laid no greater burden on him than to pick fruit from other trees, not this one. Jesus' temptations involved things that seemed morally neutral. Each action would have been easy to rationalize. So these incidents seem very different.

Compare

But in some key ways, the two incidents are quite similar.

- Adam and Eve's temptation centered on what God had said. That is, the word of God. Jesus' temptations also centered on God's word. Jesus clearly demonstrated his understanding that God's word is central to resisting Satan when he replied to each challenge with the words, "It is written. . . ."
- Satan appealed to Eve based on the lust of the flesh (the fruit was good for food), the lust of the eyes (the fruit was beautiful), and the boastful pride of life (the fruit was able to make one wise like God) (Genesis 3:6). With Jesus, Satan stuck with the same strategy. He appealed with the lust of the flesh (making the stones into bread), the lust of the eyes (all the beauty and grandeur of the world), and the boastful pride of life (showing off by jumping off the temple). John teaches that these three avenues of temptation comprise the heart of Satan's world-system (1 John 2:15-16).

Of course, the biggest contrast was the outcome: with Adam, failure; with Jesus, victory.

The Big Picture

Jesus strode in from the desert, ready to launch himself into his ministry. We already saw that Jesus was learning and growing in his life on earth. He was living as a man depending on the Holy Spirit for his strength, so his example here applies to us as well. The book of Hebrews says:

> For we do not have a high priest who cannot sympathize with our weaknesses, but One who has been tempted in all things as we are, yet without sin. Therefore let us draw near with confidence to the throne of grace, so that we may receive mercy and find grace to help in time of need." (Hebrews 4:15-16)

Jesus was changed as a result of this battle. For one thing, he understood, at a new level, what it's like to be tempted. That's important for us, because it means he can "sympathize with our weaknesses." That means we can approach God with "confidence" or "boldness." We're not afraid God might disapprove or not welcome us. Instead, he can soothe our aching souls with his warm knowledge of what we're going through.

7

JESUS AT NAZARETH

LUKE 4:14-29

Things started out well for Jesus' ministry.

> Then Jesus returned to Galilee, filled with the Holy Spirit's power. Reports about him spread quickly through the whole region. He taught regularly in their synagogues and was praised by everyone. (4:14-15 NLT)

This passage should not be overlooked, because it summarizes a lot of history. The Synoptic Gospels (Matthew, Mark, and Luke) are called synoptic because they see (optic) the same (syn) way. The fourth Gospel is John, who sees things differently. One area where this stands out is the chronology of Jesus' ministry.

Length of Jesus' Ministry

John covers three distinct Passovers at which Jesus was present (John 2:13; 6:4; 11:55). In addition, the "feast of the Jews" in John 5:1 could be Passover, or the Feast of Tabernacles. Either one would suggest another year had passed. So John has Jesus' ministry at three years plus the time between his baptism and the first Passover. That puts his ministry at about three and a half years long. Most scholars accept this length.[1]

1. Several incidental mentions of time add to this picture of three and a half years. The feeding of the 5000, recorded in all four Gospels, was near the Passover of John 6:4. Mark 6:39 mentions

The Synoptic Gospels all focus almost entirely on the last year and a half of his ministry, and mention only two Passovers. Looking closely at verses 14-15 cited above, notice Luke says, "Reports about him spread quickly through the whole region." That is, "quickly," not like our quickly, but like ancient quickly. Transport was almost all by foot, and people didn't travel to other towns very often. With no phones or TV, this statement by Luke signals a significant passage of time.

He also says Jesus, "taught regularly in their synagogues and was praised by everyone." To "teach regularly" must mean at least several times. And the synagogues are in the plural. So this describes a teaching ministry lasting a minimum of months, or more likely a year or two. This is when a lot of John's unique material and passage of time probably happened.

Of course, neither account is wrong. This is just another case of author selectivity—choosing which part of Jesus' ministry to cover.

Home Coming

So after this lengthy period of growing amazement and positive response, Jesus came back again to his home synagogue:

> When he came to the village of Nazareth, his boyhood home, he went as usual to the synagogue on the Sabbath and stood up to read the Scriptures. The scroll of Isaiah the prophet was handed to him. (vs. 16-17 NLT)

He's not standing with the scroll in his hands. Rather, there was an almost chest-high table at the center of the synagogue. The heavy scroll lies on that table and attendants help unroll and manipulate it.

> He unrolled the scroll and found the place where this was written:
>
> "The Spirit of the Lord is upon me, for he has anointed me to bring Good News to the poor. He has sent me to proclaim that captives will be released, that the blind will see, that the

the grass was green. That puts it in the spring, right before Passover. But earlier in the Synoptic Gospels is the story of the disciples plucking grain (Matt. 12:1; Mark 2:23; Luke 6:1). That must have happened near the harvest season (May) a year earlier. Jesus later said, "Do you not say, 'There are yet four months, and then comes the harvest'?" (John 4:35). That means the encounter with the woman at the well would have been in winter before the feast of John 5:1.

> oppressed will be set free, and that the time of the Lord's favor has come."
>
> He rolled up the scroll, gave it back to the attendant, and sat down. All eyes in the synagogue looked at him intently. Then he began to speak to them. "The Scripture you've just heard has been fulfilled this very day!" (vs. 17-21 NLT)

Jesus was reading Isaiah 61:1-2, but he stopped in the middle of verse 2. He read the part that says he was called, "To proclaim that the time of the Lord's favor has come." But he failed to complete the thought: "And the day of vengeance of our God."

We now know that Jesus came to make God's grace and favor available to all—the day of the Lord's favor." But "the day of vengeance of the Lord," refers to the judgment day. That still hasn't happened, even today. The rest of Isaiah's prophecy goes on to describe Jesus' second coming. He says at that time, "To all who mourn in Israel, he will give a crown of beauty for ashes" (v. 3). He predicts, "Foreigners will be your servants" (v. 5), and "You will be called priests of the Lord" (v. 6). Finally, "Everlasting joy will be yours" (v. 7).

This passage is clearly about the blessings of the future reign of the King fulfilled in Jesus. But how did Jesus' coming involve "the day of vengeance of our God?" And why did he stop reading where he did, right in the middle of a rhyming couplet? The text is clear that he deliberately "rolled up the scroll, handed it back to the attendant, and sat down" (v. 20).[2] Then he said, "Today this Scripture has been fulfilled in your hearing" (v. 21).

This is a case of "unforeseen, partial fulfillment," or what can also be called a "prophetic time gap." Any reader would see that Isaiah's prophecy was about the coming blessings of Messiah's kingdom. But it turned out that the fulfillment was going to happen in two phases. First, Jesus fulfilled verse 1 and part of 2. Then, unexpectedly, comes a gap of time—unannounced in the text—that spans over two thousand years, until "the day of vengeance of our God." Often biblical prophecy about Jesus skips from his first coming to his second coming, just like we see here.[3]

2. Commentators who don't believe in such a thing as a prophetic gap argue that Jesus just cited the first few lines to identify the passage. But then why would he give the scroll back to the attendant instead of reading on? He already had the scroll opened.

3. Many interpreters deny that prophetic gaps exist. Instead, they argue that the fulfillment of

Luke goes on that, "Everyone spoke well of him and was amazed by the gracious words that came from his lips. 'How can this be?' they asked. 'Isn't this Joseph's son?'" (v. 22).

You can sense the incredulity in their statement. Jesus knew any admiration was superficial. He knew they wanted to see a miracle. "And he said to them, 'No doubt you will quote this proverb to me, "Physician, heal yourself! Whatever we heard was done at Capernaum, do here in your hometown as well."'" (v. 23). They seem to be suggesting that a doctor who can't heal himself must be a phony. They were daring him to prove he was real. Jesus just observed, "No prophet is welcome in his hometown" (v. 24).

God's Heart for the Gentiles

Instead of catering to their desire for a miracle show, he was provocative:

> "Certainly there were many needy widows in Israel in Elijah's time, when the heavens were closed for three and a half years, and a severe famine devastated the land. Yet Elijah was not sent to any of them. He was sent instead to a foreigner—a widow of Zarephath in the land of Sidon. And many in Israel had leprosy in the time of the prophet Elisha, but the only one healed was Naaman, a Syrian." (vs. 25-27 NLT)

These cases from the Old Testament both refer to God working with Gentiles when he could have worked with Jews. His observation was probably part of a larger argument where Jesus suggested God was going to reach out to the Gentiles. Luke, the only Gentile author of a biblical book, frequently records how Jesus responded to Gentiles, especially when they believed, often in contrast to Jewish unbelief. The audience's reaction was immediate and ferocious:

---

the second portion will not come in any literal way. Instead, it will be fulfilled "spiritually" in the church. This view is partially true, in the sense that the church does take part in some blessings of the kingdom. The view is wrong, however, in saying that the kingdom promises to Israel have been cancelled. In many passages God insists that he will never reject the Jews as his people. For example, "'For this is like the days of Noah to me, when I swore that the waters of Noah would not flood the earth again; so I have sworn that I will not be angry with you nor will I rebuke you. For the mountains may be removed and the hills may shake, but my lovingkindness will not be removed from you, and my covenant of peace will not be shaken,' says the Lord who has compassion on you." (Isaiah 54:9-10). The New Testament agrees. Paul says, "As far as election is concerned, they [the Jews] are loved on account of the patriarchs, for God's gifts and his call are irrevocable" (Romans 11:28-29).

> When they heard this, the people in the synagogue were furious. Jumping up, they mobbed him and forced him to the edge of the hill on which the town was built. They intended to push him over the cliff, but he passed right through the crowd and went on his way. (vs. 28-30 NLT)

Rabbinic Judaism at this time had become an ethnic religion. Entrance to that religion for Gentiles involved a rigorous denial of their former way of life and beliefs. The Jews were possessive of their religion and resented any suggestion that God was going to turn to the Gentiles. Just like some crowds later in the book of Acts, the mention of Gentiles coming to God drove them crazy (e.g., Acts 21:21-22).

You can tell the narrator was impressed by Jesus passing right through the crowd. Had they lost their nerve and didn't want to face charges for murder? Was there some kind of majesty in Jesus that nobody wanted to attack? Was a miraculous dread cast upon the mob? We can't be sure, but it sounds supernatural.

Luke's Source

Where did Luke get this story? It's not in Matthew, Mark, or John. Jesus was already walking with disciples, so it could have been one of them. But we can also safely place another witness there—Mary, a native of Nazareth. Whether she was traveling with Jesus like later, or stayed at home, she certainly would have been in synagogue that day to hear her son teach.

Capernaum

> And he came down to Capernaum, a city of Galilee, and he was teaching them on the Sabbath. (v. 31)

Capernaum is about thirty miles from Nazareth on the northern shore of the Sea of Galilee. Archaeologists have excavated a synagogue there built in the third century, but also an earlier synagogue beneath the third century one. This older synagogue is the very place where this story took place.

Luke says, "They were amazed at His teaching, for His message was with authority" (v. 32). Mark adds, "He was teaching them as one having authority, and not as the scribes" (Mark 1:22). We have an idea of how the scribes taught when we read the Mishnah or Talmud. They constantly quote what this rabbi said or what that rabbi said, often disagreeing with each other. We also have examples of Jesus' authoritative teaching in passages like the sermon on the mount. There Jesus several times said, "You have heard it said . . ." and cites rabbinic teaching. Then, "But I say to you . . . " signifying that his authority exceeded that of the rabbis.

Confronting Demons

Jesus' authority came from the Father, and it included authority over the demonic:

> In the synagogue there was a man possessed by the spirit of an unclean demon, and he cried out with a loud voice, "Let us alone! What business do we have with each other, Jesus of Nazareth? Have you come to destroy us? I know who you are—the Holy One of God!"
>
> But Jesus rebuked him, saying, "Be quiet and come out of him!" And when the demon had thrown him down in the midst of the people, he came out of him without doing him any harm. (vs. 33-35)

Mark adds that the demon "threw him into convulsions" (Mark 1:26). This is the first case of deliverance in Luke. You see that the demon knew who Jesus was without being told. Hyperesthesia (the ability to know or feel things you have no way of knowing) is a classic symptom of demon-possession.

The demon spoke in the plural, suggesting there may have been more than one demon inhabiting the man. He challenged Jesus on whether he had come to destroy him. The demons know they are going to be judged, and they fear it (James 2:19).

Then when he identifies Jesus as "the Holy One of God," Jesus silences him. "Be quiet and come out of him." He didn't need an evil spirit to speak on his behalf. This was also during the period when Jesus was keeping a low profile concerning his identity.

The people watching Jesus had never seen anything like this:

> Amazement came upon them all, and they began talking with

> one another saying, "What is this message? For with authority and power he commands the unclean spirits and they come out." (v. 36)

In the modern, western world, Satan stays out of sight and persuades people he doesn't exist. But in this ancient world, everyone knew the spiritual realm was real. Fear of dangerous spirits afflicted ancient people, causing them to waste money on false exorcisms and false healings. Here with Jesus was real spiritual authority. John later declared that Jesus came to "destroy the works of the devil" (1 John 3:8). That work was already beginning.

And Healing

Jesus left the synagogue and went to Simon Peter's house.

> Now Simon's mother-in-law was suffering from a high fever, and they asked him [Jesus] to help her. And standing over her, he rebuked the fever, and it left her; and she immediately got up and waited on them. (vs. 38-39)

From demonic deliverance, Jesus moves to healing. The fact that the woman went from a high fever in bed to serving the guests shows it wasn't just a gradual recovery, but a true instantaneous, supernatural healing. And Luke knew the difference between disease and demon possession, unlike most ancient people.

> While the sun was setting, all those who had any who were sick with various diseases brought them to him; and laying his hands on each one of them, he was healing them. Demons also were coming out of many, shouting, "You are the Son of God!" But rebuking them, he would not allow them to speak, because they knew him to be the Christ. (vs. 40-41)

You can see the clear distinction Luke makes between illnesses and demon possession. Matthew goes even further, naming epileptics, paralytics, various diseases, and pains along with demon possession (Matthew 4:24). Epilepsy and paralysis were often seen to be caused by demons in ancient times. But not in the Bible—God, who inspired the text, knew better.[4]

4. There were cases when regular illness could accompany demonic activity (e.g. Matthew 12:22; Mark 9:18). At other times, events that might look natural are really a demon trying to kill its host,

Notice he was "laying His hands on each one of them" as he healed. Liefeld points out that this is an unusual procedure among the Jews, not found in the Old Testament nor in rabbinic literature.[5] How eloquently this expresses Jesus' warmth and compassion for people. It made healing a personal event, not just a decree.

They waited until sundown because it was Sabbath. When Sabbath ended at sundown Saturday, they came out in droves. Jesus must have served them long into the night. His miracle working and teaching were drawing people like a magnet. By now, thousands were hiking to the area.

> When day came, Jesus left and went to a secluded place; and the crowds were searching for him, and came to him and tried to keep him from going away from them. But he said to them, "I must preach the kingdom of God to the other cities also, for I was sent for this purpose." So he kept on preaching in the synagogues of Judea. (vs. 42-44)

Judea is the middle and southern part of the country, but it's also the name of the Roman province, which included both North and South. You can see Judea clearly meaning the whole country in Luke 23:5. We know from John that Jesus had an extensive ministry in Judea (the southern part). So this use refers to the whole province.

The Big Picture

As Jesus continued to travel and teach, he was also continuing John the Baptist's work of making the nation ready. He was showing the people a new and different view of God. During this part of Jesus' ministry his popularity was growing and nearing a peak. We read, "The report about Him was spreading into every locality in the surrounding district" (vs. 37).

When Jesus healed, it was for the purpose of making a statement. He exhibited his power in order to show that God had sent him and was with him. As evidence piled up, people would eventually understand his whole saving mission, but that would come later. When we read of

---

as in Matthew 17:15: "Lord, have mercy on my son. He has seizures and suffers terribly. He often falls into the fire or into the water."

5. Liefeld, *Luke*, 130. He points out it was attested once in Dead Sea literature.

the extraordinary response that came on Pentecost and the following months, this groundwork came into play.

Jesus was already widely known as a healer and worker of miracles, so when that was combined with the realization that he was the suffering servant and finally the apostles' testimony to his resurrection, people believed in great numbers. Likewise, the apostles were themselves granted the power to heal during the early days of the body of Christ, resulting in thousands of conversions in a short time.

Some people today think God should heal now just like he did then, but with the difference that the reason they are healed is merely that they are sick. That is not usually a sufficient reason for God to heal. God sovereignly decides when to heal. He cannot be manipulated on that decision. Most of the time, followers of Jesus suffer disease and death at roughly the same frequency as non-believers.

Teaching to the contrary—that healing is available to anyone with enough faith—leads to disillusionment and loss of faith when people are unable to pray their loved ones out of cancer, Alzheimer's, or other illnesses (often without using medicine). The problem is not a failure of faith, but false teaching, promising something God never promised. What he did promise is eternal life and complete healing when he returns.

God does heal today, and I've been privileged to see several remarkable cases. But in my experience, supernatural healing is rare. And when he does heal, God typically has a greater purpose. When Jesus raised Lazarus from the dead, he didn't solve the problem of death for Lazarus. He would still have to die, now for the second time. But in the meantime, Jesus made a great statement about his power over death. He was "the resurrection and the life" (John 11:25).

8

Jesus Confronts Ancient Thinking

Luke 5:1-26

Even though we're early in the book of Luke, it's important to realize that the stories in this chapter didn't happen at the beginning of Jesus' ministry. He had already been teaching and preaching for perhaps two years by this time, the majority of that in Galilee. Simon Peter's rather different encounter described in Mark 1:16-20 happened earlier, and is not the same event we read of here.

Peter already knew Jesus and Jesus had called him earlier. But now we find him back in his fishing business. He hadn't grasped what being called by Jesus meant. He was foot-dragging and short arming his response. Jesus moved in to confront him with divine power.

> One day as Jesus was preaching on the shore of the Sea of Galilee, great crowds pressed in on him to listen to the word of God. He noticed two empty boats at the water's edge, for the fishermen had left them and were washing their nets. Stepping into one of the boats, Jesus asked Simon, its owner, to push it out into the water. So he sat in the boat and taught the crowds from there. (Luke 5:1-3 NLT)

Luke calls Peter Simon until 6:14. After that, he's Peter, because Jesus gave him that name. Night was the time for net fishing the Tilapia species that still inhabit the lake. The boats were empty and the fishermen were washing their nets because they were finishing the night's work.

Their boats weren't very large. An authentic first century fishing boat sank and was preserved in mud near Capernaum. Archeologists restored it and it's on display there today, under the name "The Jesus Boat." You can see how little free-board it has, even allowing for a couple of boards missing along the gunwale. That helps explain how a load of fish could threaten to sink the boat, especially when pulling a heavy net full up from the side.

The Old Testament calls it the Sea of Galilee, but Luke calls it a lake. It is a lake, with fresh water, about fifteen miles long and seven miles wide. It's relatively shallow with the deepest place near the center at about 140 feet deep.

The crowds were a nuisance by now, so needy and persistent. But Jesus continued to patiently teach. Pushing a few feet off shore created an amphitheater effect.

> When he had finished speaking, he said to Simon, "Now go out where it is deeper, and let down your nets to catch some fish."
>
> "Master," Simon replied, "we worked hard all last night and didn't catch a thing. But if you say so, I'll let the nets down again." And this time their nets were so full of fish they began to tear! A shout for help brought their partners in the other boat, and soon both boats were filled with fish and on the verge of sinking.
>
> When Simon Peter realized what had happened, he fell to his knees before Jesus and said, "Oh, Lord, please leave me—I'm a sinful man." For he was awestruck by the number of fish they had caught, as were the others with him. (vs. 4-10 NLT)

Only pro fishermen could fully appreciate how impossible this miracle was. Peter and the others struggled to get the catch ashore. Finally, as the full recognition registered on Peter, he spun around and looked at

Jesus. Jesus stared back. Was there a slight grin on Jesus' face? It wasn't that Peter saw Jesus for the first time, but that he had seen enough.

Peter responded in a way that is not unusual when people realize they are in the presence of a holy God. His awareness of his own sin welled up, but it also tended to drive him away from Jesus. Only those well-taught in grace can avoid this instinctive reaction. Peter didn't comprehend grace very well at this point in his life. Neither did he likely comprehend it when Jesus said, "Do not fear, from now on you will be catching men" (v. 10).

Luke says, "They left everything and followed Him" (v. 11). It doesn't mean they just walked away from their over-loaded boats like zombies and left the catch to rot. It's far more reasonable to think they first divided the catch and left the income with their families to cover their expenses while Dad was on the road with Jesus.

Likewise, they would have left their boats with other family members. We see the disciples with one or more boats later in Luke's narrative, so they still owned the boats. In catching the miraculous load of fish, Jesus was probably planning the huge catch partly in order to support their families. At the same time he was overcoming any remaining unbelief in his key followers.

Grasping a Leper

Then comes a remarkable event:

> In one of the villages, Jesus met a man with an advanced case of leprosy. When the man saw Jesus, he bowed with his face to the ground, begging to be healed. "Lord," he said, "if you are willing, you can heal me and make me clean." (v. 12 NLT)

"Leprosy" was a word used for various skin diseases. They didn't know how to differentiate such skin conditions from Hansen's disease—a truly dangerous, disfiguring, and ultimately fatal bacterial infection that attacks the nerves, respiration, skin, and eyes. Victims often lose fingers or toes because they have no feeling in their extremities, resulting in burns and cuts that go unnoticed. It also causes white lesions and pale areas on the skin.

Ancient people were terrified of leprosy. They had no idea what caused it, and their only countermeasure was quarantine. If a leper showed up near uninfected people, they would throw stones to keep him away. As a result of such fear and loathing, lepers had no way to earn a living. They had to beg for food or raise their own gardens in designated colonies. The leper in this encounter was "full of leprosy," so it was a severe case.

Jesus had been healing in the area for some time, so the leper knew he was able to heal. The question was whether he was willing. Then Jesus did the astonishing:

> Jesus reached out and touched him. "I am willing," he said. "Be healed!" And instantly the leprosy disappeared. Then Jesus instructed him not to tell anyone what had happened. (vs. 13-14 NLT)

Touching a leper was unthinkable. But "touch" is probably a weak translation of *haptomai.* The more common translations are "to fasten one's self to, adhere to, or cling to." Jesus didn't just stick his forefinger out and touch him. Jesus *grasped* the leper! This matches Jesus' often repeated mission statement, that he had come to reach out to the weak, the disabled, and the marginalized (4:18).

Cleanliness Laws

It's hard not to also see this as a picture of Jesus' attitude toward sinful people. We know God abhors sin because it offends his nature (Habakkuk 1:13). He gave cleanliness laws, which in many cases reminded people of the problematic nature of sin by connecting sin with other daily elements of life. For instance, touching a dead body makes one unclean because of the linkage between sin and death.

Becoming unclean doesn't mean you are in sin, but that you have contacted something related to sin. These laws are for teaching purposes, including reminding people of the pervasive impact of humans' fall from grace. The quarantine laws for leprosy were also for protection. They clearly implied that one shouldn't touch a leper.

But here, Jesus shows another side of God's nature—he grasped the leper. He healed him. This healing clearly demonstrates Jesus' power, but even more it cries out his willingness to come to grips with sinful humans.

Jesus wasn't grossed out by the leper, and he isn't grossed out by us. He knows all about our sin, but he grasps and holds us anyway.

Jesus' Directions

> Jesus ordered him to tell no one, "But go and show yourself to the priest and make an offering for your cleansing, just as Moses commanded, as a testimony to them." (v. 14)

Jesus sent the man to the priests because the Old Testament prescribed that the priests were responsible to examine a former leper. They would officially declare he was clean and safe to reenter society (Exodus 13).

Jesus' remark that it would be a testimony to the priests fits in with the stream of tips he was sending, beginning with his astonishing discussion with the rabbis in the temple as a boy. Now he confronted them with unprecedented healing power. Soon representatives of the powerful priestly class showed up to check Jesus out.

The healed man ignored Jesus' order that he tell no one. Mark says:

> But the man went and spread the word, proclaiming to everyone what had happened. As a result, large crowds soon surrounded Jesus, and he couldn't publicly enter a town anywhere. He had to stay out in the secluded places, but people from everywhere kept coming to him. (Mark 1:45)

How could you not say something when you show up in the old neighborhood healed from an incurable disease like leprosy? Luke agrees with Mark that "large crowds were gathering" as people hobbled up on crutches, in slings, and on stretchers. Here was real healing. Their "doctors" never really healed anyone. They were still shaking rattles and smearing mostly useless poultices on sick people's skin.

Escaping to Pray

We read that Jesus "would often slip away to the wilderness and pray" (v. 16). So God's Son considered it important to spend time with God, praying and nurturing his relationship. Jesus knew what it meant to commune with God. Sometimes these sessions lasted all night. The spiritual energy and filling he got from these times of prayer sustained him in his overwhelming ministry.

We could learn a lot from that. What does it mean if I'm too busy doing ministry to spend time in prayer? It's not a pretty picture. It would be a picture of someone who trusts in himself so much that he doesn't need the spiritual nurture Jesus needed.

The Paralytic

Jesus was in a crowded house teaching.

> Some men were carrying on a bed a man who was paralyzed; and they were trying to bring him in and to set him down in front of him. But not finding any way to bring him in because of the crowd, they went up on the roof and let him down through the tiles with his stretcher, into the middle of the crowd, in front of Jesus. (vs. 18-19)

Imagine Jesus teaching in this standing-room-only house and suddenly, dust and debris begins raining down. They all look up and there the tile and stick roof is being disassembled! Then things go from startling to insane. Here comes a palate with a man on it being lowered by ropes, right down on top of the crowd! People are pushing back to get out of the way, as murmurs and cries fill the air.

Jesus could have been irate. Why are they disrupting his teaching? But no. He actually sees this desperate act as a sign of great faith. "Seeing their faith, He said, 'Friend, your sins are forgiven you'" (v. 20). Surprising. The man was looking for healing, but instead, Jesus pronounces his sins were forgiven. He knew exactly what he was doing.

"The scribes and the Pharisees began to reason, saying, 'Who is this man who speaks blasphemies? Who can forgive sins, but God alone?'" (v. 21). They make a good point. Jesus is acting like he's God here. Who does he think he is to pronounce this man forgiven? But "Jesus knew what they were thinking, so he asked them, 'Why do you question this in your hearts? Is it easier to say, "Your sins are forgiven," or "Stand up and walk"?'" (vs. 22-23).

The Rabbis on Disease

To fully understand Jesus' question, it's important to understand the religious consensus he was facing on the issue of illness. We know the rabbis' views from their writings reflecting this period. "Ancient Judaism acclaimed God as source of health and illness, with sickness a divine-mandated punishment for individual and communal sins."[1] So in their view, this paralytic deserved his fate. He must have done something pretty bad earlier in life.

You see this logic in John 9:2: "Why was this man born blind? Was it because of his own sins or his parents' sins?" This question shows that the disciples were aware of the contemporary argument among rabbis concerning those born with a disability. If illness was the result of sin, how do they explain a man born already blind? Some rabbis said it was because of the parents' sin. But Ezekiel clearly teaches:

> "The person who sins will die. The son will not bear the punishment for the father's iniquity, nor will the father bear the punishment for the son's iniquity; the righteousness of the righteous will be upon himself, and the wickedness of the wicked will be upon himself." (Ezekiel 18:20)

In reply, other rabbis argued for "prenatal sin." The infant must have sinned while in the womb![2] None of this is from the Bible. And Jesus firmly rejected this uncompassionate teaching.

Jesus' Refutation

The order of Jesus' statements was purposeful—he was confronting their view. Their theology puts an interesting spin on Jesus' question, "Which is easier?" Under their theology, Jesus couldn't heal this man unless he first forgave the sin that caused his disability. They were cornered. They stare, but can't answer. Jesus answers for them, "So I will prove to you that the Son of Man has the authority on earth to forgive sins" (v. 24). Then he matter-of-factly healed the man.

Cries of amazement broke out from the crowd. "Everyone was gripped with great wonder and awe, and they praised God, exclaiming, 'We

1. "Illness & Healing: The Bible sees folk healing as idolatrous," *My Jewish Learning*, https://www.myjewishlearning.com/article/illness-healing/. Or, see the rabbinic teaching that women die in child birth because they failed to keep the Sabbath preparation—either dividing the dough, lighting the candle, or saying a certain prayer. *Mishnah Shabbat* 2:6

2. For example, *Midrash Rabbah* Genesis 63 teaches that Esau was wicked before his birth. It's a misunderstanding of Malachi 1, which is about the people of Edom, not Esau the baby. In *Babylonian Talmud* 91b they debate whether a fetus can sin. Direct connections between key sins and illness or tragedy are abundant.

have seen amazing things today!'" (v. 26). In a relatively small village, paralyzed people weren't that common. Most of the people there knew about this man, so there was no way to fake a healing.

Jesus wasn't confirming the rabbinic view by using this dilemma. Rather, he was saying that according to their own theology, his ability to heal implied the ability to forgive sin. This left them in a painful dilemma. Was their teaching on disease false? Or was Jesus divine? Or both?

The Big Picture

In Jesus' opening salvo, he cut directly across the grain of the religious consensus of his day. Reaching out to grasp the leper with his loving hand of healing was so unthinkable. He made sure the priests would see the supernatural outcome of his action. Then he confronted the crowd, along with visiting Pharisees and rabbis, with his ability to forgive sin. And that implied, in turn, his divinity. Already he was hinting at the ultimate goal of his mission—forgiveness for all fallen humanity.

Although Jesus had proven his divine authority to forgive sins, the Pharisees and scribes gathered there didn't accept the evidence of their own eyes. Neither did they modify their theology to remove its inherent contradictions. Instead, the whole incident with the paralytic only created anger.

The common people had a different response.

> They were all struck with astonishment and began glorifying God; and they were filled with fear, saying, "We have seen remarkable things today." (v. 26)

9

LEVI FOLLOWS JESUS
LUKE 5:27-39

At this point, Jesus did something that multiplied the shock effect:

> After that he went out and noticed a tax collector named Levi sitting in the tax booth, and He said to him, "Follow me." And he left everything behind, and got up and began to follow him. (Luke 5:27-28)

Levi and Matthew, who wrote our book of Matthew are the same person (compare with Matthew 9:9). People in this culture often had more than one name.

Jesus grasped the leper. He confronted the leaders. Now he did something more shocking still—he called a tax collector to be his disciple. Modern readers could easily miss why this was such a radical move.

Tax Collectors

Nobody enjoys paying taxes, but we do appreciate having highways, police, sewer systems, schools, and national defense. Viewed this way, taxes are inevitable. But none of these benefits came from the taxes these Jews paid as we saw earlier. They paid their taxes to Israel's hated enemy, Rome.

The Romans also supplied soldiers to enforce collections. You could find yourself driving your cart of goods to market only to be stopped by a tax collector. He could inventory your goods, and demand a percentage that was not fixed. Even if you complain that you just paid taxes earlier in the journey, it meant nothing. Several spear tips would point at anyone resisting. "Is there a problem?" the Romans would ask. This was tax law at the tip of a spear—in other words, "whatever I say."

To make matters worse, the Romans had a quota system where tax collectors bid for districts. The taxes they collected repaid their bid first. Then the collectors could gather even more and pocket the difference. The whole system was an open invitation to oppression and corruption.

With all the power on their side, tax collectors were usually rich. The so-called "King's Highway" ran from Egypt to Damascus, and passed just to the north of Capernaum, where Levi worked. He would have been reaping a rich harvest from the merchant traffic there.

The Jews bitterly hated tax collectors (as did people in other Roman provinces) not only because they were unfair in collecting, but because they had turned against their own people to collaborate with the enemy. This would be no different than a French official during World War II in occupied France collecting money for the Nazis at the end of a gun.

Jewish people at this time were not wealthy. Most people were poor. The few wealthy people were mostly land-owning aristocrats or collaborators with the Romans.

Unable to defeat Rome or its tax collectors, the rabbis lashed back the best they could. They gave out a special exception—although lying or swearing false oaths are normally sin, it was okay to lie to a tax collector, or even to swear an oath with no intent of keeping it.[1]

The leaders made tax collectors' word worthless in Jewish courts. They also declared tax collectors unclean, so much so that if a tax collector ever entered a house, the whole house and everything in it became unclean.[2]

The rabbis refer to "robbers, thieves, and tax collectors." Some rabbis argued that if a tax collector wanted to repent and return to God, he must return all the money he extorted. Then, whatever was taken from

1. *Mishnah* Nedarim 3:4.
2. *Mishnah* Tohoroth 7:6.

unknown people, or the deceased, went into a common fund for the community. Other rabbis argued that for tax collectors, it was too late to convert. Still others taught that a tax collector could repent, but it couldn't be authentic unless he dropped dead on the spot!

Jews especially resented tolls (like those Levi was collecting) which they viewed as utterly unjust. On long journeys goods were often taxed several times as they passed through various districts.[3]

Tax collectors' money was unclean, and adding their money to your own money box made all your money unclean. As a result, observant Jews wouldn't take money from a tax collector. So the collectors had lots of money, but nowhere to spend it.

Because becoming a tax collector resulted in removal from the synagogue, only non-practicing Jews would take the job. Then, who would take their money? Only those who didn't care about the synagogue or uncleanness—prostitutes, criminals, other collaborators with the Romans—in short, the riff-raff of the city. The lawless class would come together with plenty of wine and food to party.

It was into one of these parties that Jesus strode with his disciples. This would be something like well-known preacher, Rick Warren going to a Columbia drug cartel dinner, and hiring one of their leaders for his staff!

Reaction

Apparently some Pharisees were in the area observing, and they saw him go into the tax collectors' house. Their question may have come later to the disciples: "The Pharisees and their scribes began grumbling at his disciples, saying, 'Why do you eat and drink with the tax collectors and sinners?'" (v. 30). To the Pharisees, "sinners" meant people who didn't bother to keep the system of observation they had developed. It could also refer to those guilty of gross sins of commission, like sexual immorality.

To the Pharisees, sinners were a nuisance and even a threat. Their evil could be contagious, so righteous people should avoid them. You wouldn't talk to them or sell to them, and you certainly would *never* enter their house, let alone join into table fellowship.

3. Gerhard Kittle, *Theological Dictionary of the New Testament*, Abridged (Grand Rapids, MI: Eerdmans, 1985), 1168-1167.

Back to the Party

The "you" here when they ask "Why do you eat . . ."is plural. That means the disciples also went to the party. But it was Jesus who answered:

> Jesus answered and said to them, "It is not those who are well who need a physician, but those who are sick. I have not come to call the righteous but sinners to repentance." (vs. 31-32)

Here Jesus laid bare the heart of his mission. He hadn't come to judge sinners, to avoid them, or to cast them out of the synagogue. He had come to love them. Notice he agrees that the tax collectors and their raw friends were sinners. He's not rationalizing their way of life, or saying sin doesn't matter. Rather, he's calling them to repentance.

To turn your heart back toward God, you have to admit you're not already following him. Tax collectors found it easier to admit they were sinners and away from God than did the Pharisees.

At the same time, when Jesus refers to "the righteous," he was not agreeing that the Pharisees and their friends were actually righteous. Rather, he knew that they considered themselves righteous, and that was a fatal barrier that made them further away from God than even these gross sinners. He later stated this straight up: "I tell you the truth, corrupt tax collectors and prostitutes will get into the Kingdom of God before you do" (Matthew 21:31).

This is one of Jesus' main points, not just for tax collectors but for us as well. God's grace is an undeserved gift. Admitting helplessness is essential in the process of receiving grace. It's not like religion, where worshippers attain to the favor of the gods. Viewed correctly, the biggest barrier to God's acceptance isn't gross sin (like the tax collectors) but self-righteous pride (like the Pharisees).

Matthew adds another comment Jesus lobbed at the Pharisees: "But go and learn what this means: 'I desire mercy, not sacrifice'" (Matthew 9:13 citing Hosea 6:6). This statement clearly shows that religious rigor and performance means little to God compared to inner character qualities like being merciful and gracious.

Real godliness involves loving others with the love Jesus imparts. Matthew was undergoing a massive spiritual life shift, discovering God's love and coming to faith. Some of his friends probably were as well. What did the Pharisees think about that? Nothing. They couldn't care less. They only thought about preserving their separation from those they considered more sinful.

Fasting

Jesus' critics ignored his statement about sinners and the righteous, and changed the subject to a relatively trivial religious practice—fasting.

> And they said to him, "The disciples of John often fast and offer prayers, the disciples of the Pharisees also do the same, but yours eat and drink."
>
> And Jesus said to them, "You cannot make the attendants of the bridegroom fast while the bridegroom is with them, can you? But the days will come; and when the bridegroom is taken away from them, then they will fast in those days." (vs. 33-35)

Why do they ask about fasting when Jesus wasn't talking about that? This matches a pattern Jesus later called "straining out the gnat and swallowing the camel" (Matthew 23:24). It's a negative habit often seen in legalistic religious people: They deflect attention away from the big thing (the camel) by focusing on the trivial thing (the gnat).

It's not that they were curious about gnats. It's a way to keep the discourse safe, by not looking at the big areas where they were failing. Facing a different (but really the same) group of Pharisees later, Jesus said they were ignoring "the weightier provisions of the law: justice and mercy and faithfulness" (Matthew 23:23).

God would rather have us focusing on these "weightier" parts of the ethical teaching in Scripture. Jesus said the most weighty things for his followers were loving God and loving others (Matthew 22:36-40). The Pharisees were doing poorly in both of those norms. But they really knew how to fast!

Jesus' critics weren't offering up this observation on fasting in a neutral tone. They saw the lack of fasting as a sign of spiritual weakness and sinful self-gratification. To them, not fasting signaled low devotion. Notice how the Pharisee in the parable of the Pharisee and the Publican boasts: "I fast twice a week" (Luke 18:12).

Was that a biblical point of view? Not at all. In fact, the Old Testament says next to nothing about fasting. The rabbis taught that people needed to fast for the Day of Atonement, but if you read the section on that day, fasting is never mentioned (Leviticus 16).

In fact, there is no law calling for fasting. Fasting had to do with mourning, so it could fit on the Day of Atonement when people confessed and mourned their sins for that year. But no such direction is given. There are incidents when people fasted, usually because of a tragedy (like Job) or to mourn their sin or to humble themselves before God (like in Ezra 8:21).

Beneath the slight mentions in the Old Testament was the growing asceticism in rabbinic Judaism. Asceticism includes the belief that denying oneself and causing pain results in higher spirituality. Such a view is alien to the Bible. The Pharisees had expanded the importance of fasting from negligible to front and center.

Jesus easily batted their complaint aside, pointing out that he and his disciples had nothing to mourn. But he also went on to speak to the larger question.

New Wineskins

> And He was also telling them a parable: "No one tears a piece of cloth from a new garment and puts it on an old garment; otherwise the new wine will burst the skins and it will be spilled out, and the skins will be ruined. But new wine must be put into fresh wineskins. And no one, after drinking old wine wishes for new; for he says, 'The old is good enough.'" (vs. 36-39)

This short illustration isn't real easy to interpret. The reader must identify six different things: new cloth, old garment, new wine, old wine, new wineskins, and old wineskins. The context is our main helper. Jesus is refuting rabbinic rules on avoiding contact with "sinners" and fasting. This illustration should have something to do with that.

Cloths and Garments

The "new cloth" was Jesus and what he was bringing—the new covenant and the new supernatural lifestyle of the Spirit. His message is that any attempt to take the new cloth and sew it onto the old will only result in a tear because of the fundamental mismatch. The old garment here stands for the whole constellation of rabbinic traditions and rules, like those being discussed in context. Jesus was telling these tradition-bound leaders that what he was bringing was too radical to fit within their traditional system.

Wine and Wineskins

In a similar way, the old wine stands for what God was doing in the Old Testament. The Covenant of Moses spelled out a way of life and worship that came from God. In Jesus' day, that old wine was contained in the old wineskins of rabbinic Judaism and its traditions.

Now, with new wine coming out of the vat (Jesus and his message) new wineskins would be needed. Old skins lose their elasticity and crack as the wine completes the last of its fermentation.[4]

With the wineskin illustration we have the additional point that the cracking of the old wineskin results in a loss of wine. The old wineskin's inflexibility is unsuitable to the new wine (like with the patch of cloth). As a result, cracks open, spilling and ruining the new wine. Yet, the wine is what matters—what God is doing. The wineskin is unimportant in itself.

Note that the wineskins, whether new or old, are human creations. They don't come from God. The rabbi's fasting and hand-washing were human additions to the Old Testament.

Today, we still create wineskins. Our church has organized itself into house churches and "spheres" or "networks" of multiple house churches. We didn't always have these wineskins, and we may not have them in the future. The test of good wineskins is whether they hold the wine. Are our wineskins effective in winning people to Jesus? For building believers up? For fostering healthy families? For healing the broken? If not, we need new wineskins.

When leaders argue, "This is the way we've always done things," it's a poor argument. They are setting a course that will lose relevance and effectiveness in a changing culture.

4. This lays to rest the mistaken belief that the "wine" in the New Testament was non-alcoholic. Why would non-alcoholic wine stretch a wineskin?

A Parting Shot

Jesus ends by saying, "And no one, after drinking old wine wishes for new; for he says, 'The old is good enough'" (v. 39). It's a basic observation about human nature. People—especially religious people—like to draw a sense of security from staying the same. Jesus knew it was going to be incredibly difficult for these tradition-bound thinkers to truly open their minds to the gospel, let alone create and adopt new wineskins.

The Big Picture

Stiff, brittle wineskins are still a problem today. Church worship styles, dress, avoidance of contemporary music, or cinema, all work against Jesus' goal of loving sinners. The nonbeliever has to enter a culturally alien environment quite different than what he is used to. That blocks effectiveness in evangelism. It should be believers entering the secular culture they aren't used to, just like Jesus and his disciples in this story.

A typical wineskin today is the unbiblical rule against consuming alcohol. It hurts evangelism. You can see that Jesus didn't follow this prohibition (v. 30). His enemies said of Jesus, "He's a glutton and a drunkard, and a friend of tax collectors and other sinners!" (Matthew 11:19). That was a lie. Jesus could eat and drink with sinners without going to excess. But insisting on unbiblical barriers between nonbelievers and the gospel is a grave mistake, and it's against God's will.

Modern Christians also suffer from focusing on the insignificant while ignoring the main point. For example, many churches fixate on fighting "foul" language—a concern hardly mentioned in Scripture. This emphasis makes non-believers feel uncomfortable and nervous when around believers. They worry that their language might give offense. Meanwhile, their non-believing friends aren't offended at all.

Some modern believers teach the mistaken idea of keeping separate from non-Christian culture based on the faulty application of Paul's quotation from Isaiah 52:11, "'Therefore, come out from their midst and be separate,' says the Lord. 'And do not touch what is unclean.'" They fail to notice that Paul cites this verse to show that New Testament believers should not be "bound" to non-believers, like in marriage (2 Corinthians 6:14).

Paul explicitly rejected the notion that believers should hold themselves separate from sinful non-believers for the same reason Jesus went to Matthew's party (1 Corinthians 5:9-11).

> I wrote you in my letter not to associate with immoral people; I did not at all mean with the immoral people of this world. . . . But actually, I wrote to you not to associate with any so-called brother if he is an immoral person. . . .

Non-believers need our presence, our friendship, and our witness to God's love. Otherwise, wine will gush out of our broken old wineskins all over the floor.

Jesus' example was to stride right into a party where "foul" language, raw behavior, and heavy drinking were in progress. He brought his relatively new followers with him, and ignored the horror observers expressed. Later he came out of the party with new believers—people who mattered to God.

10

Jesus and the Sabbath

Luke 6:1-11

Luke now gives us two stories that exemplify what commentators call the Sabbath controversy. In the first account, Jesus' disciples were picking some grain:

> Now it happened that he was passing through some grain fields on a Sabbath; and his disciples were picking the heads of grain, rubbing them in their hands, and eating the grain. But some of the Pharisees said, "Why do you do what is not lawful on the Sabbath?" (vs. 1-2)

They weren't stealing. To glean grains by hand in someone's field (not using a sickle) was permitted by law (Deut. 23:25). The critics' problem came from rabbinic definitions that made grabbing a few grains equal to harvesting the field.

To fully appreciate these encounters we need to go deeper into ancient doctrine concerning the Sabbath day.

Sabbath

The Hebrew word for Sabbath is *shabua*, which means seven. Hebrew law prescribed for both Sabbath days and Sabbath years. The Sabbath, celebration was important in Judaism, and in fact, it had become way too important. The rabbis started with the relatively simple law of the Sabbath given by God in Exodus 20:

> "Remember the Sabbath day, to keep it holy. Six days you shall labor and do all your work, but the seventh day is a Sabbath of the Lord your God; in it you shall not do any work, you or your son or your daughter, your male or your female servant or your cattle or your sojourner who stays with you. For in six days the Lord made the heavens and the earth, the sea and all that is in them, and rested on the seventh day; therefore the Lord blessed the Sabbath day and made it holy."[1] (vs. 8-11)

You can see it is quite a simple rule. The seventh day was to be kept "holy" which means "different" from other days. The main way to do this was to not work. And God specified that the no-work rule applied to all—servants, foreigners, and even work animals.

The Sabbath law was the "sign" or symbol of the Mosaic covenant, just as circumcision was the sign of the Abrahamic Covenant and the rainbow was the sign of the covenant with Noah.

Most readers would understand that it meant not going to work. For people working within a household it would mean they avoid working there. Unlike other ancient nations that commonly worked their servants and livestock seven days a week, Israel had a day for rest. It was a law of compassion.

But in the hands of legalistic thinkers this law became ground zero for expanding hair-splitting additional rules. Under their careful analysis this law grew into a body of legal thinking that fills two large volumes, or tractates, in the *Talmud*.

Laws like the Sabbath became tortured interpretations as the rabbis worked the biblical material over.

For instance, what if a beggar came to a wealthy person's window and

1. Sabbath is never mentioned before the giving of the law in Exodus 20. God rested on the seventh day, not because he was tired, but because his work was finished (Hebrews 4:7-10). As such, the rest God prescribed in Exodus becomes a suitable symbol of the rest Jesus gives his followers, and for the same reason—his work is finished. Therefore, we can rest from our works and rely on the finished work of Jesus (Hebrews 4:10). See also Deuteronomy 5:12–15 and Exodus 31:14–17 which reiterate the law, but add little in terms of detail.

put his hand through the window to receive an offered gift. His guilt or innocence depends on whether he extends his arm with his palm up to have the home owner drop the coin into his hand (that would not be working on the Sabbath, because he just held his hand out and money fell into it).But if he extends it in palm down to pick the coin up from the homeowner's hand, that would be working on the Sabbath.[2]

Even the day before Sabbath one had to be very careful. He could not put meat into an oven on Friday unless it would be fully cooked before the beginning of Sabbath at sundown.[3]

Could you put a lid on a pot on Sabbath? That depends. "If he did not cover it [a pot] while it was yet day, it may not be covered after nightfall. If it was covered but became uncovered, it may be recovered."[4] These detailed laws ran into the hundreds, and violating any one of them could result in serious punishment, including being publicly rebuked or whipped.

A woman wasn't permitted to sew on the Sabbath of course. But she was also guilty if she left a needle stuck in her garment. That would be bearing a burden on the Sabbath.[5]

Picking my chair up and carrying it to the table is okay. But dragging it to the table is a violation. That's because dragging the chair on a dirt floor would leave a tiny rut, which is really a furrow. Therefore it's plowing—forbidden, because it's part of harvesting.[6] Is there really any moral content in this rule?

Some of the rabbis admitted, "The laws of Shabbat are like mountains hanging by a thread," because hardly any of it came from Scripture and the burden on people was heavy.[7]

---

2. *Mishnah* Shabbat 7:2. This tractate teases out "forty less one" types of labor forbidden on the Sabbath. Each type of work is painstakingly defined with examples given. Such a list of illegal work is not detailed in the Bible. But the rabbis observed that they suspended building the Tabernacle during Sabbath, so things like sewing and writing or making bread were all forbidden, along with anything even remotely connected with them.
3. *Mishnah* Shabbat 1:11.
4. *Mishnah* Shabbat 4:2.
5. *Mishnah* Shabbat 6:3.
6. *Mishnah* Beitzah 2:10.
7. *Mishnah* Hagigah 1:8.

So What?

So the Sabbath laws seem very picky to us today, but what harm results? Actually, the harm is great, not just from the picky laws, but from the underlying pattern of thought. This is what angered Jesus.

Remember, the problem here is not with Judaism. Judaism is from God and was revealed in the Old Testament. And in fact, we believe that Jesus fulfills Judaism and that we who follow him are all Jewish by conversion. According to Jesus and the rest of the New Testament, Judaism correctly understood meant following Jesus. The problem was with a legalistic interpretation of Judaism that departs far from anything revealed by God. Several problems resulted.

- **View of God** – Why does God care whether you dropped the coins into someone's hand or picked them up? Or when you put a lid on a pot? What sort of being runs his people through such hurdles and why? Does God love us? If so, why does he insist we jump over these hurdles? So this is why my mom died—she forgot to get the lamp lit in time for Sabbath? The legalistic view makes God seem like a cosmic bean counter and a control freak. And God takes offense at that picture, because that's not what he's like. This is why in Matthew's account of this conflict in the grain field, Jesus quoted Hosea 6:6where God says, "I desire mercy and not a sacrifice." Jesus' words here go to the heart of who God is and what his nature is like.
- **View of Righteousness** – The legalistic version of righteousness or goodness is distorted. Doing good is important for followers of God. But under legalistic religion, goodness becomes doing picky things like not dragging a chair on Sabbath. To the legalists opposing Jesus, doing good meant remembering and keeping hundreds of these fussy, strange laws.
- **The Effect These Views Have on Outsiders** – All the negative observations regarding God and what it takes to please him create a quite negative picture to others who don't know God. The picture of God holding out a hoop for his people to jump through, and keep jumping through indefinitely is frightening. This picture doesn't come from God, but from God's enemy. First, God doesn't need anything from us. When God gives us rules or instructions, it's only for our own good. His laws either teach us or protect us.

Just as religious men's view of God was low, God's view of them, as seen through Jesus, was quite low. By the end of the book he is calling them a "brood of vipers" and "sons of hell." Their conflict culminated in Jesus' death.

Jesus' Reply

Let's return to the scene in the field where leaders had charged Jesus' disciples with sin.

> Jesus replied, "Haven't you read in the Scriptures what David did when he and his companions were hungry? He went into the house of God and broke the law by eating the sacred loaves of bread that only the priests can eat. He also gave some to his companions." (vs. 3-4 NLT)

The episode Jesus referred to happened when David and his men were fleeing from Saul and his small army (1 Samuel 21:6). David came to a village and asked for food, but they had nothing other than the sacred bread in the tabernacle. This bread was only to be eaten by the priests. But because of their hunger, David took the bread and gave it to his men. It was a case where human need was more important than keeping ritual law.

Put differently, compassion for those suffering men trumped keeping ritual rules. That's directly in line with God's heart of compassion.

The Innocent

Matthew adds an interesting comment by Jesus at this point: "But if you had known what this means, 'I desire compassion, and not a sacrifice,' you would not have condemned the innocent" (Matthew 12:7). He was referring to the disciples picking grain, but also, in principle, to David's violation of ritual law. The verse is important because it speaks in favor of something called "hierarchical ethics."

When studying ethics, or how we form moral norms, we have to respond to moral dilemmas. Moral dilemmas are situations where one has to do something wrong. For instance, Rahab of Jericho was confronted by soldiers searching for two Israelite spies. They were hiding in Rahab's place. So Rahab faced a moral dilemma—either lie to the soldiers, or hand the Jewish spies over to death.

She lied, sending the soldiers off in the wrong direction. She was praised for what she did at that time and later by James, who adds that her action was a good deed (James 2:25).

But how can telling a lie be a good deed? It can be good because ethics (moral norms) are not all of equal importance. They form a hierarchy. If you find yourself in an ethical dilemma, like Rahab did, you do the lesser evil. Everyone agrees on that. But the question is, if you do the lesser evil, is it still evil? Or is doing the lesser evil now good? According to Jesus, what David did and what his disciples did left them "innocent." In other words, Jesus taught hierarchical ethics.

Jesus' Authority

Jesus also said, "The Son of Man is Lord of the Sabbath" (v. 5). This infuriated the leaders. But Jesus knew that soon he was doing away with the Sabbath. Under the New Covenant, observing the Sabbath became optional (Romans 14:5; Colossians 2:16). Many Jewish followers of Jesus continued to observe Passover, as a way to stay in touch with their culture, but Gentiles often did not, because as Paul observes, "We are no longer under law but under grace" (Romans 6:14).

With this declaration that the Son of Man was Lord of the Sabbath, Jesus was really saying, "I'll let you know what the law teaches."

Healing on the Sabbath

Next:

> On another Sabbath he entered the synagogue and was teaching; and there was a man there whose right hand was withered. The scribes and the Pharisees were watching him closely to see if he healed on the Sabbath, so that they might find reason to accuse him. (vs. 6-7 NLT)

The last sentence is an important part of the story. The leaders are there to catch him doing something illegal. They weren't interested in God's will or what was good for the sick people. They were hunting Jesus.

> But he knew what they were thinking, and he said to the man with the withered hand, "Get up and come forward!" And he got up and came forward. (v. 8)

He didn't heal him in his seat. He wanted him front and center where everyone could clearly see with their own eyes. He no doubt had the man show the whole crowd his withered hand.

> And Jesus said to them [the scribes and Pharisees], "I ask you, is it lawful to do good or to do harm on the Sabbath, to save a life or to destroy it?" (v. 9)

The question made no sense to legalistic thinkers. Jesus was appealing to principled ethics where broad moral principles (like love and compassion) govern judgments about right or wrong. The obvious answer to his question was, "Yes, do good!"

But these men only knew a nomistic or rules-based school of ethical thinking. In their way of thinking, you come to a situation and then you look up the rule for that case. And, Jesus' question doubly made no sense because they weren't interested in what God wanted anyway. If they were interested in what God wanted, wouldn't they be more open to the possibility that Jesus was real? Why were they hunting him? They were silent.

This event upset Jesus. Mark describes Jesus, "looking around at them with anger, grieved at their hardness of heart." Jesus' angry eyes went from one to another, as if to say, "You? Do you have an answer?" "What about you?" Nobody had an answer.

> After looking around at them all, he said to the man, "Stretch out your hand!" (v. 10)

He clearly wanted everyone to see what was about to happen. Then, as they watched, "His hand was restored." This "withered" hand must have looked awful. Before their eyes it swelled and spread out to become a normal hand! Cries rang out in the crowded house as people gasped in their astonishment. Tears probably burst out of the man's eyes and those of his friends and family.

The Scribes and Pharisees must have been blown away, right? No. "But they themselves were filled with rage, and discussed together what they might do to Jesus" (v. 11). Matthew adds, "Then the Pharisees called a meeting to plot how to kill Jesus (Matthew 12:14). They were illustrating the proverb that warns, "Better to meet a bear robbed of her cubs than a fool in his folly" (Proverbs 17:12). People bent on sin feel white hot rage in the presence of the godly.[8]

The Twelve

We saw that Jesus recruited disciples before this, but here is where Luke discusses the separation of the twelve to be apostles.

> It was at this time that he went off to the mountain to pray, and he spent the whole night in prayer to God. And when day came, he called his disciples to him and chose twelve of them, whom he also named as apostles. (vs. 12-13)

The Greek word for "disciple" is *mathates*, which means a student, or a learner. Is also implies being a follower, especially in the Jewish context, because students would attach themselves to a rabbi and follow him through his work day. It becomes clear as we read on in the Gospels that many people in addition to these twelve considered themselves disciples of Jesus.

Jesus didn't invent discipleship. Rabbis before him already practiced discipleship as the main way to train new rabbis. Other tradesmen used a mentoring or apprentice approach for teaching a trade. John the Baptist and the Pharisees both had disciples before Jesus did (Matthew 11:2; 14:12; 22:16; Mark 2:18).

In a day without universities or graduate schools, personal on-the-job-training was the main way to transmit skills and knowledge to the next generation. Arguably, something is lost when training consists only of book study without field training. Jesus modeled an extra dimension: the close personal friendship the disciple-maker built with his students. Mark says Jesus chose them "to be with him" (Mark 3:14). In personal discipleship, the learner spends time with the teacher and the teacher's good qualities rub off.

In this passage, Luke explains that Jesus made a clear distinction between most of his followers and twelve key disciples he also named apostles.

---

8. How did Luke get this info about a murder conspiracy meeting? We know that later, many Pharisees and other rulers came to faith. Notice in Acts 15:5, the reference to "some of the sect of the Pharisees who had believed." One or more of them must have been at this meeting.

The word apostle means "a sent one;" someone commissioned to carry out a task. Their task would be to lead the early church in spreading the gospel in the face of unrelenting opposition. Luke gives their names:

> Simon, whom he also named Peter, and Andrew his brother; and James and John; and Philip and Bartholomew; and Matthew and Thomas; James the son of Alphaeus, and Simon who was called the Zealot; Judas the son of James, and Judas Iscariot, who became a traitor. (vs. 14-16)[9]

Replacement theologians use this number, twelve, to suggest that Jesus was establishing the true Israel, and by implication, laying aside the original Israel. Nothing in the text says that. But Jesus did say, "In the regeneration when the Son of Man will sit on his glorious throne, you also shall sit upon twelve thrones, judging the twelve tribes of Israel" (Matthew 19:28). So the twelve tribes are still there when Jesus returns, and God will deal with them as tribes of Jews. This probably was one reason they felt the need to replace Judas with Matthias (Acts 1:15-26).

These men were Jesus' chosen strategy for reaching the world. He left no organization or system behind when he left. He just left twelve men (and a number of women) who knew Jesus and could represent him to the masses. In Luke's next book we see this small band explode into a movement of many thousands of believers.

The Big Picture

Man-made religion displeases God. It displeased Jesus. That was especially true because these religious leaders were in possession of God's costly collection of Scriptures. The religious leaders were the stewards who were supposed to be disseminating that word to the people. But instead, they distorted the Scriptures and propagated a legalistic system that was fatal—it could not save.

That should be upsetting to anyone who understands spiritual things. This system also gave offense because it was uncompassionate, and it portrayed God as uncompassionate as well. This conflict between what

9. The minor discrepancies on this list between the Gospel writers is mostly due to the fact that Jewish men at this time had more than one name, like we already saw with Levi being the same as Matthew.

Jesus was bringing and what the scribes and Pharisees offered was now in full fury. Already, they wanted him dead.

11

The Sermon on the Plain

Luke 6:17-49

> Jesus came down with them and stood on a level place; and there was a large crowd of His disciples, and a great throng of people from all Judea and Jerusalem and the coastal region of Tyre and Sidon, who had come to hear him and to be healed of their diseases; and those who were troubled with unclean spirits were being cured. And all the people were trying to touch him, for power was coming from him and healing them all. (vs. 17-19)

This crowd was large, and included both disciples and other people from far away. If he was at the northern coast of the Sea of Galilee (where we last saw him), people were traveling over a hundred miles from the south in Jerusalem, and two hundred miles from the north in Tyre and Sidon. Those were long trips to make on foot. Once again, Luke carefully delineates between people with illnesses and those with demonic affliction.

The Sermon on the Mount?

As you read this sermon, you will quickly notice similarities with the

Sermon on the Mount in Matthew 5-7. Yet, while the wording is often similar or even identical, the points he makes with those words are sometimes quite different. This sermon is also much shorter than Matthew's version. Matthew's version was on a mountainside. This one is on a level place. The discrepancies are too many to be the result of editing as some believe. These are two similar but different teachings.

Some commentators advance the idea that Luke's version is not a real sermon by Jesus, but a collection of his sayings gathered by Luke with the backdrop of the level place. This doesn't fit with Chapter 7:1, where Luke says "When Jesus had finished saying all this to the people, he returned to Capernaum." That sounds more like a concrete sequence of events.

The fact that he uses some of the same phraseology and expressions is no surprise to anyone who has preached in different venues to different people. You simply have no reason to come up with all new material and language, when your current crowd has never heard your earlier material. Also, preachers use similar expressions, illustrations, and figures of speech, even when making different points.

> And turning His gaze toward his disciples, he began to say,
>
> "Blessed are you who are poor, for yours is the kingdom of God.
>
> Blessed are you who hunger now, for you shall be satisfied.
>
> Blessed are you who weep now, for you shall laugh.
>
> Blessed are you when men hate you, and ostracize you, and insult you, and scorn your name as evil, for the sake of the Son of Man.
>
> Be glad in that day and leap for joy, for behold, your reward is great in heaven. For in the same way their fathers used to treat the prophets." (vs. 20-23)

The word "blessed" is *makarios*, usually translated "happy," but can also mean "enriched." Randy Alcorn argues persuasively that the word "blessed" is a vague churchy word that doesn't communicate well. The phrase "Blessed are you," means "You should be happy."[1]

1. Randy Alcorn, *Happiness* (Wheaton, IL: Tyndale House Publishers, 2015), chap. 1-3.

Reversal Theology

All of these statements have one thing in common: They all reflect "reversal theology." We saw this earlier with the Song of Mary and elsewhere.

To understand why Jesus preached this way, you must see not only who he is preaching *to*, but also who he is preaching *against*. Every proposition in this section flies directly in the face of the Pharisaic, rabbinic teaching of his day. They believed that hunger, poverty and public disgrace were the result of God's judgment on people's sin. They saw wealth, prestige, and health as rewards for living a righteous life.

Luke later reveals that the Pharisees "were lovers of money" (16:14). They also often belonged to the landed upper class, and used that position to oppress the poor (20:47). So Jesus set forth cases that contradicted Pharisaic theology and injustice. At the same time, he reflected God's outrage that privileged, healthy, and rich people would use their privilege to shame the less fortunate.

In place of the rabbinic worldview, Jesus advances the "eternal perspective." This view refuses to base values on temporal things, like wealth, health, and fame. Instead, values come from the larger view, including how this life affects the life to come. The true value of all things is based on how those things leave us and others in eternal life. Poverty in this life won't make us poor in heaven. In fact, Jesus said, "Some are last who will be first and some are first who will be last" (13:30). God's values system is often at odds with humanity's values.

This is the crux of what Jesus was preaching in this part of his sermon. People are puzzled over why some of the godliest people are poor, while some of the most wicked are rich. Jesus was warning that the story isn't over. Justice is rare in this world, but God is going to get the last word.

Jesus wasn't saying that all poor people possess the kingdom of God. The unspoken word here is "many." Many poor will possess the kingdom. That's the point his opponents were missing. Also, he used the plural "you" because he was addressing many of his own followers who had given up worldly riches to follow him.

Notice that in Matthew's Sermon on the Mount, the message is different. In that sermon, Jesus extolled not the poor, but the "poor in spirit." He praised not the hungry, but those who "hunger and thirst after righteousness" (Matthew 5:3, 6). Those who claim this is just Luke's edit end up implying that Luke the author was authorized to change the meaning of Jesus' statements. That's unwarranted. It's better to see this as a different sermon.

On some of the other beatitudes Jesus makes the same point in both sermons, so it's partly the same and partly different. That's exactly what you would expect from two different talks by the same speaker to two different audiences.

Having given the positive, Jesus went on to give the antithesis:

> "But woe to you who are rich, for you are receiving your comfort in full. Woe to you who are well-fed now, for you shall be hungry. Woe to you who laugh now, for you shall mourn and weep. Woe to you when all men speak well of you, for their fathers used to treat the false prophets in the same way." (vs. 24-26)

His repeated "woe" isn't a threat, but an expression of sorrow or regret. NLT translates, "What sorrow awaits you who are rich," etc. Jesus was not ascetic. He didn't believe that enjoying yourself or having a good reputation would ruin your life or make you unspiritual. His concern was with those who put their trust in wealth or pleasure, and especially those who believe such things are the proof of God's blessing and approval. When referring to "you who laugh" (v. 25), he probably means those who laugh at less fortunate people.

The True Standard for Goodness

After denying the rabbinic view that amounted to a form of Karmic law, Jesus continued to discuss what it takes to be considered truly righteous:

> "But I say to you who hear, love your enemies, do good to those who hate you, bless those who curse you, pray for those who mistreat you. Whoever hits you on the cheek, offer him the other also; and whoever takes away your coat, do not withhold your shirt from him either. Give to everyone who asks of you, and whoever takes away what is yours, do not demand it back. Treat others the same way you want them to treat you." (vs. 27-31)

This description sees a righteous life as being extremely generous. It's also very difficult to follow. Only a superficial look at this passage would fail to see the problem with keeping these rules consistently. And what if you keep it part of the time, but not always? Jesus makes no provision for that.

His rabbinic-instructed audience must have heard his call with dismay. And things didn't get any easier:

> "If you love those who love you, what credit is that to you? For even sinners love those who love them. If you do good to those who do good to you, what credit is that to you? For even sinners do the same. If you lend to those from whom you expect to receive, what credit is that to you? Even sinners lend to sinners in order to receive back the same amount. But love your enemies, and do good, and lend, expecting nothing in return; and your reward will be great, and you will be sons of the Most High; for he himself is kind to ungrateful and evil men. Be merciful, just as your Father is merciful." (vs. 32-36)

Wait, lend with no repayment? Isn't that just giving money away? Loving your enemies? Yes, just like God, who is "kind to ungrateful and evil people." His hearers thought they were in the clear if they didn't murder anyone. But Jesus said, "Whoever says, 'You fool,' shall be guilty enough to go into the fiery hell" (Matthew 5:21-22). So one minor slip up is bad enough to send someone to hell? That's what he said.

The strict standard Jesus advanced in this sermon is a clue to his main point. In order to establish their own righteousness, the Pharisees and other rabbis had radically reinterpreted the Law of Moses, shifting God's expectations downward. They wanted a lower bar that they could clear, or at least appear to clear.

Jesus gave an example of the Pharisees' version: "You have heard that it was said, 'You shall love your neighbor and hate your enemy.'" (Matthew 5:43). That standard is totally man-made. It comes nowhere near God's true standard for righteousness: "love your enemies" (v. 35).

Man-made standards are arbitrary and lead nowhere. That's why Jesus compared the rabbinic path to a guide who can't see. "A blind man cannot guide a blind man, can he? Will they not both fall into a pit?" (v. 39). In other words, sinful humankind is in no position to define sin.

They will always miss the point in favor of trivial, silly rules. The result is not real goodness, but pride and self-righteousness as people pretend to follow their own rules. Jesus was saying that if you want to claim that good works are the path to heaven, you have to accept God's definition of good works. And you have to perform those works at all times, in thought, word, and deed.

In Matthew's version of the sermon Jesus says, "Therefore you are to be perfect, as your heavenly Father is perfect" (Matthew 5:48). Modern interpreters often stumble over this part of Jesus' message. They argue that he is using hyperbole—intentional exaggeration for effect.

Other readers argue that Jesus means perfection should be our aim, not that we are really perfect. But he doesn't say to make perfection our aim. He says to be perfect like the Father. Ironically, these commentators are lowering God's standards in a way similar to Jesus' opponents! Instead, people should realize the futility of thinking that fallen humans could satisfy God through good works.

The despair one feels when looking honestly at Jesus' incredibly high standard is supposed to compel a cry for mercy; a cry for grace. But before people can appreciate grace, they have to see that they fall hopelessly short of God's standards. Paul would later say, "Obviously, the law applies to those to whom it was given, for its purpose is to keep people from having excuses, and to show that the entire world is guilty before God" (Romans 3:19). God knew that his law would expose sin. And abandoning the project of being righteous is the perfect prelude to receiving grace.

Jesus was born under law (Galatians 4:4), and as such, he was a preacher of the law. He preached grace also, as you can see in the story of the Samaritan woman at the well in John 4. But for the religious class, he needed to first re-establish the lofty grandeur of God's perfect law.

Matthew makes it clear that Jesus also said in reference to this same train of thought, "I did not come to abolish [the law] but to fulfill it" (Matthew 5:17). Luke didn't record that statement, but it's implied.

Jesus' fulfillment was three-fold. First, he fulfilled the Old Testament predictions of the suffering servant. Then, he fulfilled the Old Testament trajectory—the story line in the Old Testament stops in the middle of nowhere. A centuries-long story that seemed to be headed somewhere just ends without fulfilling its promise. The completion comes in the New Testament. Finally, he fulfilled the Old Testament demands by becoming "our righteousness" (2 Corinthians 5:21).

This was Jesus' purpose. He was correcting the flawed view of God's law that brings it down to a level where some might think they successfully obey it.

That's why Matthew added,

> "Whoever then annuls one of the least of these commandments, and teaches others to do the same, shall be called least in the kingdom of heaven; but whoever keeps and teaches them, he shall be called great in the kingdom of heaven. For I say to you that unless your righteousness surpasses that of the scribes and Pharisees, you will not enter the kingdom of heaven." (Matthew 5:19-20)

In order to appreciate the shock value of this saying you need to understand how holy the people thought Pharisees were. Outdoing the Pharisees when it came to following the law was unthinkable. If anyone was good enough for God it was them. No, Jesus said, they're not even close.[2]

Log and Speck

Then, continuing his argument against rabbinic teaching, he gave his classic challenge:

> "Why do you look at the speck that is in your brother's eye, but do not notice the log that is in your own eye? Or how can you say to your brother, 'Brother, let me take out the speck that is in your eye,' when you yourself do not see the log that is in your own eye? You hypocrite, first take the log out of your own eye, and then you will see clearly to take out the speck that is in your brother's eye." (vs. 41-42)

Who is finger-pointing and judging their brothers? The Pharisees and their followers! For this crew, identifying the speck in others' eyes was a

2. Another school of interpretation called Dispensational Theology argues that this sermon is addressed to future people living in the Millennium, and therefore doesn't apply to us. There is no sign of that in the wording of the sermon. These ethical standards apply directly to us, just as they did to them.

national pastime. We just saw two examples of this when the Pharisees criticized Jesus and the disciples for grabbing a handful of grain or eating with sinners.

The religious mentality operates on a comparative standard. It's not that I never sin, but that I sin less than that person. Under this view, it becomes important to identify sinners who are so much worse than me.

The fact that Jesus was preaching the law in order to awaken religious people to their need for grace doesn't mean his moral teaching in this sermon is hyperbole or that it only applies to someone else, as some claim. Jesus was only preaching the true intent of the law. And God's law doesn't change. His demands are no less than the full undiluted law, practiced in thought, word, and deed all the time and without any exception. If you can't do that, your only hope is the imputed righteousness of Jesus (Philippians 3:9).

The Benefits of Godly Living

God's standards for salvation are absolute, in the sense that they are relative to God's absolute righteousness. But conforming our lives to Jesus' moral teaching is entirely beneficial in this life. To focus on removing the log from my eye before worrying about the speck in my brother's eye is nothing less than humility.

The order is clear: by first looking at the log in my eye, I will immediately notice my rage toward an adversary declining. God will graciously show me that my expectation that my adversary behave well is directly at odds with the fact that I'm not behaving well. That's why Jesus says anyone who fails to remove his own log is a hypocrite. If believers followed Jesus' call in this section, conflict in the body of Christ would decline to the vanishing point.

The Tree and its Fruit

Jesus went on to insist that "each tree is known by its own fruit" (v. 44). It's a basic principle of good discernment: deeds count for more than words. People, especially religious leaders, know what to say to create the impression they want people to see. But fallen humans are notoriously dishonest: "The human heart is the most deceitful of all things and desperately wicked" (Jeremiah 17:9).

Jesus puts the burden of discerning good from bad leaders squarely on the individual believer. You can't trust your denomination's ordination rules to do this for you. Most villains in church history were ordained. Anyone who does the reading sees rapists, thieves, murderers, and cult leaders parading through the history of Christianity before the undiscerning, naive eyes of God's people. Multi-millionaire preachers make no effort to conceal their riches, often given by misguided poor people.

We see religious criminals stealing money in Jesus' day. He declared that they were making the temple a "den of thieves" (19:46). He said the Pharisees hearts were "full of robbery and wickedness" (11:39). So although Jesus had his own day in view, his warning also applies to future wrongdoing. Look carefully at a leader's lifestyle to learn the truth.

Hearers versus Doers

Jesus finished his talk by insisting people act on his teachings, not just listen to satisfy their curiosity. "Why do you call me, 'Lord, Lord,' and do not do what I say?" (v. 46). Biblical faith always has an action component, and that willingness to take the step of faith reveals whether your faith is real. Scripture also teaches that ministry is for serving people, not using them to enrich yourself.

Being a follower of Jesus means building your life based on him and his teaching. That's a building that will resist any storm. But nominal Christianity—Christian in name only—or, Christianity that says "Lord, Lord," but doesn't really follow, has always been a major problem.

The Big Picture

In the sermon on the plain, Jesus announced God's judgment on the arrogant and the proud, the exact opposite of the lowly and humble. Humility is one of the greatest values Jesus taught. He comes back to it often. And humility is the precondition for an authentic turning to God in faith and dependence. Trusting God to establish you is so different from trying to establish yourself.

The apostle Paul later described the Jewish dilemma this way: "For not knowing about God's righteousness and seeking to establish their own, they did not subject themselves to the righteousness of God" (Romans

10:3). The rabbinic tradition seriously underestimated God's righteousness as shown in his law.

As a result, they thought it was possible to establish their own righteousness at a level that would satisfy God. This tragic mistake ended up causing the majority of first century Jews to reject Jesus. They failed to comprehend that "Christ is the end of the law for righteousness to everyone who believes" (Romans 10:4).

12

Jesus Heals
Luke 7:1-50

Jesus went back to Capernaum, and there a group of Jewish elders approached him on behalf of a godly Roman centurion—a commander over a hundred soldiers. He's not Cornelius, another centurion who later came to faith in Acts 10. There's no way the same author, Luke, would fail to mention that connection if it were there.

This Gentile officer was what the book of Acts calls a "God-fearer." God-fearers were Greco-Roman Gentiles who had concluded that biblical monotheism had the answers that their polytheism lacked. Yet, they hadn't undergone circumcision and the other rites needed for full conversion to Judaism. Most of the synagogues we read about in Acts had a significant number of these God-fearers in attendance, and many were responsive to the gospel.

The Jewish elders approached Jesus asking that he heal this centurion's beloved servant, who was sick and near death. They explained that he deserved this healing because of his good works—he loved the Jews and he built them their new synagogue (7:5). Their thinking was typical of Jews in this era. The question was whether he deserves to have God bless him. Jesus didn't challenge their logic. He agreed to go.

On the way, the group met another group headed toward them. These were friends of the centurion. He had sent them with the message;

> "Lord, do not trouble yourself further, for I am not worthy for you to come under my roof; for this reason I did not even consider myself worthy to come to you, but just say the word, and my servant will be healed. For I also am a man placed under authority, with soldiers under me; and I say to this one, 'Go!' and he goes, and to another, 'Come!' and he comes, and to my servant, 'Do this!' and he does it." (vs. 6-8)

This remarkable message reveals several things.

First, you can tell the centurion knew about the rabbinic teaching that Jews were not to enter the house of a Gentile. Yet, he humbly submitted to it, declaring himself "unworthy" to have Jesus enter his home. Jesus, of course, ignored this unbiblical, rabbinic teaching.

Secondly, the centurion understood how authority worked, and correctly concluded that Jesus didn't need to walk to his home.

Finally, he had believed in Jesus. He said, "Just say the word, and my servant will be healed." Had he heard Jesus preach? Had he been present earlier when Jesus healed people? Jesus "marveled at him," blown away by his faith. "He turned and said to the crowd that was following Him, 'I say to you, not even in Israel have I found such great faith'" (v. 9).

The servant was healed.

This Gentile officer becomes typical of thousands of God-fearing Gentiles who would come to faith in the coming years. His humble attitude is far from being entitled, nor did he agree with his Jewish friends that he deserved the favor. Like everyone who is strong in faith, he is so in touch with his own lack of deserving that it leaves him amazed that God sees fit to bless him.

Raising a Dead Boy

A funeral procession came walking out of the small village of Nain, about thirty-two miles southwest of Capernaum. It was a scene of utter tragedy. The dead young man was a widow's only son. That meant she had lost everything and would now face the agony of that loss and the stark future that awaited widows, who were not highly valued.

Luke says, "When the Lord saw her, his heart overflowed with compassion" (v. 13). Jesus; not unmoved; not other-worldly; not ethereal; but bursting with raw, tearful sorrow. He understood and felt the horror of death.

This scene is similar to a later one when Jesus wept at Lazarus' funeral, even though he knew he was about to raise him from the dead (John 11:35). Knowing that wasn't enough to keep Jesus from feeling his friends' agony as they cried out in mourning. He wept.

We should feel very glad that Jesus wept at Lazarus' tomb and also, no doubt, at this tragedy. He's not distant. He's not impassive. He enters into our pain with real empathic understanding (Hebrews 4:15).

> "Don't cry!" he said. Then he walked over to the coffin and touched it, and the bearers stopped. "Young man," he said, "I tell you, get up." Then the dead boy sat up and began to talk! And Jesus gave him back to his mother. (vs. 13-15 NLT)

He didn't touch the "coffin" as translated here. It was a funeral bier—a platform made of sticks or boards. That explains why the boy could sit up. Coffins were not in common use at this time in Israel, especially among the poor. They covered the dead with a shroud.

How awestruck the mother must have been! Some recent movies about Jesus portray him as often smiling. This was not the case in many earlier depictions. But here we certainly have to imagine Jesus beaming with a joyful smile as he hugged the widow.

> Great fear swept the crowd, and they praised God, saying, "A mighty prophet has risen among us," and "God has visited his people today." And the news about Jesus spread throughout Judea and the surrounding countryside. (vs. 16-17 NLT)

Jesus was still gradually revealing himself at this time. The crowd's conclusion—that he was a mighty prophet—underestimated his true nature. That "God has visited" was more accurate. Nain is in Galilee, not Judea. But this is using Judea as the name of the Roman province, which includes Galilee.

Reassuring John the Baptist

As Jesus' renown was growing, John the Baptist sent two of his disciples to ask Jesus, "Are you the coming one, or should we keep looking for someone else?" (v. 20). He had earlier declared that Jesus was "The lamb of God who takes away the sin of the world" (John 1:29). He also had explained that God revealed to him Jesus' identity when the Holy Spirit descended like a dove (John 1:32-34). Why was he asking this question?

Matthew, who records this same interaction, adds that John was in prison by this time (Matthew 11:2). John probably expected Jesus would have made a move by now. He probably also expected Jesus to be a reigning king. His statement about Jesus taking away the sin of the world was probably a prophetic utterance, and John may not have fully understood the implications. In any case, taking away the sin of the world wouldn't be incompatible with being a king. This episode suggests that he was unclear. He certainly didn't know about any second coming.

It's hardly surprising that John was doubting his earlier picture of things. He had probably been in prison for a year or longer at this time. What was God doing? Was there another stage in God's plan that he had overlooked? Why was Jesus still hushing people when he healed them?

Jesus' reply was a slightly veiled "yes." He told John's disciples to go back and report what they saw—healings, miracles, and deliverance—all marks of the Messiah (Isaiah 35:5–6; 61:1ff.).

Jesus' Challenge

Then Jesus turned to the crowd:

> "What did you go out into the wilderness to see? A reed shaken by the wind? But what did you go out to see? A man dressed in soft clothing? Those who are splendidly clothed and live in luxury are found in royal palaces!" (vs. 24-25)

John's austerity was well known. It was clear to all that he wasn't operating for any self-serving motive. Jesus went on:

> But what did you go out to see? A prophet? Yes, I say to you, and one who is more than a prophet. This is the one about whom it is written, 'Look, I am sending my messenger ahead of you, and he will prepare your way before you.' I say to you, among those born of women there is no one greater than John; yet he who is least in the kingdom of God is greater than he." (vs. 26-28)

Jesus seems to feel that people related to John like they would to a fad.

He was the hot item at the time, but did they fully realize who they were dealing with? Jesus doesn't seem to think so. His questions are rhetorical but provocative. We earlier saw that John was a prophet—the first prophet to appear in four hundred years.

Elijah?

He was also the forerunner predicted in Malachi 3:1, which Jesus cites here. But Matthew's account includes something else Jesus said:

> "And if you are willing to accept it, John himself is Elijah who was to come. He who has ears to hear, let him hear." (Matthew 11:14-15)

This is a shocking statement. We already saw that the leaders asked John if he was Elijah, and he answered that he was not (John 1:21). So how can we explain Jesus saying John was Elijah after all?

In answer, first notice the following statement, "He who has ears to hear, let him hear." That's a saying Jesus used when speaking parables or something metaphorical (Matthew 13:9, 43; Mark 4:9, 23; Luke 14:35). It suggests his listeners should look for more than the surface meaning.

It's also notable that he adds the condition, "If you are willing to accept it." That makes it sound like John either is, or is not Elijah, depending on whether they accept it. How can that be?

The explanation is that John was not Elijah, but he was a *type* of Elijah. The prophecy in Malachi where God said, "Behold, I am going to send you Elijah the prophet before the coming of the great and terrible day of the Lord" (4:5), was well known to Jews of this period. Mark tells how the disciples, after Jesus' transfiguration, asked, "Why do the teachers of religious law insist that Elijah must return before the Messiah comes?" (Mark 9:11). This legitimate question would have been on all Jews' minds.

Jesus' answer to their question on that occasion is quite interesting:

> "Elijah does first come and restore all things. And yet how is it written of the Son of Man that he will suffer many things and be treated with contempt? But I say to you that Elijah has indeed come, and they did to him whatever they wished, just as it is written of him." (Mark 9:12-13)

Careful reading shows that Jesus first declared that Elijah is indeed going to come back before the coming of Messiah, as Malachi predicts. He is speaking of the future, and adds that he will "restore all things." That is a clear reference to Malachi, who predicted that Elijah would "restore the hearts of the fathers to their children and the hearts of the children to their fathers" (Malachi 4:6).

Jesus was saying that Malachi's prophecy will be fulfilled, and that it was not fulfilled yet in his day. That means John was not the fulfillment of Malachi 4:6, because by the time Jesus said this in Mark, John the Baptist was already dead. Jesus said the fulfillment would be in the future in his day ("Elijah does come . . .").

Finally, consider Jesus' last comment that Elijah had already come and was met by persecution. Could he be referring to John the Baptist? No. His last phrase says, "Just as it is written of him." None of our gospel books were written at the time Jesus said this. He can only be referring to the original Elijah from 1 and 2 Kings, who was also persecuted by Jezebel and Ahab.

Problem solved. Although many conservative scholars don't believe Elijah is going to come in the future, Jesus clearly said he will. He also asked them a question, which should have been a clue. Right after saying Elijah does come, he asks, "Yet why do the Scriptures say that the Son of Man must suffer greatly and be treated with utter contempt?" (Mark 9:12). Why would Jesus change the subject away from John and Elijah? He's hinting that they have overlooked something—namely, the first coming of the Messiah.

Malachi said that Elijah is going to come before the "great and terrible day of the Lord." That refers to the *second coming* of Jesus and the judgment day. But the disciples were looking for Elijah before the *first coming*. They didn't realize Jesus would come twice.

The Old Testament never talks about two comings for the Messiah. It never says there won't be two comings. It just never say there will be. Passages about the suffering servant refer to the first coming, but Jews at this time didn't see these as teaching two comings of the Messiah. Jesus is basically saying, "You're overlooking the first coming."

But we're not done. Matthew also recounts the same conversation on the way down from Jesus' transfiguration. The disciples asked Jesus the same question about why the rabbis taught that Elijah must come before the Messiah, and he gives the same answer: "Elijah is coming and will restore all things," (Matthew 17:11) using the future tense. But then comes a big surprise. Matthew adds, "Then the disciples understood that he had spoken to them about John the Baptist" (Matthew 17:13).

Wait, that can't be. We just saw that Jesus' comments about Elijah were from written Scripture ("just as it is written of him"). That couldn't possibly refer to John, because nothing had been written about John at that time.[1] The disciples were wrong! They assumed Jesus was talking about John, but they hadn't listened carefully to what he said, including "just as it is written of him."

Jesus probably knew they had reached the wrong conclusion, but he didn't bother to correct them, or others who reached the same conclusion. This was an important role John played. Jews, who expected Elijah to come back shortly before the Messiah, would view Elijah's absence as proof that Jesus was not the Messiah.

That's when Jesus would point to John and say, "If you care to accept it, he is Elijah." John was a dead ringer for Elijah. They both lived out in the wilderness by themselves, they dressed alike (compare Mark 1:6 with 2 Kings 1:8), they both prophesied against a wicked king and queen, and they both called the nation to repentance.

As a result, nobody would stumble into disbelieving Jesus just because Elijah was missing. John was not Elijah, but he was similar enough that people, including the disciples, couldn't tell the difference.

Why didn't Jesus just clearly explain that there were two separate comings and Elijah was for the second one? He had his reasons for concealing the full plan, as we'll see.

Jesus' Assessment of John

Back in Luke, Jesus finished his comments to the crowd, saying:

1. Most scholars miss this fact or ignore it. A strong consensus prevails that Malachi 4:5-6 has already been fulfilled by John the Baptist, and nothing further is to be expected. So my reading is in the minority. I can only observe that Jesus referred to Elijah saying, "just as it is written of him," which can't possibly refer to John. It must therefore refer to the original Old Testament Elijah. To claim it refers to John is a departure from a grammatical-historical reading. Also, Jesus says here in Matthew, "Elijah will come," at a time when John was already dead. So John was a type of Elijah, but Elijah will also come before Jesus' second coming.

> "I tell you, of all who have ever lived, none is greater than John. Yet even the least person in the Kingdom of God is greater than he is!" (v. 28 NLT)

For Jesus to say John was as great as anyone who ever lived is amazing when you think about all the heroes of faith in the Old Testament. His greatness probably grew out of his role—to introduce the Messiah to the world.

But what does the second statement about those "least in the kingdom" mean? Most likely, he's predicting that believers under the New Covenant will be greater in the sense that they are literally indwelt by the Holy Spirit. Believers who are merged with God's spirit have an intimacy with God that Old Covenant believers never knew. Or is Jesus talking about people in heaven or even in the future kingdom of the Messiah?

Finally,

> When they heard this, all the people—even the tax collectors—agreed that God's way was right, for they had been baptized by John. But the Pharisees and experts in religious law rejected God's plan for them, for they had refused John's baptism. (vs. 29-30 NLT)

The polarizing impact John had on the nation resulted in an accurate demarcating between those who were truly open to God from those who were more set on defending the status quo. Jesus' field of ministry was the former.

A Riddle

Turning to his critics, Jesus concluded with a short ironic riddle:

> "To what can I compare the people of this generation?" Jesus asked. "How can I describe them? They are like children playing a game in the public square. They complain to their friends,
>
> 'We played wedding songs,
> and you didn't dance,
> so we played funeral songs,
> and you didn't weep.'

> For John the Baptist didn't spend his time eating bread or drinking wine, and you say, 'He's possessed by a demon.' The Son of Man, on the other hand, feasts and drinks, and you say, 'He's a glutton and a drunkard, and a friend of tax collectors and other sinners!' Yet wisdom is vindicated by all her children." (vs. 31-35 NLT)

Jesus was observing that nothing was good enough for his unbelieving critics. Whether it was John's austerity, or Jesus' fun-loving willingness to feast and drink, or his gracious acceptance of sinful people, all the opposition could do is finger-wag and condemn.

Jesus was certainly not a glutton or a drunk, even though many people at these parties probably were. Jesus' acknowledgment that he feasted and drank wine is significant. He wasn't ascetic or other-worldly. Feasting is a blast, as long as you don't lose control over it, and so is drinking some good wine. The Bible says,

> In Jerusalem, the Lord of Heaven's Armies
> will spread a wonderful feast
> for all the people of the world.
> It will be a delicious banquet
> with clear, well-aged wine
> and choice meat. (Isaiah 25:6)

So we will be feasting in heaven, and Jesus will be pouring the drinks! The abhorrence some Christians have for drinking alcohol is a man-made tradition, not supported in Scripture.[2] Jesus rejected such additions, saying, "Neglecting the commandment of God, you hold to the tradition of men." And then, "You nicely set aside the commandment of God in order to keep your tradition" (Mark 7:8-9).

The cost for adding to God's word can be very high. This human addition prohibiting alcohol has resulted in a new hurdle blocking people's access to the gospel. Who knows how many people who enjoy having a beer and watching the game have turned away after realizing that if they came to Jesus, they would never be able to do that again—even though, in truth, Jesus himself would have happily joined in with them.

2. See the clear biblical permission to drink alcohol in moderation Mischelle Sandowich, "(Almost) Everything You Need to Know About Alcohol and the Bible," *Reformed Earth* (blog), September 13, 2022, https://mischelle.substack.com/p/god-and-alcohol.

Anointed by a Sinful Woman

A Pharisee named Simon was possibly open to Jesus' claims, or at least curious. He invited Jesus to come to lunch at his house. While they were reclining on pads—not sitting on chairs—a local woman approached Jesus from behind. Jesus would have been lying on his side at an angle with his head near the table edge, his feet extending out into the room. This explains how the woman could approach his feet and pour expensive perfume on them from an alabaster vial.

Luke notes that the woman was a sinner—perhaps a prostitute. She was so moved by Jesus' acceptance that she began to weep, and her tears fell on his feet as well. She even kissed his feet as she wiped them with her long hair (vs. 36-38).[3]

Then we read,

> Now when the Pharisee who had invited him saw this, he said to himself, "If this man were a prophet he would know who and what sort of person this woman is who is touching him, that she is a sinner." (v. 39)

The implication of his thought is that if Jesus were really a prophet he wouldn't let this sinful woman touch him. That's because in Pharisaic teaching, you shouldn't touch a "sinner" because they were contagious. Touching one who is unclean made you unclean. This was a key part of the thinking behind the ritual washing before eating a meal (Luke 11:38; see below).

The Power of Forgiveness

Jesus either discerned, or had it revealed, what the Pharisee was thinking. He said, "Simon, I have something to say to you" and then continued,

> "A moneylender had two debtors: one owed five hundred

3. Some readers wonder if this might be the same event recounted in John 12:1-8, Mark 14:3-9, and Matthew 26:6-13. It certainly is not. This event featured a sinful woman (as even Jesus agreed), while the other event recounted in John, Mark, and Matthew had Mary, the sister of Martha pouring the ointment. Nothing suggests Mary was an immoral woman. All three of the later anointing accounts say it happened in Bethany at the house of Simon the Leper (near Jerusalem). This event in Luke happened in Galilee—far from Jerusalem. The later anointing happened at the very end of Jesus' ministry. This one in Luke was much earlier. It is quite possible that Mary had heard of this event, and decided to repeat it, with slight alterations. She might even have heard that this woman poured perfume from an alabaster vial, and thought, "Hmm. I have one of those."

> denarii, and the other fifty. When they were unable to repay, he graciously forgave them both. So which of them will love him more?"
>
> Simon answered and said, "I suppose the one whom he forgave more."
>
> And Jesus said to him, "You have judged correctly." (vs. 40-43)

This mini-parable underscores again how important it is that we be honest about our sin if we want to enjoy grace. Simon the Pharisee probably wasn't guilty of the same sins as this woman. But he had his own sins in ample measure, neatly concealed from his vision by religious works. Then:

> Turning toward the woman, he said to Simon, "Do you see this woman? I entered your house; you gave me no water for my feet, but she has wet my feet with her tears and wiped them with her hair. You gave me no kiss; but she, since the time I came in, has not ceased to kiss my feet. You did not anoint my head with oil, but she anointed my feet with perfume. For this reason I say to you, her sins, which are many, have been forgiven, for she loved much; but he who is forgiven little, loves little."

Jesus wasn't saying that her love saved her, but that her love was the sign that she had been forgiven.

> Then he said to her, "Your sins have been forgiven."
>
> Those who were reclining at the table with Him began to say to themselves, "Who is this man who even forgives sins?" And He said to the woman, "Your faith has saved you; go in peace." (vs. 44-50)

His pronouncement that she was forgiven must have been for the benefit of Simon and his other guests. Jesus implied earlier that her sins were already forgiven, and that's why she was so moved.

The other guests grumbled to one another "Who is this man who even forgives sins?" (v. 49). Their question has the sense, "Who does this man think he is." But Jesus resolutely ignored their suspicions: "And he said to the woman, 'Your faith has saved you; go in peace'" (v. 50). Jesus left no grey area when it came to his authority to forgive sins. Neither did he leave doubt about what leads to forgiveness—saving faith.

The Big Picture

The incidents in Luke 7 greatly clarified who Jesus was, what he was like, and the line he was drawing in the sand opposing Pharisaic theology.

Jesus never got to see John again. His death wounded Jesus mightily. He had to go off by himself to mourn (Matthew 14:13).

The sinful woman event shows Jesus' heart for lost people who are willing to come to him. Instead of viewing her as scum that should only be avoided, he welcomed her and forgave her. Throughout the Gospels this nexus between Jesus and raw sinners recurs.

Jesus himself explained this affinity when he said that those who are forgiven much love much. People who think they have little or no sin in their lives (like those gathered that day) have little appreciation of God's grace. Their focus was less on forgiveness and more on performance. Behind that was the sorry fact that they were more characterized by pride than by humility.

13

Supporting Women, Parables

Luke 8:1-18

Spiritual Women

In an amazing account, Luke notes that many of Jesus' key supporters and followers were women.

> Soon afterwards, he began going around from one city and village to another, proclaiming and preaching the kingdom of God. The twelve were with him, and also some women who had been healed of evil spirits and sicknesses: Mary who was called Magdalene, from whom seven demons had gone out, and Joanna the wife of Chuza, Herod's steward, and Susanna, and many others who were contributing to their support out of their private means. (Luke 8:1-3)

This was unprecedented. Rabbis never had female followers, and they had a low view of women. They argued that women were so incompetent that, "It's better to burn the Torah than have it fall into the hands of a woman."[1] Women sat separately in the synagogue and didn't participate

1. *Talmud* Sotah, 3:4, 119.

in the debates or even speak. They were not taught to read or write. They were certainly not permitted to teach Torah.

Jesus discarded all this negative tradition. And we should note that none of the tradition was biblically based. But here we see that a significant portion of Jesus' following were women. Luke later tells how Jesus defended a woman's desire to learn, saying, "Mary has chosen the good part, which shall not be taken away from her" (10:42).

These women weren't just hanging around. They were key workers enabling his mission. The group traveled, and that probably meant moving a camp from place to place, so Jesus' followers had plenty of work to do. These women were also buying much of the food and other provisions. They probably weren't sent out to preach, for the simple reason that this culture would not accept females preaching, and it would have been too dangerous. Weak males may consider it their business to keep women down, often with violence.

"Joanna the wife of Chuza, the manager of Herod's household" mentioned here appears again at the cross. That took courage and faithfulness. Most of his disciples fled or lied about their ties with Jesus. This is also the best explanation for how Luke and other Gospel writers know about inside happenings in Herod's court. They clearly had an inside source, and his name was probably Chuza (see 3:19-20; Matthew 14:1-12; Mark 6:19-20).

Here we also learn that Mary Magdalene had been demon possessed.

After naming a few women, Luke adds that "many others" were following. That language suggests perhaps dozens of lady followers. They may have been single or widowed, because if married, their husbands would not have let them travel with Jesus. Or, some of them could have been following along with their husbands.

So Jesus rejected the first century view that women were foolish and incapable of learning and serving God. Later in the early church, women continued to be at the center, including power house church planters like Priscilla with her husband Aquila. One lady, Junia, is named as an apostle! (Romans 16:7).

The Parable of the Soils

> When a large crowd was coming together, and those from the various cities were journeying to him, he spoke by way of a parable: "The sower went out to sow his seed; and as he sowed, some fell beside the road, and it was trampled underfoot and the birds of the air ate it up. Other seed fell on rocky soil, and as soon as it grew up, it withered away, because it had no moisture. Other seed fell among the thorns; and the thorns grew up with it and choked it out. Other seed fell into the good soil, and grew up, and produced a crop a hundred times as great." As he said these things, he would call out, "He who has ears to hear, let him hear." (vs. 4-8)

Then later his disciples began questioning Him as to what this parable meant, so he explained:

> "Now the parable is this: the seed is the word of God. Those beside the road are those who have heard; then the devil comes and takes away the word from their heart, so that they will not believe and be saved. Those on the rocky soil are those who, when they hear, receive the word with joy; and these have no firm root; they believe for a while, and in time of temptation fall away. The seed which fell among the thorns, these are the ones who have heard, and as they go on their way they are choked with worries and riches and pleasures of this life, and bring no fruit to maturity. But the seed in the good soil, these are the ones who have heard the word in an honest and good heart, and hold it fast, and bear fruit with perseverance." (vs. 9-15)

Lessons

This famous parable contains several key insights.

First, the seed is the word of God, or according to Matthew, "the word of the kingdom" (Matthew 13:19). The seed is the same no matter where it falls. It's the soils that are different.

The soils stand for the different ways people respond to the word.

Some either ignore the word, or reject it. Those are the seeds beside or on the path. Satan snatches the seed away. So Satan can go inside people's hearts to snatch the word away. He does this mostly through accusation and deception, claiming that the believers who brought the message are up to something bad or that following God will be dreadful.

The seed falling on the rocky soil stands for superficial hearers. These people seem to believe temporarily, but the word "has no firm root." So persecution, or trials (as in Matthew's version) or temptation (as here) expose the truth—they are not authentic believers.

Some people sort of follow for awhile perhaps because they like the social atmosphere in the body of Christ, or even a potential boy or girlfriend. They look like other believers. They may act like believers. But it's only for awhile. Persecution squeezes out false believers, and maybe that's why God allows it.

In the third case, soil lands on ground full of thorns. Although the seeds germinate and grow, they never bear fruit. These are distracted hearers. They get caught up with the "worries and riches and pleasures of this life." Worldly believers might actually have the Spirit, but God can't use them to advance his kingdom, because they are too devoted to the things of the world.

Finally, some seed falls on good ground. These are people with "an honest and good heart" and they bear a huge harvest with "steadfastness." In Matthew's version he adds that this harvest was 30, 60, or 100 fold. So people are differently gifted, resulting in different quantities of fruit. But God only expects us to be faithful to what he has given us.

Why Parables?

When Jesus was alone with his disciples, they asked him why he spoke in parables. We learn this from Matthew's account, but it's implied in Luke. In reply, Jesus said,

> "You are permitted to understand the secrets of the Kingdom of God. But I use parables to teach the others so that the Scriptures might be fulfilled: 'When they look, they won't really see. When they hear, they won't understand.'" (v. 10, quoting Isaiah 6:9)

In other words, Jesus revealed that speaking in parables was like a coded message only comprehensible to believers, or at least to willing people. He refers to the hardened hearts of people in Isaiah's day to exemplify the dynamics of unbelief leading to a hardened heart. Notice in Matthew's account, he quotes the further part in Isaiah where he says, "For the hearts of these people are hardened, and their ears cannot hear, and they have closed their eyes—so their eyes cannot see, and their ears cannot hear, and their hearts cannot understand" (Matthew 13:15, quoting Isaiah 6:10).

People who have hardened hearts distort what they hear. Their inability to understand or comprehend communication from God is not the result of poor hearing, but of unwillingness. In a related passage, the apostle Paul said, "A natural man does not accept the things of the Spirit of God, for they are foolishness to him; and he cannot understand them, because they are spiritually appraised" (1 Corinthians 2:14).

Jesus adds another warning later: "So pay attention to how you hear. To those who listen to my teaching, more understanding will be given. But for those who are not listening, even what they think they understand will be taken away from them" (v. 18 and compare Matthew 13:12). He was warning that access to God's word is a rare privilege, not to be trifled with.

Whenever people fail to take the word seriously, including acting on it, "even what they think they understand will be taken away from them." This statement means that your spiritual knowledge is either increasing or decreasing. It doesn't stay neutral. "Use it or lose it," is the rule for responding to revelation from God.

The punishment for not listening to God's word is that he removes access to it. The TV screen simply goes dark. God warns people about this type of discipline in Amos:

> "Behold, days are coming," declares the Lord God,
>
> "When I will send a famine on the land,
>
> Not a famine for bread or a thirst for water,
>
> But rather for hearing the words of the Lord.
>
> People will stagger from sea to sea
>
> And from the north even to the east;

> They will go to and fro to seek the word of the Lord,
>
> But they will not find it." (Amos 8:11-12)

What a terrible fate! When God stops speaking, where do you turn? Hebrews teaches that it's never too late:

> Take care, brethren, that there not be in any one of you an evil, unbelieving heart that falls away from the living God. But encourage one another day after day, as long as it is still called "Today," so that none of you will be hardened by the deceitfulness of sin. (Hebrews 3:12-13)

Here, the "deceitfulness of sin" refers to the fact that people whose hearts are hardening usually don't realize what's happening. Apathy concerning the things of God easily becomes a habit. Compromise that seems reasonable at one level, before long seems reasonable at many levels.

But the ray of light here is the word "today." If it's still called "today," it's not too late to change your heart and turn back to God for instruction.

The Kingdom of God

Jesus said he was disclosing "the secrets of the Kingdom of God" (v. 10). Matthew's account aligns this parable with several other parables often called the kingdom parables. All of these parables have one thing in common. They contradict current popular expectations for the nature of the kingdom of God. Jewish teaching held that the Messiah would arrive in power and take over the world. The kingdom of God on earth would follow.

But that's not the picture Jesus paints. Instead, he gives the parable of the soils. Under this picture, the Kingdom of God won't be imposed on the earth by force. Instead, people will have the freedom to respond as they wish; some positive, some negative. The kingdom will grow gradually, more like a field of grain than any sudden takeover.

The same goes for the succeeding parables here in Luke and in Matthew. Matthew includes the parable of the wheat and the tares, where the children of God and the children of the Evil One grow together (Matthew 13:24-30). They won't be separated until the harvest, which Jesus identified: "The harvest is the end of the age" (Matthew 13:39).

It's not that the world takeover of King Messiah has been canceled. It's still coming, but later. Jesus didn't come right out and say that he wasn't going to come as king until later. A sharp eye can see that implication in his reference to the end of the age. But given the paradigm in which his audience was trained, they weren't going to get the picture. And Jesus planned it that way, as he himself said. The "secrets" of the kingdom were not granted to this audience.

The Lampstand

Luke recounts another parable or simile that fits with the picture of the gradual spread of the gospel:

> "No one lights a lamp and then covers it with a bowl or hides it under a bed. A lamp is placed on a stand, where its light can be seen by all who enter the house. For all that is secret will eventually be brought into the open, and everything that is concealed will be brought to light and made known to all." (vs. 16-17 NLT)

This version is different than the similar recounting in Matthew, and also comes from a different context—Matthew's account of the lamp was during the Sermon on the Mount, much earlier.

Here is Matthew's version:

> "You are the light of the world. A city set on a hill cannot be hidden; nor does anyone light a lamp and put it under a basket, but on the lampstand, and it gives light to all who are in the house. Let your light shine before men in such a way that they may see your good works, and glorify your Father who is in heaven." (Matthew 5:14-16)

This illustration clearly refers to evangelism. He says they are the light of the world . . . letting their light shine before people, so they will glorify God.

Luke's version has less to do with speaking or acting, and more to do with listening. The imperative is "So take care how you listen" (v. 18). In this case, hiding the lamp means not listening to the word. Instead, we are to "hear the word in an honest and good heart, and hold it fast, and bear fruit with perseverance," like the good soil in verse 15.

If we listen well, and act upon what we hear, God will see that we hear more. But if we're faking it, or not taking it seriously, he takes away "even what he thinks he has." So our knowledge of the kingdom is dynamic; either growing or shrinking, depending on what we do with what we already know.

His Mother and Brothers

Finally, Luke gives us a strange little quip:

> Someone told him, "Your mother and brothers are standing outside, wanting to see you."
>
> He replied, "My mother and brothers are those who hear God's word and put it into practice." (vs. 20-21 NIV)

We know his brothers were not believing in him (John 7:4-5). Earlier, when a big crowd gathered around Jesus we read, "When his family heard what was happening, they tried to take him away. 'He's out of his mind,' they said" (Mark 3:21). Of course, that was not Mary's view.

We don't know what they wanted him for, but it could have been something trivial that would have taken him away from his work. In any case, Jesus stressed that the family of God would now take first place over one's natural family. That's especially true when your family members are nonbelievers who are unable to grasp the importance of the things of God.

We regularly see young believers taken out because they failed to set down boundaries with their unbelieving families. Some young people seem almost unable to say no to anything their families call for. It frequently takes them away from the body of Christ and their spiritual walk suffers.

The Big Picture

As Jesus and his large following, including a good number of women, traveled about in Galilee, people were fascinated, but in many cases, for opportunistic reasons. They were benefiting though his healings. They were also excited about the messianic age and the overthrow of the Romans. But most still failed to understand his nature or his mission. As he gradually pulled back the curtain, these people became disillusioned. Jesus was thinning out his following, gradually separating the true believers from the opportunists, whom he characterized as having hardened hearts.

14

Jesus Displays His Power

Luke 8:22-56

Calming the Storm

> Now on one of those days Jesus and his disciples got into a boat, and he said to them, "Let us go over to the other side of the lake." So they launched out. But as they were sailing along he fell asleep; and a fierce gale of wind descended on the lake, and they began to be swamped and to be in danger. (8:22-23)

Jesus must have been exhausted to keep sleeping. But I've had the same experience sleeping during a storm on Lake Erie. A rocking boat can encourage sleep.

> They came to Jesus and woke him up, saying, "Master, Master, we are perishing!" And he got up and rebuked the wind and the surging waves, and they stopped, and it became calm. And he said to them, "Where is your faith?" They were fearful and amazed, saying to one another, "Who then is this, that he commands even the winds and the water, and they obey him?" (vs. 24-25)

Jesus' calming of the storm was a nature miracle. Nature miracles clearly showed Jesus' supremacy over nature. That was important in a day when people believed that natural events were caused by spirits. Still today, many cultures have a spiritual view of nature.

These were experienced fishermen raised on this lake, so this was not a case of them being hysterical over a minor storm. Also, the boats they used were not safe in large waves.

Why did Jesus rebuke their lack of faith? It wasn't that they cried, "Master, Master," seeking help. It was the part about "We are perishing" that showed a clear lack of faith. If they knew Jesus was the Messiah, what were the chances that God might lose his Messiah and all his followers in a storm? None.

The disciples' murmurings, "Who is this?" shows that they still hadn't fully grasped who they were dealing with. Their apparent confusion about Jesus' identity was part of a normal growth process. But we will see increasingly that Jesus was exasperated by their slow progress in comprehension.

Power over the Demonic

Demon possession is relatively rare in our part of the world. But international missionaries encounter it much more frequently. Apparently, the Evil One is more intent on reinforcing materialism in our part of the world. If westerners saw demon possessed people wandering about, they might begin to question their anti-supernatural assumptions. Jesus' ministry was extraordinarily active with demon possession, possibly because the demons knew something important was underway in that area.

They arrived at the east shore of the Sea of Galilee.[1] "And when he came out onto the land, he was met by a man from the city who was possessed with demons; and who had not put on any clothing for a long time, and was not living in a house, but in the tombs" (v. 27). This naked man running up to Jesus and his disciples probably looked insane. But it wasn't insanity. Luke says he was possessed with demons.

1. Matthew says it was the "country of the Gadarenes" (Matthew 8:28), while Luke and Mark say it is in the "country of the Gerasenes" (v. 26). Historians believe these districts overlapped which explains the discrepancy. There are also manuscript differences, leading to confusion. Most scholars place this event on the east coast of the Sea of Galilee.

Mark adds more detail:

> This man lived in the burial caves and could no longer be restrained, even with a chain. Whenever he was put into chains and shackles—as he often was—he snapped the chains from his wrists and smashed the shackles. No one was strong enough to subdue him. Day and night he wandered among the burial caves and in the hills, howling and cutting himself with sharp stones. (Mark 5:3-5)

Cutting himself with rocks is typical of the self-destructive tendencies often seen in possessed people.

The ability to break chains is partly due to the fact that ancient chains were not like ours today. These were bent iron rings, and much easier to break than a modern, steel chain, but not that much easier. "Smashing the chain" sounds like he was using rocks to bash the chain apart. They clearly considered it remarkable. Reports of demon-possessed people frequently refer to surprising strength.

The howling could be the fits or paroxysms possessed people often manifest. In shamanistic possession quests, the shaman usually speaks in tongues, which they interpret to be the languages of the animals. They see speaking these languages as a sign that possession has been achieved.

> Seeing Jesus, he cried out and fell before him, and said in a loud voice, "What business do we have with each other, Jesus, Son of the Most High God? I beg you, do not torment me," for it had seized him many times; and he was bound with chains and shackles and kept under guard, and yet he would break his bonds and be driven by the demon into the desert. (vs. 28-29)

The man ran at Jesus, according to Mark, but fell to his knees on the way. Based on the tense used, Jesus had already spoken a word of authority, commanding the demons to come out. That probably halted the man, preventing an attack.

The man, or really the demons within the man, knew immediately who Jesus was without any introduction. He cried out, "What business do we have with each other, Jesus, Son of the Most High God? I beg you, do not torment me!" (v. 28).

It's a real bad sign when someone knows things they had no way of knowing. It suggests they have a source of knowledge other than their senses. Most occult phenomena, like psychics, are fake. They use people's desire to know the future, to be healed, or to make decisions as avenues for profit. Other phenomena are autogenic, or self-caused. The placebo effect is real, and people can cause change in themselves because they believe in the psychic or shaman.

The third source of change is actual, real, spiritual power or insight. Here is where one encounters demonic activity. The result of engaging in such practices can be demonic influence in your life that could range from occasional oppression to the most serious level—demon possession.

Believers don't need to worry about becoming possessed. But they can come under demonic influence to a significant extent. Peter said to Ananias, "Ananias, why has Satan filled your heart to lie to the Holy Spirit?" (Acts 5:3).

The Holy Spirit sometimes gives believers a similar ability to know things about another person, whether through the gift of prophecy or perhaps the spiritual gift of knowledge (1 Corinthians 12:8-10). Notice Paul says that when believers prophecy, the visiting non-believer has "the secrets of his heart" revealed (1 Corinthians 14:24-25). Arguably, Satan counterfeits most of God's gifts. Most psychics and shamans claim they work for God, so believers should beware and avoid any involvement with the occult.

The demon possessed man also cried out, "I beg you, do not torment me!" (v. 28). In Matthew's account we see an additional detail: "Have you come here to torment us before the time?" (Matthew 8:29). This intriguing question suggests that the demons knew the Messiah would come and judge them, but they apparently thought it would happen later. They were surprised to see him this early. That in turn suggests that they, too, didn't know about two separate comings for the Messiah.

Why Ask His Name?

At this point, "Jesus asked him, 'What is your name?' And he said, 'Legion'; for many demons had entered him" (v. 30). This is the only time in the New or Old Testament that anyone asked a demon for his name. We notice that Jesus earlier ordered the demon out, but he's still in possession of the man. This could be why Jesus asked him his name.

He may have wanted to know why this demon wasn't immediately complying with his orders.

Some demons are more powerful than others. They may temporarily resist a command. You see this in Matthew when the disciples were unable to deliver a boy, even though they had been able to deliver people earlier. They asked Jesus, "Why couldn't we cast out that evil spirit?" Jesus replied, "This kind can be cast out only by prayer" (Mark 9:28-29). Notice his words, "This kind." In other words, there are different kinds of demons, and some are apparently harder to cast out.

So, when Jesus asked his name the demon answered, "'Legion'; for many demons had entered him" (v. 30). This may be why they had more power than most. This isn't the man speaking, it's his demon. So this is a case of multiple personality. Multiple personality disorder was way over-diagnosed in the 80s and 90s. But it does show up rarely. It could reflect psychosis, faking to get attention, or that another personality inhabits the person.

The demons were also "imploring Jesus not to command them to go away into the abyss" (v. 31). This might be the same abyss Jude refers to when he mentioned certain fallen angels whom God "has kept in eternal bonds under darkness for the judgment of the great day" (Jude 6). Peter says, "God did not spare angels when they sinned, but cast them into hell and committed them to pits of darkness, reserved for judgment" (2 Peter 2:4). These verses don't seem to refer to fallen angels in general, but to a certain group of angels in primordial history around the time of Noah. The demons in this man apparently knew about this judgment.

Some Pigs

Then comes the bizarre part:

> Now there was a herd of many swine feeding there on the mountain; and the demons implored him to permit them to enter the swine. (v. 32)

Apparently, if the alternative is between going into the abyss and going into some swine, it's an easy choice.

> And he gave them permission. And the demons came out of

> the man and entered the swine; and the herd rushed down the steep bank into the lake and was drowned. (vs. 32-33)

This is an incredible scene—a herd of many swine running down the hill into the lake. Did God or the demons make them self-destruct? Most likely it was God. The demons are left disembodied after all. Some interpreters suggest that demons enjoy being in a physical body, but there's not enough evidence. We don't know why they asked to enter the pigs. The fact that they were able to do so becomes important, because it demonstrates that demons can inhabit animals, just like Satan apparently inhabited a serpent in the Garden of Eden.

Liberal commentators bemoan Jesus' cruelty in this scene. New Testament scholar Michael Green observes wryly:

> Much ink and compassion have been spilled upon the pigs by scholars who no doubt enjoy their bacon for breakfast and their pork for dinner.[2]

Not to mention that the destiny for all these pigs was the dinner table. Why else would they raise swine? The farmers in this area were probably Jewish, so why did they have a herd of swine? That's not kosher. Were the pigs for Jewish markets? That seems unlikely. They were probably being raised for Romans living in nearby Decapolis, or "ten cities" built in Roman fashion. If so, herding was unethical for Jews.

Reaction

Luke goes on to describe how villagers in the area heard about the miracle and came running out to see. There sat the demon possessed Wild man, "clothed and in his right mind." Their response is surprising: "They became frightened" (v. 35). Why?

When people who don't know God personally, see raw supernatural power doing something they never thought could be done, it can cause fear. These villagers didn't understand the benevolent and loving nature of God.

Paul reminds us of an earlier episode when Moses came down mount Sinai with his face glowing from his recent encounter with God. "The

2. Michael Green, *The Message of Matthew: The Kingdom of Heaven*, Revised edition (Westmont, IL: IVP Academic, 2020), 120.

sons of Israel could not look intently at the face of Moses because of the glory of his face" (2 Corinthians 3:7).

They had no good reason to fear God's glory, but the fact that they did signified their distance from God. They didn't know him well, and that made him seem scary. Moses had to put a veil over his face when talking to them. But—and here's Paul's point—"Whenever a person turns to the Lord, the veil is taken away." Then, "with unveiled face, beholding as in a mirror the glory of the Lord, we are being transformed into the same image" (2 Corinthians 3:16, 18).

This fear of God's power matches what follows in Luke:

> And all the people of the country of the Gerasenes and the surrounding district asked him to leave them, for they were gripped with great fear; and he got into a boat and returned. (v. 37)

Why not ask him to stay in case some other danger arose? No, they were repelled from Jesus. They probably weren't too happy about their loss of income from the pigs, but more importantly, they weren't open to the spiritual gift Jesus was bringing.

There must have been some back and forth in this discussion. To spread to the "surrounding district" would take some time. But in the end Jesus saw no openness. That's why he left, in the same way he would soon instruct his disciples to avoid endlessly pushing truth on people who already said no.

The Healed Man

The formerly demonized man wanted to join the apostolic band:

> But the man from whom the demons had gone out was begging him that he might accompany him; but he sent him away, saying, "Return to your house and describe what great things God has done for you." So he went away, proclaiming throughout the whole city what great things Jesus had done for him. (vs. 38-39)

Being one of the apostles was never an option. But God used his testimony, probably with great power.

Jairus' Daughter

The band sailed back across the lake, probably to Capernaum. It didn't take long for a crowd to gather. "The people welcomed Him, for they had all been waiting for Him" (vs. 41). The crowd becomes significant later.

> And there came a man named Jairus, and he was an official of the synagogue; and he fell at Jesus' feet, and began to implore him to come to his house; for he had an only daughter, about twelve years old, and she was dying. (vs. 41-42)

Here is an agony only a parent could fully understand. I had a twelve year old daughter at one time, and I remember reading this and imagining what it would be like. How desperate and frantic I would have been if it was my daughter.

A Sick Woman

> But as he went, the crowds were pressing against him. And a woman who had a hemorrhage for twelve years, and could not be healed by anyone, came up behind him and touched the fringe of his cloak, and immediately her hemorrhage stopped. (vs. 43-44)

Mark adds that this woman, "had endured much at the hands of many physicians, and had spent all that she had and was not helped at all, but rather had grown worse" (Mark 5:26). We are familiar with the kind of "medicine" she would have received based on healing treatments for discharge that have survived. Here is an example suggested in the *Talmud*:

> Let them procure three . . . Persian onions, boil them in wine, make her drink it, and say to her, "Cease your discharge!"
>
> But if not, she should be made to sit at cross-roads, hold a cup of wine in her hand, and a man comes up from behind, frightens her and exclaims, "Cease your discharge!"

This one suggests picking out a barley grain from the dung of a white mule. Then,

> When she eats it and holds it in one day, her discharge will

> cease for one day, if for two days, her discharge will cease for two days, if for three days, it will cease forever.[3]

Before the advent of modern medicine, medical care was usually nothing but superstition. This is a sad story of a harmless woman in a fallen world having her life destroyed through no fault of her own. Her suffering was made worse because of the Jewish loathing for touching another's blood or having it in their house.

She must have earlier seen Jesus heal, because she thought to herself, "If I just touch his garments, I will get well" (Mark 5:28). She seems to have an impersonal, sort of electrical theory of healing. She wants to snatch the healing anonymously and slip away. So, she pushed through the crowd surrounding Jesus and finally managed to reach out and touch his cloak.

In the surging crowd, Jesus immediately halted:

> And Jesus said, "Who is the one who touched me?" And while they were all denying it, Peter said, "Master, the people are crowding and pressing in on you." But Jesus said, "Someone did touch me, for I was aware that power had gone out of me." (vs. 45-46)[4]

So the electrical theory was right? This is such an intriguing event. Jostling along, people trying to get close, not wanting to miss anything. And yet, in the midst of all this, Jesus feels power go out from him. What made her touch different from all the rest? That became clear soon.

> When the woman saw that she had not escaped notice, she came trembling and fell down before him, and declared in the presence of all the people the reason why she had touched him, and how she had been immediately healed. (v. 47)

Then we learn the true significance of the story.

> And he said to her, "Daughter, your faith has made you well; go in peace." (v. 48)

Why was she healed? Because she touched his cloak? No, many were doing that. It was because she acted in faith. That's what God saw—the

---

3. *Talmud* Shabbath, 110b.

4. Notice Jesus doesn't know who touched him. It's another case where Jesus' emptying of himself left him without omniscience.

attitude of her heart. That's why Jesus insisted on identifying her. He wanted her to know the real reason she had been healed.

The Bad News

While he was still speaking, someone came from the house of the synagogue official, saying, "Your daughter has died; do not trouble the Teacher anymore." The news must have come like a stab in the heart. But Jesus quickly intervened and challenged his faith.

> But when Jesus heard this, he answered him, "Do not be afraid any longer; only believe, and she will be made well."
>
> When he came to the house, he did not allow anyone to enter with him, except Peter and John and James, and the girl's father and mother. (vs. 49-51)

Peter, James, and John were definitely the first team among the disciples. Jesus didn't go by equality. These three must have had qualities that Jesus saw would suit them to be leaders of the other disciples after his departure. Two of them—Peter and James—would die as martyrs. A principle of disciple-making is that focusing on fewer disciples leads to enhanced transmission.

> Now they were all weeping and lamenting for her; but he said, "Stop weeping, for she has not died, but is asleep."
>
> And they began laughing at him, knowing that she had died. (vs. 52-53)

The term for laughing here means they were scoffing at him.

Jesus was using the comparison between death and being asleep to mean that she was not finally dead, but only temporarily, like sleep. Falling asleep later became a standard way to refer to believers dying in the early church.

> He, however, took her by the hand and called, saying, "Child, arise!" And her spirit returned, and she got up immediately; and he gave orders for something to be given her to eat. Her parents were amazed; but he instructed them to tell no one what had happened. (vs. 54-56)

"Her spirit returned," shows that she was truly dead. He touched her first, which was his pattern when healing, as we have seen.

Considering the widespread destruction that bodily tissues undergo rapidly at the point of death—the absence of oxygen affects not only the brain, but all bodily organs—you realize the damage was extensive even within minutes of death, let alone hours. That means that part of the miracle of raising the dead is that such damage would have to be substantially repaired before life could be restored. Her body would need immediate food and water to sustain that healing.

Once again, Jesus ordered the witnesses to tell no one what they saw. But that was unlikely to happen.

The Big Picture

In this chapter, Jesus demonstrated his power over nature, over evil spirits, over illness, and over death.

Over nature: The calming of the storm was a nature miracle. As mentioned earlier, ancient people revered and feared nature. They believed that natural events were the result of nature spirits or gods. Appeasing potentially angry spirits or gods kept heathen worshippers busy.

Biblical Judaism didn't teach that view. Amazingly, the entire Old Testament doesn't contain a single incantation or other instruction for healing, like other ancient scriptures do. But many Jews in Jesus' day had also adopted superstitions concerning nature

Nature miracles were important in Jesus' ministry because they demonstrated that God is not subject to the laws of nature that he himself created. In place of the reverence and worship the ancient world displayed toward nature, Jesus displayed God as over and apart from nature.

Over evil spirits: Jesus dismissed even a remarkable concentration of demonic power with a simple word of command. As the first century unfolded, Jesus' power over the demonic was one of the things Greco-Romans found attractive. Ancient people lived in fear of the demonic, never sure whether they had offended a powerful spirit. They attributed way too much to demons—every disease, every disaster, every misfortune. But they saw that Christians didn't share their fear because "Greater is he that is in you than he who is in the world" (1 John 4:4).

This source of evangelistic appeal is still evident today, especially in animistic cultures.

Over disease: The woman was healed instantly from a grievous twelve-year disease. But it was not through an impersonal touching of the cloak. God saw her faith.

Over death: Paul says Jesus' final foe is death (1 Corinthians 15:26). Jesus came to out-die all deaths. His own resurrection was "the first fruits of those who are asleep" (1 Corinthians 15:20). When he returns, death will have been "swallowed up in victory" (1 Corinthians 15:54). The ease with which he raised the little girl to life signaled the trajectory of his mission, and our one great hope.

15

Introduction to Ministry

Luke 9:1-17

At this point, Jesus was ready to send his disciples out on a preaching tour.

> And he called the twelve together, and gave them power and authority over all the demons and to heal diseases. And he sent them out to proclaim the kingdom of God and to perform healing. (vs. 1-2)

A crucial part of making disciples is field training. Watching, hearing, and discussing are all good ways to learn. But you don't know how far disciples have come until you turn them loose to practice what they've been taught. We learn this in the first place from Jesus. His men were being sent out to do something they had never done before.

Mark records that he sent them out two by two (Mark 6:7). That becomes a pattern throughout the New Testament with maybe only one exception: Phillip the Evangelist's early ministry was solo (Acts 8). That's very unusual. Paul nearly always worked with a traveling missionary band.[1]

1. One exception is when Paul ended up alone in Athens because he left his partners in Macedonia to consolidate the gains there. Paul had to flee to avoid death. He had an escorting group that took him to Athens, but then they left him there by himself (Acts 17:15).

He gave them power over demons and to heal. Their mission was to "proclaim the kingdom of God." Proclaiming the kingdom was probably what Mark describes as Jesus' earlier message:

> Jesus came into Galilee, preaching the gospel of God, and saying, "The time is fulfilled, and the kingdom of God is at hand; repent and believe in the gospel." (Mark 1:14-15)

Although Mark's statement was from earlier in Jesus' ministry, nothing had changed. What would this message of the kingdom mean to first century Jews? Only one thing: The Messiah has arrived, and the messianic kingdom would now begin. Yet, as we've seen, the kingdom was not going to be what they expected. The core issue was that people needed to believe that Jesus was the Messiah. He gave the disciples instructions:

> And he said to them, "Take nothing for your journey, neither a staff, nor a bag, nor bread, nor money; and do not even have two tunics apiece." (v. 3)

Jesus wanted to teach his disciples how to trust God for their sustenance. Mature servants of God learn that you can't wait until all the funding and needed conditions are already in place before you act. Instead, you often need to act first, and trust that God will supply any shortfall. At the same time, what they were trusting God for was not irrational—that someone would share food and shelter was hardly far-fetched. But it did take significant faith to launch out without a backup plan.

It's also wise to start small in ministry, like these men did. Going to a village and even a single house to preach is inexpensive, relatively simple and they could build on any response they got. Most ministry begins with one person. If you win someone over, you can expand from there.

Later, at the last supper, Jesus reminded them what they had learned during this sending. "He said, 'When I sent you out without money belt and bag and sandals, you did not lack anything, did you?' They said, 'No, nothing'" (22:35-36). They were learning to trust God for their provision. But then he said that for the next sending they would need to plan ahead and take provisions. That's the norm when launching out on new ministry.

The Man of Peace

Then, Jesus added another strategic instruction:

> Whatever house you enter, stay there until you leave that city. (v. 4)

Matthew adds that when selecting in which house to stay, they should "inquire who is worthy in [the town], and stay at his house" (Matthew 10:11). In other words, they were to look for someone who was respected in the village. If he was willing, they were to work through that respected local person to influence others.

The host would invite family and friends to come to his house to hear the apostle speak and see him heal. In a later sending, Jesus called this host the "man of peace" (10:6). It could be a woman of peace. You see that in Acts 16:14ff, where Lydia is the woman of peace. She was the first convert in Philippi, and she took the apostolic band into her large house and held meetings there.

The man or woman of peace has become an important principle in missions today. Workers moving into unreached towns still look for the key man or woman of peace—the person God is going to use to reach substantial numbers in a given locality. They can accomplish many times more than strangers coming in from outside.

When Jesus said "stay at his house," his point is that they were to stay put and allow time for their host and the Holy Spirit to work. They should not flit around, taking superficial shots here, there, and the other place. Diffuse movements with short stays are rarely effective in winning people over to faith, or building them up in the faith. But notice the condition for staying in place—that people are responsive to the gospel. If they weren't responsive, Jesus gave different instructions.

Handling Rejection

Jesus went on:

> "And as for those who do not receive you, as you go out from that city, shake the dust off your feet as a testimony against them."

> Departing, they began going throughout the villages, preaching the gospel and healing everywhere. (vs. 5-6)

Jesus anticipated failure as one likely outcome at least part of the time. He taught his disciples to see failure as a problem with the audience, not with themselves. This is the same point he made in the parable of the soils. The gospel is simply too polarizing to be accepted all the time or even most of the time. Instead of questioning themselves and whether they did a good job proclaiming the gospel, they were to shake the dust off their feet. It's a gesture that says, "I'm through with you."

Why would Jesus direct his disciples to move on, rather than trying harder? It's a principle of ministry in the New Testament. First, it's best for the rejecting audience. When people aren't responsive, continuing to push the point just makes matters worse. They resent the ongoing calls and it makes them less likely to become responsive later.

Jesus said, "Do not throw your pearls before swine, or they will trample them under their feet, and turn and tear you to pieces" (Matthew 7:6). He wasn't saying people are pigs. He was talking about literal pigs. Pigs don't see any value in pearls. They don't know what pearls are, and if you throw some over in their direction, they're more likely to think you're attacking them. The result, in the hilarious words of the King James Version is that they "turn ye on and rend ye." It's a pointless effort.

You're not giving up when you move on from an unresponsive hearer. You can always come back later, and the situation may have changed. It happens all the time. The same person who was adamant in refusing the gospel at one time, later sees the need level increase in his or her life. The result can be new openness.

Also, at the same time this city is refusing the gospel, another city might be wide open. By moving on from unresponsive towns, they made it more likely that they would find the responsive field.

Seeking out the responsive field is an act of faith. Instead of believing that you can convert someone if you keep driving your point, you are accepting that the key to reaching people is the action of the Holy Spirit working in their hearts. Our role is to find responsive people by sowing the seed widely. Once someone expresses interest, persuasion and the good news will carry weight.

The Return

> When the apostles returned, they gave an account to him of all that they had done. (v. 10)

Debriefing after a time of ministry is always great fun. Nothing is more exciting than seeing God work through you and your friends. Mark notes that, "They were casting out many demons and were anointing with oil many sick people and healing them" (Mark 6:13). Anointing with oil was a way of signifying identification, similar to laying on hands. The one anointing was the channel of divine healing power. Surely this caused a quantum leap upward for their faith!

Jesus wanted to take some time off with his disciples, but it wasn't to be:

> Taking them with him, he withdrew by himself to a city called Bethsaida. But the crowds were aware of this and followed him; and welcoming them, he began speaking to them about the kingdom of God and curing those who had need of healing. (vs. 10-11)

Bethsaida is north of the Sea of Galilee and east of the Jordan River. It's a semi-arid area used for grazing sheep and goats rather than planting grain. This was the area the disciples called "a desolate place" (v. 12).

The Feeding of the Five Thousand

> Late in the afternoon the twelve disciples came to him and said, "Send the crowds away to the nearby villages and farms, so they can find food and lodging for the night. There is nothing to eat here in this remote place."
>
> But Jesus said, "You feed them." (vs. 12-14 NLT)

Hadn't they just been on a trip where they saw God's power move through them including miraculous healing? Jesus was clearly hoping they would now scale up their confidence in the power of believing prayer.

Luke points out that the crowd included "about 5,000 men" (v. 14). That's a huge crowd, even if we discount some estimates of crowd size reaching heights of ten and twenty thousand when including women and children. Probably most of those present were men. Most married couples had children, and wouldn't go hiking out to a deserted area with kids in tow and no plan for how to eat or drink. There were probably some women and children, but mostly men.

Jesus' challenge that the disciples feed the crowd would seem ridiculous to the natural mind. And naturalistic thinking is exactly what the disciples answered with.

> "But we have only five loaves of bread and two fish," they answered. "Or are you expecting us to go and buy enough food for this whole crowd?" (v. 13 NLT)

John adds the detail that "Andrew, Simon Peter's brother, said to him [Jesus], 'There is a lad here who has five barley loaves and two fish, but what are these for so many people?'" (John 6:8-9). From his question, you can tell Andrew felt a bit foolish for bringing up such a paltry offering, especially if the others standing there burst into laughter. Throughout, the disciples saw only a material problem. They showed no signs of understanding God's power.

Jesus had a different view.

It was only after receiving the loaves and fish that Jesus had the crowd sit down "in groups of about fifty each." (v. 14). In his hands, perhaps in a basket, he held the loaves and fish. Would he have fed the multitude even if Andrew never brought these morsels forward? The text doesn't clearly say here. But in the symbolic spin Jesus put on this incident later, their offering of the three loaves and two fish stand for humans offering themselves to be used by God in ministry. God takes our paltry offering and multiplies it.

> So the people all sat down. Jesus took the five loaves and two fish, looked up toward heaven, and blessed them. Then, breaking the loaves into pieces, he kept giving the bread and fish to the disciples so they could distribute it to the people. (vs. 15-16 NLT)

The disciples did the actual passing out, no doubt using their travel baskets to hold their batches. They must have taken many trips back and forth before they could feed such a crowd.

Metaphor?

Is this a picture of how ministry works? Jesus' own commentary on the miracle suggests it is. Only John records this discourse in John 6. The day after the feeding, the crowd followed Jesus around the lake to another site. They were hoping he would feed them again. But this is when Jesus gave a more spiritual interpretation of the feeding:

> "Do not work for the food which perishes, but for the food which endures to eternal life, which the Son of Man will give to you." (John 6:27)

When the crowd reminded him of manna, he added,

> "For the bread of God is that which comes down out of heaven, and gives life to the world. . . . I am the bread of life; he who comes to me will not hunger, and he who believes in me will never thirst." (John 6:33-35)

He was using the universal desire for food—hunger—as a metaphor for how he could meet their inner need. So, following Jesus' logic, we can see the feeding of the 5,000 as a metaphor for ministry. In ministry, we distribute the bread of life—Jesus. Other principles follow.

Availability

First, the size of the boy's lunch compared to the size of the crowd was truly pathetic, just like our efforts to meet the spiritual needs of our day. Yet, he did put that paltry offering in Jesus' hands. It's a good picture of how God works through people. Jesus isn't asking for our ability. He's asking for our availability.

Human Agency

Next, he fed the crowd through his disciples. The picture mentioned earlier, where they went out to distribute and back to refill from Jesus' hands, fits well here. It's a picture of human agency, where God works through willing humans.[2] This agency is so much a part of God's plan that he will even leave work undone until willing people show up so he can use them. Examples abound, such as the task of world mission outreach that lay dormant for hundreds of years. Once believers accepted

2. John describes the distribution as done by Jesus: "Jesus then took the loaves, and having given thanks, He distributed to those who were seated" (John 6:11). Luke says it was the disciples who passed it out. Was it Jesus or the disciples who handed out the food? Actually, this is two ways of saying the same thing. When God works through human agency it's the same as him doing the work himself.

the biblical mandate for world mission, the modern missionary movement proceeded to reach millions of people all over the world.

The disciples went out to the people and gave out food, but every time quickly returning to Jesus for another supply. To feed five thousand, they must have made that trip repeatedly. That matches how true servants of God serve. Paul said, when describing his own ministry, "Not that we are adequate in ourselves to consider anything as coming from ourselves, but our adequacy is from God" (2 Corinthians 3:5).

Servants of God have to continually come to God and draw close to him in order to replenish their spiritual power. Jesus described it this way: "I am the vine, you are the branches; he who abides in me and I in him, he bears much fruit, for apart from me you can do nothing" (John 15:5).

Sufficiency

"They all ate as much as they wanted" (v. 17). So following the logic of the feeding as a picture of ministry, this suggests the people's needs were fully met, not partially. The "bread of God which comes down out of heaven," would be fully sufficient to meet the needs of the world.

Ministry as a Means of Growth

Finally we read, "Afterward, the disciples picked up twelve baskets of leftovers!" (v. 17). They already said this was a desolate place, so where were they getting these baskets? Clearly, these must be their own travel baskets. That's why there are twelve of them. In these times people often traveled with a wicker basket that had a strap for slinging it over the shoulder.

The twelve would be eating loaves and fish for days to come. They fed the crowd, but the disciples got more food than anyone. That's because ministry, or serving love, is a "means of growth." This is one of the channels through which God's grace flows to nourish growing believers.

Other channels include fellowship, prayer, Scripture, and suffering. But ministry is just as important as these other means. If people leave out any one of these means their growth will stall eventually. Imagine a believer who plans to grow spiritually, but refuses to pray. That's absurd. But trying to grow without practicing serving love is just as absurd.

The Big Picture

During this part of Luke's account, Jesus was working on elevating his disciples' understanding of ministry principles. He alone knew what their future would be. He knew his time was short—he would be leaving soon. Instead of leaving behind an organization or a government, he would leave this handful of men and another handful of women. God would use them to launch the worldwide spread of the gospel.

One missing element in these training experiences was the new role of the Holy Spirit. Just before his ascension he told them to go to Jerusalem and wait until "you will receive power when the Holy Spirit has come upon you; and you shall be my witnesses . . ." (Acts 1:8).

That couldn't happen yet. Jesus later explained, "But I tell you the truth, it is to your advantage that I go away; for if I do not go away, the Helper [the Holy Spirit] will not come to you" (John 16:7). So they would need to remember what they learned with Jesus present, and later learn how to translate those lessons to a new approach focused on relying on the Holy Spirit's power.

Today, the picture of Andrew holding the small loaves and fish is funny. You can imagine the other disciples scowling, "Are you serious? Why are you wasting our time when we're trying to solve a problem?" But the little meal was important. Jesus didn't create food out of nothing. He multiplied the loaves and fishes. The human part of the equation is part of the picture.

Those of us who go forward to serve God often feel just like Andrew did when he said, "What are these among so many?" It's a common sense observation. What's the point? We feel so helpless and weak. But if we dare to place our inadequate, even paltry, selves into Jesus' hands, he will multiply that offering out of all expectation. This act of trust needs to be an ongoing way of life. It isn't that every time we place ourselves in his hands a miracle happens. Rather, as we learn to daily assume this posture, we will eventually see fruit.

16

Who is Jesus? Luke 9:18-26

Who Do You Say I Am?

It was time for the disciples to undergo a complete breakthrough on the question of Jesus' identity.

> And it happened that while he was praying alone, the disciples were with him, and he questioned them, saying, "Who do the people say that I am?"
>
> They answered and said, "John the Baptist, and others say Elijah; but others, that one of the prophets of old has risen again." (Luke 9:18-19)

The disciples knew better than to believe any of these theories. But Jesus wasn't worried about his reputation with the masses. His reason for asking this question follows when he asked, "But who do you say that I am?" (v. 20). Is this the most important question before all humanity? The answer we give to this question will determine how we respond to God's next question—What are you going to do about it?

Peter had it right: "Peter answered and said, 'You are the Christ of God.'" (v. 20). Matthew gives a more complete quote: "You are the Christ, the Son of the living God" (Matthew 16:16). Jesus was pleased that Peter was seeing the truth so clearly. "Blessed are you, Simon Barjona, because flesh and blood did not reveal this to you, but My Father who is in heaven" (Matthew 16:17).

How much did Peter understand? Is there a difference between being the son of God and being God? Perhaps, in Peter's mind. His later effort to set Jesus straight concerning his death indicated that he had not fully grasped Jesus' deity (Matthew 16:22).

The disciples knew God was working powerfully through Jesus. But they may have still expected an earthly king. That certainly was what the crowds believed. Right at this time, John records that Jesus sensed "that they were intending to come and take him by force to make him king." That was one reason Jesus escaped the limelight and "withdrew again to the mountain by himself alone" (John 6:15).

Because of this potentially explosive thirst to see Jesus take his throne, and the consequences that would follow, he again hushed his followers: "Jesus warned his disciples not to tell anyone who he was" (v. 21).

First warning

He also began to teach them on the other part of his mission they didn't expect.

> "The Son of Man must suffer many terrible things. He will be rejected by the elders, the leading priests, and the teachers of religious law. He will be killed, but on the third day he will be raised from the dead." (v. 22 NLT)

This statement seems plain enough, and one would assume that from now on they would be expecting these events. But that's wrong. Even though we have seventeen different accounts of Jesus giving this warning, not one of his disciples ever understood what he was saying! A number of accounts clearly state that they didn't understand.[1] In the other accounts, it doesn't say, but we can infer they didn't understand.

The later accounts of Jesus' crucifixion and resurrection make it crystal clear that nobody knew what was going on. Not one person was waiting

1. In this list, the passages with an asterisk report how Jesus' hearers responded. In every case, his hearers did not understand what he was saying. Some accounts say the saying was "hidden" from them. Matthew 16:21*, 17:22-23, 20:17-19; Mark 8:31*, 9:9-10, 31-32*, 10:32-34, 45; Luke 9:22, 9:44-45*, 18:31-34; John 3:14, 10:15-18, 12:32-33*, 16:17-18*.

at his tomb for the resurrection. Instead, they were terrified when they saw Jesus raised from the dead (e.g. 24:37). Even at the empty tomb, the angels had to tell the women, "Remember what he told you back in Galilee, that the Son of Man must be betrayed into the hands of sinful men and be crucified, and that he would rise again on the third day" (24:6-7). No, they didn't remember. They were there with spices to anoint his dead body.

Dense Disciples?

Modern readers are sometimes amazed at how dense the disciples seem to be in their inability to comprehend these straightforward statements from Jesus. But we today already know the story of his death and resurrection, so it's easy for us to see what he meant.

To put ourselves in their shoes, we have to recognize the power of something called "paradigmatic thinking." This problem begins with a reigning paradigm, which is a model or pattern of understanding. Once you have one model firmly in mind, you try to fit new data into that model, in order to make sense of it. That makes it very difficult to change to a different view. It's not *impossible* to change. When people finally conclude that their paradigm is in the wrong, they undergo a "paradigm shift." This is what happened to Jesus' followers after the resurrection.

The Jews of Jesus' day had a strong paradigm in place when it came to the Messiah. It wasn't just that the Messiah would be a king and reign over the earth, but also that his reign would be eternal. For example, Isaiah says,

> There will be no end to the increase of his government or of peace, on the throne of David and over his kingdom, to establish it and to uphold it with justice and righteousness from then on and forevermore. (Isaiah 9:7)

There is no dying Messiah in this picture. They thought passages like Isaiah 53 that speak of his dying were about someone else.[2] Because the

2. Their misunderstanding of Isaiah's servant songs became more inevitable because of the Septuagint's poor translation from Hebrew into Greek. (The Septuagint was the Bible most people knew at this time.) The crucial last half of Isaiah 53 is virtually unintelligible. Emiliano Urciuoli, "'Ein Erratisher Block': The Pre-Jesuanic and Pre-Christian Exegesis of Isaiah 53," *Henoch* 32, no. 1 (2010): 66-100. They even switched from first person singular to second person plural in verse 10, making it look like the suffering will happen to the community rather than an individual.

disciples' paradigm was so strong, they tended to look for other interpretations of what Jesus said. We see a clear example of this in Mark 9. After seeing the transfiguration of Jesus,

> He gave them orders not to relate to anyone what they had seen, until the Son of Man rose from the dead. They seized upon that statement, discussing with one another what rising from the dead meant. (Mark 9:9-10)

You can tell they were unwilling or unable to take Jesus' statement literally. Instead, they assumed it must be metaphorical or symbolic—maybe a figure of speech. Literal death for the Messiah had no place in their paradigm. And this event from Mark happened *after* our passage here in Luke 9.

Another reason they didn't comprehend might have been direct concealment by God. Later in this chapter, Jesus again said,

> "Let these words sink into your ears; for the Son of Man is going to be delivered into the hands of men." But they did not understand this statement, and it was concealed from them so that they would not perceive it; and they were afraid to ask Him about this statement. (vs. 44-45)

The phrase "it was concealed from them" with the passive voice suggests that someone else, perhaps God, was concealing the meaning from them. This language appears in several other passages. Could it be that God didn't want them to understand too much, but at the same time, he wanted them to later remember that Jesus had predicted the events at his death and resurrection?

That's what Jesus himself later said, "But these things I have spoken to you, so that when their hour comes, you may remember that I told you of them" (John 16:4). It sounds like he knew they wouldn't understand until later, but once they did understand, they would also remember that he had told them in advance.

John admits on another occasion, "His disciples didn't understand at the time that this was a fulfillment of prophecy. But after Jesus entered into his glory, they remembered what had happened and realized that these things had been written about him" (John 12:16).

If God concealed the full meaning of some of Jesus' sayings—mainly those about the cross and his resurrection—he must have had a reason. And he did have a reason, as we will see. As the story of Jesus' passion unfolded, instead of the disciples anticipating the drama, it came to them as one gut-wrenching shock after another. We can only imagine what would have happened if they knew what was coming, but we can be quite sure that they didn't know.

It's also important to remember that they were not indwelt by the Holy Spirit like we are. The Spirit's "illumining" ministry is when he enables us to comprehend spiritual matters in a way the natural man cannot (1 Corinthians 2:10).

We can't know all the answers, but this pattern of Jesus telling his disciples exactly what would happen, and them not comprehending it, is a fascinating feature of their relationship.

The Cost of Discipleship

The scene has changed, and Jesus is now apparently addressing the crowd.

> And he was saying to them all, "If anyone wishes to come after me, he must deny himself, and take up his cross daily and follow me." (v. 23)

He announces his requirements for those who would "come after me." Is he talking about the requirements for personal salvation? That's what Lordship Theologians claim. Or is he talking about a second decision where people fully commit to following him?

You see Paul talking about such a second decision in Romans 12:1 where he urges Christian "brethren" to "present your bodies a living and holy sacrifice, acceptable to God." In the view of many, including myself, Jesus' statement here in Luke is like that in Romans 12—a call to a second decision of all-out commitment to discipleship. "Coming after Jesus" means discipleship—a further step.

Four reasons back this view.

First, Jesus' conditional language makes it clear that coming after him is not permitted apart from this full commitment. But he has announced salvation already for several people who barely knew him: Think of the man lowered through the roof or the woman who touched his garment.

He assured both of them their sins were forgiven based on faith. They could hardly have been informed about this new, higher requirement. So the Lordship position pictures Jesus being inconsistent with himself.

Secondly, those who often work in personal evangelism know that people typically come to Jesus with many problems and little or no knowledge of God. They only gradually begin to gain victory as they grow in their relationship with God. Only after they come to know God more closely, do they eventually comprehend the need for a second decision to totally commit. We rarely see new converts making such a decision. So the Lordship view doesn't match the process of growth seen in young believers.

Thirdly, the Lordship salvation position is internally inconsistent. Most Lordship theologians believe in salvation by faith apart from works. Many of them are even Calvinists. Yet, if denial of the self and carrying the cross are required for salvation, it makes no sense to claim salvation is free. It's no different than saying a million equals zero.

Finally, Lordship theologians' claim that good works, devotion, and willingness to suffer are not the prerequisites, but the necessary *result* of salvation. That also fails the test of consistency. How many good works are required? How much devotion? What if a new believer falls into sin? Does that mean he or she is no longer a believer? Or never was one? When pressed, Lordship theologians have to admit that believers falling into sin is compatible with salvation, and it happens all the time.

Denying Self

We conclude that Jesus was challenging those who considered themselves his followers to step up the rest of the way. To deny one's self is to deny what self wants, that is, to leave off self-serving. As fallen humans, self-serving is the way we come out of the womb. Jesus wants us to learn to live like he did—the sacrificial way. Jesus ignored what was beneficial to him and devoted himself to meeting others' needs.

Bearing the Cross

For Jesus, that included shouldering his cross, literally. The Romans made execution victims carry the crossbeam of their crosses. The victim knew it was a one-way journey. For us, because Jesus says, "pick up you cross daily," he means picking up our crosses metaphorically. The "cross" is not the ordinary, human troubles like having a flat tire in the rain. Shouldering the cross refers to the extra suffering that comes from serving God, including persecution, spiritual attack from our enemy, and even wounds from the people of God.

It isn't asceticism, where suffering is an end in itself. This is suffering for a purpose—the salvation and building up of people inside and outside the body of Christ. We also call it "ministry," another word for serving love. Jesus is serious that anyone who wants to follow him needs to plan on a life of servitude at a level that includes sacrifice and suffering. Of course there are enjoyable parts as well.

What did the twelve and Jesus' other disciples think about this statement? The cross hadn't happened yet, so they must have felt confusion. Jesus had earlier talked about the bridegroom being taken away. But this was the first time he mentioned the cross in the life of believers. Did they wonder if he was predicting that they would die by crucifixion?

Saving Your Life

Jesus then declared one of his most profound and deep sayings:

> "For whoever wishes to save his life will lose it, but whoever loses his life for my sake, he is the one who will save it. For what is a man profited if he gains the whole world, and loses or forfeits himself?" (vs. 24-25)

The word here for "life" is not one of the usual words for life (*zoan* or *bios*). Instead this word is *pseuche*, from which we get psychology. *Pseuche* is usually translated soul, mind, or heart. In this context, it could be understood as "self."

To lose one's self is the result of serving self. Autonomy means self-rule. That is the direction that loses your life. Jesus just said his followers had to deny self and the two verses are linked by the word "for," meaning "because." In other words, denying yourself amounts to relinquishing your autonomous soul—your determination to do things your own way. But it also leads to saving your soul or self as God intended for his followers. His point is that we can't have it both ways. We can't insist on directing our own lives, but also expect to benefit from God's direction.

The Stakes Are High

Jesus adds:

> "For what is a man profited if he gains the whole world, and loses or forfeits himself? [or 'loses his soul" NASB]" (v. 25)

Again he added the connecting "for," so this is part of the same train of thought. Jesus was only calling his followers to do what's best for them. What if someone offered you a suitcase full of ten million dollars if you shoot yourself in the head? Not a very attractive offer. If he made it twenty million it wouldn't change anything. Even the whole world, as Jesus says, is a poor offering. What good is a fortune if you're dead and unable to enjoy it?

Following Jesus whole-heartedly isn't something you measure out while carefully considering other options. If Jesus is real, there are no other options, only counterfeits—promises that end in pain—things that should have been rewarding but end up empty and disappointing. So the only sane response is to deny self, pick up your cross and follow Jesus.

People who don't understand that, including Christians, cannot undergo true discipleship. Their hesitant, partial commitment is based on distrust of God. They have to reconsider each directive to see if it's too costly. They aren't sure that all-out following is safe, and they suspect that other options might be more beneficial. That mindset blocks the work of the Spirit and makes spiritual mediocrity inevitable.

Ashamed of Me and My Words

Jesus concluded:

> If anyone is ashamed of me and my message, the Son of Man will be ashamed of that person when he returns in his glory. (v. 26 NLT)

Jesus was held in contempt by many then and still today. His death was the worst kind of public disgrace. It's also embarrassing to be shouted down and accused of all manner of wrong-doing, manipulation, and abuse when you try to spread the gospel. In postmodern culture, any attempt to bring others to faith is considered violent imperialism and arrogance. Any stand for objective morality will be interpreted as rejecting others.

Making believers feel ashamed is a key tactic for Satan. Serious followers of Jesus know we don't follow him in order to gain popularity. Part of our loyalty to Jesus is that we are willing to bear this shame with him. Jesus said, "If the world hates you, keep in mind that it hated me first" (John 15:18).

Is Jesus referring to compromised Christians who refuse to bear his shame? Such believers go underground and keep their faith as their own little secret. It's unusual for Jesus to say he will be ashamed of them, although that would certainly be deserved. We know from Paul that when the judgment of believers happens, "each person will receive their praise from God" (1 Corinthians 4:5). So any disapproval would be temporary. All our worthless deeds—our wood, hay, and stubble—will be burned up (1 Corinthians 3:13).

Or is Jesus referring to those who come close to faith, but turn away because of the shame they believe will result? How many times have we heard someone say something like, "I get the feeling Jesus is real, but if I accept him, I'll be rejected by my family?" In Jesus' culture you could be completely ostracized. John reported, "The Jews had already agreed that if anyone confessed Him to be Christ, he was to be put out of the synagogue" (John 9:22).

The Big Picture

Jesus' following at this time was a mixed group. After the feeding of the 5,000 and his follow up talk, "Many of His disciples withdrew and were not walking with Him anymore" (John 6:66). The more he clarified that his way of life was sacrificial, the more his following thinned out. Many were attracted to Jesus because they thought they might gain an advantage. When he explained that they might lose some of the advantages they already had, attraction turned to aversion. Within months his following dwindled to a handful.

17

Jesus' Transfiguration

Luke 9:27-36

To the Mountain

Jesus said:

> "I tell you the truth, some standing here right now will not die before they see the Kingdom of God." (Luke 9:27 NLT)

Matthew's account of the statement was more complete:

> "There are some of those who are standing here who will not taste death until they see the Son of Man coming in his kingdom." (Matthew 16:28)

His words make clear that it's Jesus they will see, coming in his kingdom, that is, in his kingly glory, not the kingdom itself.

The chapter break should be here, not after this verse, but before it. Jesus' mysterious statement seems more mysterious because the chapter break makes it seem like two different stories.[1] If you read straight through, it's

1. Always remember that the chapter divisions and verse numbers didn't come until hundreds of years after the Bible was finished. We never hear any mention of them in the early church fathers or

clear that we don't need any far-out explanation for who these witnesses are, or what they will see. Just follow the context.[2]

> About eight days later Jesus took Peter, John, and James up on a mountain to pray. And as he was praying, the appearance of his face was transformed, and his clothes became dazzling white. (vs. 28-29 NLT)

So these four went up alone to pray on the mountain. There, God pulled back the curtain and they saw Jesus as he is in glory! By comparing verses 37 and 32, it seems clear that this event happened at night. Had this same thing happened on other nights when he went aside to pray sometimes all night, but nobody saw it?

Matthew's account adds details:

> His face shone like the sun, and his clothes became as white as the light. (Matthew 17:2)

So energy streamed from Jesus' face, apparently so bright you couldn't look at it!

> Suddenly, two men, Moses and Elijah, appeared and began talking with Jesus. They were glorious to see. And they were speaking about his exodus from this world, which was about to be fulfilled in Jerusalem. (vs. 30-31 NLT)

Jesus must have introduced Moses and Elijah to the disciples, because they already know who they are later in the same account. But it sounds like most of the conversation was between Jesus, Moses, and Elijah. The disciples were actually asleep when the encounter began (v. 32). Jesus may not have wanted them to hear the full discussion.

How strange and overwhelming this experience must have been! To meet Moses and Elijah as they are in glory.... To see Jesus light up like that.... Why Moses and Elijah? Moses was the author of the Pentateuch (the first five books of the Old Testament) and Elijah was a famous example in the sequence of preaching prophets who wrote the rest of the Old Testament. Jews often referred to the Old Testament as "the law

---

in rabbinic writing. So, when interpreting, read the text as it was written and then decide whether the chapter divisions are correct.

2. There are other potential meanings. He could have been referring to Pentecost and the coming of the power of the Spirit. Or, he could have been referring to his resurrection. But neither of those match his language well.

and the prophets." So these two may stand for the Old Testament, which was the base upon which Jesus stood and which he fulfilled.

In addition, it's hard to miss the parallels between Jesus and Moses. Both went up a mountain to encounter God. Both radiated light. With both, God was signifying who people should listen to as their authority in spiritual matters. In Jewish thought at this time, the Messiah would fulfill Moses' words that "God will send you a prophet like me" (Deuteronomy 18:15).

The Two Witnesses?

Some interpreters think there's another reason these two showed up. We already saw that Elijah will return just before Jesus' second coming. And that may be why God took his body to heaven. That way, when Elijah comes back, it won't be by birth, but a returning of his original body, kept by God—the body they were seeing in this account.

Interestingly Moses' body was of interest to God as well. First we read that God buried Moses (Deut. 34:6). Then, he sent Michael the archangel to fetch the body, according to Jude 9: "Michael the archangel, when he disputed with the devil and argued about the body of Moses. . . ." Why would God send Michael to get Moses' body? That's extraordinary. Some interpreters think this is not coincidence, but has a greater purpose.

In the book of Revelation, John has a vision of "two witnesses" (Revelation 11:3). These two prophet-like men appear near the end of history as we know it and preach for three and a half years according to the text. They have unusual powers. One is to shut up the sky from raining. Elijah also did that for three and a half years! Also, "they have power over the waters to turn them into blood, and to strike the earth with every plague" (Revelation 11:6). Those were miracles that Moses did! So these similarities lead many readers to believe that the two witnesses in Revelation 11 are, in fact, Moses and Elijah. The witnesses are never named, so we can't be sure. But it would fill in some blanks.

Their Discussion

Luke says they, "were speaking of his departure which he was about to accomplish at Jerusalem" (v. 31). We know what that involved. But did they? If Jesus' death and resurrection were at the center of the so-called messianic secret, then, according to Ephesians 3:9 that secret had "for ages been hidden in God." So God alone knew what he was planning to do. Moses and Elijah may have been asking questions. They may have been given part of the whole story. But Paul says the mystery was a plan kept secret from the beginning of time.

Peter's Enthusiasm

> As Moses and Elijah were starting to leave, Peter, not even knowing what he was saying, blurted out, "Master, it's wonderful for us to be here! Let's make three tabernacles—one for you, one for Moses, and one for Elijah." (v. 33 NLT)

Peter is probably suggesting temporary shelters, like those used in the Feast of Tabernacles. You can tell Luke thought it was funny because he added a comment about Peter not knowing what he was saying. It seems that Peter liked this experience so much he didn't want it to end!

That's not hard to imagine. Any believer standing in this setting would hope it didn't have to end. But although God occasionally grants spectacular experiences, they never last for long. If they did, we would probably take them for granted.

In fact, the quest for ecstatic experiences can become an unhealthy idol for believers. Some believers are so fixated on spiritual experiences that they devote large swaths of time to seeking them. They can even become miserable and lose faith when no experience comes. Healthy believers always have access to more minor experiences like feeling the joy of the Lord. But the really big experiences, the ones involving miracles, are relatively rare and temporary. They usually have a purpose as did this one.

Peter's suggestion that they build three structures may have implied that he was seeing Jesus on the same level as Moses and Elijah. That fits into what happened next.

The Cloud and the Voice

> While he was saying this, a cloud formed and began to overshadow them; and they were afraid as they entered the cloud. Then a voice came out of the cloud, saying, "This is my Son, my Chosen One; listen to him!" (vs. 34-35)

Was it a cloud of water vapor? Or was it a cloud of light like the one that showed up when God entered the temple? That could have been a glowing cloud of energy (1 Kings 8:10). Again in Exodus 16:10, "the glory of the Lord appeared in the cloud." It sounds like the cloud may have been lit up within. Whatever it was, it scared the disciples: "terror gripped them as the cloud covered them" (v. 34).

Then came the voice of God: "This is my Son, my Chosen One. Listen to him" (v. 35). Was God telling Peter to shut up and listen? More likely, God was calling attention to the difference between Jesus and these two great Old Testament heroes of faith. God was declaring that Jesus would supersede the Law and the Prophets with a New Covenant.

The story ends when the disciples plant their faces in the ground cringing in fear. Then we read:

> And Jesus came to them and touched them and said, "Get up, and do not be afraid." And lifting up their eyes, they saw no one except Jesus Himself alone. (Matthew 17:7-8)

Such tenderness! He's stooping down to reach out to them. He knew how weak and helpless they were. Jesus' transcendence and closeness are both on display in this story.

The Big Picture

Mount Herman is the traditional site given for the transfiguration, and that's very plausible. Matthew says it was a "high mountain," and Herman is far taller than any of the minor mountains in that area.

Mount Herman stands at the northern end of the Jordan valley. From its slopes one can look down the whole valley to a point east of Jerusalem on a clear day. As they gazed down that spectacular gorge, Jesus knew he was headed down that valley into a world of agony and disgrace. He would need all his courage to stay the course.

His most intimate friends had just seen what he looked like in glory. That would hopefully strengthen their resolve to face whatever came their way. This is the lasting usefulness of extraordinary spiritual experiences. Decades later, Peter was facing his own execution within days or even hours (2 Peter 1:14). In that extreme situation his mind drifted back to this event on the mount of transfiguration. He wrote:

> For we did not follow cleverly devised tales when we made known to you the power and coming of our Lord Jesus Christ, but we were eyewitnesses of his majesty. For when he received honor and glory from God the Father, such an utterance as this was made to him by the Majestic Glory, "This is my beloved Son with whom I am well-pleased"—and we ourselves heard this utterance made from heaven when we were with him on the holy mountain. (2 Peter 1:16-18)

In the face of the terror of crucifixion, Peter reflected on his past, including this event. As he remembered, he knew that voice was real. That gave him the courage he needed to face the ordeal ahead.

God sometimes grants a special experience to his followers. It may be a new vision of what he's like. I could be a prophetic word, referring to knowledge the person had no way of knowing. It's often an illuminated passage of Scripture. Those experiences can sustain us even years later like this one did for Peter.

To realize that advantage, we have to first of all remember the times God showed us something. Too often, we sit calling for more, but never reflecting on those times God has already spoken in the past. Instead, with the help of the Holy Spirit, we can reflect and re-experience those earlier events with all their faith-strengthening power.

18

More Displays of Power

Luke 9:37-50

A Demon Possessed Boy

> The next day, after they had come down the mountain, a large crowd met Jesus. A man in the crowd called out to him, "Teacher, I beg you to look at my son, my only child. An evil spirit keeps seizing him, making him scream. It throws him into convulsions so that he foams at the mouth. It batters him and hardly ever leaves him alone. I begged your disciples to cast out the spirit, but they couldn't do it." (9:37-40 NLT)[1]

Mark adds that the man also said, "Have mercy on us and help us, if you can" (Mark 9:22). Jesus detected the man's unbelief. "'What do you mean, "If I can"?' Jesus asked. 'Anything is possible if a person believes.' The father instantly cried out, 'I do believe, but help me overcome my unbelief!'" (Mark 9:23-24).

1. In Matthew's account, the father says his son was epileptic, or "moonstruck." They believed epilepsy got worse during successive full moons. Of course, none of this has any bearing on the child's true condition—the ancients were completely ignorant as to what epilepsy was. The real problem was demon possession, as Luke says.

Jesus seemed to accept that prayer, but he was distressed that so many had seen so much and still doubted. He said, "You unbelieving and corrupt people! How long must I be with you and put up with you?" Then he said to the man, "Bring your son here" (v. 41).

You can see Jesus was exasperated. He clearly felt the disciples should have by now been able to cast this demon out. Matthew includes a conversation later where the disciples asked Jesus why they were unable to cast the demon out. He said, "Because of the littleness of your faith . . ." (Matthew 17:20). He also said "this kind only comes out by prayer" (Mark 9:29), but he clearly felt they were slow learners and weaker in faith than they should have been.[2]

Jesus strode forward:

> While he was still approaching, the demon slammed him [the boy] to the ground and threw him into a convulsion. But Jesus rebuked the unclean spirit, and healed the boy and gave him back to his father. And they were all amazed at the greatness of God. (vs. 42-43)

Another Warning

But just as people were rejoicing about the deliverance, Jesus gave his disciples another warning of what was coming:

> But while everyone was marveling at all that He was doing, He said to His disciples, "Let these words sink into your ears; for the Son of Man is going to be delivered into the hands of men." (vs. 43-44)

Jesus seems to not want people to merely focus on what blessings he could deliver. Serious work of a far more weighty nature lay ahead. He may have felt a strong contrast between the celebration going on in the village and his own heavily burdened heart. His prefix, "Let this sink into your head," suggests that he knew they had not comprehended the first warning.

His mind was riveted on what was coming, and he wanted them to respond. But no:

2. Matthew's version adds that "This kind only comes out with prayer and fasting" (Matthew 17:21). But early manuscripts are missing the "and fasting." It's a later addition, added because of the early churches' growing fascination with fasting and asceticism.

> But they did not understand this statement, and it was concealed from them so that they would not perceive it; and they were afraid to ask him about this statement. (vs. 45)

So this declaration takes its place along with the others that nobody comprehended. But an additional negative comes here: "They were afraid to ask Him about this statement." Afraid of what? Probably, afraid of looking stupid. But we never see Jesus respond to honest questions that way. It was really a sign of pride that they didn't want to admit that they had no idea what he was talking about.

Who Is the Greatest?

They still couldn't connect the dots. Instead:

> An argument started among them as to which of them might be the greatest. But Jesus, knowing what they were thinking in their heart, took a child and stood him by his side, and said to them, "Whoever receives this child in my name receives me, and whoever receives me receives him who sent me; for the one who is least among all of you, this is the one who is great." (vs. 46-48)

Whatever the disciples understood about Jesus at this point, it's clear that their character development was negligible. Even many non-believers would be embarrassed if caught in an argument like this. Yet it happened several times. They were still discussing this favorite topic at the last supper! (Luke 22:24). So they neither understood Jesus' mission nor his character.

People who believed Jesus, including the disciples, still believed that he had arrived to be king of the world. If that happened, those near him could reasonably expect to receive high office or other benefits. We know two of the disciples, James and John, approached Jesus with their mother to ask for the first and second place in the kingdom (Mark 10:35-37).

The other disciples were only angry because James and John were trying to get the drop on them. These arguments about who was the greatest were the tip of a larger iceberg. They had been listening to Jesus talk about the sacrificial way of life, but it sailed right over their heads. Their self-serving desire to use Jesus to gain importance, power, and even perhaps wealth was blocking their hearts from truly grasping Jesus.

The child he sat before them—was it a three-year-old? A four-year-old? Kids this age have a mysterious absence of competitive ego. Even when beaming and showing you what a great drawing they did, the ego is missing. The sharing is clean and wholesome. Children have no problem asking for help, unlike their self-sufficient elders. When offered a gift, you'll never hear a child say, "Oh, I couldn't possibly accept that."

Matthew describes Jesus putting a child before his disciples—possibly the same incident, Then he said:

> "Truly I say to you, unless you are converted and become like children, you will not enter the kingdom of heaven. Whoever then humbles himself as this child, he is the greatest in the kingdom of heaven." (Matthew 18:3-4)

Many aspects of children are not desirable in adults. Paul says, "When I was a child, I used to speak like a child, think like a child, reason like a child; when I became a man, I did away with childish things" (1 Corinthians 13:11). Childish thinking is over-simplistic. They are gullible and undiscerning. Jesus points to the desirable part—"whoever humbles himself."

Territoriality

> John answered and said, "Master, we saw someone casting out demons in your name; and we tried to prevent him because he does not follow along with us."
>
> But Jesus said to him, "Do not hinder him; for he who is not against you is for you" (vs. 49-50).

Wait. Jesus also said, "He who is not with me is against me; and he who does not gather with me scatters" (11:23). How do we reconcile these two statements?

The difference is that between "me" and "you." The "me" is Jesus. The "you" refers to his followers. The standard is not the same. People are required to be with Jesus, that is to believe him and follow him. No such universal requirement applied to his followers. For human workers, it's enough that others are not against you.

This effort to block others from doing God's work for no better reason than they weren't affiliated with the twelve amounted to an effort to protect their territory. It's rivalry and pride on the group level instead of the individual level. But it's a base instinct that contradicts the humility Jesus was trying to teach with the child.

It became a huge problem in later church history. Many people don't know that for hundreds of years, people were not allowed to interpret or teach the Bible unless they got credentials from the church. The penalty for preaching or teaching without permission was death. Even after the Reformation the same thing applied. State churches allowed nobody but their licensed preachers to preach or teach, even in a small home meeting.[3]

The Big Picture

Jesus was burdened by the spiritual density of the crowds and his own disciples. That frustration burst above the surface at one point. Yet, even when he catches his disciples boasting and competing, he patiently sets them straight using a child. This tug-of-war between Jesus and his disciples' unspiritual outlook continued right into the last supper. Not until the Holy Spirit came to indwell them did they undergo the lasting and deep transformation Jesus was longing for.

We, his followers today, also feel frustrated when obstinate selfish pride shows its face, either in ourselves or in others. God will graciously show us even the secret pride hiding in our hearts. But only God can cure pride and bestow true humility. When we humble ourselves before him, he will grant a growing ability to be humble before people.

3. For an example of a group undergoing imprisonment and death for reading and teaching the Bible during the medieval period, see Dennis McCallum, "The Waldensian Movement From Waldo to the Reformation," Dwell Community Church (website), https://www.dwellcc.org/essays/waldensian-movement-waldo-reformation. For a later case under Reformed and Lutheran rule, see Dennis McCallum, "Phillip Jacob Spener's Contribution to Protestant Ecclesiology," Dwell Community Church (website), https://www.dwellcc.org/essays/phillip-jacob-speners-contribution-protestant-ecclesiology.

19

Southward

Luke 9:51-10:24

This section begins with Luke's announcement that the final trek was at hand:

> As the time drew near for him to ascend to heaven, Jesus resolutely set out for Jerusalem. (Luke 9:51 NLT)

The next ten chapters of Luke focus on this fateful journey and Jesus' teaching on route. He didn't go straight to Jerusalem. Instead, he meandered so he could visit as many villages as possible. Most of this material is unique to Luke. Matthew and Mark don't have it. Where did it come from? Clearly, based on the detail given, it came from someone who was there. It must be from one or more of the "many" sources Luke refers to at the beginning of the book.

We know Jesus was traveling with the twelve, but also a significant group of others, including women. One of those women was Mary, Jesus' mother. We know she was with the group during this trip because she shows up in Jerusalem at the end of the trip, and there's no way she went there by herself. Her kids were adults by now, and her husband was dead. So she was an empty nester widow.

We saw earlier that she was a key source for Luke, either directly, or through a written piece, or through a family member. Remembering this trip and all its details would be natural for a mother who knew this was the key trip for her son, the Messiah. She might have been debriefed after the ascension, when the early believers were getting things written down.

Although these chapters follow a sequence traveling south from Galilee to Jerusalem (9:52; 10:38; 13:22; 13:32-33; 17:11; 18:31, 35; 19:1, 28-29), one story is inserted that is probably out of place (Luke 10:38-42, Mary and Martha lived in Bethany, near Jerusalem). We saw earlier that exact chronology was often not important to ancient writers, and they saw nothing wrong with arranging their accounts thematically. So it's also possible that various teachings have been inserted without worrying about the proper order. His meandering to various villages also took him into Samaritan territory.

Samaritans

> He sent messengers ahead to a Samaritan village to prepare for his arrival. But the people of the village did not welcome Jesus because he was on his way to Jerusalem. (vs. 52-53 NLT)

This fits everything we've seen earlier about Jewish-Samaritan relations. The mere fact that they were headed to Jerusalem was enough to cause rejection from this Samaritan village. Surely by now the disciples' reactions will be more gracious, right? Not quite.

> When James and John saw this, they said to Jesus, "Lord, should we call down fire from heaven to burn them up?" But Jesus turned and rebuked them. So they went on to another village. (vs. 54-56 NLT)

This incident shows why the Zebedee brothers were known as the "sons of thunder." The Samaritans' guilt here pales before the violent wishes of Jesus' disciples. Racism would be a major barrier to the spread of the gospel as Luke, the Gentile, records in his following book of Acts.

Would-Be Followers

As they move southward, Jesus interacts with people offering to follow him:

> As they were walking along, someone said to Jesus, "I will follow you wherever you go."

> But Jesus replied, "Foxes have dens to live in, and birds have nests, but the Son of Man has no place even to lay his head." (vs. 57-58 NLT)

Here, Jesus calls the man's attention to the Spartan conditions in which he and his band lived. Jesus may not have been as austere as John the Baptist, but he did live without a home, as he says. Constant traveling, speaking, and camping out on the ground add up to a harsh way of life. We aren't told the man's response.

> He said to another person, "Come, follow me."
>
> The man agreed, but he said, "Lord, first let me return home and bury my father."
>
> But Jesus told him, "Let the dead bury their own dead! Your duty is to go and preach about the Kingdom of God." (vs. 59-60 NLT)

A reader might see this as incredibly rude and insensitive. But the expression "bury my father" doesn't mean his dad was already dead. Jewish tradition called for a quick burial of the dead, so if the dad was already dead, the man would have been at home making arrangements or attending the funeral, not out on the road talking to Jesus.

Instead, the man was saying that his dad was old, and he wanted to wait until his dad died. That could happen in days or months, even years. And death is when the property and other inheritances are passed out. If he's on the road when Dad dies, who knows what would happen to his inheritance?

The statement, "Let the dead bury their own dead," probably carries the sense, "There are plenty of already spiritually dead people who can take care of that." It's a call not to put conditions on following. Luke again doesn't say what the man's response was.

> Another said, "Yes, Lord, I will follow you, but first let me say goodbye to my family."
>
> But Jesus told him, "Anyone who puts a hand to the plow and then looks back is not fit for the Kingdom of God." (vs. 61-62 NLT)

Ancient farmers dragged their plowshares behind an ox or other work animal. The plowman stood behind the plow, guiding it and the ox using two handles and a long stick. It was rough work and required constant attention and strength to keep the plow from drifting off to one side or the other. Looking back over your shoulder would immediately result in error.

This is Jesus' picture, showing how his followers must focus and not be distracted. He doesn't want to hear that we're putting other things "first" before heeding his call. Saying goodbye doesn't seem unreasonable, but there could have been other reasons Jesus rejected the request. Maybe the man's family was distant? Maybe "saying goodbye" actually meant spending a week or two with them? Maybe Jesus had previous history with him? The heart of the issue is that Jesus comes first.

We don't know how the man responded. The fact that none of the accounts gives the person's response suggests it doesn't matter. The question that does matter isn't their response, but ours.

The Sending of the Seventy-Two[1]

At some point during these final months, Jesus again sent disciples to surrounding villages. This time he sent seventy-two followers to cities he planned to visit later. He gave them instructions very similar to those he earlier gave the twelve when he sent them (see 9:1ff), and he again sent them out two by two as usual throughout the early church.[2]

He said, "The harvest is plentiful, but the laborers are few; therefore beseech the Lord of the harvest to send out laborers into His harvest" (v. 2). That suggests that they were not just making short proclamations, but were trying to train up others to continue spreading the word. This is also why he told them not to move from house to house (v. 7). Then, as now, there are more responsive people who could be reached if only we had more quality workers. That suggests the wisdom of building deeply, not just broadly.

He warned them of their vulnerability: "I send you out as lambs in the midst of wolves" (v. 3). A lamb would be completely helpless in the presence of wolves. But then he added more vulnerability by saying, "Carry

1. Study of the variant readings of Luke 10:1 reveals strong manuscript evidence that it should read seventy-two, not seventy, as in later versions.
2. Mark 6:7; Luke 7:18–19; Acts 13:2, 15:27, 39-40, 17:14, 19:22.

no money belt, no bag, no shoes" (v. 4). So they were going to be utterly depending on God for their protection. This means turning away from any human means of security. They could have gone out in groups of ten. They could have made provisions. They could even have carried weapons. But Jesus is making sure they get the point about complete dependence in faith.

He brought this lesson up later: "He said to them, 'When I sent you out without money belt and bag and sandals, you did not lack anything, did you?' They said, 'No, nothing'" (22:35). But interestingly, on the night before his death he said they should now pack a sword and other provisions (22:36). That suggests that planning and provisioning are the norm for outreach projects and church planting. This sending out with nothing was a special training event.

His call to "greet no one on the way" meant they shouldn't get side-tracked with lengthy talks on the road. They needed to get directly to their assigned village without delay.

His instruction that they greet people saying, "Peace be to you," is the Greek version of the Jewish "Shalom!" It's harder to understand the next part:

> "Whatever house you enter, first say, 'Peace be to this house.' If a man of peace is there, your peace will rest on him; but if not, it will return to you." (vs. 5-6)

The "man [or woman] of peace," as we saw earlier, is the local opinion leader who God uses to spread the word through his friends and relatives. Jesus doesn't envisage much cold contact evangelism, but outreach through key local people. (Of course it requires cold contact to meet the man or woman of peace in the first place).[3] This is a key principle in the field of missions, still practiced by successful mission teams today.

The language about their peace remaining on the man of peace or returning to them seems to be a way of saying that they should stay with responsive home owners but if they aren't responsive, the disciple should move on to a different house.

His instruction that they eat whatever their host gave them, may refer to

3. See Jesus practicing this himself with the woman at the well. She became his woman of peace, and opened the door to the city (John 4).

the more lax standards for ritual cleanliness practiced in some of these villages—especially Samaritan towns. He suggests, like Paul later, that they not ask questions (1 Corinthians 10:27). It's not important enough to disrupt the mission.

As before, in any village that rejects the message the worker is to shake the dust off as a statement of rebuke. Jesus follows this with a series of denunciations:

> "I say to you, it will be more tolerable in that day for Sodom than for that city. Woe to you, Chorazin! Woe to you, Bethsaida! For if the miracles had been performed in Tyre and Sidon which occurred in you, they would have repented long ago, sitting in sackcloth and ashes. But it will be more tolerable for Tyre and Sidon in the judgment than for you. And you, Capernaum, will not be exalted to heaven, will you? You will be brought down to Hades!" (vs. 12-15)

You can tell Jesus was angry when he spoke these words. That's a fair representation of God's attitude when people reject his word. Especially when Jesus had performed so many miracles in their presence, it was truly an outrage that people in these cities would turn their noses up in rejection.

On the other hand, after his resurrection many people in these cities recognized Jesus as Lord. That contributed to the explosive expansion of the body of Christ recorded in the book of Acts.

Finally, Jesus gave them their authorization: "The one who listens to you listens to me, and the one who rejects you rejects me; and he who rejects me rejects the one who sent me" (v. 16).

Jesus also implies in this denunciation that evidence does have an effect on people who see it. He is clear that evidence like the miracles performed in these cities would have been enough to convert those in cities like Tyre and Sidon. That disproves the view of some that evidence is irrelevant in evangelism.

The Return

We hear nothing about the trips the seventy-two took, but move directly to their return. This matches the perspective of someone in Jesus' band of followers, especially women, who would not have been sent out. They saw the seventy-two go and they saw them return, with nothing in between. It's a mark of authenticity. A writer inventing a story (like skeptical scholars claim) would have created accounts of what went on during their journeys.

> The seventy returned with joy, saying, "Lord, even the demons are subject to us in your name."
>
> And he said to them, "I was watching Satan fall from heaven like lightning." (vs. 17-18)

Jesus' reply is cryptic. We have no reason to link this statement with Revelation 12:9-10, where Satan and his angels are cast out of heaven onto the earth. The context of that passage hardly fits this episode. Those who see the book of Revelation as revealing the future understand that passage relates to the end times. Even those who reject a futuristic reading see it pointing to something other than this verse—the cross, the resurrection, etc.

The plain truth is that we aren't sure what Jesus was referring to. It's safe to say that when believing workers go out to proclaim the gospel, including casting out demons, it affects the spiritual realm. So too, their ability to drive Satan back foreshadowed the future spread of the gospel. Satan's followers were being cast out, and this was somehow visible to Jesus. He goes on:

> "Behold, I have given you authority to tread on serpents and scorpions, and over all the power of the enemy, and nothing will injure you. Nevertheless do not rejoice in this, that the spirits are subject to you, but rejoice that your names are recorded in heaven." (vs. 19-20)

This powerful promise that they, and we, have authority and power to overcome Satan is no different than 1 John 4:4, "You are from God, little children, and have overcome them; because greater is he who is in you than he who is in the world." Our problems with Satan result not from any lack of power or authority on our part, but from preoccupation with the world and unbelief. These leave us oblivious and blind to what the enemy is doing. Still, this verse should be of great comfort to believers who are afraid of evil spirits.

The even more reassuring and more important part is that our names are written in the Book of Life. That should be our focus as well as theirs. The gospel and our sharing of it is far more important than any duels we may have with the demonic.

Was Jesus foreseeing the future tendency to become fascinated with the occult and demons? Perhaps. He clearly sets the priority here. Later in church history, foolish "Christians" would torture and kill thousands of innocent people in the belief that they were witches, warlocks, wizards, or possessed by demons.[4]

The Privilege of Knowing

> At that very time [Jesus] rejoiced greatly in the Holy Spirit, and said, "I praise you, O Father, Lord of heaven and earth, that you have hidden these things from the wise and intelligent and have revealed them to infants. Yes, Father, for this way was well-pleasing in your sight." (v. 21)

The intelligentsia of Jesus' day were the scribes, Pharisees, and priests. They were busy trying to figure out how to kill Jesus. The "infants" were the peasants, craftsmen, shop owners, and their families in the villages they were visiting. Almost all of Jesus' disciples came from the common people. Matthew may have been somewhat more educated in order to work as a tax collector. The only other likely educated disciple was from Judah, the more sophisticated region in southern Israel—Judas Iscariot.

Why did the state of affairs make Jesus happy? It was less that the high-brow scholars were blinded that made Jesus happy, but that the infants were believing. But there was a certain justice in the fact that the elite felt like they already knew the way, and were too proud to admit they might be in the wrong.

It wasn't that no wise or intelligent people believed, but that few did. Paul was an example of a world-class scholar who followed Jesus. So was Apollos. As Paul later put it,

> Consider your calling, brethren, that there were not many wise according to the flesh, not many mighty, not many noble; but God has chosen the foolish things of the world to shame

4. For an overview, see Mark P. Donnelly, *The Big Book of Pain: Torture & Punishment Through History*, Reprint edition (London: The History Press, 2011).

> the wise, and God has chosen the weak things of the world to shame the things which are strong, and the base things of the world and the despised God has chosen, the things that are not, so that he may nullify the things that are, so that no man may boast before God. (1 Corinthians 1:26-29)

Nothing is more offensive to God than pride—the original sin. He won't tolerate proud people boasting in his presence. The weak and the ignorant might not be sophisticated, but they were humble enough to accept what Jesus was offering.

Finally,

> "All things have been handed over to me by my Father, and no one knows who the Son is except the Father, and who the Father is except the Son, and anyone to whom the Son wills to reveal him." Turning to the disciples, he said privately, "Blessed are the eyes which see the things you see, for I say to you, that many prophets and kings wished to see the things which you see, and did not see them, and to hear the things which you hear, and did not hear them." (vs. 22-24)

Once again, Jesus called on his friends to appreciate what they were seeing, because it was a rare privilege. Any time God reveals himself to a sinful, undeserving person it's an exceptional blessing.

You can also see the deity of Christ in this passage. He and the Father are put on the same plane here.

The Big Picture

Although Jesus' following was already declining, he pushed ahead, even expanding his outreach through the seventy-two. Most of these seventy-two probably later became leaders in the new movement after Jesus' ascension. We know that local churches sprang up all over Galilee, Samaria, and to the east of the Jordan.

At the same time he wasn't making his conditions for being a disciple any easier. Every time he added another layer to the picture of a true disciple, more people turned away. But Jesus knew he didn't need the multitudes as much as he needed a reliable group of fully committed disciples.

20

WHO IS MY NEIGHBOR?

LUKE 10:25-42

In a synagogue or home, Jesus was speaking, when a scribe stood up to challenge him.[1] Some translations say it was a lawyer, but their lawyers were different than ours. The only law in view here was the Law of Moses. The man is a clergyman. The result was one of Jesus' most memorable parables.

Salvation By Law

> One day an expert in religious law stood up to test Jesus by asking him this question: "Teacher, what should I do to inherit eternal life?"
>
> Jesus replied, "What does the law of Moses say? How do you read it?"
>
> The man answered, "'You must love the Lord your God with all

1. Notice that this is not the same dialog recounted in Matthew 22:34-40 and Mark 12:28-34. That dialog happened in Jerusalem. This one happened well before he got to Jerusalem. In Matthew and Mark's account, Jesus gives the two great laws, while here it is the scribe who gives them. The fact that they both gave the same two laws is not really surprising because we know rabbinic discussion frequently mention these laws.

> your heart, all your soul, all your strength, and all your mind.' And, 'Love your neighbor as yourself.'" (Luke 10:25-27 NLT)

We see nothing surprising here. The scribe gives the standard theological position of the day—obey the law! The surprise is Jesus' reply:

> "Right!" Jesus told him. "Do this and you will live!" (v. 28 NLT)

Wait, we already established that Jesus taught salvation is by faith apart from works! Now he's saying works are adequate after all. This is the same approach he took with the Sermon on the Plain. It's also the same approach Paul took in the book of Romans. First Jesus confronted the man with the law—Plan A.

The scribe wriggled to avoid the obvious:

> The man wanted to justify his actions, so he asked Jesus, "And who is my neighbor?" (v. 29 NLT)

This is what Jesus was expecting. If you look at even the two laws this man gave, the word "all" plays an important and daunting role. God's law doesn't give easy to follow laws, like praying three times a day. This first law calls for *all* one's heart, *all* one's soul, *all* one's mind, and *all* one's strength. Nobody has ever kept that law for a whole life, or even for a single hour!

An honest look at the law of God reveals he never says to keep the laws more than others do; never says to keep them more often than you break them; he just says, "Keep them." That means all the time, without exception, and in thought, word, and deed. Good intentions mean nothing. Keeping the whole law but offending in one point makes you guilty of all (James 2:10). Viewed that way, it's quite hopeless.

So was the law to love your neighbor as you love yourself. The scribe's effort to weaken the law was classic: "Who is my neighbor?" We know the rabbis claimed this only applied to fellow Jews. But a neighboring group lived right next to them—the Samaritans. We saw earlier how the rabbis prayed that they would never have to look upon a Samaritan. They hated them.

The Good Samaritan

Jesus didn't answer the man's question in typical rabbinic

fashion—wrangling over what is or is not allowed. Instead he told a story picturing true sacrificial love like that intended in the Law—love that goes way beyond legal duty, all the way to love like God's love.

> "A Jewish man was traveling from Jerusalem down to Jericho, and he was attacked by bandits. They stripped him of his clothes, beat him up, and left him half dead beside the road.
>
> By chance a priest came along. But when he saw the man lying there, he crossed to the other side of the road and passed him by.
>
> A Temple assistant walked over and looked at him lying there, but he also passed by on the other side." (vs. 30-32 NLT)

Jesus has both men who passed by being clergy. Although the NLT misses this, the NASB correctly says, "a priest was going down." That means he was going away from Jerusalem, not toward it. So he was already finished with any temple work he needed to do. It's the same with the "Temple assistant." That means any excuse they may have had to the effect that they couldn't touch the man because touching a dead person would make them unclean was nullified.

They both sinned. What was the sin called? It's called *doing nothing*. In the face of suffering and need, doing nothing is not good enough.

> "Then a Samaritan came along, and when he saw the man, he felt compassion for him. Going over to him, the Samaritan soothed his wounds with olive oil and wine and bandaged them. Then he put the man on his own donkey and took him to an inn, where he took care of him. The next day he handed the innkeeper two silver coins, telling him, 'Take care of this man. If his bill runs higher than this, I'll pay you the next time I'm here.'" (vs. 33-35 NLT)

Referring to this story, Jesus later said, "Go and do the same." So he considered the story a pattern we should follow.

The first thing we see is that the Samaritan "felt compassion." That is, he let himself care. And it wasn't the compassion that the priest may have felt—"Tsk tsk, poor fella. The crime is really bad on this road. Someone should do something about it." And then passes by, shaking his head. What's missing? He failed to do anything.

Merely feeling sorry falls way short of what God expects. Thinking about the story as a pattern for serving the poor and suffering in our world today, we see that believers shouldn't wait for the poor to come to them. We should cross over and take initiative like the Good Samaritan did.

Next the Samaritan bandaged the man's wounds after anointing them with oil and wine. The wine disinfected, and the oil soothed. He used his own wine and oil. He may have torn the bandages from his cloak. In sum, he met the man's immediate needs by sacrificing his own belongings. Again when serving the poor today, the first need is often relief work. We can't succeed in long-term development work if people are starving.

Then, the Samaritan put the man on his own donkey. He would have to walk up the long ascent to Jerusalem, while the beaten man rode on his donkey. So again, the Samaritan was sacrificing what was his for the other man's sake.

When they reached town, the Samaritan took the injured man to the inn and tended his wounds. Then, the next day he left money with the inn keeper to care for the man. In other words, he met his more long-term needs. He even added that he would pay more still if needed when he returned. Just doing short term relief work among the poor isn't good enough. They need help getting out of poverty in a lasting way. Here, the sacrifice can grow exponentially. Years of giving, serving, and instruction are often needed to make lasting change among the poor.

We can also observe that most of the poor in our world are of a different race than white westerners, just like with this man and the Samaritan. So any lingering issues of racism will block effectiveness in serving love. Racism directly defies God's clear teaching that he created all people in his own image.

After finishing his story, Jesus turned to the scribe:

> "Now which of these three would you say was a neighbor to the man who was attacked by bandits?" Jesus asked.
>
> The man replied, "The one who showed him mercy." (v. 36-37 NLT)

He can't bring himself to say, "the Samaritan." He just calls him "the one."

> Then Jesus said, "Yes, now go and do the same." (vs. 37 NLT)

We aren't told how the scribe responded after that. If he responded correctly, he would have pleaded for Plan B: giving up on pretending to be righteous, admitting his own inability, and throwing himself on the mercy of God.

Why did Jesus have the doer of good be a Samaritan? He could have told it with a Samaritan victim and a Jewish savior. By reversing the roles, the story becomes even more provocative. Here is a Samaritan doing for a half-dead Jew what his own fellow Jews wouldn't do. It would have been beyond disturbing to this Jewish crowd. It's an example of why the leadership wanted him dead.

Astonishing Stand on Women

The following incident showed Jesus' attitude toward women being educated and becoming Christian workers. A woman named Martha and her sister Mary invited Jesus and his disciples to dinner. As Martha cooked, "Mary sat at Jesus' feet listening to his words" (v. 39), but,

> But Martha was distracted with all her preparations; and she came up to him and said, "Lord, do you not care that my sister has left me to do all the serving alone? Then tell her to help me!" (v. 40)

So here is Martha in the kitchen where she belonged (in their view), doing the cooking while the men folk discuss matters of importance. This picture perfectly fits ancient Jewish expectations except for one part—Mary sitting out with the men, listening to the rabbi teach instead of being in the kitchen with her sister. This scene would have been considered highly improper.

> But the Lord answered and said to her, "Martha, Martha, you are worried and bothered about so many things; but only one thing is necessary, for Mary has chosen the good part, which shall not be taken away from her." (vs. 41-42)

It's hard for modern readers to grasp how shocking this incident would be to this ancient culture. A rabbi defending the idea of a woman learning the word? No way! But Jesus routinely included women among his disciples. The early church would follow his example with key church planters like Priscilla, and even an apostle named Junia (Romans 16:3, 7).

Some commentators argue that this event proves that sitting at Jesus' feet is more important than ministry or service. Yet, in the previous parable Jesus stressed the importance of serving and meeting needs of our neighbors. Dichotomies like that are not necessary. In this setting, Jesus is saying that what he was teaching was more important than preparing dinner. Later, they could go ahead with the meal. Martha was fussing and not moving with the situation; trying to drive her agenda and timing. She wanted to control the situation. She could have joined Mary for the teaching, and then gone in to prepare dinner.

The Big Picture

Women were held back in Jesus' day and a low view of women and their capabilities prevailed. But at least they were in relationship, and protected in some key ways. Far more rejected were the Samaritans. Jesus ignored both prejudices and included them all.

Women were there in the upper room where the disciples were "continually devoting themselves to prayer, along with the women" (Acts 1:14). Women were the first to witness the resurrected Jesus. Later, they received spiritual gifts, just like the men. Jesus and the early church reversed the prejudice against women. It didn't last that long, fading away in the post-apostolic period.

Likewise, Jesus reached out to the Samaritans at Sychar (John 4), and they were later caught up in a very early spiritual awakening resulting in most of the city of Samaria coming to faith in Jesus. From there, they reached out to "many of the villages of the Samaritans" (Acts 8:25). This happened before the gospel made it out to the Gentile world.

Love stands at the center of God's will for people. But prejudice blocks the expression of love.

21

Jesus on Prayer

Luke 11:1-23

Jesus' Model

> It happened that while Jesus was praying in a certain place, after he had finished, one of his disciples said to him, "Lord, teach us to pray just as John also taught his disciples." (Luke 11:1)

The disciples had seen Jesus go off for entire nights of prayer. At other times he prayed in their presence or went off by himself for shorter periods. At this point, his modeling came to fruition. They had seen enough. It wasn't that they never prayed, but that they sensed that Jesus had something going on with his prayer life that they were lacking.

> And he said to them, "When you pray, say: 'Father, hallowed be your name. Your kingdom come. Give us each day our daily bread, and forgive us our sins, For we ourselves also forgive everyone who is indebted to us. And lead us not into temptation.'" (vs. 2-4)

This is a similar, but slightly different version of the Lord's Prayer. It's doubtful that he taught them the same prayer twice. Probably Matthew moved it from its original location in time and gathered it along with some other teachings into the sermon on the mount. Matthew's discourses are known to be edited in this way.

Irony

The version of the prayer in Matthew resulted in one of the most bizarre ironies ever: Immediately before giving this example prayer, Jesus said, "And when you are praying, do not use meaningless repetition as the Gentiles do, for they suppose that they will be heard for their many words" (Matthew 6:7). Instead, he said, "Pray like this," and gave them the Lord's Prayer.

The irony is that in the centuries since, the church made the Lord's Prayer into a classic example of meaningless repetition. Some churches just say it every week. In others, you might be called on to repeat it ten times back-to-back. They completely missed the intent of this prayer. It was never to give people specific words to repeat, but to give examples of the themes that should be a part of a believer's prayer.

He specifically mentions eight themes:

1. He begins with the word "Father." So the first thing we need to do when praying is remember who we're talking to, and the nature of our relationship. We need to think, not necessarily of the earthly father we knew, but of an ideal father. The father-child bond should ideally be close and nurturing. A good father cares for his children, provides for them, loves them, and teaches them. He loves it when his kids come to him asking for help, or asking him questions. Kids in a good relationship with their dad love to run to him and jump up on his lap, enjoying closeness with him.

   To come to God as your father means you approach him as one who loves you; as one who is pleased that you have come to talk; as one who understands you like no other. Not even you can understand yourself like he does. The father relationship reveals that your relationship with God is not institutional or legal—like your relationship to the IRS or your place of work—but personal and intimate.

2. In Matthew he addresses God saying, "Our Father." That means that we come to God in prayer together, corporately. Luke's version leaves out the "our" but later says, "Give us each day..." in the

plural. So he too assumes coming to God corporately—as part of his body of followers.

3. Next, Jesus prays, "Hallowed be your name." This strange saying often sails over modern readers' heads. The word "hallowed" is the same word from which we get "holy." It means separate, special, or different. In this context, it means God is not commonplace, but totally different and greater than any other. In other words, we are addressing an exalted, lofty God. We need to remember when we pray that God is eminent (close, like a father) but he is also transcendent (like the almighty sovereign of the universe).

   The NET version translates it, "may your name be honored." That's correct. This phrase stands for praising God—an important part of any time of prayer. We need some time marveling at the grandeur of God.

   So the first steps in prayer involve focusing on God, not on yourself, not on your actions, but on God and your relationship with him.

4. The next plea is, "Your kingdom come." Matthew adds, "Your will be done, on earth as it is in heaven." This is a prayer that the earth return to what God intended—not a rebel planet with daily atrocities, but a place where people follow God and live fulfilled and joyful lives.

   We know this future is coming when Jesus returns. But in the meantime, we, his followers, are already trying to win people over to become followers of God. When people are converted from unbelief to faith, God's will is done on earth. And the new believer will continue to do God's will on earth. So the prayer that God's will be followed here in our fallen world is really a prayer for ministry, and the spread of the gospel.

   So Jesus' order in his model prayer is first, God; then our relation to God (e.g. forgiven, adopted, given a new identity, etc.). Next comes ministry. That is, praying for others. This order is significant and suggests the order of importance.

5. Next Jesus said, "Give us each day our daily bread" (v. 3). Here is where we pray for our own needs. There's nothing wrong with praying for our own needs, but it should follow after more important

things. The others-centered perspective is Jesus' way, not the self-centered perspective.

Notice this part of Jesus' suggested prayer is simple and based on God's promise to meet our daily needs (Matthew 6:25-30). He calls us to pray for today, not for the next ten years. Focusing on the long term future only causes anxiety.

6. Next, Jesus suggests we pray for forgiveness (v. 4), It raises important questions, because the rest of the New Testament, from Pentecost on, always speaks of believers' forgiveness as a past, completed event. Note that the prayer is addressed to God as father, so Jesus is teaching this lesson to believers.

   You can see a clear example of the typical New Testament view in Ephesians, where Paul says, "Be kind to each other, tenderhearted, forgiving one another, just as God through Christ has forgiven you" (Ephesians 4:32). Notice the past (actually "aorist") tense. It means our forgiveness is a singular, past event.

   Not all believers realize this. Many churches teach their people that they must be forgiven as they go, day by day. The biggest source for this teaching is the passage before us, the Lord's Prayer.[1] But Jesus lived under the Old Covenant, the Mosaic Covenant (Galatians 4:4). In that covenant, we see no teaching of once-for-all forgiveness like we do in the New Covenant.[2] But the Old Covenant has been set aside, as Hebrews makes clear: "He cancels the first covenant in order to put the second into effect" (Hebrews 10:9). So it would

1. The other source of forgiveness-as-you-go view is 1 John 1:9, "If we confess our sins to him, he is faithful and just to forgive us our sins and to cleanse us from all wickedness." But this passage is not an instruction for believers when praying. Instead, John is contrasting the sin-denying heretics' view with that of true believers. This becomes clear in the context: "If we claim we have no sin, we are only fooling ourselves and not living in the truth. But if we confess our sins to him, he is faithful and just to forgive us our sins and to cleanse us from all wickedness. If we claim we have not sinned, we are calling God a liar and showing that his word has no place in our hearts" (vs. 8-10). John is writing against proto-gnostics who denied that any sin of the physical body mattered. His point is not that we must confess sin-by-sin, but rather that we must admit in principle that we need forgiveness and that our sin is real.

2. Some other key examples of this forgiveness given at one time and including all our past, present, and future sins include Hebrews 10:10, 14, "By this will we have been sanctified through the offering of the body of Jesus Christ once for all. . . . For by one offering He has perfected for all time those who are sanctified." The "once for all" language confirms that forgiveness happens at one time, and includes all our sin, past, present, and future. That's why Paul can declare, "Therefore there is now no condemnation for those who are in Christ Jesus" (Romans 8:1).

be more appropriate for us to *thank* God for his forgiveness, not to *ask* him for forgiveness. And we should all do that on a daily basis.

7. The seventh theme is our willingness to forgive others. Jesus considered this a high-level obligation for his followers. His parable of the unforgiving servant in Matthew 18:21-35 shows how a refusal to forgive looks from God's point of view. That the king would forgive a fortune worth 375 tons of silver, but his ungrateful servant refused to forgive a small debt of a few coins. This is how God sees our reluctance to forgive from the heart. For us who have received ultimate forgiveness, it's a moral outrage.
8. Finally, comes the prayer that God will not lead us into temptation. It's not that we ever are completely free from temptation. Neither does it imply that God would tempt us unless we pray against it. James makes it clear that "he himself does not tempt anyone" (James 1:13). The likely sense is "Do not lead us into too much temptation." It's a basic prayer for our spiritual growth, including avoidance of sin. Matthew's version adds, "but deliver us from evil" (Matthew 6:13 NASB), or, "deliver us from the Evil One" (NLT, NIV). It's probably deliverance from the Evil One, because it has a definite article "the evil." If so, this is a call to spiritual warfare via prayer. We pray to God, for others, for ourselves, and against the Evil One.

The familiar, traditional ending of the Lord's Prayer, "For yours is the kingdom and the power and the glory forever. Amen," (Matthew 6:13) is not found in early manuscripts. It was added later as the church became more formalistic. They added this ending for use in a growing liturgy, or worship recitation.

Perseverance in Prayer

Jesus continued teaching on prayer using some example scenarios.

> Then he said to them, "Suppose one of you has a friend, and goes to him at midnight and says to him, 'Friend, lend me three loaves; for a friend of mine has come to me from a journey, and I have nothing to set before him'; and from inside he answers and says, 'Do not bother me; the door has already been shut and my children and I are in bed; I cannot get up and give you anything.' I tell you, even though he will not get

> up and give him anything because he is his friend, yet because of his persistence he will get up and give him as much as he needs. So I say to you, ask, and it will be given to you; seek, and you will find; knock, and it will be opened to you. For everyone who asks, receives; and he who seeks, finds; and to him who knocks, it will be opened." (vs. 5-10)

Wait. How is this reluctant, unwilling, preoccupied neighbor a picture of God? This story makes it sound like God is not a good friend, and we have to pester him until he grudgingly gives us what we need, mainly because he's annoyed.

A Fortiori

None of this is right. This story advances a type of argument called *a fortiori*. An *a fortiori* argument follows the form, "If this, how much more that?" We don't use this type of argument often today, but Jesus used it a lot. In this kind of argument, there are two similar things and two contrasting things. You could view it this way: "If A leads to B, how much more will C lead to D?" The key to a persuasive *a fortiori* argument is that the first points of comparison—B and D—need to be similar. But the next points of comparison—A and C—need to be as different as possible. The contrast is what gives the argument its force.

So in this story, Jesus argues, "If a reluctant, unwilling, and poor friend becomes willing to help, how much more will a loving, willing father meet our need?" If you admit that the first interaction is plausible, how much more plausible would a persistent interaction with God be?

Generous God

So the point of this argument is that God is exactly the opposite of the reluctant friend. You see this in Jesus' follow up:

> "So I say to you, ask, and it will be given to you; seek, and you will find; knock, and it will be opened to you." For everyone who asks, receives; and he who seeks, finds; and to him who knocks, it will be opened. (vs. 9-10)

No, God is not reluctant, he's eager to give. But the issue of timing is still in his hands. There may be important reasons why God might withhold an answer for a period of time. First, if he gave us whatever we ask immediately, it would be ruinous to our growth in faith. We would be spoiled kids: no patience, no real appreciation, just taking everything for granted. It's the waiting in expectancy that grows faith. When you finally see a prayer answered after persevering in prayer for months or even years, your faith takes a quantum leap upward.

At other times, God may be aware of factors that make it disadvantageous to grant the request until later. Certain pieces may need to fall into place before the answer will achieve maximum benefit. We saw earlier how God waited four hundred years before sending the Messiah, probably because it was a more advantageous time to send him. He made Abraham and Sarah wait over twenty years for the birth of Isaac, also for strategic reasons.

The waiting element in hearing answers to prayer leads to Jesus' call for perseverance in prayer. When I was a new believer, I used to think that asking for something once and then never bringing it up again showed faith. Later, after studying Jesus' teaching on prayer, I realized I was wrong. Actually, asking repeatedly shows more faith. Under the thought, "I already prayed for that," it's too easy to simply forget the issue. It's also far more likely that we will fail to recognize an answer to our prayer when it finally comes.

Of course God won't answer some prayers ever, because he knows it's not what we need and would be harmful. It's only when we pray in accord with God's will that we can pray confidently and without wavering (1 John 5:14). Of course, for people who know God, the last thing we would want to see is God doing something that is not his will.

A Loving Father

Jesus added another example:

> "Now suppose one of you fathers is asked by his son for a fish; he will not give him a snake instead of a fish, will he? Or if he is asked for an egg, he will not give him a scorpion, will he? If you then, being evil, know how to give good gifts to your children, how much more will your heavenly Father give the Holy Spirit to those who ask Him!" (vs. 11-13)

When praying, it is absolutely essential that you comprehend that you are praying to a God who loves you. Jesus' questions envisage a son asking his father for something good, a fish or an egg. Would you, if you were the father, give him something nasty or dangerous, like a scorpion or a snake? No. Most fathers wouldn't do that. Yet, Jesus reminds his hearers, you treat your son well even though you are evil. How much more would a good God give something awesome, like the Holy Spirit, to his kids?

It's another *a fortiori* argument, and a powerful one! Scripture teaches that humans—all of them—are selfish and born with a dread of God's authority. We don't know how to love well, and even in a relationship most characterized by love, like a father and son, we are nowhere close to God's love.

Comprehending God's love is an ongoing project that lasts a lifetime. Growing believers get to experience new waves of realization as their relationship with God grows. The apostle John explains the life-changing impact of realizing God's love:

> We have come to know and have believed the love which God has for us. God is love, and the one who abides in love abides in God, and God abides in him. By this, love is perfected with us. . . . (1 John 4:16-17)

He goes on to say, "We love because he first loved us" (v. 19). Perhaps the hardest thing to believe in the Bible is the true extent of God's love. Nothing is harder to believe, and nothing changes our lives more. Once we begin to realize the depth of God's love, our prayer life will soar upward.

Blasphemy

> One day Jesus cast out a demon from a man who couldn't speak, and when the demon was gone, the man began to speak. (v. 14 NLT)

Some were leaning toward believing. Matthew observed, "All the crowds were amazed, and were saying, 'This man cannot be the Son of David, can he?'" (Matthew 12:23)

But the opposition was still growing.

> Some of them said, "No wonder he can cast out demons. He gets his power from Beelzebul, the prince of demons." (v. 15 NLT)

Beelzebul was originally a false god of the Philistines, specifically worshipped in the city of Ekron (1 Kings 1:2, 6, 16). His name at that time was Baal-Zebub, one of the Baals. Various texts, mostly from the inter-testamental period, refer to him as the prince of demons. But the name at times seems to be referring to Satan himself.[3] Regardless of exactly where the name came from, in essence they were accusing Jesus of accessing satanic or demonic power to cast out demons. Matthew says it was the Pharisees who made this charge (Matthew 12:24).

> Others, trying to test Jesus, demanded that he show them a miraculous sign from heaven to prove his authority. (v. 16 NLT)

Those "demanding a sign" were "trying to test him." The language makes it clear that they were cynical, daring, even taunting. So if he doesn't give a sign, they won't believe, and if he does give a sign, they'll attribute it to Satan.

> He knew their thoughts, so he said, "Any kingdom divided by civil war is doomed. A family splintered by feuding will fall apart. You say I am empowered by Satan. But if Satan is divided and fighting against himself, how can his kingdom survive? And if I am empowered by Satan, what about your own exorcists? They cast out demons, too, so they will condemn you for what you have said. (vs. 17-19 NLT)

Jesus points out the implausibility of their claim, because Satan is too smart to go against his own kingdom. And at the same time, why has this charge of exorcism via Satan never come up before with earlier exorcists? Their problem is not with Satan. Their problem was with Jesus' authority.

> But if I am casting out demons by the power of God, then the Kingdom of God has arrived among you. (v. 20 NLT)

3. Some scholars believe the correct translation of Beelzebub is "Lord of the flies." Nobel Prize winner William Golding wrote a novel by that title. Or, it could come from a different Hebrew word meaning "Lord of the house." Jerome substituted Beelzebub in the Latin Vulgate, which became the traditional spelling in the medieval period. The original Greek here in Luke is Beelzebul.

This is the real meaning of Jesus' command over evil spirits. It's the power of the Kingdom of God they are witnessing.

Binding the Strong Man

The discussion about Satan leads to Jesus explaining how spiritual warfare really works:

> "For when a strong man is fully armed and guards his palace, his possessions are safe—until someone even stronger attacks and overpowers him, strips him of his weapons, and carries off his belongings. He who is not with me is against me; and he who does not gather with me, scatters." (vs. 21-23 NLT)

In context, the strong man is clearly Satan and the demons. He is pictured here as guarding his palace and his possessions. Then comes a stronger man—Jesus. He attacks and overpowers the strong man, and takes away his armor. Now the strong man is vulnerable. This reminds us of Jesus' earlier promise that he would give us "authority over all the power of the enemy and you can walk among snakes and scorpions and crush them." (10:19)

The new, stronger man also distributes the plunder. What would that be? We know Satan claimed earlier that the world and its kingdoms belonged to him (4:6), and Jesus didn't contest that claim. Who will liberate the prisoners in the strong man's palace? Jesus! Power greater than Satan can only come from God. He does use us, but in ourselves we have nothing to put up against the prince of the power of the air (Ephesians 2:2). Instead, we summon God's power in prayer against the enemy. This is called "binding the strongman" in Matthew 12:29.[4]

The Big Picture

Jesus made some of his most memorable points on prayer during this

4. An alternative interpretation sees the binding of Satan as a one-time event where Jesus once-and-for-all bound Satan's power. But nothing in the passage says it's a one-time event. The usual argument given by the one-time interpreters is that binding Satan refers to Revelation 20:1-2, where Satan is bound for a thousand years. But the context in Revelation has nothing to do with the scene before us here in Luke. Only the word "bind" would link these two passages, widely separated in time and content. The binding of Satan in Revelation results in him being cast "into the abyss" where he will "not deceive the nations any longer" (v. 3). That's hardly a good description of history since Jesus' day. That binding in Revelation is in the future. This binding in Luke refers to events in Jesus' own day and following.

period. As he revealed the loving heart of father God, his enemies could think of no better explanation for his miraculous power than Satan. Like Satan would be healing people and casting out demons? No. But the opportunity led to some of the most important teaching Jesus gave on spiritual warfare.

22

Polarization
Luke 11:23-36

The power of Jesus' word was polarizing the crowd. While some were believing, others were scoffing and equating Jesus with Satan. In the face of such opposition, Jesus added:

> "He who is not with me is against me; and he who does not gather with me, scatters" (Luke 11:23).

"Gathering" here refers to gathering a flock of sheep. Gathering the sheep is a job for shepherds, but it was the shepherds who were fighting against Jesus. As a result, the sheep were being scattered—the worst thing for sheep. Some leaders were actively fighting Jesus, saying he worked for Satan. Others were standing around watching, but not believing. That's not good enough, according to this warning.

Jesus said that if you're not with him, you're against him. Watching and wondering is okay for a while. But it's still unbelief. Biblical faith includes the willingness to take action. People who stand around waiting for something to happen need to be warned that they're waiting for something that may never come. At a certain point, it's time to take a step of faith. And if you step toward Jesus, he'll step toward you.

Ironically, while Jesus talked about how "hireling" self-serving leaders let the flock get scattered (John 10:11–13), who is really scattering them? It's the wolf—Satan. So, while they're accusing Jesus of working for Satan, it is actually they who are doing the evil one's work!

Limits to Exorcism

Jesus also warned the people that being delivered from demonic oppression is not an end in itself:

> "When an evil spirit leaves a person, it goes into the desert, searching for rest. But when it finds none, it says, 'I will return to the person I came from.' So it returns and finds that its former home is all swept and in order. Then the spirit finds seven other spirits more evil than itself, and they all enter the person and live there. And so that person is worse off than before." (vs. 24-26 NLT)

This warning makes it clear that being delivered from demonic possession or oppression is only a temporary opportunity. The delivered person needs to take advantage of the new freedom to get right with God. Evil spirits are relentless, and they will counterattack. Even when Jesus won his battle with the Evil One in chapter 4, we read that Satan only retreated "until a more opportune time" (4:13).

God's enemy is tireless and attacks relentlessly. It's one of the central reasons for perseverance in prayer—our enemy is going to persevere, so we need to match that.

His Mother

> As he was speaking, a woman in the crowd called out, "Blessed is the womb that bore you and the breasts at which you nursed!" Jesus replied, "On the contrary, blessed are those who hear the word of God and observe it." (vs. 27-28 NLT)

This curious exchange sounds like Jesus might be disowning his mother. But it actually doesn't say anything bad about Mary. He does seem to want people to move on from glorifying his birth, let alone parts of his mother's body, to deeper matters of God's word.

We should also remember that God knows the future. This exchange might have been given in order to warn against the future extreme veneration of Mary. As great as Mary was, she had to take her place at the cross too. At that point, she too "heard the word and observed it."

Show Us a Sign

> As the crowds were increasing, he began to say, "This generation is a wicked generation; it seeks for a sign, and yet no sign will be given to it but the sign of Jonah. For just as Jonah became a sign to the Ninevites, so will the Son of Man be to this generation." (vs. 29-30)

It's possible to call for a sign as entertainment. Some in the crowd were clearly cynical and verse 16 makes clear: "Others, to test him, were demanding of him a sign from heaven." One of the limitations to signs is that most people are going to say, "Wait, I wasn't watching," or "I wasn't there. Do it again." But doing it again still won't be enough.

The ongoing unbelief in the face of many miracles proved that this crowd was only idly curious. Mark adds, "Sighing deeply in his spirit, he said, 'Why does this generation seek for a sign?'" (8:12). It burdened him that people were so focused on signs, but not on following. Still, Jesus did perform more signs after this, so he was speaking in generalities—he wasn't going to cater to idle curiosity. His statement, "No sign will be given to it," probably referred to the crowd in question, not to other, later crowds.

This passage also shows that Jesus believed Jonah was real, and that overrules any suggestion that Jonah's story is just a moral fable. Matthew makes it explicit that the parallel was between Jonah's sojourn in the great fish and Jesus' burial and resurrection (Matthew 12:40). Based on this statement, if Jonah was a non-historical genre, Jesus' death and resurrection must also be non-historical. And Jesus was declaring that this—his resurrection—would be the premier "sign" they could expect to prove he was from God.

Ancient Cities

To picture his frustration, Jesus gave two scenarios that exemplify the stubbornness he was seeing:

> "The Queen of the South will rise up with the men of this

> generation at the judgment and condemn them, because she came from the ends of the earth to hear the wisdom of Solomon; and behold, something greater than Solomon is here." (v. 31)

And,

> "The men of Nineveh will stand up with this generation at the judgment and condemn it, because they repented at the preaching of Jonah; and behold, something greater than Jonah is here." (v. 32)

In both of these examples, those being converted had little or no access to the Scriptures or to attesting miracles. Yet, they believed. These examples clash sharply with Jesus' opponents, who had seen many miracles, but remained skeptical.

Lighting a Lamp

Jesus then said,

> "No one, after lighting a lamp, puts it away in a cellar nor under a basket, but on the lampstand, so that those who enter may see the light. The eye is the lamp of your body; when your eye is clear, your whole body also is full of light; but when it is bad, your body also is full of darkness. Then watch out that the light in you is not darkness. If therefore your whole body is full of light, with no dark part in it, it will be wholly illumined, as when the lamp illumines you with its rays." (vs. 33-36)

Eyes are for seeing, but our perception of reality can become distorted, even darkened. We saw earlier that those with hardened hearts lose their ability to comprehend spiritual matters. Your attitude directly affects your perception of reality. Here, Jesus warned that unbelief has a negative snowballing effect.[1]

1. This is a good example of Jesus using similar or even identical language to make different points. In Matthew 6, Jesus says, "Your eye is like a lamp that provides light for your body. When your eye is healthy, your whole body is filled with light. But when your eye is unhealthy, your whole body is filled with darkness" (vs. 22-23). So that's extremely close to what he said here. But in Matthew, he is discussing the lure of materialistic avarice, and how greed distorts your vision. Here, he's using the need for light as an illustration of having a mind receptive to his teaching. The teachings are different, the settings are different, but the wording is very similar. Your eyes are the gateway to your perception, which could be either perception of Jesus' teaching (here in Luke) or perception of the danger of money lust (in Matthew).

The Big Picture

In business, they say, "Money comes to money." So true! But Jesus is concerned about something else: "Unbelief comes to unbelief." Also true. Harboring any suspicion about God quickly becomes habit forming. If God isn't going to come through here, why think he'll come through there? If God's word isn't true here, why think it's true there? Real trust in God and his word comes as a package deal.

Jesus' opponents were by now far down the path to irreversible unbelief. But many others were watching the conflict in a mindset of neutrality. Here Jesus warns the crowd that neutrality is not good enough. A positive commitment of the will to believe and follow Jesus is essential.

Even nominal Christianity—where people passively think they are Christians, but it's in name only—are in this same mindset. Nominal Christianity is rampant in the modern west. With little persecution, and having been raised going to church, people assume they must be Christian. They can't remember becoming one. They have no coherent conversion account, they don't follow in any committed way, but they know they aren't Muslims, or any other faith, so they must be Christian.

Don't count on it. People doing evangelistic ministry often have dealings with nominal Christians who later actually receive Christ. Their testimony is that they can't believe what they were missing. They certainly did not have the Spirit before their conversion, even though they thought they were true believers. It's one of the great perils of living in a culture where Christianity has become a tradition.

Jesus also used the sentence about not covering a lamp versus putting it on a lampstand in Matthew 5:14-15. But there, he was referring to his disciples' evangelism. Here, in Luke, putting the lamp on the stand refers to people needing enlightenment for themselves. So, like most teachers, Jesus used and reused illustrations for different purposes at different times. There is no contradiction here.

23

Woe To You!
Luke 11:37-54

Hand Washing

The next scene began at a dinner.[1]

> As Jesus was speaking, one of the Pharisees invited him home for a meal. So he went in and took his place at the table. His host was amazed to see that he sat down to eat without first performing the hand-washing ceremony required by Jewish custom. (vs. 37-38 NLT)

This handwashing custom had nothing to do with sanitary handwashing, like we do today. They had no knowledge of bacteria or other causes of disease. This kind of washing grew out of superstitious beliefs about spiritual contagion—the belief that people's evil could rub off.

It was distantly based on the Old Testament use of washing as in Leviticus 15. But those washings had do to with quarantine from possible infections of the genitals or other open sores. "Unclean" in this context in Luke refers to moral contamination.

1. Matthew has most of this discourse set on the temple mount during the last week of Jesus' life. Mark and Luke place it earlier and not in Jerusalem. It's not necessarily the same event. The content fits so well, and the statements are so pithy, Jesus may well have uttered some of the same comments at Pharisees in different settings. Or, one or more Gospel writers has moved these sayings for effect. It's not clear that Mark's account is in a different location or time from Luke.

The washings in Jesus' day were ceremonial, and had to do with the false doctrine of sin contagion. The rabbis taught that coming into contact with sinful people or their unclean property made you unclean. Then, if you ate with unclean hands, the moral filth would be taken into yourself.

So they would hold their hands with fingers upward, and an eggshell of water was poured, running down the fingers and off at the wrist. Then, they pointed the fingers down and water was dribbled onto the wrists, running off the fingertips. The subject rubbed one palm with the opposite fist, and then the reverse. That's it. There was a blessing to recite while doing the washing. You could wash your own hands one at a time. Or sometimes a servant would do both of your hands at once.

Jewish teaching at this time was formalistic as we have seen. They made a huge deal of this washing. According to Rabbi Asi, concerning anyone who eats bread without washing his hands, "It is as if he engaged in sexual intercourse with a prostitute.[2]

Jesus' View

Jesus rejected this practice because it was based on false doctrine. Mark includes more background for Jesus' rejection of the practice.

> The Pharisees and all the Jews do not eat unless they carefully wash their hands, thus observing the traditions of the elders; and when they come from the marketplace, they do not eat unless they cleanse themselves; and there are many other things which they have received in order to observe, such as the washing of cups and pitchers and copper pots. (Mark 7:3-4)

Notice Mark's identification of the source of these teachings—the elders, not the Bible.

The vessels need to be cleansed when returning from the market, because that's where you come into contact with Gentiles, Samaritans, or prostitutes. Even occupying air recently contaminated by a sinner would cause uncleanness. They had no way to know if they were contaminated,

2. *Talmud* Sotah 4b. Another example is *Talmud* Shabbat 62b, "Three matters bring a person to a state of poverty as a divine punishment from Heaven: One who urinates before his bed while naked, and one who demeans the ritual washing of the hands, and one whose wife curses him in his presence." Read other reasons and techniques for washing vessels in B. Pesachim 30b.

so constant washing was the answer. Interestingly, the outside of a hot pot was the part most likely to become impure, according to this view, because defiled air would blow against it. Jesus saw that as a picture of their thinking as we'll see.

Jesus thought their external fussing was absurd. When they asked him why he and his disciples didn't wash:

> Jesus replied, "You hypocrites! Isaiah was right when he prophesied about you, for he wrote, 'These people honor me with their lips, but their hearts are far from me. Their worship is a farce, for they teach man-made ideas as commands from God.'" (Mark 7:6-7 NLT)

He correctly labeled the handwashing as "man-made." Even though washing is prescribed rarely in the Old Testament, the rabbis in Jesus' day had so expanded the practice that it no longer resembled the original. In particular, the belief that being around certain kinds of people made you impure was false. In the Old Testament, nonbelievers were usually called "sojourners," meaning foreigners. God's word says, "You must show love to foreigners, for you yourselves were once foreigners in the land of Egypt" (Deuteronomy 10:19, also Exodus 23:9). So they were to love foreigners, not avoid them. No wonder Jesus said, "You ignore God's law and substitute your own tradition" (Mark 7:8 NLT).

Jesus Pressed His Attack

He tried to explain why the rabbis were wrong:

> Jesus called to the crowd to come and hear. "All of you listen," he said, "and try to understand. There is nothing outside the man which can defile him if it goes into him; but the things which proceed out of the man are what defile the man." (Mark 7:14-15 NLT)

His explanation seems clear enough, but it didn't work:

> When he had left the crowd and entered the house, his disciples questioned him about the parable. And he said to them, "Are you so lacking in understanding also?" (Mark 7:17-18)

You can feel Jesus' frustration and amazement at their blindness. He tried again:

> "Do you not understand that whatever goes into the man from outside cannot defile him, because it does not go into his heart, but into his stomach, and is eliminated?" (Mark 7:18-19)

Jesus treats food for what it is—matter. We metabolize and discard food; that should be obvious. But food isn't spiritual, and doesn't affect the spirit. In this he showed that he wasn't subject to the superstitious views of his age—not just in Judaism, but in all religions—that assigned various spiritual properties to foods.

Mark adds the aside, "Thus he declared all foods clean" (Mark 7:19). That's an important statement, given that the Old Covenant used dietary laws as we saw earlier for teaching or for health reasons. Those laws had all served their purpose, and Jesus set them all aside. He went on:

> "That which proceeds out of the man, that is what defiles the man. For from within, out of the heart of men, proceed the evil thoughts, fornications, thefts, murders, adulteries, deeds of coveting and wickedness, as well as deceit, sensuality, envy, slander, pride and foolishness. All these evil things proceed from within and defile the man." (Mark 7:20-23)

Here is the appeal of a formalistic, external view of sin and righteousness. Admitting that my lust, selfishness, and deceit are generated by me—not inflicted on me from the outside—that offends human pride. It's easier to think, "I'm righteous enough, but these sinners keep smearing their scum all over me!" Jesus found that view intolerable.

Jesus' View

This brings us back to the dinner in Luke, where Jesus laid the related charge:

> "You Pharisees are so careful to clean the outside of the cup and the dish, but inside you are filthy—full of greed and wickedness! Fools! Didn't God make the inside as well as the outside? So clean the inside by giving gifts to the poor, and you will be clean all over." (vs. 39-41 NLT)

Cleaning the outside of cups and dishes is a metaphor here, but it was also literally what they did. In Numbers 31:22-23 the Jews were ordered to cleanse pots and pans they had won from their enemy, the Midianites.

So this was an unusual situation, calling for recognition that this booty was from unbelievers. The vessels may well have been used in evil religious practices. Such cleansing would have been quite rare.

But under Pharisaic teaching, just superficial contact with unclean people imparted uncleanness. Their fussing over external cleanliness is typical of their focus on the outward, not on the inward, where the real problem lay. On the other hand, giving to the poor was an example of a real good deed, not silly fussing over externals. Again, we see the contrast between the inner transformation Jesus advanced, and the external religiosity he deplored.

Jesus Pressed His Attack Further

Jesus was probably looking around at dumbfounded, uncomprehending faces, or even disapproving frowns. He went on:

> "What sorrow awaits you Pharisees! For you are careful to tithe even the tiniest income from your herb gardens, but you ignore justice and the love of God. You should tithe, yes, but do not neglect the more important things." (v. 42 NLT)

This is the "straining out the gnat and swallowing the camel" we studied earlier in connection with their fascination with fasting. Here, the focus is on washing, but it's the same problem. They were ignoring truly important spiritual and moral teaching, like explaining how loving God is, and how that love leads us to gain a loving character.

At the same time, they were distracting attention to relatively pointless, or even false details of outward performance. To God, outward religion without authentic following in the heart is worthless, and is actually an insult to God.

And what about the Pharisees' motivations? Jesus threw the blanket back revealing what was really going on:

> "What sorrow awaits you Pharisees! For you love to sit in the seats of honor in the synagogues and receive respectful greetings as you walk in the marketplaces. Yes, what sorrow awaits you! For you are like hidden graves in a field. People walk over them without knowing the corruption they are stepping on." (vs. 43-44 NLT)

This was an age and a culture that admired religiosity, unlike our secular culture today. And Jesus knew that the Pharisees were playing to this admiration, basking in the impression that they were deep men of God.

Old Testament law taught that touching a corpse or walking over a grave made one unclean for seven days—not that it was a sin, but that it was to remind people that the consequence of sin is death (Numbers 19:16).

As a result, Jews clearly marked graves with white-washed stones. But the Pharisees were like graves with no markers. The people were being taken in by their fake version of spirituality without realizing it. It was defiling because self-righteous showing off is contagious. The people were falsely concluding that this is what it meant to follow God.

And The Scribes Too

Not only Pharisees were present.

> "Teacher," said an expert in religious law, "you have insulted us, too, in what you just said." (v. 45 NLT)

These were the rabbis; experts in the Old Testament Scriptures. They were also the creators of the vast body of "oral law," or *halakhah*. The scribes claimed that God gave these extra laws to Moses on Mount Sinai but had not been written down.

From there, they claimed the body of law had been passed down orally from his time to theirs—fourteen hundred years later. In that way, they were able to claim divine inspiration for their teachings, when in fact, they were man-made, and not from God. Not a shred of evidence points to it going back to Moses. In fact, it was developed in the inter-testamental period, from 400 BC to the first century AD.

The rabbis later wrote this oral law down after the destruction of the temple in AD 70. That writing became the *Mishnah*, completed around AD 220, but made up of teaching from the time of Jesus and earlier. Later, rabbis continued to debate and expand the *Mishnah* many times over. When these teachings or "*Gemara*" were added to the *Mishnah*, the result was the *Talmud*, completed around AD 400.

Jesus called their teaching "man-made tradition" and charged that the effect of their elaborations was that "You are experts at setting aside the commandment of God in order to keep your tradition." (Mark 7:9).

Then he lit into the rabbis:

> "Yes," said Jesus, "What sorrow also awaits you experts in religious law! For you crush people with unbearable religious demands, and you never lift a finger to ease the burden." (v. 46 NLT)

Jesus wasn't exaggerating when he described their laws as "unbearable religious demands." We've seen numerous examples already in previous chapters, and those are just the tip of the iceberg.

Is having traditions and oral law necessarily that bad? Yes!

First, this law was not from Moses. By claiming that it came through Moses, these men were adding their own opinions to Scripture, and they weren't authorized to do that. Leaders need to always keep crystal clear the difference between the word of God and the word of man. Anytime people add to God's word, they end up nullifying his word.

Secondly, as we saw earlier, these picky detailed rules paint an extremely negative, even ugly, picture of God as a demanding, hard to please enforcer of nonsense rules. As Jesus said, people's faith is crushed by this legalistic thinking.

A Dire Prophecy

> "What sorrow awaits you! For you build monuments for the prophets your own ancestors killed long ago. But in fact, you stand as witnesses who agree with what your ancestors did." (vs. 47-48)

The scribes outwardly revered the prophets who wrote the Old Testament, but they weren't honoring the Scriptures the prophets wrote. Ironically they were already trying to figure out how to kill Jesus.

So Jesus uttered a prophecy from God, saying he was going to send more apostles and prophets and the leadership would kill them as well (v. 49). Luke goes on in his next book to recount how they fulfilled that prophecy, first by killing Jesus. Then they killed a righteous leader named Stephen. Then, under the leadership of a ferocious Pharisee named Saul, they killed, tortured, and imprisoned believers in an all-out attack intended to annihilate Jesus' followers.

Finally, Jesus warned,

> "So that the blood of all the prophets, shed since the foundation of the world, may be charged against this generation." (v. 50)

Why was that generation any different than earlier ones? For one thing, their forebears attacked prophets sent to predict the Messiah. These leaders were attacking the Messiah himself! Then, too, the volume of miracles they witnessed far exceeded anything since at least the time of Moses.[3]

This idea of Jesus' skeptics escalating their acts of evil matches the parable of the evil tenants later in Luke (20:9-16).

The Big Picture

Jesus vigorously denounced the religious status quo and the leaders who created it. He summarized his verdict saying,

> "What sorrow awaits you experts in religious law! For you remove the key to knowledge from the people. You don't enter the Kingdom yourselves, and you prevent others from entering." (v. 52 NLT)

That's really the point. It's bad enough that these religious men weren't entering into the kingdom, or that they were replacing God's word with their own. But they were also preventing others from entering. That made them enemies who Jesus had to fight. It wasn't a case of different sides trying to win a debate. The issue here was people missing the grace of God and losing their souls. Out of his love for the people who were missing a relationship with God, Jesus had to express fury.

His words failed to draw any response from his critics except more anger and hate.

> As Jesus was leaving, the teachers of religious law and the Pharisees became hostile and tried to provoke him with many

3. Jesus says his generation will be guilty of the death of prophets "from the blood of Abel to the blood of Zechariah, who was killed between the altar and the house of God" (v. 51). We aren't sure who Zechariah was, based on his description here. He was probably the biblical Zechariah, author of the book by that name. Taking Josephus's order of the canon, Jesus' placing of Zechariah as last in a series could well refer to the canonical order rather than a chronological order.

> questions. They wanted to trap him into saying something they could use against him. (vs. 53-54 NLT)

Jesus knew he was aggravating his opponents. It was all part of the plan.

24

Jesus on Materialism

Luke 12

Large crowds were still showing up, numbering in the thousands. But teaching like that in Luke 12 would soon thin out those crowds.

Before teaching the multitudes, Jesus went aside to his disciples and said, "Beware of the leaven of the Pharisees, which is hypocrisy" (Luke 12:1). Hypocrisy in the context of the Pharisees is a type of lying where you pretend you're more spiritual or righteous than you really are. Having the community show up to hear what you have to say can be quite exhilarating and people are tempted to compete and show off in order to gain a hearing. God is displeased.

You get a feel for how dangerous hypocrisy is by looking at the case of Ananias and Sapphira in Acts 5. They pretended to be more sacrificial than they really were by claiming they had sold a piece of land and given the proceeds for the needs of God's people. In fact, they had only given part. So they were exaggerating what they gave, probably in order to impress their friends with their spirituality. Is that so terrible?

God let people know what he thought when he struck both of them dead! As believers, they probably went to heaven, so they didn't suffer. But their friends left alive stood staring at two dead bodies. That left quite an impression—don't go this way! The early church was just getting underway, so God probably decided to nip hypocrisy in the bud. Given the religious environment in Jerusalem, it would have been natural for believers to imitate what they had grown up with under the Pharisees and scribes.

We've already seen how the Pharisees and scribes were show-offs, and how Jesus deplored it. Hypocrisy is extremely dangerous. It replaces honest, humble transparency with showy, false attention-getting. It's highly contagious. Just a few members flaunting their awesomeness is enough to make struggling young believers feel unable to open up. They cover up their sin problems. And that removes one of the keys to victory over sin—bringing it into the light.

Everything Uncovered

Jesus critiqued hypocrisy with one clear fact. We can fool people, but we can't fool God. And he's going to bring everything to light anyway:

> "There is nothing covered up that will not be revealed, and hidden that will not be known. Accordingly, whatever you have said in the dark will be heard in the light, and what you have whispered in the inner rooms will be proclaimed upon the housetops." (vs. 2-3)

Secrecy is where sin grows and worsens. Coming out with the truth to trusted friends is the gateway to accessing God's wisdom and the support you need.

At the root of self-righteous faking is the deeper problem of man-pleasing. People without God in their lives (and many who do have him in their lives) draw their sense of wellbeing from the approval of others. Or, to avoid self-doubt, they avoid disapproval from others. In either case, they end up basing their security and sense of identity on the opinions of other people—a constantly at-risk source of security. Not surprisingly, it leads to more insecurity.

Jesus puts his finger on the problem:

> "I say to you, my friends, do not be afraid of those who kill the body and after that have no more that they can do. But I

will warn you whom to fear: fear the One who, after he has killed, has authority to cast into hell; yes, I tell you, fear him!" (vs. 4-5)

It's not that Jesus wants us to be scared of God. His point is, why are we scared of what people think when they are so far below God? If you're going to be worried about what someone thinks, why not worry about what God thinks?

And when it comes to what God thinks, the news is good.

> "What is the price of five sparrows—two copper coins? Yet God does not forget a single one of them. And the very hairs on your head are all numbered. So don't be afraid; you are more valuable to God than a whole flock of sparrows." (vs. 6-7 NLT)

So it's not only God's power and sovereignty that point toward focusing on what he thinks, it's also his omniscience and love. Jesus is clear that God's knowledge penetrates into even the tiniest details of life. In Matthew's version of this same discourse Jesus said, "Are not two sparrows sold for a cent? And yet not one of them will fall to the ground apart from your Father" (Matthew 10:29). It doesn't mean that God pushed the sparrow out of the nest, but that even the most minute things are permitted by God. Knowing and causing are different concepts.

This is really an *a fortiori* argument. If God can keep track of sparrows and the number of hairs on your head, how much more can he keep track of significant events and trends in your life? It shuts down the common thought: "How can the creator of the universe care about my little problems?" He does! And it's no strain for him to care about millions of people at once. We don't have any way to understand omniscience, because we have no frame of reference for it. But Jesus and the rest of Scripture are clear about God's absolute omniscience and his heartfelt care for our lives. It's an article of faith for people who believe God's word.

Confessing or Denying

Jesus then offered a stark choice:

> "And I say to you, everyone who confesses me before men, the Son of Man will confess him also before the angels of God;

> but he who denies me before men will be denied before the angels of God." (vs. 8-9)

The word here for "confess" means to say the same thing, or to agree. That means accepting his teaching and claims. To deny him could mean to deny something you already have. But the word *arneomai* can also mean to reject, to refuse something offered. That seems to be the usage here. The question is whether people accept or reject Christ.

Along the same lines, he said,

> "And everyone who speaks a word against the Son of Man, it will be forgiven him; but he who blasphemes against the Holy Spirit, it will not be forgiven him." (v. 10)

The statement is enigmatic for the simple reason that he doesn't define what constitutes blaspheming the Spirit. Blasphemy is a strong term, signifying railing against, insulting, or mocking. It's probably like the leaders saying Jesus' miraculous power came from Beelzebub.

Some have suggested that blaspheming the Spirit is simply refusing the gospel until you die. But the tense of the verb here is *aorist*, which means blaspheming is an event that happens at a point in time. It could refer to a point of no return, where the Spirit has fully revealed Jesus to a person, and the answer is still no (John 16:8, 13). In that case, a person's state becomes hopeless.

At a deeper level, it's not important that we don't know exactly what blaspheming the Spirit is. What is important is that we know such a thing exists. That was important for Jesus' hearers to know. Jesus was warning that they could mock and deny him for a time, but there's a limit. Clearly, we all reach that limit when we die. But this passage suggests we can reach that limit while we're still alive.

God said through Hosea, "Ephraim is joined to idols; Let him alone" (Hosea 4:17). He told Jeremiah, "Pray no more for these people, Jeremiah. Do not weep or pray for them, for I will not listen to them when they cry out to me in distress" (Jeremiah 11:14). That's about as bad as it gets, when God himself has given up on you. But he knows the state of people's hearts, and he knows when it's hopeless. Knowing that there is a limit—a place of no return—is a needed warning for those resisting the gospel. You never know when you might cross an invisible line of no return.[1]

When You're Arrested

In connection with his earlier prophecy about the violence to come, he told his followers,

> "When they bring you before the synagogues and the rulers and the authorities, do not worry about how or what you are to speak in your defense, or what you are to say; for the Holy Spirit will teach you in that very hour what you ought to say." (vs. 11-12)

It's not an instruction to avoid preparing for your sermon or teaching. This is about a specific situation that you may never experience—having to give a defense to an arresting power.

The Rich Fool

A man in the crowd tried to tattle on his brother for not sharing the family fortune, but Jesus refused to get involved. Instead, he began to teach on money.

> Then He said to them, "Beware, and be on your guard against every form of greed; for not even when one has an abundance does his life consist of his possessions." (v. 15)

"Greed" in Greek is *pleonexia*—the desire for more. It's a self-reinforcing force in the lives of most people. To explain how God looks at greed, Jesus told the parable of the rich fool:

> "The land of a rich man was very productive. And he began reasoning to himself, saying, 'What shall I do, since I have no place to store my crops?'" (vs. 16-17)

It was the land that was productive, not the man. The man was already rich as this verse makes clear. He was fortunate. He was under God's

1. Is this point of no return the same as John's "sin unto death?" (1 John 5:16). That's possible, but again, John doesn't define what this sin is. And a major problem is the question of how anyone would know that a sin unto death has occurred. Some answer that a sin unto death means a sin resulting in physical death, like Ananias and Sapphira (Acts 5:1-10), or those Corinthians Paul said had died for disciplinary reasons (1 Corinthians 11:30). But there is no clear reason to link either of these passages with the notion of blaspheming the Holy Spirit.

blessing. To be rich and to own a very productive farm . . . this story starts out with a happy setting. It could have stayed happy and even become happier. But something is missing. Where is the acknowledgment of his blessedness? Where is the thanksgiving?

The rich man only had one problem—he was reaping more grain than he had room for. At that point, he made a fatal decision. He decided to accumulate unnecessary wealth.

> "Then he said, 'This is what I will do: I will tear down my barns and build larger ones, and there I will store all my grain and my goods.'" (v. 18)

He spoke of barns in the plural. So he's going to tear down two or more barns and replace them with larger barns. Why? What's the point? He's not suggesting he needs the extra grain, because he's already producing more than he can consume or store. He imagines a life of pleasure:

> "And I will say to my soul, 'Soul, you have many goods laid up for many years to come; take your ease, eat, drink, and be merry.'" (v. 19)

All of this is a plan in the rich man's mind. But we can assume that he also carried his plan out, because God refers to his great riches in the next verse.

Note that resting, eating, drinking, and being merry are not sinful. That's not what Jesus criticized. The sinfulness came in because of the base the rich man laid for his partying. God had no place in his plans. He trusted that accumulated riches would be an adequate basis for a merry life. Was there a point where the man realized he had enough? Doubtful. That's not how *pleonexia* works. At each level of attainment, the one in the grip of greed sees where a bit more is needed.

If he had based his feasting on celebrating what he had accomplished for God, and on his future with God, his partying would have been a good thing.

Suddenly, God intruded with his opinion:

> "But God said to him, 'You fool! This very night your soul is required of you; and now who will own what you have prepared?'" (v. 20)

This is no different than Jesus' haunting earlier question, "For what is a man profited if he gains the whole world, and loses or forfeits himself?" (9:25). It might seem like an unexpected fate suddenly befell the rich man. But he knew this was coming. He didn't know when, but he certainly knew it was coming. Now all his planning and achievement come under God's verdict: You fool!

Did he go to hell? The parable doesn't say that. This could easily be a believer acting as a fool. If the man was a believer, what he did was even more foolish.

Jesus gave the meaning of the parable:

> "So is the man who stores up treasure for himself, and is not rich toward God." (v. 21)

Storing up treasure for yourself is bad. Jesus said point blank, "Do not store up for yourselves treasures on earth" (Matthew 6:19). It's unnecessary, and other people need that money, so it's selfish.[2] Once he made the decision to store up treasure, it almost guaranteed that he would not be rich toward God because, as Jesus said, "Where your treasure is, there your heart will be also" (v. 34).

Avarice

Jesus wasn't teaching against philosophical materialism. He was teaching against greed for wealth or material gain. People lapse into avarice because of unbelief that God will care for them. The unbelief results in worry and anxiety, which in turn causes the avaricious person to long for ever more money and possessions. It's a vicious circle.

> And He said to His disciples, "For this reason I say to you, do not worry about your life, as to what you will eat; nor for your body, as to what you will put on. For life is more than food, and the body more than clothing." (vs. 22-23)

2. An interesting case to consider is saving for retirement. In modern, western culture, people save and invest money, usually in vast amounts, so they can retire from their career and continue to receive an income. In most cases, financial advisors are planning for twenty-five or more years of income (between when they retire and their death). Some of the income comes from social security (if you've paid into it) and investment profit. But that still leaves hundreds of thousands of dollars that a typical couple needs to save up. Is that laying up treasure on earth? Often it is, especially when the intent is to bequeath a fortune to the kids. On the other hand, saving a responsible sum that enables you to avoid being a burden to others can be reasonable.

Worry is inversely proportional to trust. As your trust in God's goodness rises, your anxiety decreases. Anxiety is pointless and destructive. Jesus asked, "Which of you by worrying can add a single hour to his life's span?" The correct answer is "no one." In fact, anxiety shortens your life.

> "If then you cannot do even a very little thing, why do you worry about other matters? Consider the lilies, how they grow: they neither toil nor spin; but I tell you, not even Solomon in all his glory clothed himself like one of these. But if God so clothes the grass in the field, which is alive today and tomorrow is thrown into the furnace, how much more will He clothe you?" (vs. 26-28)

This is another *a fortiori* argument. If God arrays the flowers or the grass, which are destined for the fire, and have only brief, temporary value, how much more would he care for his very valuable and eternal people? And he gives the reason for their problem of worry: "You men of little faith!" (v. 28).

> "And do not seek what you will eat and what you will drink, and do not keep worrying. For all these things the nations of the world eagerly seek; but your Father knows that you need these things. (vs. 29-30)

The nations here (*ta ethne*) are the peoples who don't know God. They are "of the world" that is, the cosmos, or world system. Satan constructed the world system for the expressed purpose of drawing people away from God. He is able to confuse people, resulting in them putting their trust in money, often based on fear.

Paul says,

> And even if our gospel is veiled, it is veiled to those who are perishing, in whose case the god of this world has blinded the minds of the unbelieving so that they might not see the light of the gospel of the glory of Christ. (2 Corinthians 4:3-4)

"The god of this world" here is Satan. He is able to blind the minds of unbelieving people to the point where they focus on money as though it lasts forever. They are blind to the fact that their money is very temporary, and like with the rich fool, will suddenly become worthless.

Instead of that pattern, Jesus says:

> "Sell your possessions and give to charity; make yourselves money belts which do not wear out, an unfailing treasure in heaven, where no thief comes near nor moth destroys. For where your treasure is, there your heart will be also." (vs. 33-34)

Some read this and conclude that Jesus wants his people to be poor after giving all they own away. To the contrary, God wants his people to become rich, especially when they gain true riches that last forever. Earthly wealth is always at risk, so no wonder it produces anxiety.

Wealth that disappears shortly after you earn it is not worthwhile. Jesus was expressing disappointment that people were expending so much effort and worry on something that simply isn't worth it.

Making enough money to eat and get needed clothes is fine; not buying a whole new wardrobe every year to keep up with fashion. And Jesus promised in this discourse that God will make available the means to meet those needs: "Seek His kingdom, and these things will be added to you" (v. 31). Matthew's version adds, "Seek *first* the kingdom of God. . . ." "First" here means of highest priority.

Many believers are unaware that most worrying is a sin. But Jesus said right here, "Do not keep worrying" (v. 29). That's an imperative, to be obeyed if we're going to follow Jesus. Worrying about something never changes it. It just wears you out emotionally and, trashes your faith and joy. This is such a serious matter that it's believed to be the most common command in Scripture. Observers claim, "Fear not," or similar, is in the Bible 365 times—equal to once for each day of the year. I haven't counted, but I know there are a lot.

Probably the most important cure for anxiety is thanksgiving. The apostle Paul said:

> Be anxious for nothing, but in everything by prayer and supplication *with thanksgiving* let your requests be made known to God. And the peace of God, which surpasses all comprehension, will guard your hearts and your minds in Christ Jesus. (Philippians 4:6-7, emphasis mine)

The order here is crucial—first we abandon our anxiety in favor of prayer, and that prayer must include thanksgiving. It's a key trigger to the soul—a time of remembering God's faithfulness and how it applies to the current situation. And it's a time of remembering what he promised in his word. Thanksgiving flips a switch that turns on our ability to appreciate. Only then will the peace of God guard your heart.

Readiness

The rich fool wasn't ready for what happened when the Lord came to bring him to account. Jesus warned the crowd:

> "Be dressed in readiness, and keep your lamps lit. Be like men who are waiting for their master when he returns from the wedding feast, so that they may immediately open the door to him when he comes and knocks. Blessed are those servants whom the master will find on the alert when he comes; truly I say to you, that he will gird himself to serve, and have them recline at the table, and will come up and wait on them." (vs. 35-37)

This short simile has strong echoes of the parable of the ten virgins in Matthew 25.[3] In fact, this might be a condensation of that story. Both stories imply that the master will depart for an indefinite time. Jesus was hinting again that he has two comings, but they didn't grasp that.

In Matthew's account, ten virgins are waiting for a wedding party. Five were said to be wise because they brought extra oil in case the groom came later than expected. The other five were foolish because they failed to bring extra. When the foolish virgins began to run out of oil, they asked the wise virgins for some of theirs. But the wise virgins pointed out that they now needed their extra, lest they, too, run out.

So, as the foolish virgins went into town to buy more oil, the bridegroom arrived. The whole procession went in, and the door was locked. When the foolish virgins arrived later, they knocked on the door and pleaded to be let in. But the groom said he didn't know them (Matthew 25:1-13).

Jesus' point in both this parable in Matthew and the statements here in Luke is the same—nobody knows when the Son of Man will return.

3. What are we to make of Matthew and Mark delivering this material after the Olivet discourse? The accounts are not identical, but close. Scholars argue that this part comes from the Q source with additional material. Did Luke just put it here because Jesus was talking about the final judgment? Or did Jesus give these statements more than once? It hardly matters. The concepts are the same.

People feel like they want to be ready, but they need to know the time and date so they can plan ahead. But that's not how it works. Nobody knows the time or the date. Only one thing guarantees readiness, and that's to be ready all the time. Readiness becomes an attitude, a mindset that controls the rest of your life. Each thought and plan goes before the examination of the readiness board in your mind. Does this enhance or decrease my readiness? Can I do this without damaging my readiness?

Jesus summarized his meaning:

> "You too, be ready; for the Son of Man is coming at an hour that you do not expect." (v. 40)

For Leaders

Then Peter asked if the lesson was for the Twelve, or for the rest of the public. At that point, Jesus told another parable:

> And the Lord said, "Who then is the faithful and sensible steward, whom his master will put in charge of his servants, to give them their rations at the proper time? Blessed is that servant whom his master finds so doing when he comes. Truly I say to you that he will put him in charge of all his possessions." (vs. 42-44)

The difference here is that this servant has extra responsibility and higher accountability. He is a leader, a manager of the master's household. So even as the Twelve were given the stewardship of feeding and caring for the people of God, subsequent leaders fill the same role.

Leaders in the church throughout church history have proven to be a very mixed lot. As Jesus foresaw:

> "But if that slave says in his heart, 'My master will be a long time in coming,' and begins to beat the slaves, both men and women, and to eat and drink and get drunk; the master of that slave will come on a day when he does not expect him and at an hour he does not know, and will cut him in pieces, and assign him a place with the unbelievers." (vs. 45-46)

The rough handling these bandits get shows how God views those who would use church positions to serve themselves and take advantage of their people. This is one of the most serious crimes one can commit. Jesus later confirmed the point with strong language (17:1-2).

Different Punishments

We saw earlier that when God gives out rewards in heaven, some receive more than others. Likewise, when giving out punishments, not all are alike.

> "And that slave who knew his master's will and did not get ready or act in accord with his will, will receive many lashes, but the one who did not know it, and committed deeds worthy of a flogging, will receive but few." (vs. 47-48)

This is the passage that gave rise to the medieval concept of levels in hell. Whether that's true or not, it is clear that punishment will be more severe for some than others. That's fair. Why should some isolated tribe member who failed to respond to common grace suffer the same sentence as Adolf Hitler? According to some scenarios (like Dante's *Inferno*) the suffering for some might be so light that it's really not suffering at all.

This is the Catholic concept of "limbo." It's a place where people are in no pain other than the fact that they regret not making it into heaven. Protestants mostly reject this concept, mainly because they see it as yet another Catholic invention. But in this case, there is some biblical warrant. I think it's worth asking how any eternal punishment could be described as receiving "but few" lashes. It must be very mild indeed.

The legal principle in view is clear enough:

> From everyone who has been given much, much will be required; and to whom they entrusted much, of him they will ask all the more. (v. 48)

The principle here is that culpability depends on what you've been given. That's why false preachers will be judged so harshly. They know exactly what they're doing. Likewise, every time a person hears the gospel they become more culpable than before. This is why babies go to heaven (2 Samuel 12:23). No doubt some disabled people do as well.

Division

Jesus then squared up and announced something that was sure to shock his hearers:

> "I have come to cast fire upon the earth; and how I wish it were already kindled! But I have a baptism to undergo, and how distressed I am until it is accomplished! Do you suppose that I came to grant peace on earth? I tell you, no, but rather division; for from now on five members in one household will be divided, three against two and two against three. They will be divided, father against son and son against father, mother against daughter and daughter against mother, mother-in-law against daughter-in-law and daughter-in-law against mother-in-law." (vs. 49-53)

Casting fire upon the earth refers to the offensive that Jesus was about to launch through the early church. For the first time, the people of God would launch an all-out attack on the world system, winning people and gaining ground for God. The fire he cast onto the earth is the fire of spiritual warfare (2 Corinthians 10:3-5; Ephesians 6:10-18).

The Messiah is called "the prince of peace" (Isaiah 9:6). Throughout Old Testament prophecy the Messianic era is one of peace. "And they will hammer their swords into plowshares and their spears into pruning hooks. Nation will not lift up sword against nation, and never again will they learn war" (Isaiah 2:4).

But that's for later. Jesus said no, rather, he brings division. This militant aspect of Jesus offends many. Instead of the picture of Jesus carrying a lamb, here he is wielding a sword.

He specifically mentions division in the home, and anyone active in evangelism has seen this over and over again, when a family attacks a new believer's faith, even issuing ultimatums. The best strategy is to win over the non-believing family as well, but that isn't always possible. The new believer is left wondering what to do. Surrender? Failure to surrender could mean the loss of tens of thousands of dollars in tuition support. A person could even be ejected from his or her family. That was especially true in Jesus' day.

Over the years, we have found that new converts who go too far in trying to appease angry relatives fare the worst. The family becomes an ever-tightening net, eventually stifling out the young believer's walk.

Family threats to remove a believer from the family or to cut them off financially are often saber-rattling. When the believer graciously says he's sorry they feel that way, but it won't change his beliefs, the family soon begins to realize that their ploy didn't work, and they change their tactics. It's not uncommon at this point to see a new openness from the rest of the family.

The main point in Jesus' saying is that believers are going to have to be prepared to suffer and to fight. We fight for our own faith when suffering rejection and persecution. We fight by trying to overcome evil with good" (Romans 12:21).

The Big Picture

Jesus knew he still wasn't really gaining traction with the multitudes. They were curious, they were watching, listening, but too many were not deciding to definitely believe. It's sadly possible to listen to a lot of Bible teaching without it resulting in an active commitment of the will. He told them,

> "When you see a cloud rising in the west, immediately you say, 'A shower is coming,' and so it turns out. And when you see a south wind blowing, you say, 'It will be a hot day,' and it turns out that way. You hypocrites! You know how to analyze the appearance of the earth and the sky, but why do you not analyze this present time?" (vs. 54-56)

Mark and Matthew have something close to this statement in the Olivet Discourse. There, it's about the need to recognize the end times. Here in Luke, it refers to the crowd failing to recognize the obvious presence of God's power backing his son. They were smart enough to analyze the weather, but too blind to see what was right before their eyes. Once again, Jesus was angry that people could see so many miracles and fail to connect the dots.

Jesus knew the time was short for his ongoing ministry, so he warned the people:

> "While you are going with your opponent to appear before

> the magistrate, on your way there make an effort to settle with him, so that he may not drag you before the judge, and the judge turn you over to the officer, and the officer throw you into prison. I say to you, you will not get out of there until you have paid the very last cent." (vs. 58-59)

This quip is about being smart enough to realize when further resistance is futile. Note that in this day they had debtors' prisons. To them, not repaying a loan was the same as stealing. We've gotten away from that in modern times.

In this illustration, Jesus implies that they really do owe the debt—similar to the sentence of death they owe God. So the last place you want to settle matters is before the judge. That can have only one outcome—prison. The time to surrender is now, and nothing was blocking them from that but their own pride.

Chinese author, Watchman Nee explains what he calls "the thing in hand."

> Suppose a father asks his son to do a certain thing. The son answers, "Right now I have something in my hand; as soon as I finish it I will do what you order." "The thing in hand" is the thing which the son is doing prior to his father's orders.[4]

Or we could say the thing in hand is what he is doing "*instead* of the father's orders." It amounts to the same thing. Many of Jesus' listeners were non-committal. They weren't necessarily against Jesus, but they weren't throwing their trust into him either. As a result, their debt remained, and the clock was ticking.

4. Watchman Nee, *The Release of the Spirit* (New York: Sure Foundation Publishers, 1965), 31.

25

Repentance
Luke 13

In the same setting, Jesus again attacked the rabbis' karma-like worldview:

> Now on the same occasion there were some present who reported to him about the Galileans whose blood Pilate had mixed with their sacrifices. And Jesus said to them, "Do you suppose that these Galileans were greater sinners than all other Galileans because they suffered this fate?" (Luke 13:1-2)

It's important to realize that a rabbi of his day would answer, "Well, Pilate did kill them, and I'm sure God wouldn't be unfair, so yes! They must have done something pretty bad to deserve their fate."

Jesus utterly rejected their view:

> "I tell you, no, but unless you repent, you will all likewise perish. Or do you suppose that those eighteen on whom the tower in Siloam fell and killed them were worse culprits than all the men who live in Jerusalem? I tell you, no, but unless you repent, you will all likewise perish." (vs. 3-5)

Jesus rejected the religious tendency to read God's hand of judgment into natural tragedies. That superstitious view suggests that the recipients of tragedy are more sinful than others. Jesus instead affirms the sinfulness of all people. Blaming God is also arrogant, because the observer has no way to know whether God was involved in causing a tragic event.

Not only first century Jews, but modern-day fundamentalists habitually make these claims, bringing disgrace on God. One well-known preacher dared to announce that the 2003 tsunami that killed a quarter-million people was God's judgment on Islam and Hinduism. Another declared that the tragic flooding of New Orleans from Hurricane Katrina was God's judgment for the sin of that city. As we saw earlier, this is the same sin of presumption Job's friends committed.

Jesus' denial here is also important because it affirms the scientific worldview over the spiritualistic view. The best explanation for why the tower fell on these people is physics. A shaky tower, gravity, and the location of the people under the tower resulted in their death—simple cause and effect. But if the real explanation is that God dropped the tower to punish those people, why study physics at all? Those who attribute all events to the actions of spirits or of God are reflecting animism—a pre-scientific worldview not backed by Scripture or by Jesus as this passage shows.

Of course God could have caused the event. Our worldview can best be described as "uniformity of cause and effect in an open system." That means that a real cause and effect sequence is in motion that can be measured and described by science. But God can and does intrude into the cause-and-effect sequence; that's why it's an open system.

Any suggestion that God never causes anything is the blind-faith position of materialism. But the suggestion that everything is caused by God is also an unwarranted claim denied by Jesus. Of course God created the system, so in that sense he is the ultimate cause. But unless he says he did it, we have no reason to ascribe specific events to God's action. In this case, Jesus said it was not an act of God.

The Unfruitful Fig Tree

Again Jesus warned them that the time to respond in faith was limited:

> And he began telling this parable: "A man had a fig tree which had been planted in his vineyard; and he came looking for fruit on it and did not find any. And he said to the vineyard-keeper, 'Behold, for three years I have come looking for fruit on this

> fig tree without finding any. Cut it down! Why does it even use up the ground?' And he answered and said to him, 'Let it alone, sir, for this year too, until I dig around it and put in fertilizer; and if it bears fruit next year, fine; but if not, cut it down.'" (vs. 6-9)

This parable is strikingly similar to one in Isaiah 5:1–7. That version starts out almost identical to Jesus' version here. But in that one, it's already too late. In this one, he offers one more chance to change. One more year to be fertilized, weeded, and cultivated. If it again bears no good fruit, it will be cut down.

The extra year probably stands for Jesus' own ministry and the remarkable miracles recorded in the early chapters of Acts. Jesus was warning the people that they need to respond to what God was showing them, and the time was limited. Was it coincidence that Jesus had been in his ministry for about three years at this time?

The farmer who plants an olive tree has every right to expect it to bear fruit. This is hardly wrong or out of line. Especially in the face of so many miracles and wonders, they had no excuse for their unbelief.

An Afflicted Woman

> He was teaching in one of the synagogues on the Sabbath. And there was a woman who for eighteen years had had a sickness caused by a spirit; and she was bent double, and could not straighten up at all. When Jesus saw her, he called her over and said to her, "Woman, you are freed from your sickness." And he laid his hands on her; and immediately she was made erect again and began glorifying God.
>
> But the synagogue official, indignant because Jesus had healed on the Sabbath, began saying to the crowd in response, "There are six days in which work should be done; so come during them and get healed, and not on the Sabbath day." (vs. 10-14)

She probably had kyphosis, a condition that results in a humpback. The fact that Jesus laid his hand on her suggests she was not currently possessed by a demon, because in cases of deliverance, he would not put his hand on the person. But when healing he almost always touched the person. He also called it a "sickness." Perhaps an earlier involvement with the demonic had left her in this condition.

The important point is that as before, keeping a strict interpretation of the law meant more to this synagogue leader than the release of the woman after eighteen years of suffering.

> The Lord answered him and said, "You hypocrites, does not each of you on the Sabbath untie his ox or his donkey from the stall and lead him away to water him?" (v. 15)

The answer to Jesus' question is not given, but from the rabbinic literature we know the correct answer is yes. They wouldn't hesitate to take an animal to water or meet other needs. So Jesus uses an *a fortiori* argument: If your animals get cared for, how much more this daughter of Abraham who has suffered so long? (v. 16).

This is the last instance in Luke where Jesus appears teaching in a synagogue. The hostility of the Jewish authorities apparently increased to the point where he was no longer free to address people there.

The Mustard Seed and the Yeast

Jesus gave two small parables or similes without clarification:

> So he was saying, "What is the kingdom of God like, and to what shall I compare it? It is like a mustard seed, which a man took and threw into his own garden; and it grew and became a tree, and the birds of the air nested in its branches."
>
> And again he said, "To what shall I compare the kingdom of God? It is like leaven, which a woman took and hid in three pecks of flour until it was all leavened." (vs. 18-21)

The reader has to discern what is going on and the lesson implied.

First, we see that Matthew included both of these parables almost word-for-word in his collection of "kingdom parables" beginning with the parable of the soils. Luke had that parable back in chapter 8.

In Matthew's collection, the parables were pointing to a kingdom unlike what they were expecting. Instead of a sudden takeover of the world, the kingdom parables point to gradual growth from a tiny beginning to something big. They also include that the kingdom will not be made up of only believers, as predicted in the Old Testament, but will be a mixture of the good and the bad.

What about these two? Many interpreters think that since yeast is a symbol of corruption in the Old Testament, the parable of the yeast is predicting the spreading corruption within the church. Others think the main point is just a growth process rather than a sudden takeover. The yeast multiplies and permeates the loaf, just like God's people will multiply to fill the earth. Both happened.

The same goes for the mustard seed. It grows from tiny to big, in fact, so big that birds can nest in its branches. Looking at Matthew's kingdom parables, Jesus explained that in the parable of the soils, the birds stood for Satan snatching the word out of someone's heart. So birds are bad. But this parable lacks the context that Matthew gave. Jesus may be predicting unexpected growth along with corrupt infiltration by negative players. Or is it simply that a usually small seed grew large enough for birds to nest in it? If this is predicting corruption in the future church, that's much easier to see from our viewpoint today than it would have been at that time.

Undeniably, one of Jesus' most amazing predictions was that a small band of Jews would eventually blanket the entire earth with the gospel. Today, every nation state on earth has witnessing believers in it.

On the Road Again

Jesus continued his circuitous journey toward Jerusalem, teaching and answering people's questions as he went.

> And he was passing through from one city and village to another, teaching, and proceeding on his way to Jerusalem. And someone said to him, "Lord, are there just a few who are being saved?" And he said to them, "Strive to enter through the narrow door; for many, I tell you, will seek to enter and will not be able. Once the head of the house gets up and shuts the door, and you begin to stand outside and knock on the door, saying, 'Lord, open up to us!' then he will answer and say to you, 'I do not know where you are from.'" (vs. 22-25)

The grim truth is that this door is narrow. Why would people "seek to enter and not be able?" Because it's too late! Nothing prevents people from entering but their own refusal. Any striving necessary isn't striving to qualify for rescue from God, but striving with one's own resistance and pride. Once again, Jesus warns that there is a limit, and once you cross that limit, signified here by shutting the door, it's too late.

To people bothered by this truth, consider what it would be like if there were no limit? People could go on indefinitely denying God and at any point change their minds, even a million years from now. That's not going to happen.

Notice that the master rejects their plea to enter based on their lack of relationship with him. Whether it's Luke's "I don't know where you're from," or Matthew's "I never knew you" (Matthew 7:13), the issue is whether or not you formed a personal relationship with the head of the house.

Jesus went on to talk about hell:

> "In that place there will be weeping and gnashing of teeth when you see Abraham and Isaac and Jacob and all the prophets in the kingdom of God, but yourselves being thrown out." (v. 28)

It's one thing to crack party jokes about how you would rather party in hell with your friends than sing hymns in heaven. What that leaves out is the isolation people will experience in hell, and that they go there after seeing what they could have had. To be banished from the presence of God and his people, too late, condemned people will realize what they missed.

The Great Banquet

Meanwhile, Jesus describes the people of God reclining to a big feast, a celebration of the kingdom of God. His cryptic comment that "Some are last who will be first and some are first who will be last" (v. 30) is one he repeated often.[1] Among those who were considered last are the hated Gentiles (signified by those "from east and west and from north and south), happily dining and drinking wine with Jesus. While some

1. For example, Matthew 19:30, 20:16; Mark 10:31.

of those considered first will be his rabbinic critics, who falsely assumed that they had the future with God locked down.

Warning About Herod

Some Pharisees approached Jesus with a warning:

> "Go away, leave here, for Herod wants to kill You." And he said to them, "Go and tell that fox, 'Behold, I cast out demons and perform cures today and tomorrow, and the third day I reach my goal.' Nevertheless I must journey on today and tomorrow and the next day; for it cannot be that a prophet would perish outside of Jerusalem." (vs. 31-33)

Were these Pharisees worried for Jesus' wellbeing? Or were they trying to manipulate him into leaving their area? It didn't matter to Jesus because he knew his fate lay in Jerusalem. He also knew Herod was not going to be the agent of his death. But as Jerusalem has come up, he cried out his heart for the city of God:

> "O Jerusalem, Jerusalem, the city that kills the prophets and stones those sent to her! How often I wanted to gather your children together, just as a hen gathers her brood under her wings, and you would not have it!" (v. 34)

The compassion Jesus felt for his people and their great city bursts forth from his heart. But it's a sad message because, while he was willing to gather them together, they were not willing to be gathered. As a result of their refusals, God was going to move on to other peoples.[2]

> "Behold, your house is left to you desolate; and I say to you, you will not see me until the time comes when you say, 'Blessed is he who comes in the name of the Lord!'" (v. 35)[3]

2. This verse doesn't fit well with the Calvinistic notion of irresistible grace (where people cannot say no to God's choosing them) or unconditional election (where God chooses and calls people for his own reasons apart from any condition like saving faith). You can see that Jesus was the one who wanted to gather them, but it was their refusal that prevented Jesus' desire to save. It was not, "I was going to gather you, but I decided not to." Rather, it was, "I was going to gather you, but *you* decided not." Some try to dodge this clear statement by saying Jesus only wanted to gather the children in the city, not the whole city. But a fair reading makes clear that it's not the children *in the city* but the children *of the city*—in other words, everyone in Jerusalem. Making it about children does nothing to change the proposition, and it renders the whole statement unintelligible.

3. Matthew has this statement later, during the last week of Jesus' life. Matthew's position makes more sense, because he has just come up the road to Jerusalem and sees it at the time of this saying.

Some suggest this refers to the destruction of Jerusalem in AD 70. It could, especially because he makes a similar statement later in which he specifically links it to the coming destruction of the city (19:41-44). "Your house being left desolate" comes from a verb meaning to step away or remove. NLT translates it "your house is abandoned." If understood that way, it could refer to God moving on from their house i.e. the temple. It certainly is a reproof and a lament for their rejection of Jesus.

The Big Picture

Even though there were still multitudes listening to Jesus in curiosity and even tentative joy, a subtle dark gloom reigns over the journey south. Jesus' opposition is hardening. Soon, polarization would be complete and they would close in.

Jesus stands above the scene, well aware of where this was all headed. Along with the negatives comes Jesus' amazing prediction in the mustard seed and leaven—that what he was beginning would grow to great size and would in fact become the biggest faith on earth, eventually winning billions to eternal life. Also some of his most important teaching was yet to come on this journey.

Luke might have moved it here for unknown reasons, but as we've already seen, they weren't that interested in strict chronology.

26

Time for Dinner

Luke 14:1-24

In this chapter Jesus gives a series of lessons that happen to come during dinners. This material, unique to Luke, must have come from someone who was in the houses described, based on the immediacy and fine detail in these accounts.

Healing on the Sabbath

> One Sabbath day Jesus went to eat dinner in the home of a leader of the Pharisees, and they were watching him closely. There was a man there whose arms and legs were swollen. (Luke 14:1-2 NLT)

As a "leader of the Pharisees," this host may have been a member of the Sanhedrin—the ruling council of the Jews. The sick man probably had edema, a swelling of the joints caused by inflammation, diabetes, or poor circulation. This important man and his colleagues were "watching him closely," not because they were interested in truth, but because they were waiting for him to incriminate himself. Jesus could have waited a day to heal the man, but he wanted to confront the group with their hypocrisy.

> Jesus asked the Pharisees and experts in religious law, "Is it

> permitted in the law to heal people on the Sabbath day, or not?" (v. 3 NLT)

In the silence that followed, the scribes and Pharisees reveal their duplicity. They knew exactly what the rabbinic teaching on this was. But they weren't there to discuss theology. They were laying a trap. "When they refused to answer, Jesus touched the sick man and healed him and sent him away" (v. 4).

He probably sent the man away so he wouldn't be distracted by any foolish argument that might follow.

> Then he turned to them and said, "Which of you doesn't work on the Sabbath? If your son or your cow falls into a pit, don't you rush to get him out?" (v. 5 NLT)

Yes, both of these were exceptions to the rule about working on the Sabbath, and they knew that. But again, "they could not answer" (v. 6). They knew the answer to Jesus' question was yes, but they didn't want to leave any impression that Jesus might be in the right.

Jesus on Humility

Perhaps at the same dinner:

> When Jesus noticed that all who had come to the dinner were trying to sit in the seats of honor near the head of the table, he gave them this advice: "When you are invited to a wedding feast, don't sit in the seat of honor, for someone more distinguished than you may have been invited by him, Then the host will come and say, 'Give this person your seat.' Then you will be embarrassed, and you will have to take whatever seat is left at the foot of the table! "Instead, take the lowest place at the foot of the table. Then when your host sees you, he will come and say, 'Friend, we have a better place for you!' Then you will be honored in front of all the other guests. For those who exalt themselves will be humbled, and those who humble themselves will be exalted." (vs. 7-11 NLT)

Jesus could see human pride with great clarity. Here he puts the choice before them and us: either humility or humiliation. God understands our desire to be admired and appreciated. In its unfallen context, this urge was not sinful at all. God said of the first humans, "Let us create man in our own image and let them rule" (Genesis 1:26). That built-in desire to rule is our desire for significance. Through leading well, humans are capable of doing great good. Since the fall, this attribute has been twisted into pride.

God would have us use our gifting to do good for others, and let him, God, do the glorifying. As Jesus promises in this passage, those who humble themselves will be exalted. That is, God will exalt, or glorify us if we leave off glorifying ourselves. Those, on the other hand, who insist on self-glorification, Jesus said, "They have their reward in full" (Matthew 6:5). Whatever pseudo-glory we gain here in this life will disappear like a puff of smoke.

Not only should we reject self-aggrandizement, we also need to aim for the lowest seat. That refers to turning away from all the daily opportunities for prideful hints:

- Exaggerating when retelling a story with yourself coming out a little better
- Selective telling of history by leaving out the embarrassing truth of my own motives, or the detail that makes sense of what others did
- Lying, either to claim for yourself that which is not true, or to hide shameful sin from others' view
- Always volunteering for the showy ministry that gets a lot of attention, but not for the background serving that nobody notices
- Cutting down competitors for attention or admiration
- Engaging in image management by trying to make sure people aren't telling others about the dirt they know is in your life.

And the list goes on.

Instead, we are called to use our genius to elevate others around us. For us, the question is not how many do you have under you, but how many have you raised up? (Ephesians 4:11-16). And, have you raised anyone up to a place higher than yourself? If you busy yourself raising others up, you won't be troubled by so many temptations to self-glorify.

Considering how common and overpowering the temptation is to self-glorification, it's a good thing that God is so gracious. If I got what

I deserved on this, the picture would be grim. But as David exalts, "He does not punish us for all our sins; he does not deal harshly with us, as we deserve" (Psalm 103:10). Still, I have to wonder. Who knows how much God has had to restrain progress in ministry because his people are waiting for the chance to seek glorification in it?

Reaching Out to the Marginalized

Jesus probably noticed all the upper-class people at the dinner.

> And he also went on to say to the one who had invited him, "When you give a luncheon or a dinner, do not invite your friends or your brothers or your relatives or rich neighbors, otherwise they may also invite you in return and that will be your repayment. But when you give a reception, invite the poor, the crippled, the lame, the blind, and you will be blessed, since they do not have the means to repay you; for you will be repaid at the resurrection of the righteous." (vs. 12-13)

Jesus points out the difference between giving that is truly sacrificial versus giving that includes an expectation of repayment. The human heart is sneaky and deceptive. Jesus is not at all unrealistic in suggesting that people will give out in order to take back. That was especially likely with this high society group at the dinner.

The Rejected Feast

One of the guests cried out a typical Jewish sentiment:

> When one of those who were reclining at the table with him heard this, he said to him, "Blessed is everyone who will eat bread in the kingdom of God!" (v. 15)

Eating at God's celebration feast was well taught in the Old Testament. Jesus responded with another parable:

> "A man was giving a big dinner, and he invited many; and at the dinner hour he sent his servant to say to those who had been invited, 'Come; for everything is ready now.'" (vs. 16-17)

You can tell that the host and his guests have talked about it earlier because he says, "everything is ready now." The servant doesn't need to explain the feast. This fits high-class practice in the first century. Leifield explains that two invitations would be sent. The first was to determine how many portions to prepare. The second was sent when the dinner was ready, because preparing this kind of feast took a long time.[1] Clearly, Jesus was referring to the second invitation.

This is significant because these guests had already agreed to come to the feast. That makes their later refusal doubly bad. Their earlier agreement matches the prior dealings the Jewish people had with God.

> "But they all alike began to make excuses. The first one said to him, 'I have bought a piece of land and I need to go out and look at it; please consider me excused.'" (v. 18)

So, he bought a piece of land but didn't look at it first? How likely is that? And won't it still be sitting there tomorrow? Why does he need to go look at it right at dinner time?

> "Another one said, 'I have bought five yoke of oxen, and I am going to try them out; please consider me excused.'" (v. 19)

Wait. So this wealthy man just bought ten oxen (only possible for the rich) and he's saying he has to go out and try them in a yoke. What, one pair at a time? This is what he's doing instead of coming to the feast? He didn't examine the oxen when he bought them?

> "Another one said, 'I have married a wife, and for that reason I cannot come.'" (v. 20)

Hmmm. Married people eat. He can't bring his wife to the feast? He just now found out he's getting married? He didn't know that a week ago when he agreed to the first invitation?

All of these excuses are incredibly lame! In fact, they make so little sense that they're probably lies. The truth is, they just don't want to come. This is Jesus' picture of those who were rejecting him. And we can infer that the rest of the story reflects how God views the situation.

> "And the servant came back and reported this to his master. Then the head of the household became angry and said to his servant, 'Go out at once into the streets and lanes of the city

1. Liefeld, *Luke*, 978.

> and bring in here the poor and crippled and blind and lame.'" (v. 21)

Here is a practical explanation for why Jesus so often preached reversal theology. The poor, the crippled, the lame, and the blind were simply more responsive than the complacent, self-satisfied upper class. Those who own and benefit from the status quo are always the most resistant to change. In Jesus' story, the servant left for another trip trying to gather up guests from the street. He came back and reported:

> "'Master, what you commanded has been done, and still there is room.' And the master said to the servant, 'Go out into the highways and along the hedges, and compel them to come in, so that my house may be filled.'" (vs. 22-23)

The striking point here is the attitude of the host. He is absolutely determined that his house be filled with guests enjoying his feast. This is God's determination that people be rescued. When he sends the servant out the third time, it's probably with a broomstick he can use to poke around under hedgerows where homeless people slept. This is no passive invitation, but a determined drive to find guests. He says to "compel them to come in."

Finally, Jesus says,

> "'For I tell you, none of those men who were invited shall taste of my dinner.'" (v. 24)

The host knew he was being insulted by the phony excuses and obvious deception from his original guests. Not coming to the feast in this story and context refers to going to hell.

The Big Picture

Having Jesus over to dinner could be risky! You might find your self-serving, your pride, and your insincerity being called out. Considering how the Pharisees reacted to other talks Jesus gave, we can safely assume that most of them felt increased rage after this dinner. Phariseeism didn't feature humility, caring for the poor, the lame, or the sick. They no doubt also realized that his parable of the rejected dinner was aimed at them.

We aren't told what happened as Jesus and whoever was with him (his mother? some key disciples?) left to go back to where they were staying. After this dinner, the scene abruptly shifts back to the multitudes.

27

Counting the Cost
Luke 14:25-35

Jesus knew that the multitudes that came out to watch him were going to lose interest in the end. He may have decided to thin out the crowd at this point.

> Now large crowds were going along with him; and he turned and said to them, "If anyone comes to me, and does not hate his own father and mother and wife and children and brothers and sisters, yes, and even his own life, he cannot be my disciple." (Luke 14:25-26)

This incredibly high bar doesn't refer to conditions for salvation. He is clear that it refers to being his disciple. The group of theologians who argue that these are conditions for personal salvation are known as "Lordship theologians." We discussed their position briefly earlier in Luke 9.

They come from a broad swath of larger theological positions—Reformed, Wesleyan, Holiness, Dispensational and Free Will schools all contain some Lordship theologians. Because Catholics and Orthodox theologians believe the same thing about these passages, the Lordship view is easily the predominant view. But our conclusions should be based on exegesis (interpretation via the grammatical historical method), not by popularity.

The opposing view—that these conditions refer to a later commitment people make after conversion—is called the "free grace" view. I will be defending this view.

Hate?

First, both sides in this debate agree that the expression, "hate his own father and mother and wife and children and brothers and sisters" is not calling believers to hate their families. Rather, this is an *idiom*—a figure of speech with a meaning different from the literal definition of the words. For instance, when we say someone is level-headed, we aren't saying his head is flat like a table. It means the person has good judgment. When we say, "He's got a big head," we're not actually talking about the size of a person's head. Rather, it means the person is proud.

When used in comparison (like in this statement by Jesus) the word for hate—*miseo*—should be understood to mean "loved less" as in the NASB margin. Jesus was calling his disciples to put him first, even over family relations. It doesn't mean that *miseo* always means this—only in this comparative use.

Those who grow to know God's perfect wisdom and love realize that nothing would be better for their families than putting Jesus first in life. That actually leads to mature, sacrificial love, including toward your family. So love of Jesus and of your family are fully compatible. But why is it so essential that love of Jesus comes first?

The answer has been expressed by the old saying, "If Jesus isn't Lord *of all*, he isn't Lord *at all*." Failure to put Jesus in first place means something else is in first place, like your family. But it's at the very point where your family may want you to go in a particular direction, or to not go in a particular direction, that following Jesus and loving your family may come into conflict.

They may want you to favor your career more than your ministry. They may want you to prioritize certain things more than what Jesus wants. You need to have already anticipated this possibility and you need to have already decided that you'll hold the line for Jesus' will. Otherwise you may end up being misguided or even manipulated.

Following Jesus needs to be unconditional. If you're willing to follow as long as this or that condition doesn't come up (e.g. your family's approval), that's not following. You're not following as long as you are the one making the choices.

Ask yourself, why would believers need to put conditions on following Jesus? Isn't it because of distrust? Instead of giving themselves over in an unconditional way, some people reserve the right to examine God's call to see if it fits into their plans; to see whether it's really a good idea; to see whether it might conflict with other priorities. That distrust, that suspicion that Jesus might give you a bad direction, is fatal to real following. It's not following at all.

The Cost

Jesus continued,

> "Whoever does not carry his own cross and come after me cannot be my disciple." (v. 27)

This is the most complete commitment possible. He used this picture before (9:23). To carry your cross is nothing less than all-out commitment to the point of the worst thing imaginable—a painful death. Sincere believers need to wrestle with this notion honestly, not superficially like Peter who blithely said he would go with Jesus to prison and to death. He soon revealed that his confidence in himself was misplaced.

We might likewise wonder if we would chicken out in the face of a cruel death, and of course, we don't know. But the intent is what Jesus seeks. He wants our agreement that following him will take us to the best place possible, even if it includes pain. Only whole-hearted trust will enable anyone to take such a step. And this is exactly what Jesus called for.

Counting

Jesus warned people to count the cost and make sure they had what it took:

> "For which one of you, when he wants to build a tower, does not first sit down and calculate the cost to see if he has enough to complete it? Otherwise, when he has laid a foundation and is not able to finish, all who observe it begin to ridicule

> him, 'This man began to build and was not able to finish.'" (vs. 28-30)

Yes! It would be unthinkably foolish to begin a building project not knowing if you have the funds to complete it. In a modern setting this would hardly be possible. We settle financing and have letters of credit ready before we ever break ground. But I actually saw what Jesus describes when I ran a painting and decorating company earlier in life.

We were working for multi-millionaires in a new development filled with incredible mansions. One in particular was so huge and impressive, sitting on top of a hill, that I wanted to get the contract for it. We never saw much activity in the unfinished house.

Asking around, I ran into an old general contractor who knew about the property. He recounted with a grin how a fancy lawyer had decided to be a building contractor and started this house and several others as "speck houses" built before anyone bought them. He stopped talking, so I probed. "So what happened?"

A big smile spread over his face. "He lost his ass!" he chuckled.

The pleasure and humor this old guy got from the half-finished house is exactly what Jesus was referring to. Nobody wants people laughing at their foolishness. So it's best to make sure we have what we need to finish the job. Jesus didn't want people lightly declaring readiness without realizing the cost.

Another illustration had to do with armies:

> "Or what king, when he sets out to meet another king in battle, will not first sit down and consider whether he is strong enough with ten thousand men to encounter the one coming against him with twenty thousand? Or else, while the other is still far away, he sends a delegation and asks for terms of peace." (vs. 31-32)

This scenario calls for urgent action. The king is about to be badly defeated, and he needs to act quickly and decisively. By sending the delegation, he is basically admitting that he's not strong enough to join battle. That would be analogous to Jesus' superficial followers in the multitude admitting to themselves that they weren't ready for real commitment.

He continued, "So then, none of you can be my disciple who does not give up all his own possessions" (v. 33). It's not an exaggeration. When you make the second decision, you put all your stuff in the car. Then you hand Jesus the keys and say, "You drive."

It's important to realize that this decision must be made in advance, without knowing where Jesus will drive. We don't need to know what the future holds. All we need to know is that we can trust Jesus.

All-Out Following

To give yourself over to complete following is the result of simply realizing that:

- If God is real,
- If Jesus rescued you through the cross,
- If God is all-knowing,
- If he is loving—including loving you,

then nothing makes sense except following him with everything that you are.

Of course, if any of those propositions is false or doubtful, then everything breaks down. Unbelief slips in, undermining the advisability of all-out following. So young believers or doubting older believers need to deeply examine what they believe, until they are able to say yes to each of these.

Then we become like Peter, when Jesus suggested to his disciples that maybe it would be better for them to quit following him, like so many others were. Peter didn't have to think long. "Lord, to whom shall we go? You have words of eternal life" (John 6:68). There is simply no sane alternative to all-out following once we fully realize who Jesus is.

Savory Salt

Jesus adds one last thought:

> "Therefore, salt is good; but if even salt has become tasteless, with what will it be seasoned? It is useless either for the soil or

> for the manure pile; it is thrown out. He who has ears to hear, let him hear." (vs. 34-35)

A main source for salt in Judea was the Dead Sea. The lake is saturated with minerals and salts, but not all is table salt. Several other minerals make up more of the total load of salts than our table salt.[1] Salt gathered there, if left out in the rain, would gradually lose its saltiness, because the Sodium chloride is easily soluble, while some other minerals are less so (like calcium).

Some commentators argue that salt's preserving ability is in view. But Jesus points to its taste. In a parallel passage in Matthew, being salt and being the light of the world are linked. Salt tastes good, and it makes food taste good, so it's attractive. The warning here is that if we lose our saltiness, we won't be attractive. And if we aren't fully committed, we will lose our saltiness. How compelling can our faith be to the world if it doesn't even command allegiance from its own people?

Nobody knows what Jesus meant when he said the unsalty salt isn't worth throwing on the manure pile. The claim that salt enhances the fertilizing power of manure is not true. Salt would worsen the manure. Magnesium could help. It's more likely that Jesus meant that the bland salt is good for nothing, including throwing on the manure heap—i.e. good for nothing at all.

1. The dissolved solids in the Dead Sea are made up of 53% magnesium chloride, 37% potassium chloride and 8% sodium chloride. Only sodium chloride is table salt. Potassium chloride also tastes salty (used in sodium free salt), but not as salty as sodium chloride.

28

Looking Into God's Heart

Luke 15

Once again, the scene shifts. It's not unlikely that many of the pseudo followers departed, leaving the tax collectors and other sinners to press in around Jesus. Some of his enemies were there too.

> Now all the tax collectors and the sinners were coming near him to listen to him. Both the Pharisees and the scribes began to grumble, saying, "This man receives sinners and eats with them." (Luke 15:1-2)

Once again, the hungry hearts of the "sinners" stand in stark contrast to the self-contented "*harrumpf*" of the disgruntled leaders. These men simply didn't understand what God is like. Jesus continued trying to get through to them by giving three parables that illustrate God's attitude toward lost people.

The Lost Sheep

> "What man among you, if he has a hundred sheep and has lost one of them, does not leave the ninety-nine in the open pasture and go after the one which is lost until he finds it?

> When he has found it, he lays it on his shoulders, rejoicing. And when he comes home, he calls together his friends and his neighbors, saying to them, 'Rejoice with me, for I have found my sheep which was lost!' I tell you that in the same way, there will be more joy in heaven over one sinner who repents than over ninety-nine righteous persons who need no repentance." (vs. 4-7)

He pictures God as one who is not passively observing what's going on. He is emotionally engaged enough to call for a party celebrating his success in finding the lost sheep. His statement about joy in heaven is amazing. These must be the angels, or perhaps previously rescued humans? What a surprising claim! And Jesus would know. This really pictures the heavenly host hanging on each decision, waiting for a cause to celebrate. What a contrast with the dour, rejecting attitude of Jesus' critics.

The "ninety-nine righteous who need no repentance" is confusing, because Jesus already taught that everyone needs repentance in his sermon on the plane. Several readings are possible. First, he may be referring to unfallen angels who never sinned, and therefore need no repentance.

Or could he be referring to other populations of high order creatures on other planets? It's quite possible that a creative God would create beings other than us. But if so, they never fell into sin, based on the "once for all" language in the book of Hebrews.

Or, perhaps most likely, he is referring to those who *think* they're righteous and in no need for repentance. The key point is the joy God feels when lost people come to him.

The Lost Coin

Jesus continued pressing his case:

> "Or what woman, if she has ten silver coins and loses one coin, does not light a lamp and sweep the house and search carefully until she finds it? When she has found it, she calls together her friends and neighbors, saying, 'Rejoice with me, for I have found the coin which I had lost!' In the same way, I

> tell you, there is joy in the presence of the angels of God over one sinner who repents." (vs. 8-10)

The silver coin was a drachma, which was equal to a day's wage for a grown man. Today an average adult daily wage is close to two hundred and seventy dollars ($70,000 per year). So the coin was valuable; not like one of our coins. The woman is easy to identify with. If you've ever lost something valuable, like your phone or your keys, it's maddening. You keep tracing and retracing your steps, straining to remember where you've been. This woman simply couldn't think of anything else until she reclaimed her coin.

Remember the context for these parables is verses 1 and 2 about the lost sinners crowding around him. The shepherd in the earlier parable and the woman in this one are pictures of God's insistence that he win what he has lost. Jesus would later make it clear that "The Son of Man has come to seek and to save that which was lost" (19:10). The common theme of all the parables in this chapter is loss, and God's determination to recover what was lost. The next parable is one of Jesus' most famous. This time, it's the loss of a son.

The Prodigal Son

At this point, Jesus gave what is to my eye the greatest parable he ever told. I loved it when as a new believer, I identified very much with the prodigal son himself. I was turning to God out of a life of drugs and partying, but also prison and other consequences. Geldenhuys correctly observes: "In no other religion in the whole world does one come to know God as the one who in His love seeks the lost person to save him through his grace."[1]

> To illustrate the point further, Jesus told them this story: "A man had two sons. The younger son told his father, 'I want my share of your estate now before you die.' So his father agreed to divide his wealth between his sons. A few days later this younger son packed all his belongings and moved to a distant land, and there he wasted all his money in wild living." (vs. 11-13 NLT)

For the younger son to demand his inheritance while his father was still

1. Geldenhuys, *Luke*, 403.

alive was shockingly disrespectful in that culture. Later, when he sold his part of the farm and struck off on his own to a "distant country," it speaks even more of his contempt for his father. Finally, his wild living, including prostitutes (v. 30), shows without doubt that this son is a good-for-nothing sinner. Jesus isn't trying to describe a slightly misguided young man. An important part of his message comes from the willful wickedness of this son.

The party lifestyle didn't go as expected:

> "About the time his money ran out, a great famine swept over the land, and he began to starve. He persuaded a local farmer to hire him, and the man sent him into his fields to feed the pigs." (vs. 14-15 NLT)

The physical starvation here could also represent inner spiritual starvation. The misery of life away from God comes as a low-key sense of dissatisfaction in life; an awareness that there must be more. People living without God in their lives are contradicting their own architecture—the way they were created to be—and it hurts. Jesus earlier said, "Do not work for the food which perishes, but for the food which endures to eternal life, which the Son of Man will give to you" (John 6:27).

The NASB has the correct sense, that he "joined himself" to the farmer. It's indentured servitude. He has voluntarily become a slave.

It would be hard for modern western readers to fully grasp the disgust and revulsion first century Jews would feel toward this way of life. Pigs were unclean animals according to the law. Farming them would be disgusting. The rebel young man was reaping the harvest he had sown. Jesus was purposely grossing his hearers out.

Some years ago, a friend took me to the hog farm he grew up on. I was quite impressed by the nauseating stench. Jesus went on:

> "The young man became so hungry that even the pods he was feeding the pigs looked good to him. But no one gave him anything." (v. 16 NLT)

Slopping the hogs—an ancient practice—is when hog farmers toss their discarded and left over food cuttings and other garbage into a "slop bucket." Later, they take the slop and mix in grain, carob pods, or other undesirable waste and pour it out into the hog trough. The pigs go crazy snorting, squealing, and slurping up the dark smelly mass, often getting their front feet up into the trough as they eat.

Jesus added the final piece of the picture: "No one was giving anything to him." His worldly friends were all happy to help him spend his money and drink the free wine. They were all "besties." But when the money ran out, they seemed to forget who he was. Nobody cared about this foolish young one, except one old man.

Repentance

The rebellious young man reached the climax of the story when his burning hunger drove him to plunge his hand into the hog slop. Lifting the smelly mess toward his lips, something snapped inside. "Wait a minute . . ." he must have said as his eyes were opened to the pitiful awareness of what he had become! And for what?

Tears surely filled his eyes as the mysterious inward event called repentance spread out, filling his heart. Jesus described it as, "He came to his senses" (v. 17). As he repented, he immediately saw things as they were in truth; himself, kneeling in stinking mud next to grunting, unclean swine, dying of hunger. He recalled the memory of his kind, fair father, generously paying even his servants. All the glamour of revolt and hedo nism reduced to stench and pain.

Jesus takes us inside the son's mind where he immediately knows what to do. He says,

> "I will get up and go to my father, and will say to him, 'Father, I have sinned against heaven, and in your sight; I am no longer worthy to be called your son; make me as one of your hired men.'" (vs. 18-19 NLT)

Notice the classic elements indicating true repentance:

- "I will get up and go to my father." He's not going to lay around feeling sorry for himself. He's not going to be like Adam, crouching in shame behind a bush. He knows exactly where to go—to his father. And remember, the father in this story stands for God.
- "I have sinned against heaven." He frankly admits he has sinned. No caveats, no qualifications. And he acknowledges that his sin is not

just a sociological event on the horizontal plane. In the first place he has sinned against God.

- "And in your sight." He also had sinned against his family—the people in his life—and the father plays both roles here.
- "I am no longer worthy to be called your son." He has a keen awareness of his own unworthiness. No hint of entitlement here. He hasn't even dared to come asking to be returned to his place as a son.
- "Make me as one of your hired men." He's ready to humbly serve, taking a bunk in the employee's quarters.

This masterful portrayal of the dynamics and psychology of sin and repentance comes from one who never did either one. Only supernatural insight, straight from the Holy Spirit could enable this portrayal.

The Father

This parable is about the father, more than anyone. Jesus was trying to explain what God's heart is like, and how different he is from Jesus' sneering judgmental opponents. He went on with his story:

> "But while he was still a long way off, his father saw him and felt compassion for him, and ran and embraced him and kissed him." (v. 20 NLT)

Notice several things about the father:

- He earlier gave the son his share of the estate and watched him go away. God created free will beings made in his own image. We, like this son, have the freedom to reject God.
- He didn't chase after his son into the distant country. He didn't grovel to an unrepentant rebel. He let the natural course of events break the son down.
- The phrase, "while he was still a long way off," implies that the father was keeping watch, expectantly—hopefully—for the son's return. Every day he was scanning the horizon.
- When he saw the son, was he consumed with rage? No. That would have been deserved, but instead he "felt compassion" for him. Then, the old man even ran to him, so unusual in that culture for an old

man to run. He would have had to gather his robe up in order to run. It eloquently picturing his eagerness for the son's embrace.

- He embraced and kissed his dirty, smelly son, cutting short the son's proposal to be hired. In light of the son's repentance, everything was instantly forgiven.
- He turned to his servants with urgency: "Quickly bring out the best robe and put it on him, and put a ring on his hand and sandals on his feet" (v. 22 NLT). He immediately dressed his son in his new identity. He was no longer a swineherd but a son.
- "And bring the fattened calf, kill it and let us eat and celebrate!'" Yum. Wagu beef! Killing a fattened calf was only done on rare occasions. Jesus pictures a great feast (v. 23 NLT).
- "'For this son of mine was dead and has come to life again; he was lost and has been found.' And they began to celebrate" (v. 24 NLT). The celebration began, just like in the previous two parables. According to Jesus, God and his angelic hosts rejoice and party when a lost, sinful person repents! The Pharisees and scribes simply didn't understand how much God loves people—including hardcore, sinful ones, like the tax collectors and other sinners gathered around Jesus.

The Older Brother

This beautiful story of reconciliation and joy is suddenly spattered with filthy human nature.

> "Now his older son was in the field, and when he came and approached the house, he heard music and dancing. And he summoned one of the servants and began inquiring what these things could be. And he said to him, 'Your brother has come, and your father has killed the fattened calf because he has received him back safe and sound.'" (vs. 25-27)

Did he love his brother? Did he have his father's heart in view, including the joy he must be feeling? If so, he would be joyful too. But if he was locked into a self-centered view, we could expect this:

> "But he became angry and was not willing to go in; and his father came out and began pleading with him.

> But he answered and said to his father, 'Look! For so many years I have been serving you and I have never neglected an instruction of yours. And in all that time you never gave me even one young goat for a feast with my friends. Yet when this son of yours comes back after squandering your money on prostitutes, you celebrate by killing the fattened calf!'" (vs. 28-30 NLT)

Again, we see several points in the older son's response. All of them remind us of the mindset Jesus' critics hold.

- For this son, it's all about "me." His focus is not on his brother, not on his father, or anyone else.
- His focus is on his good works and on deserving. In typical religious thinking, he compares himself with others, and sees his own superiority.
- He resents the father's kindness and grace. His relationship with his father is not good. He shows an inability to grasp how his father is feeling. Resentment is evident, and it's doubtful that it began here.
- He complains that his dad never gave him a goat to celebrate with. Why would the father give him no goat? There can be little doubt: He never asked! After all, the father goes on to say, "All that is mine is yours" (v. 31). Based on the characters in this parable, we can hardly doubt that if the older brother had asked for a goat, the answer would have been yes. The older son stands for a mentality of entitlement, including the poor prayer lives entitled people have.

Since the younger brother already got his third, only the older brother's share—two thirds—was left. So there was permanent loss to the younger brother, just as believers will suffer loss if they refuse to follow God fully. But the loss will be in missing a happier life, and losing rewards in heaven, not losing the father's love (1 Corinthians 3:15).

The father concludes:

> "'But we had to celebrate and rejoice, for this brother of yours was dead and has begun to live, and was lost and has been found.'" (v. 32 NLT)

God is a joyful, happy God, especially when a lost person changes his or her heart and turns back to him. Just like in the two previous parables, Jesus envisions a party in heaven whenever a lost person is found.

The Big Picture

Alfred Edersheim quotes a rabbinic version of Jesus' statement: "There is joy before God when those who provoke Him perish from the world," and he adds, "There is no rabbinic equivalent to God's seeking of sinners."[2] The seeking God is truly an amazing and wonderful vision. Can you imagine this older man gathering his robes up and running out to the son? What an extraordinary picture of God's response to repentance! Not just waiting until we come to him, but running out to us.

Jesus later defined his own ministry: "The Son of Man has come to seek and to save that which was lost." (19:10). This is the heart of God. He is a seeking, rescuing God. And Jesus later added, "As the Father has sent me, I also send you" (John 20:21).

God wants us to not only appreciate his seeking love, but to become that way ourselves. He even expects us to take part in the project of winning the lost. Having a heart for lost people is essential to spiritual health. Not all believers have this. Some are too similar to the Pharisees and scribes—they feel aversion to sinful, lost people. As a result, they are unable to reach those people with God's love.

Even whole churches can become aversive to sinful, lost people. When that happens, all we can observe is that such groups are quite unlike Jesus.

2. Alfred Eidersheim, *The Life and Times of Jesus the Messiah*, vol. 2 (Whitefish, MT: Sagwan Press, 2015) 256.

29

Jesus on Money
Luke 16:1-31

The Unrighteous Steward

Luke mentioned during this episode that "The Pharisees, who were lovers of money, were listening to all these things and were scoffing at Him" (v. 14). That awareness led Jesus to launch into two additional parables related to money:

> Jesus told this story to his disciples: "There was a certain rich man who had a manager handling his affairs. One day a report came that the manager was wasting his employer's money. So the employer called him in and said, 'What's this I hear about you? Get your report in order, because you are going to be fired.'" (Luke 16:1-2 NLT)

The grammar makes it clear that the rich man's decision has already been made. "The manager thought to himself, 'Now what? My boss has fired me" (v. 3 NLT). There is no possibility that the manager could retrieve his job, and he realizes that. He doesn't make the mistake of thinking, "If I just do a great job on finishing the books, maybe the boss will keep me on." This steward was too smart to believe that. Instead, he turned his back completely to the rich man and looked out at the new realities of his life. "I am not strong enough to dig; I am ashamed to beg" (v. 3 NLT). In other words, he sees no hope in conventional ways to make an income. Then the light dawns:

> "'Ah, I know how to ensure that I'll have plenty of friends who will give me a home when I am fired.'" (v. 4 NLT)

He realized what he was going to need—some contacts that would give him employment and a place to stay. He sets about his task proactively:

> "So he invited each person who owed money to his employer to come and discuss the situation. He asked the first one, 'How much do you owe him?' The man replied, 'I owe him 800 gallons of olive oil.' So the manager told him, 'Take the bill and quickly change it to 400 gallons.' 'And how much do you owe my employer?' he asked the next man. 'I owe him 1,000 bushels of wheat,' was the reply. 'Here,' the manager said, 'take the bill and change it to 800 bushels.'" (vs. 5-7 NLT)

The manager embezzles a large sum from his master. These products would cost thousands of dollars today. Of course, he couldn't care less about saving money for the master. He and the debtors are forging bills and sealing each with wax and a signet ring. They must have burned the old bills. At that point, nobody could prove the forged bills were fake.

The rich man must have looked at the altered paperwork and thought, "These numbers look wrong." But the manager would shrug and say, "That's what it says." Next comes the surprising conclusion:

> "And his master praised the unrighteous manager because he had acted shrewdly; for the sons of this age are more shrewd in relation to their own kind than the sons of light." (v. 8)

Wait. Is Jesus teaching that it's good to cheat and steal? No, Jesus is not the master in this story, He is the storyteller. The master and the steward are imaginary characters behaving in worldly ways with worldly values. The rich man realized the steward got him. The steward's action was swift, decisive, and effective. Even though the master was the victim of the scam, he had to admire the worldly savvy the steward showed. He recognized a good con when he saw one.

Jesus' Comments

At this point, Jesus began his commentary. He said, "The sons of this age are more shrewd in relation to their own kind than the sons of light" (v. 8). So we have two groups: "the sons of this age" and "the sons of light."

This parable is another *a fortiori* argument. It runs, "If worldly people, using lying and cheating, can get results that impress their masters, how much more should God's followers use their creativity and dedication to achieve results that would please him?" As in all *a fortiori* arguments, one part of comparison is desirable and one part is negative. Which part of this story is good and desirable? It's the steward's decisiveness and creativity, not his lying or stealing. The steward correctly concluded that he had no future with his master. Therefore he didn't waste time and energy investing into his old job.

In the same way, Jesus is arguing that continuing to try to please the world when we're headed for an eternal future is foolish. His followers should see that they have no future in the world system, and therefore should take decisive measures to better their lot in the real future.

Eternal Friends?

Jesus went on to explain:

> "And I say to you, make friends for yourselves by means of the wealth of unrighteousness, so that when it fails, they will receive you into the eternal dwellings." (v. 9)

Notice he says of wealth "when it fails you" not "if it fails you." There is 0.0% chance that our wealth will not fail us. All worldly wealth fails eventually.

How do you make friends by means of wealth—friends who are apparently in heaven, giving out eternal dwellings? To invest in heaven you need to invest in people who are going there. In other words, people who we win through the gospel will be in heaven with us, and they will be our grateful friends there. The same would go for people into whom we invested by teaching, counseling, serving, or other means of building up believers.

Such investing into others with a view toward eternity includes giving our wealth to fund ministry. Both evangelistic ministries and those intended to build up the people of God require funding from the people of God. God considers such giving to be "faithfulness" as Jesus went on to explain:

> "He who is faithful in a very little thing is faithful also in much; and he who is unrighteous in a very little thing is unrighteous also in much. Therefore if you have not been faithful in the use of unrighteous wealth, who will entrust the true riches to you?" (vs. 10-11)

Jesus describes wealth as a "very little thing." After all, where we are going, they use gold to pave the streets. Any value that wealth has is strictly temporary. At some point in the future, all worldly wealth will instantly lose its value, just as we saw in the parable of the rich fool.

That's true with only one exception: the money we give to invest in evangelism and building up of believers goes to heaven with us, embodied in rescued believers. So Jesus was really disclosing how to take your money with you when you die.

What if we don't give to eternal purposes? What if we decide to keep our wealth to ourselves? That, according to this parable, would be "unrighteous" use of wealth. This parable teaches against a sin of omission. God entrusts us with wealth, which we may enjoy, but also we need to use it for gospel outreach and other ministries.

God is watching how faithful we are with our wealth. How faithful are we to prioritize eternal matters? If we are faithful, he will entrust us with more; perhaps more wealth, or something even more valuable—the "true riches" (v. 11). What are these true riches? In context, verse 9 explains that the true riches are the friends we make with our wealth, who eventually end up in heaven. In other words, if we are faithful with our wealth, God will allow us to be stewards, contributing to the conversion and well-being of his people.

People who set out to build a personal ministry know what a privilege and joy it is when God uses them to powerfully affect others' lives. And according to this parable, the extent to which God trusts them with ministry is directly linked to their faithfulness with money.

Another lesson in this parable has to do with the nature of faithfulness.

When Jesus said, "He who is faithful in a very little thing is faithful also in much," he reveals that faithful character is not linked to the size of the responsibility in view. A man could say, "I might not be that faithful in this tiny, unnoticed ministry, but if I was a prominent preacher, I would be faithful." Don't believe it. True faithfulness is seen not in showy large ministries, but in small things, especially those done when nobody is looking. Large, public leadership roles could easily attract those who put on one face in public, but live another way in private.

This applies right across the board. A young man in school says, "Right now, I hardly have any income, but when I graduate I'll become a giver." Or, "Right now I have a porn hang-up, but when I get married I'll lay that aside." But that's not how sin works. And this parable warns against that kind of thinking.

The truth is, you will be no more faithful in a big ministry than you are in a small ministry, like taking care of God's money. You see the same mindset in Paul's insistence that new prospective elders "lead well in their own home," because, "if a man does not know how to lead his own household, how will he take care of the church of God?" (1 Timothy 3:4-5).

That Which Is Your Own

Then, Jesus said, "And if you have not been faithful in the use of that which is another's, who will give you that which is your own?" (v. 12). We know that all human possessions really belong to God because, "The earth is the Lord's, and all it contains, the world, and those who dwell in it" (Psalm 24:1). So anything God entrusts to us is "another's." We only hold it temporarily as a stewardship for God. What then, would be "that which is your own?"

Here he is referring to reward in heaven. We know that when we were put into Jesus, God also adopted us as his children. The apostle Paul says, "The Spirit Himself testifies with our spirit that we are children of God, and if children, heirs also, heirs of God and fellow heirs with Christ" (Romans 8:16-17). So as heirs with Jesus, we will "inherit the earth" (Matthew 5:5).

Who to Serve

Jesus concludes, "No servant can serve two masters; for either he will hate the one and love the other, or else he will be devoted to one and despise the other. You cannot serve God and wealth" (v. 13).

Few believers set out with the intent to be servants of wealth. But too often, they underestimate the power riches have over people's hearts. It begins with some small occasional looking to wealth for enjoyment and good feelings. But the lift one gets from a buying spree or new toy is so fleeting that it actually creates more desire than it does satisfaction. The dissatisfaction leads to a desire for more—*pleonexia*—and greed sets in.

This is especially dangerous in the wealthiest country in history. Not that we have some incredibly wealthy people—most countries have that. The difference in the modern west is that most people are wealthy by world and historical standards. You can drive for hours around any western city and see nothing but beautiful neighborhoods with laid out lawns and landscaping, beautiful, large homes, and two cars in the drive.

So I'm supposed to feel guilty because I'm successful? No, you should feel privileged! And responsible! You certainly have to beware of the power of wealth. You have a great opportunity to affect the course of eternity future. You can definitely help care for the poor. You're free to enjoy your wealth, but be careful. Don't serve wealth. Serve God.

Everything Jesus calls for is quite sane. There's no fanaticism here; just good, common sense. One old saint pointed out that it's hardly foolish to invest what we can't keep to get something we can't lose. The only question that resolves our conflicted feelings is this: Is Jesus real?

What if you decide to serve God and money too? If you can pull that off, the one who gave this teaching is false! He said it can't be done.

And the Pharisees

> Now the Pharisees, who were lovers of money, were listening to all these things and were scoffing at him. (v. 14)

Jesus spoke the words here and in the following verses in the context of conflict. Even though the Pharisees were so picky about minor, technical so-called sins, they had no problem with living for money or for being egotistical. Luke says they were lovers of money. People in the grip of avarice become immediately hostile whenever someone questions their right to hold onto great wealth.

Jesus came straight at them:

> "You are those who justify yourselves in the sight of men, but

> God knows your hearts; for that which is highly esteemed among men is detestable in the sight of God." (v. 15)

What is detestable in the sight of God? Justifying yourself before men. Phariseeism focused on the outward, including showy displays of piety in a culture that admired religiosity. Jesus had earlier warned against showing off in this way: "Beware of practicing your righteousness before men to be noticed by them" (Matthew 6:1). He gave examples like praying on the street corner, smearing ash on your face when fasting, or sounding trumpets when you give at the temple (Matthew 6:2, 5, 16).

These all have one thing in common—they are religious works. It's hard for us today to imagine someone standing on a street corner with hands uplifted, praying, because it would be too weird. But in that day, people admired these lengthy, repetitive prayers. To God, they were "detestable."

We saw earlier that Jesus said to the Pharisees, "You love the chief seats in the synagogues and the respectful greetings in the marketplaces" (11:43). They were also teaching that their wealth was a sign that God was on their side. But again, while people might admire their success, God thinks what they were doing was "detestable."

The True Standard

Jesus goes on to declare the real standard for knowing morality:

> "The Law and the Prophets were proclaimed until John; since that time the gospel of the kingdom of God has been preached, and everyone is forcing his way into it. But it is easier for heaven and earth to pass away than for one stroke of a letter of the Law to fail." (vs. 16-17)

The arrival of John the Baptist was the ignition point for the new program Jesus brought, even though the full blessings of the Holy Spirit wouldn't arrive until Pentecost.

But even though the Mosaic covenant was soon to be set aside, that didn't mean the moral laws in the Old Testament were nullified, as Jesus makes clear here. The moral laws grew out of God's character and that never changes. What changed is our relationship to God's law. We are no longer under law, but under grace (Romans 6:14). Our New Covenant is, "not in the old way of obeying the letter of the law, but in the new way of living in the Spirit" (Romans 7:6).

The apostle Paul, while discussing how salvation is apart from works of law, anticipates a complaint that might arise: "Do we then nullify the Law through faith? May it never be! On the contrary, we establish the Law" (Romans 3:31). When we understand the true role of the law—not for salvation, but for comparing human behavior with the righteous nature of God—we establish the law, because we're using it as God intended.

Jesus' point here is that while the Pharisees had their own traditional set of ethics, in many cases those rules were far from biblical teaching. The only authoritative source of moral norms is Scripture—from which not a "stroke of a letter" will fail (v. 17).

The expression, "Everyone is forcing his way into it," should probably be translated "everyone is eager to get in" (NLT). These eager ones were the tax collectors and other "sinners" gathered around Jesus.[1]

Divorce

Jesus went on to give an example of the distorted sense of morality common in rabbinic teaching. "Everyone who divorces his wife and marries another commits adultery, and he who marries one who is divorced from a husband commits adultery" (v. 18). The biblical standard is monogamous marriage for life. Any sex outside that marriage is adultery. In other places Jesus clarified that there are admissible grounds for divorce, but here, he's speaking in general and opposing the hyper-permissive rabbinic view on divorce.

We know this permissiveness from the New Testament and also from later samples of rabbinic teaching, like that of Hillel, who says, "A man may divorce his wife against her will for any reason whatsoever; but a woman may only divorce her husband against his will if he is insane, a leper, or impotent, or if he has not had sexual relations with her for three years."[2]

So, these rabbis would prosecute someone for the slightest violation

1. Matthew has Jesus making this statement when John the Baptist's disciples came to make sure Jesus was the Christ. This was when John was in prison. So in that context the notion of violence made sense. Here, Luke has Jesus saying the same thing in a completely different context. Obviously, he could have uttered the same statement more than once.
2. *Mishnah* Gittin 9:10.

of working on the Sabbath, but they had no problem with such cruel treatment of women. A divorced woman in this culture may not easily remarry. Divorcees were considered undesirable. They typically were not trained in any trade, and often could not get jobs. They might end up in prostitution. The husband might keep the kids, or he might drive them out with their mom. No child support would be paid. Divorcing a woman was a sentence of lifelong misery for her. The male could go on to another woman with his income intact.

That they would be so cavalier about breaking the marriage promise spoke volumes about their true spiritual state.

Jesus started this exchange with the classic parable of the unrighteous steward. He returned to that theme with the now famous parable of the rich man and Lazarus.

The Rich Man and Lazarus

With the crowd and the Pharisees still gathered around Jesus, he went right on to administer a dose of reversal theology:

> "Now there was a rich man, and he habitually dressed in purple and fine linen, joyously living in splendor every day. And a poor man named Lazarus was laid at his gate, covered with sores, and longing to be fed with the crumbs which were falling from the rich man's table; besides, even the dogs were coming and licking his sores." (vs. 19-21)

Luke already said that the Pharisees delighted in their riches. They also interpreted being rich as indicating God's blessing and favor. They saw poor people as under God's displeasure and judgment. The poor deserved their poverty. Jesus, who utterly rejected this view, set up this story with extreme descriptions of both types.

The rich man dressed in purple and fine linen—so much more expensive then than garments would be today. The "joy" and "splendor" of his lifestyle are mainly meant to contrast with the poor man.

Jesus described the poor man in the most lurid terms. First, he laid disabled at the rich man's gate, apparently unable to walk. That means every time the rich man went in or out, he passed by this spectacle. The poor man's plight was well known to the rich man, but he did nothing. To spice the picture up, we learn the poor man was "covered in sores." Then, to add revolting color, "The dogs were coming and licking his sores."

Jesus was pushing all the buttons to heighten the Pharisees' and scribes' disgust. Like some people today, they viewed the poor, sick, and disabled as an annoying mess, to be avoided by people who didn't want to become unclean. But suddenly, the narrative changes:

> "Now the poor man died and was carried away by the angels to Abraham's bosom; and the rich man also died and was buried. In Hades he lifted up his eyes, being in torment, and saw Abraham far away and Lazarus in his bosom. And he cried out and said, 'Father Abraham, have mercy on me, and send Lazarus so that he may dip the tip of his finger in water and cool off my tongue, for I am in agony in this flame.'" (vs. 22-24)

Everything has reversed! Now the rich man is the helpless beggar, while Lazarus is in bliss with Abraham. How they got into their respective fates isn't part of this story. For one thing, Jesus isn't explaining what *will* happen, he's describing what *should* happen.

Under a standard of fairness, God would feel anger toward the rich man for his callous disregard for the needs of his poor neighbor. He was selfish—he couldn't even spare a crust of bread for this pitiful man lying right at his gate? Let alone bring him in, clean him up, and feed him well? So God's view of the rich man's way of life illustrated Jesus' earlier statement, "That which is highly esteemed among men is detestable in the sight of God" (v. 15).

Notice that Lazarus is "carried away by the "angels," while the rich man was simply "buried" (v. 22). That fits with the earlier statements about the joy the righteous angels feel when one person is saved.

Again, Jesus' point isn't that this is what *will* happen, but that this *could* happen. That was unthinkable in the theology of these leaders. Jesus went on:

> "But Abraham said, 'Child, remember that during your life you received your good things, and likewise Lazarus bad things; but now he is being comforted here, and you are in agony.'" (v. 25)

That's actually pretty fair, especially considering that the rich man had it in his power to change the situation.

> "'And besides all this, between us and you there is a great chasm fixed, so that those who wish to come over from here to you will not be able, and that none may cross over from there to us.'" (v. 26)

You can see here that this is not a parable about terms for salvation, or the nature of the afterlife. True, there no doubt is a chasm between the saved and the lost, so they don't hang out with each other. But neither would they be talking to each other like in this parable. This is just a story, and the details shouldn't be pushed too far.

In the parable of the rich man and Lazarus, we see one who had no higher purpose in life than to use his riches for selfishness and pleasure. Only too late he realized that his posh life was under the judgment of God.

Unbelief

At this point, Jesus created an exchange that brought to light the underlying problem—unbelief. The rich man went on talking to Abraham:

> "'Then I beg you, father, that you send him [Lazarus] to my father's house—for I have five brothers—in order that he may warn them, so that they will not also come to this place of torment.' But Abraham said, 'They have Moses and the Prophets; let them hear them.'" (vs. 27-29)

God's word is his provision for humans to know who he is and how to follow him. And the scribes and Pharisees were the curators of that collection of books. But Jesus had earlier said they set aside the Scriptures for the sake of their traditions (Mark 7:9). The Scriptures were rich in teaching the moral obligation to help the poor—a teaching the rich man had ignored. His brothers were probably doing the same.

> "But he said, 'No, father Abraham, but if someone goes to them from the dead, they will repent!'
>
> But Abraham said to him, 'If they do not listen to Moses and the Prophets, they will not be persuaded even if someone rises from the dead.'" (vs. 30-31)

Surely the rich man was right in saying that a supernatural resurrection from the dead would persuade his brothers, right? Wrong. And here we come to an intriguing part of this parable. Jesus began the parable by giving the poor man's name—Lazarus. It's very striking, because in all Jesus' parables, he never names any of the characters; just this one.

Jesus was also aware of future events, not because of his divine nature's omniscience. Rather, he received knowledge of the future from the Holy Spirit, as did other prophets. Part of that future was a man named Lazarus. You can tell from the dialog in the first part of John 11 that Jesus knew in advance what was coming with Lazarus.

Lazarus, brother to Mary and Martha, was not poor or helpless, like this man. But he was going to be raised from the dead in front of a group of onlookers. When word traveled to nearby Jerusalem, "The chief priests and the Pharisees convened a council, and were saying, 'What are we doing? For this man is performing many signs' . . . from that day on they planned together to kill Him" (John 11:47, 53).

That's great. So "kill Jesus and get Lazarus too—and this time make sure he *stays* dead!" Unbelief can withstand any amount of evidence, including resurrection. That's because unbelief is usually not based on evidence or reason, but on a willful determination to sin.

The Big Picture

In an earlier discourse, Jesus put a point on the issue with the Pharisees when he asked: "How can you believe, when you receive glory from one another and you do not seek the glory that is from the one and only God?" (John 5:44). It's a rhetorical question. The answer is that you cannot believe under these circumstances. Andrew Murray explains:

> It is indeed pride that makes faith impossible . . . in their very nature pride and faith are irreconcilable . . . we never can have more of true faith than we have of true humility. We need only think for a moment what faith is. Is it not the confession of nothingness and helplessness, the surrender and waiting to let God work? The acceptance of our place as dependents, who can claim or get or do nothing but what grace bestows?! . . . Faith seeks the glory that comes from God, that only comes where God is All. As long as we take glory from one another, as

> long as we ever seek and love and jealously guard the glory of this life—the honor and reputation that comes from men—we do not seek, and cannot receive the glory that comes from God. Pride renders faith impossible.[3]

Yes! Here is what the religious mentality doesn't accept. True faith begins with the admission of helplessness, but religion can easily become a venue for self-glorification. When that happens, faith is instantly supplanted with self.

Throughout this chapter of Luke, Jesus was repeatedly at odds with his audience. he summed this up when he said, "That which is highly esteemed among men is detestable in the sight of God" (v. 15). God's perspective is eternal. Humans' perspective is usually temporal. God stresses self-sacrificial love. Humans stress benefit for self. No wonder they rarely see eye to eye.

3. Andrew Murray, *Humility* (London: Marshall Brothers, 1895), 8.

30

Keys to Following God

Luke 17:1-19

Guilty Leaders

The chapter division doesn't belong here. Jesus is continuing his discourse about how God views people as being lost or found.

> He said to his disciples, "It is inevitable that stumbling blocks[1] come, but woe to him through whom they come! It would be better for him if a millstone were hung around his neck and he were thrown into the sea, than that he would cause one of these little ones to stumble." (Luke 17:1-2)

Here Jesus talks about the other side of his earlier description of the celebration in heaven when someone believes. What about when a young believer is led away from God? Rage! This is too important for God to shrug off.

Jesus is referring to the millstone or "runner stone"—a large disk of heavy rock with a hole in the middle that rotated over the "bedstone" to make

1. The word for stumbling block is *skandalon*, originally referring to a stick holding up a trap.

flour. He's imagining the false teacher's head being stuck through the hole before being cast into the sea. Death would quickly follow.

Murder is a crime too serious to treat in a soft manner. After all, murder is the taking of another's life. It must be punished. But what if, instead of taking someone's physical life, you take the life of his or her soul? That would be even worse! The result would be eternal. It's hard to imagine anything that would be more upsetting to God.

His warning directly applies to our thieving, lying, scamming preachers today. Unbelieving preachers and priests don't proclaim the gospel, because they don't believe it. Others, even believers, use the church as a pipeline to self-enrichment. James, Jesus' brother, warns, "Let not many of you become teachers, my brethren, knowing that as such we will incur a stricter judgment" (James 3:1). He may have had this saying of Jesus in mind.

On the other hand, we should remember what Jesus said in 12:37 "Blessed are those servants whom the master will find on the alert when he comes; truly I say to you, that he will gird himself to serve, and have them recline at the table, and will come up and wait on them."

Forgiveness

Jesus said,

> "Be on your guard! If your brother sins, rebuke him; and if he repents, forgive him. And if he sins against you seven times a day, and returns to you seven times, saying, 'I repent,' forgive him." (vs. 3-4)

We saw earlier when studying the Lord's Prayer, that forgiveness is a moral obligation for all followers of Jesus. It would be terribly hypocritical to accept forgiveness from God but refuse to extend it to others. This expectation that we forgive is very broad. Paul says,

> So, as those who have been chosen of God, holy and beloved, put on a heart of compassion, kindness, humility, gentleness and patience; bearing with one another, and *forgiving each other, whoever has a complaint against anyone; just as the Lord forgave you, so also should you.* (Colossians 3:12-13 emphasis added)

You can see that there are no exceptions to this rule to forgive. "Whoever" and "anyone" doesn't leave much wiggle room. And our forgiveness is to match Jesus' forgiveness. Where would we be if Jesus forgave most of our sins, but not all of them? We would be in hell.

Luke's account is unusual, because he adds the apparent condition that the sinning brother repents. In other passages, including the one above from Paul, there is no such condition. In Matthew's account of this saying (Matthew 18:21-22) Jesus gave no condition.

So to harmonize these passages, one must go by the least common denominator. In other words, we should forgive when someone repents, but we should also forgive when they don't repent. Unrepentance could dictate a different response on our part, perhaps including discipline. But it would not be reason to refuse forgiveness.

Is rebuking someone compatible with forgiving? It is. Even though you forgive someone, you might realize that person still would benefit from a reproof. It's not spoken out of anger, but for the wrongdoer's own good.

More Faith?

> The apostles said to the Lord, "Increase our faith!"
>
> And the Lord said, "If you had faith like a mustard seed, you would say to this mulberry tree, 'Be uprooted and be planted in the sea'; and it would obey you." (vs. 5-6)

Jesus is teaching that the amount of faith is less important than the object of faith. If we're putting faith in something that is not God's will, no amount of faith will make a difference. On the other hand, when putting a small amount of faith into something that fits God's expressed will, you reap a harvest of more faith, as God validates your faith and teaches you to trust more.

Why don't we see more flying mulberry trees? Because Jesus isn't suggesting that people use their faith to accomplish nonsense goals. Rather, he's saying that in believing prayer you unleash supernatural power—power that could easily move a mulberry tree, or even a mountain (Matthew 17:20). And God isn't going to wait until our faith is perfect, which will never happen. But he will grant believing prayer as long as it coincides with his will, as John says, "This is the confidence which we have before him, that, if we ask anything according to his will, he hears us" (1 John 5:14).

A Servant's Attitude

Jesus next unfolds an important component of true, biblical faith: humility and submission to God.

> "Which of you, having a servant plowing or tending sheep, will say to him when he has come in from the field, 'Come immediately and sit down to eat'? But will he not say to him, 'Prepare something for me to eat, and properly clothe yourself and serve me while I eat and drink; and afterward you may eat and drink'? He does not thank the servant because he did the things which were commanded, does he? So you too, when you do all the things which are commanded you, say, 'We are unworthy servants; we have done only that which we ought to have done.'" (vs. 7-10)

To understand what Jesus is calling for, consider the antithesis: an attitude of being entitled. Entitled people think they deserve blessing. If they ever give out, they expect to be praised or paid off in some way. Jesus is arguing that an entitled attitude has no place in the life of a humble servant.

Instead, followers who see things as they really are can't believe how fortunate they are to be accepted as God's servant. They are so in touch with their own unworthiness that it makes them overwhelmingly grateful. They consider doing their duty to be a blessing. Every opportunity to serve is another privilege.

Unentitled servitude is the only fitting attitude for followers of Jesus. In fact, Jesus said, "No longer do I call you slaves, for the slave does not know what his master is doing; but I have called you friends, for all things that I have heard from my Father I have made known to you" (John 15:15). Even though we are no longer slaves, but adopted children (Galatians 4:7), the attitude of servanthood should remain the same.

Remember, Jesus said he came to be a servant (22:27). We will never out-give Jesus. But no matter how gracious he is, it never justifies an entitled attitude. Whenever we tolerate an entitled attitude we lose our ability to be grateful, because we think we deserve blessings. This is aptly illustrated with the following story.

Ten Lepers

> While he was on the way to Jerusalem, he was passing between Samaria and Galilee. As he entered a village, ten leprous men who stood at a distance met him; and they raised their voices, saying, "Jesus, Master, have mercy on us!" When he saw them, he said to them, "Go and show yourselves to the priests." And as they were going, they were cleansed. (vs. 11-14)

As we saw earlier, ancient people didn't necessarily know how to diagnose Hanson's disease. But once a village concluded that someone had leprosy, they were treated accordingly—required to stay outside the village (where we see them here), and to keep a distance from other people. That's why they cried out to Jesus from a distance. He must have walked over to them.

He announced their healing, even though it wasn't immediately visible. Leviticus 14:1-32 gives the law on leprosy. There we learn that the priests were the medical officers who certified when a leper was healed. At that point, people would accept them again into the community. So by sending them to the priests, Jesus was implying that they would be healed.

Sure enough, not instantly, but as they walked, their symptoms disappeared. Why did their healing take time, instead of being instantaneous like the leper in chapter 5? Maybe Jesus was setting up a situation where they had the option to return with thanksgiving or not. If they had been healed in his presence they obviously would have thanked him, just out of politeness. Being at a distance revealed their true heart.

> Now one of them, when he saw that he had been healed, turned back, glorifying God with a loud voice, and he fell on his face at his feet, giving thanks to him. And he was a Samaritan. (vs. 15-16)

Of course he went back! How could he do otherwise? But nine others felt differently. The Samaritan didn't feel entitled. He knew he had no reason to expect that Jesus would heal his long fatal disease and turn around his agonizing, unfortunate life.

He was a Samaritan, but why bring that up? Probably, it suggests that the Jews were more likely to feel entitled because of their history as God's people. Then too, Luke, the gentile author, is always interested in God's dealings with other non-Jews.

> Then Jesus answered and said, "Were there not ten cleansed? But the nine—where are they? Was no one found who returned to give glory to God, except this foreigner?" And he said to him, "Stand up and go; your faith has made you well." (vs. 17-19)

It takes a lot to astonish the son of God. But you can sense the astonishment in Jesus words. Is it really possible that nine out of ten lepers were walking along, suddenly noticed their deadly disease was gone, and said, "Hmm. Nice," and went on their way? Yes, under the entitled attitude people can absorb incredible blessing with little or no gratitude.

Lack of gratitude leads to profound spiritual blindness. Anyone who fails to take the time and mental energy to think through what they are thankful for will begin to take blessings for granted. They may hardly notice even amazing blessing.

Healthy, growing believers know that if God never did anything good for us after the cross, we could express nothing but thanksgiving forever! But the entitled believer harbors soul-shredding ungratefulness that will ruin their relationship with God. The unthankful heart is like a bucket with no bottom. No amount of blessing makes any difference.

The Big Picture

Imagine a friend of mine who has been cheating on his taxes. He now owes a hundred thousand dollars in back taxes. The government is taking his house and sentencing him to a lengthy time in prison.

But I meet up with him, and tell him, "My wife and I have been saving up for retirement, and we decided we don't want to see you go to jail, so we're going to pay off this tax debt."

He smiles, grasps my hand in joy. Then he says, "This is wonderful, and . . . well, I think you should throw in a new set of living room furniture."

I look at him, stunned. "What?"

"You know, you've seen my furniture. It's pretty worn. I could really use a new set." Then, with a frown, "I know you have the money . . ."

What's wrong with this picture? Is it wrong to ask God for more than he's already given? Not if we're grateful. Not if we're able to appreciate all that God is and all that God has done already. Not if we are asking only what would glorify God. God is eager to give. But if he continues to give to ungrateful followers, it will only make matters worse. Like spoiled children who always get whatever they want, ungrateful believers never appreciate God's generosity, and that leads to a negative relationship. They don't grow.

Jesus was teaching his followers about forgiveness, gratitude, the nature of faith, and a servant attitude. He was warning them against feeling entitled.

31

The Days of the Son of Man

Luke 17:20-37

The chapter division belongs here, because the rest of the chapter deals with Jesus' second coming, and the end of history as we know it. The Pharisees were questioning Jesus: "Now having been questioned by the Pharisees as to when the kingdom of God was coming" (17:20).

Remember, in their minds this was not a question about the second coming. The Old Testament was their only source of information about the promised kingdom, and it says nothing about two comings for the Messiah. So they were asking Jesus why he hadn't begun his kingdom already. Or if there was some reason for waiting, what were they waiting for?

Jesus answered:

> "The kingdom of God is not coming with signs to be observed; nor will they say, 'Look, here it is!' or, 'There it is!' For behold, the kingdom of God is in your midst." (vs. 20-21)

Why did Jesus say the kingdom "is not coming with signs to be observed," when he later said there would be signs? (21:25). The best explanation is that he is answering the Pharisees of his own day, who would not see any of the signs he later predicted. In other words, "There are no signs that you guys are going to see."

Notice a difference in translation on this verse. NIV translates it "The kingdom of God is within you." Taken this way, it would mean that the kingdom is inward, in the sense that people enter by faith. But why would Jesus say the Pharisees had the kingdom in their hearts (plural)?

More likely, he said the kingdom was already "in their midst" (NIV, NASB). That is, that he, Jesus—the king—was already in their midst. In either case, there would be no signs people of that generation could look for to announce the coming of the kingdom, other than the miracles he had already performed. His other statement in chapter 21, that there would be signs, was for future generations.

Days of the Son of Man

The following discussion is a different talk, given, not to the Pharisees, but to his disciples, perhaps days later (v. 22). To properly interpret this passage, the reader has to determine how it relates to the so-called "Olivet Discourse" found in Matthew 24, Mark 13, and later in Luke 21. Those three passages are clearly different accounts of a discourse with some similarities to this one. That discourse happened during the final week of Jesus' life according to all three accounts.

This discourse in Luke 17 has some remarkable similarities, and even identical language at a number of points. But Luke has this discussion earlier, while Jesus is still near Galilee. It's a good example of how similar language can be used in different settings to express different points. We must be careful not to read Luke 17 as a fourth recounting of the Olivet Discourse. We can learn by comparing them, but must not force the issue. They are harmonious, but they are two different talks.

Surprise

To his disciples Jesus said, "The days will come when you will long to see one of the days of the Son of Man, and you will not see it" (v. 22). His main message here is that his disciples were *not* going to see the days of the Son of Man. His concern is that they not succumb to fake claims that those days have arrived.

Some in the early church bought into exactly this error. In 2 Thessalonians 2 Paul warns them, "Don't be so easily shaken or alarmed by those who say that the day of the Lord has already begun" (v. 2).

Jesus went on:

> "They will say to you, 'Look there! Look here!' Do not go away, and do not run after them. For just like the lightning, when it flashes out of one part of the sky, shines to the other part of the sky, so will the Son of Man be in his day." (vs. 23-24)

There will be no baby in a feeding trough for this coming. Jesus declares that he will come in triumph like lightning that lights up the whole sky. Everyone will know the Son of Man has come. "So will the Son of Man be in his day." It doesn't really mention a second coming, even though that's what he's talking about. They could have easily understood that this is a future event in Jesus' life.

Then he adds,

> "But first he must suffer many things and be rejected by this generation." (v. 25)

Here is a definite hint about the two comings, but still ambiguous. He is going to suffer, but does that necessarily mean he would ascend to heaven and return millennia later? No, and nobody was thinking in those terms. But a sharp eye might pick up that there are two phases to the plan.

Is the expression "the days of the Son of Man" the same as the Old and New Testament expression "the day of the Lord?" The day of the Lord is a frequent expression, especially in the Old Testament prophets. Careful study shows that it doesn't always refer to an actual day, but to a range of days beginning with the great tribulation and spanning through the coming of the Messiah, and beyond into his kingdom.[1]

The main theme is the Messiah's coming and the day of God's judgment. The Old and New Testament also consider the coming period of tribulation to be a judgment from God. Sometimes the expression refers to lesser days of judgment. So the expressions are certainly related and

1. For example Isaiah 13:6, 9; Lamentations 2:22; Ezekiel 30:3; Amos 5:18, 20; Joel 3:14; Obadiah 15; Zephaniah 1:8, 14, 18, 2:3; 1 Corinthians 5:5; 1 Thessalonians 5:2.

probably synonymous. It's the day God comes and takes over, sets things right, punishes unbelief and sin, and sets up his kingdom.

Unexpected

Jesus went on:

> "Just as it happened in the days of Noah, so it will be also in the days of the Son of Man: they were eating, they were drinking, they were marrying, they were being given in marriage, until the day that Noah entered the ark, and the flood came and destroyed them all." (vs. 26-27)

In the days of Noah, people probably laughed at the spectacle of Noah and his family building an ocean-going barge far from the nearest ocean. The people were completely oblivious to the coming flood that would spell their doom. So this preoccupation with the things of the world and complete lack of spiritual awareness will also be typical of the last days.

> "It was the same as happened in the days of Lot: they were eating, they were drinking, they were buying, they were selling, they were planting, they were building; but on the day that Lot went out from Sodom it rained fire and brimstone from heaven and destroyed them all. It will be just the same on the day that the Son of Man is revealed." (vs. 28-30)

Lot lived in the wicked ancient city of Sodom. As he busied himself with accommodating to Sodom's values, the doom of the city drew near. When the people in Sodom least expected it, fire rained down on their city, destroying them all. Once again, surprise is in view. Later, the apostle Paul stressed the same thing.

> For you yourselves know full well that the day of the Lord will come just like a thief in the night. While they are saying, "Peace and safety!" then destruction will come upon them suddenly like labor pains upon a woman with child, and they will not escape. (1 Thessalonians 5:2-3)

Near the time of the coming of the Day of the Lord, people will cry, "Peace and safety!" Is it a plea for peace that will cause people to accept anything in order to escape the chaos? Or more likely, is this a cry of relief from people who believe they finally have solved the world's problems?

Back in Luke, both verses 27 and 29 end with the phrase "destroyed them all." Whether it was the flood of Noah, or fire in the days of Lot, the ones swept away were the non-believers. These allusions are not (as some think) referring to the rapture of believers (where God translates believers from mortal to immortal). These verses refer to the judgment of God destroying non-believers. It is significant, however, that in both Sodom and Noah's flood, God went to great lengths to get his people out before the judgment fell.

Comparing with Matthew

Jesus warned that people will need to respond quickly to escape this event. They won't have time to get their things from the house (v. 31). He said something very similar in his Olivet Discourse:

> "Therefore when you see the Abomination of Desolation which was spoken of through Daniel the prophet, standing in the holy place (let the reader understand), then those who are in Judea must flee to the mountains. Whoever is on the housetop must not go down to get the things out that are in his house. Whoever is in the field must not turn back to get his cloak.... For then there will be a great tribulation, such as has not occurred since the beginning of the world until now, nor ever will." (Matthew 24:15-21)

We will cover this passage in more detail when we get to Luke's version of the Olivet Discourse. For now, we can notice that the danger people are fleeing is signaled by something called "the Abomination of Desolation." He adds that the term comes from the Old Testament book of Daniel. There, it was an act of defiling the temple. Notice that the danger signaled by this event is "a great tribulation such as has not occurred since the beginning of the world until now, nor ever will" (Matthew 24:21).

Jesus used very similar language about not going down in the house to get one's belongings. But he adds that "those who are in Judea must flee to the mountains." So these instructions are for people living in Judea when this Abomination of Desolation happens.

It's not about the fall of Jerusalem in AD 70, as some claim.[2] True, the

2. One school of interpretation called Preterism argues that everything in this discourse and in the whole New Testament (including the book of Revelation) has already been fulfilled during the first

Romans defiled the temple after their siege of Jerusalem, but by then it would have been too late to flee to the mountains. It was impossible to escape Jerusalem once the Romans invested the city. Neither would that war fit the description of a great tribulation worse than any in the history of the world, past or future. Rather, it's referring to the great tribulation of the last days. That's when the so-called Battle of Armageddon happens.

In Matthew 24:26-27 we also find this language:

> "So if they say to you, 'Behold, he is in the wilderness,' do not go out, or, 'Behold, he is in the inner rooms,' do not believe them. For just as the lightning comes from the east and flashes even to the west, so will the coming of the Son of Man be."

That's almost identical to language in Luke 17. But Matthew adds:

> "And then the sign of the Son of Man will appear in the sky, and then all the tribes of the earth will mourn,[3] and they will see the Son of Man coming on the clouds of the sky with power and great glory." (Matthew 24:30)

So the Olivet Discourse and this discourse in Luke 17 are referring to Jesus' second coming, not to the siege of Jerusalem in AD 70, except for a few verses in Luke 21, as we will see. The disaster from which people should flee is the great tribulation. Apparently, getting out of cities, especially Jerusalem, and into the mountains will result in a better chance of surviving the war.

Lot's Wife?

Back in Luke, after comparing the end of the destruction of Sodom, Jesus adds, "Remember Lot's wife" (v. 32). Why remember her? She was the one who, after two angels dragged Lot's family out of Sodom, was given the instruction "Escape for your life! Do not look behind you" (Genesis 19:17). But she did look back, and became a pillar of salt!

---

century. I am not going to recount the debate over Preterism in detail because the view is rare in American culture, usually only found in seminaries and certain churches. I will only make a few observations where the implausibility of this view comes up. For those interested in studying the subject in depth, I recommend my colleague's book, James Rochford, *Endless Hope or Hopeless End: The Bible and the End of Human History* (Columbus, OH: New Paradigm Publishing, 2016).

3. Jesus is alluding to Zechariah 12:10, "They will look on me whom they have pierced; and they will mourn for him, as one mourns for an only son, and they will weep bitterly over Him like the bitter weeping over a firstborn." The time context for Zechariah's prophecy is also the last war of the world according to chapter 13 and 14.

Why did Jesus bring this event up? Lot's wife looking back probably stands for having a divided heart. She was still attached to life in Sodom. At least, the story underscores the need to flee with utmost urgency. Lot's wife looking back is probably parallel to people going back to their houses to retrieve their property.

Rescue or Judgment

As Jesus moved to his conclusion, he made some enigmatic statements.

> "Whoever seeks to keep his life will lose it, and whoever loses his life will preserve it." (v. 33)

We saw him make this same statement in 9:24. There, it referred to people denying themselves, and taking up their crosses daily as disciples. Here, it probably refers to abandoning the goods in your house in order to save your life.

> "I tell you, on that night there will be two in one bed; one will be taken and the other will be left. There will be two women grinding at the same place; one will be taken and the other will be left." (vs. 34-35)

As we saw earlier with Sodom's destruction and Noah's flood, the one being "taken" is swept away to judgment. That judgment happens at Jesus' second coming. Revelation 19 says,

> "And I saw heaven opened, and behold, a white horse, and he who sat on it is called Faithful and True, and in righteousness he judges and wages war. . . . And [the non-believers] were killed with the sword which came from the mouth of him who sat on the horse. (vs. 11, 21)

So Jesus slays the godless upon his return. "The sword coming out of his mouth" probably means he simply speaks a command, and they all fall dead.

Where?

The disciples respond with an ambiguous question: "Where Lord?" Jesus' answer is equally enigmatic. "Where the body is, there also the vultures will be gathered." (v. 37) It seems like he's brushing off their question. In a sense saying, "Just as the gathering of vultures shows there is a carcass nearby, so these signs will indicate that the end is near" (NLT). When you see vultures circling, you usually can't see the carcass or identify what it is. But you know it must be there, or they wouldn't be circling. So this is similar to his saying that nobody knows the day or the hour, but they should know the general time.

The Big Picture

Most religious worldviews see history as cyclical. They see us going through successive cycles often for millions of years. Scholars of religion believe they get this cyclical view from nature. The seasons repeat themselves. Key themes are birth, fertility, followed by death and rebirth of the gods. Most see life continuing on like this indefinitely.

None of this is true. We now know that history is linear, as argued in the Bible. History extends from the date of creation, to the *telos* (end). This is the teleological or linear view of history. If there had been a previous time when humans developed the skyscrapers and highways we see today, we would know it. This is the only time human history has happened.

Jesus was warning his disciples of things to come. Referring to some of this same material, he said, "Behold, I have told you in advance" (Matthew 24:25). Instead of going in circles, Jesus taught that history comes to an end with the his second coming. Neither will humanity progress into a golden future of health and peace. Instead, humanity's future is Armageddon; but not for all. We learn from this discourse that rescue is going to be individual. Why are two women grinding at the mill and only one is taken? It's because one believed, and the other didn't.

According to Jesus, many people are going to be surprised when the days of the Son of Man arrive, just like they were in the days of Noah. In that episode we read that after Noah and his family entered the ark, "God closed it behind them." (Genesis 7:16). In that moment it suddenly became too late to change one's mind. That's going to happen again with the coming of the days of the Son of Man.

Jesus also said these days would be like the days of Sodom. That primarily referred to their surprise and unpreparedness. But we wonder, how much more will it be like it was in Sodom? Sodom had a consensus of evil. Not only the men, but "those young and old" attempted to rape the two men sent to them (Genesis 19:4).

They were also guilty of "pride, gluttony, and laziness, while the poor and needy suffered outside her door" (Ezekiel 16:40). When a culture adopts a consensus of evil, anything can happen. Accounts of these days indicate it will be very dangerous, especially for followers of Jesus. We need to decide now that we will not compromise or value our possessions too much; good advice at all times.

32

Prayer Parables
Luke 18:1-17

The Unrighteous Judge

> Now he was telling them a parable to show that at all times they ought to pray and not to lose heart, saying, "In a certain city there was a judge who did not fear God and did not respect man. There was a widow in that city, and she kept coming to him, saying, 'Give me legal protection from my opponent.' For a while he was unwilling; but afterward he said to himself, 'Even though I do not fear God nor respect man, yet because this widow bothers me, I will give her legal protection, otherwise by continually coming she will wear me out.'" (Luke 18:1-5)

It's our old friend, the *a fortiori* argument. Jesus was teaching on the importance of persevering in prayer, as Luke stated in his intro: "to show that at all times they ought to pray and not to lose heart" (v. 1). The jarring impression is that Jesus was portraying God as reluctant and uncaring (like in an analogy) and will only answer prayer if he's pestered until he can't stand it anymore. I remember that impression when I read this as a horrified, new believer.

But in an *a fortiori* argument following the pattern "If this, how much more that," the judge and God are not alike at all. They are as different as can be. Jesus, after all, calls the judge "unrighteous" as he finishes the argument:

> And the Lord said, "Hear what the unrighteous judge said; now, will not God bring about justice for his elect who cry to him day and night, and will he delay long over them? I tell you that he will bring about justice for them quickly." (vs. 6-8)

In other words, Jesus was saying, "If a no-good, heartless judge responds to perseverance, how much more will a warmhearted, good father respond to perseverance from his children?" The extreme difference between the judge and God makes the argument stronger.

He chooses a widow in this story probably because of the weak position they held in that culture. Widows were virtually powerless and depended on others to get justice.

The saying, "will he delay long over them?" is best understood to mean, "Will he keep putting them off?" It means that God won't wait any longer than necessary. In the context of chapter 17 and verse 8b "However, when the Son of Man comes, will he find faith on the earth?" it refers to the vindication of God's people at his second coming.

His question about whether he will find faith when he comes probably refers to the low state of the community of believers during the "great apostasy" predicted for the last days (e.g. 2 Thessalonians 2:3).

He says, "he will bring about justice for them quickly" (v. 8a), implying the answer will come soon. But the word "quickly" could also mean "suddenly." That reading makes more sense. The second coming will come suddenly, just as he had been warning in the previous chapter.

Perseverance in Prayer

This leads to one reason why perseverance in prayer is necessary. Even when praying in accord with God's will, the question of timing remains in his hands. There may be reasons for delay that we don't know. For instance, God is waiting until the full number of servants of God and martyrs is fulfilled before he comes again (Revelation 6:11).

He may wait to answer prayer for a number of reasons. Sometimes, he uses delay in answering prayer to strengthen our faith. This was clear in the life of Abraham and Sarah, who had to wait over twenty years for a promised son. People who fail to persevere in prayer don't grow in faith. Instead, they often don't even notice when the original prayer was answered. But when you persevere throughout the wait, your faith takes a quantum leap upward when the answer comes.

Another reason to persevere is that our enemy, the Evil One, perseveres. He's not going to back off, so we can't back off.

God may know of background factors that call for waiting—things we have no knowledge of, like we saw earlier with the long wait after the Old Testament for Jesus' first coming. He might delay allowing your ministry to expand because he knows you're not mature enough to handle that.

The struggle you have while persevering forces you to confront deeper questions. Why am I following God? Why is my heart set on developing ministry? Is God not for me? As you struggle with these thoughts, you hopefully reach the right conclusions. Struggles like these are like putting stress on your muscles while lifting weight. The stress is what leads to growth.

This parable teaches that when waiting for Jesus to return, and it seems like a long wait, don't be discouraged. Keep praying and waiting on God to complete his plan.

The Pharisee and the Tax Collector

Jesus' next parable may be the clearest declaration he ever gave on the collision of works and grace. Luke spells out the audience: "He told this parable to some people who trusted in themselves that they were righteous, and viewed others with contempt" (v. 9).

> "Two men went up into the temple to pray, one a Pharisee and the other a tax collector. The Pharisee stood and was praying this to himself: 'God, I thank You that I am not like other people: swindlers, unjust, adulterers, or even like this tax collector. 'I fast twice a week; I pay tithes of all that I get.'" (vs. 10-12)

Jesus created this profile thoughtfully. The Pharisee stands praying, which was traditional, but it was also a good way to show off. Jesus mentioned their long, showy prayers elsewhere, and said they were for appearance's sake (20:47).

Jesus, choosing his words, said the Pharisee spoke "to himself." That's because the thrust of the Pharisee's prayer was more to justify himself than to commune with God.

He thanks God that he's "not like other people." But where did other people come into his train of thought? At the core of the religious mentality is a comparative standard for religious performance. In this story, he has picked the easiest of all people to compare himself to—a tax collector. We saw earlier, when studying Levi, that being a tax collector only appealed to the small non-religious part of the population. Apart from being turncoats collaborating with the national enemy, they were notoriously immoral in other ways.

If we want to compare ourselves, there is only one person to compare ourselves to—God himself (Matthew 5:48).

Jesus' audience would perceive that he has set before them the most strictly moral and religious man alongside the worst, calloused evildoer.

The Pharisee gives the evidence of his awesomeness: "I fast twice a week; I pay tithes of all that I get" (v. 12). So that's it?

We notice here more features of the religious mentality.

First, these acts are external. They say nothing about the Pharisee's heart. To see his heart, look at his self-righteousness as he compares himself, noting his own superiority.

Second, both of these acts are relatively easy. They come nowhere close to loving the Lord with all your heart, soul, mind, and strength. Let alone loving your neighbor as yourself.

Thirdly, even in these simple acts, the Pharisee has moved outside of what Scripture calls for. As we saw earlier, the Old Testament never calls on people to fast. But this religious standard has him fasting twice a week. We also saw how they had twisted the tithing law to include picky things like tithing your mint, dill, and cumin.

Finally, these religious acts can easily be carried out by someone who is not close to God and only wants to show off his own religiosity.

That means the Pharisee's self-assessment is external, easy, unbiblical, and ignores motivation. Even so, most of Jesus' audience would be nodding their heads, "Of course. Who could be more holy than a Pharisee?"

Jesus went on,

> "But the tax collector, standing some distance away, was even unwilling to lift up his eyes to heaven, but was beating his breast, saying, 'God, be merciful to me, the sinner!'" (v. 13)

To many in his audience, including any lurking Pharisees, their reaction to this would be, "Of course! He'd better plead for mercy." But according to some rabbis, a tax collector had already gone too far to be forgiven. He shouldn't even be allowed in the temple.

Then comes the punch line:

> "I tell you, this man [the tax collector] went to his house justified rather than the other; for everyone who exalts himself will be humbled, but he who humbles himself will be exalted." (v. 14)

To the tax collector, God extends a warm hand and with a smile grants his plea for mercy. He is "justified"—a term that means acquitted, or declared not guilty. That would have stunned Jesus' audience. You must be kidding! A tax collector? No way!

But the other part would probably be even more stunning: the tax collector is justified "rather than the other." In other words, God turns his back on the Pharisee. To the self-righteous, God says, "I have nothing for you."

Contrary to what the Pharisee thought, he was also a sinner, just like the tax collector, although his sins took a different form. But Jesus was saying that the Pharisee was actually in more danger of God's judgment than the tax collector. At least the tax collector knew he was guilty and in need of mercy and forgiveness. The Pharisee's self-constructed religious framework kept him from seeing his own need for forgiveness.

Jesus closed with one of his common sayings: "Everyone who exalts himself will be humbled, but he who humbles himself will be exalted" (v. 14). Nothing is more offensive to God than his fallen creatures feeling proud of themselves. This is especially true when it comes to feeling proud of your own righteousness. God intends to eradicate pride, the original sin and the source of Satan's fall. Paul says, "God has chosen the weak things of the world to shame the things which are strong . . . so that no man may boast before God" (1 Corinthians 1:27, 29).

Blessing the Babies

In keeping with the same theme, Luke recounts,

> And they were bringing even their babies to him so that he would touch them, but when the disciples saw it, they began scolding them. But Jesus called for them, saying, "Permit the children to come to me, and do not hinder them, for the kingdom of God belongs to such as these. Truly I say to you, whoever does not receive the kingdom of God like a child will not enter it at all." (vs. 15-17)[1]

It's wonderful to discover that Jesus loved children. He was the kind of man who understood the cuteness, simplicity, and purity in little kids. Were they climbing on him and playing with him? Mark says, "He took them in his arms and began blessing them, laying his hands on them" (Mark 10:16). He knew the importance of loving touch. He warned his disciples, "Beware that you don't look down on any of these little ones" (Matthew 18:10)

And Mark adds that when Jesus saw his disciples scolding the children, "he was indignant" (Mark 10:14). So it upset him to see them interfering with his contact with kids. What were they thinking? Was it that Jesus is too important to be bothered by kids?

Jesus' theological point is in line with the parable of the Pharisee and the tax collector. When he says, "Whoever does not receive the kingdom of God like a child will not enter it at all" (v. 17), the child's humility is in view. Matthew's account includes,

> Anyone who becomes as humble as this little child is the greatest in the Kingdom of Heaven. And anyone who welcomes a little child like this on my behalf is welcoming me. (Matthew 18:4-5)

The main meaning for the word Jesus used here, "welcoming," means to

1. This passage was later wrongly used to justify infant baptism. Jesus doesn't discuss baptism here. He was blessing the children, not baptizing them. And while it mentions babies (v. 15), it also mentions children (v. 16-17), a different word for older children.

take by the hand. A small child will often reach out to hold your hand, especially if the going is rough and easy to slip on. He has the sense to know he needs a stronger, steady hand to grasp.

Children don't even know what pride is. As we saw earlier when studying Luke 9, Jesus valued the humility of children. They frankly depend on their parents without any embarrassment. They know they need help, and they aren't reluctant to ask for it. Jesus calls us to be that way too, not proud and self-sufficient like the Pharisee.

The Big Picture

Parables like this one failed to cause Pharisees and other self-righteous people to see the error of their ways. Instead, these parables were stoking the fire of hate that would lead to Jesus' murder.

The picture of Jesus and the children should comfort our hearts. We see nothing dour or distant in Jesus. He was the kind of person who liked having kids climb all over him.

That same welcoming, accepting love comes to us as Jesus offers to welcome anyone who, like the tax collector, will admit our helplessness and need.

33

Coming to Jesus
Luke 18:18-19:10

As Jesus continued journeying south, his account now syncs up again with Matthew and Mark. Luke has come to the end of his special, unique source.

The Rich Young Ruler

> Once a religious leader asked Jesus this question: "Good teacher, what should I do to inherit eternal life?" (Luke 18:18 NLT)

Luke calls him a ruler, but NLT is probably right in calling him a religious leader. The rulers were the Romans. This man could have belonged to the Sanhedrin, or was leader of a synagogue, although Matthew says he was young (Matthew 19:22). That meant "young" in their view, not in our view. Jews wouldn't sit under a rabbi's teaching until he was at least thirty years old.

Jesus challenged his description, "good teacher."

> "Why do you call me good?" Jesus asked him. "Only God is truly good. (v. 19)

What was Jesus saying here, and why was he saying it? It's clear that the man's title, "good teacher" is not an adequate description of Jesus. He was much more than a teacher. But mainly, he's calling into question whether the ruler understood what constitutes "good."

As the story progresses, it becomes clear the ruler sees "good" from a human viewpoint mediated through the rabbinic consensus, not from God's viewpoint. The ruler was a believer in the current false teaching holding Israel in its grip, namely that by generally following the reduced rabbinic version of the law, one could satisfy God's requirements. Jesus went on,

> "You know the commandments: 'You must not commit adultery. You must not murder. You must not steal. You must not testify falsely. Honor your father and mother.'" (v. 20)

This curious collection of laws all came from the second tablet of the Ten Commandments, about relating to one's neighbor. But he left off the tenth—not coveting anything that belonged to your neighbor. The Jews often viewed the tenth commandment against coveting as referring to greed. Was Jesus selecting laws that were easier to follow in that culture? The ruler had no doubt about his answer:

> The man replied, "I've obeyed all these commandments since I was young." (v. 21)

So, this man felt like the apostle Paul, who said, "As for righteousness, I obeyed the law without fault" (Philippians 3:6). That was when Paul was a Pharisee. Later, he realized the true demands of God's law—not the diminished version the rabbis cooked up; not that we keep the law some of the time; not that we keep the letter of the law but not the spirit of the law; not that we keep the law more than the other guy does. After meeting Jesus Paul could face the truth:

> But those who depend on the law to make them right with God are under his curse, for the Scriptures say, "Cursed is everyone who does not observe and obey *all* the commands that are written in God's Book of the Law." (Galatians 3:10 NLT; quoting from Deuteronomy 27:26, emphasis added)

Every last law, all the time. That's the standard. He said later the law was given "so that every mouth may be closed and all the world may become accountable to God" (Romans 3:19). This ruler's question, "Which ones?" shows he didn't understand that. Mark comments at this point: "Looking at the man, Jesus felt genuine love for him" (Mark 10: 21). So he was seriously trying to guide the ruler to see truth, not manipulating him.

Jesus deftly and effortlessly exposed the truth about the ruler:

> "There is still one thing you haven't done. Sell all your possessions and give the money to the poor, and you will have treasure in heaven. Then come, follow me." (v. 22)[1]

The first commandment God gave to Moses was, "I am the Lord your God. . . . You shall have no other gods before me" (Exodus 10:2-3). So God is to be first in our lives, and we should have no other god. Someone who fits this description should have no problem getting rid of his stuff in exchange for an opportunity to follow Jesus.

But no. "When the man heard this he became very sad, for he was very rich" (v. 23). The ruler's riches were more important to him than God. He was not following the law, not even the first law.

The correct response to Jesus' proposition was not to walk away, but to admit, "I guess I'm not following the law." And then beg for mercy. "Is there any other way?" Then the law would be fulfilling its true purpose—exposing the need for grace. Jesus would answer, "Yes! The way of faith." But this man's belief that he was already obeying the law was blocking him from pleading for grace. He couldn't see the need.

So Jesus watched him walking away and turned back to his disciples, musing.

> "How hard it is for those who are wealthy to enter the kingdom of God! For it is easier for a camel to go through the eye of a needle than for a rich man to enter the kingdom of God." (vs. 24-25)

They were shocked. This is the opposite of what they had been taught. Rabbinic teaching argued that the righteous are rewarded by God, and

1. This passage was later the basis for medieval "mendicant monks" who disowned all possessions and money. They lived by begging ("mendicant" comes from the Latin word for begging) and scavenging. When seeing this verse in the context of the rest of the New Testament, it's clear that the mendicant reading is not supported. Private ownership of property is taught and protected (e.g. Acts 5:4; Ephesians 4:28), and believers are expected to work for their food and other needs, not to beg and become a burden on others (e.g. 1 Thessalonians 4:11; 1 Timothy 5:8). This verse in Luke was a special situation, meant to expose the ruler's heart, not to be followed by all.

their riches are a sign of his favor. That's why they ask, "Then who in the world can be saved?" (v. 26).

Jesus answered, "What is impossible for people is possible with God" (v. 27). That, of course, is true of all salvation, not just rich people. No human is good enough to merit eternal life. But Jesus is also suggesting that it's even harder for the rich to be converted.

Experience and history bear that out. The acclaim and comfort the rich enjoy can blunt their sense of spiritual need. It's not that the rich can't be won to faith, but that it's rare (1 Corinthians 1:26-27). Historically, the gospel has moved through the middle and lower classes far more than the upper classes.

Paul's argument in 1 Corinthians is that trying to reach the rich so they can reach the rest of society is wrong-headed. The wealthy have historically seen the body of Christ as something they can control and use to their advantage, or as a threatening alternative loyalty. We have also often enough seen a strong servant of God receive a big inheritance or other fortune and it quenched their zeal for the things of God.

What About Us?

At that point, Peter burst out,

> "We have left our own homes and followed you."
>
> And Jesus said to them, "Truly I say to you, there is no one who has left house or wife or brothers or parents or children, for the sake of the kingdom of God, who will not receive many times as much at this time and in the age to come, eternal life." (vs. 28-30)

In other words, we will never out-give God. Mark is more explicit about how God will reward any who give up possessions or people for his sake:

> They will receive a hundred times as much now in the present age, houses and brothers and sisters and mothers and children and farms, along with persecutions; and in the age to come, eternal life. (Mark 10:30)

How do we receive houses, mothers, brothers, and farms? He's referring to the people of God. While our full reward awaits arrival in heaven, we are not without reward in this life. For those who build into a healthy, loving community of believers, the rich brotherhood and inter-connectedness is a reward in itself.

And, of course he includes, "along with persecutions." There will be a price to pay any time the people of God move forward. We will suffer attack. But Jesus assures us here that he will personally make it worth our while.

These are sufficient and good reasons to be willing to sacrifice for the name of Jesus. Viewed with the eyes of faith, it's only temporary sacrifice.

Real Sacrifice

Perhaps talking about sacrifice made Jesus think about what he knew was coming:

> Then he took the Twelve aside and said to them, "Behold, we are going up to Jerusalem, and all things which are written through the prophets about the Son of Man will be accomplished. For he will be handed over to the Gentiles, and will be mocked and mistreated and spit upon, and after they have scourged him, they will kill him; and the third day he will rise again." (vs. 31-33)

This disclosure is amazingly detailed and easy to understand. It's at least the fourth time Jesus has given this type of warning. One of Isaiah's "Servant Songs" predicted the spitting:

> "I gave my back to those who strike me, And my cheeks to those who pluck out the beard; I did not cover my face from humiliation and spitting." (Isaiah 50:6)

A sharp reader might have seen the implication—that Jesus is the suffering servant. But the reaction from the disciples is disappointing:

> The disciples understood none of these things, and the meaning of this statement was hidden from them, and they did not comprehend the things that were said. (v. 34)

We've seen this before. But it becomes more and more surprising as Jesus repeats and elaborates the warnings. Luke's source (probably one of the disciples) says it three different ways: "They understood none of these things," "It was hidden from them," and, "They did not comprehend." How is that possible?

Perhaps the second statement, "It was hidden from them," means that God himself hid the meaning. The wording, with the passive of *krupto*, could easily be translated, "it was kept secret from them." If the disciples understood too much at this point in history, things might not have played out right.

Whether it was being concealed from them, or they were just too locked into their own paradigm, it's clear from the crucifixion and resurrection narratives that they still didn't understand even at that late hour. It wasn't until Jesus "opened their eyes to understand the Scripture" (24:45) that they finally understood

Bartimaeus

Jesus finally made it to the bottom of the mountain range where Jerusalem was built. He's in the Jordan valley, near the Dead Sea, approaching the city of Jericho. From here he begins to ascend the winding road upward, four thousand feet in elevation.

> As Jesus was approaching Jericho,[2] a blind man was sitting by the road begging.[3] Now hearing a crowd going by, he began to inquire what this was. They told him that Jesus of Nazareth was passing by. And he called out, saying, "Jesus, Son of David, have mercy on me!" Those who led the way were sternly telling him to be quiet; but he kept crying out all the more, "Son of David, have mercy on me!" (vs. 35-39)

He clearly knew who Jesus was, and cried out to him using the title, "Son of David," so he believed Jesus was the Messiah.

> And Jesus stopped and commanded that he be brought to him;

2. Mark and Matthew say Jesus was leaving Jericho, but Luke says he was entering Jericho. The apparent contradiction is probably a reflection of the fact that there were two cities of Jericho in the first century. The ancient site (famous from the book of Joshua) was at this time a small village about two miles from the new city built by Herod the Great. This incident could have happened between the two cities. So he was either entering or leaving Jericho depending on which town was in view.

3. Matthew says there were two blind men. That can't be a contradiction, because if there were two, there had to also be one. This could be a case of selectivity. Mark and Luke focused on one man, possibly because he did the talking.

> and when he came near, Jesus questioned him, "What do you want me to do for you?" (vs. 40-41)

How strange that Jesus would ask this question! Wasn't it obvious? He did this more than once. When healing the paralytic at the Pool of Bethesda he stooped down to the man and asked him, "Would you like to get well?" (John 5:6). Interestingly that man didn't answer Jesus' question. He just complained about how nobody cared enough to help him. So this could be a metaphor for prayer. The man at Bethesda just complained, but never asked to be healed. Not so with this man:

> And he said, "Lord, I want to regain my sight!"
>
> And Jesus said to him, "Receive your sight; your faith has made you well." Immediately he regained his sight and began following Jesus, glorifying God; and when all the people saw it, they gave praise to God. (vs. 41-43)

Apparently his friend, who was also blind, was standing there, and Jesus healed him as well (Matthew 20:30, 34).

Zacchaeus

The main road from the eastern side of the Jordan crossed over to the west and went through Jericho. That made the city a key location for taxing traffic heading up to Jerusalem.

> Jesus entered Jericho and made his way through the town. There was a man there named Zacchaeus. He was the chief tax collector in the region, and he had become very rich. (vs. 1-2 NLT)

Zacchaeus was a "chief tax collector." That means he held the license for the region and hired regular collectors to work under him. This is unlike Matthew, who was a regular collector (5:27–30). He must have heard about Jesus, because he was zealous to see and hear him.

> He tried to get a look at Jesus, but he was too short to see over the crowd. So he ran ahead and climbed a sycamore-fig tree beside the road, for Jesus was going to pass that way. (vs. 3-4 NLT)

Middle aged men don't usually climb trees today, and they would have even less back then. With their robes, it was awkward to climb and it was considered undignified. The sight caught Jesus' eye. That he was up in a tree spoke eloquently of his heart hunger.

> When Jesus came by, he looked up at Zacchaeus and called him by name. "Zacchaeus!" he said. "Quick, come down! I must be a guest in your home today." (v. 5 NLT)

Did he ask a local in the crowd who it was? Zacchaeus would have been well known and hated in Jericho. Or did the Holy Spirit reveal his name? The important part in the eyes of the crowd was that he planned to enter Zacchaeus' house.

> Zacchaeus quickly climbed down and took Jesus to his house in great excitement and joy. But the people were displeased. "He has gone to be the guest of a notorious sinner," they grumbled. (vs. 6-7 NLT)

Again Zacchaeus' "great excitement and joy" speak well of his eagerness to hear Jesus. Jesus heard the predictable grumbling because he was going into the house of a sinner. This time, it wasn't just the leaders complaining, but all the people, because Zacchaeus was so notorious for his taxing and collaboration with the Romans.

The following part was a conversation between Jesus and Zacchaeus. It sounds like it happened in public. Was this after having lunch when they came out?

> Zacchaeus stood before the Lord and said, "I will give half my wealth to the poor, Lord, and if I have cheated people on their taxes, I will give them back four times as much!" (v. 8 NLT)

God must have already been working in Zacchaeus' heart. His conscience may well have been bothering him for some time because he was stealing from his own people. An awakened conscience is a common sign that God is dealing with someone. John the Baptist said earlier that people should "bring forth fruit in keeping with repentance" (3:8).

> And Jesus said to him, "Today salvation has come to this house, because he, too, is a son of Abraham. For the Son of Man came to seek and save those who are lost." (v. 9-10)

This is one of Jesus' clearest descriptions of his mission. And if it was

Jesus' mission, it should be our mission too. Yes, Zacchaeus was lost, "notorious sinner," but that's exactly the kind of person Jesus was looking for. He earlier said he was sent to the "lost sheep of Israel" (Matthew 15:24). The plight of the lost should penetrate the heart of every believer with an urgency to seek and to save what was lost.

The Big Picture

When dealing with the rich young ruler, Jesus said, "How hard it is for those who have riches to enter the kingdom of God!" But here with Zacchaeus we see that it is possible. In fact, both the rich and the poor are accountable before God, as Jesus would soon clarify with the parable of the minas. One thing is clear: God is willing to accept even rotten people like Zacchaeus, or people as simple as children.

Jesus had once again stressed the reasonableness of self-sacrifice to the rich young ruler, and in predicting his own death. And he had healed two blind men in front of a shocked multitude. To the thousands about to ascend to Jerusalem, things must have seemed like they were heading toward a thrilling climax!

34

The Parable of the Minas

Luke 19:11-27

Before ascending the road to Jerusalem, Jesus taught using a complicated parable.

> While they were listening to these things, Jesus went on to tell a parable, because he was near Jerusalem, and they supposed that the kingdom of God was going to appear immediately. (Luke 19:11)

This introduction implies that the crowd was mistaken when thinking that the kingdom of God was about to begin. Instead, it wouldn't come for a significant length of time. That's not what replacement theologians claim. They argue that the kingdom had either already begun, based on Luke 17:21, "The kingdom of God is in your midst." Or, some argue that it would begin within the next two months at Pentecost. Neither claim is true. Instead, it will be like in this parable.

> So He said, "A nobleman went to a distant country to receive a kingdom for himself, and then return. And he called ten of his slaves, and gave them ten minas and said to them, 'Do business with this until I come back.'" (vs. 12-13)

The country he went to was distant, so in their day, that journey would take a long time. His expectation that they do business with their minas suggests a lengthy period of time before his return—especially given the time needed to multiply the minas five or even tenfold. Neither of these elements suggests that Jesus would receive the kingdom within two months (at Pentecost).

In fact, the king's returning refers to the second coming of Jesus, an event we're still waiting for. Notice that the king's servants give an account upon his return—an event that also happens at Jesus' second coming, not at Pentecost. At the time Jesus gave the parable, people didn't realize there would be two comings, let alone that they would be separated by millennia.

Stewardship

In giving this story, Jesus is also explaining how stewardship works from God's point of view. Stewardship is when an owner entrusts his money to another to invest and take care of. Today people have financial planners or stockbrokers to do the same thing. The nobleman in this story isn't *giving* his money to the servants; he's *entrusting it to them temporarily*, with the expectation that they will grow his investment, and show a profit.

Jesus continued his story:

> "But his citizens hated him and sent a delegation after him, saying, 'We do not want this man to reign over us.'" (v. 14)

This aside doesn't seem to fit the main flow of the stewardship story. But it shows that substantial numbers of the nobleman's subjects hate him. They put themselves in the position of active opposition to the nobleman, and later king. Not a good idea.

Settling Accounts

> "When he returned, after receiving the kingdom, he ordered that these slaves, to whom he had given the money, be called to him so that he might know what business they had done." (v. 15)

We use the term "accountability" for this part. In a stewardship scenario, the steward is accountable to show that he's doing his job. They were trained for this task, so there's nothing surprising about being called in to give account.

> "The first appeared, saying, 'Master, your mina has made ten minas more.' And he said to him, 'Well done, good slave, because you have been faithful in a very little thing, you are to be in authority over ten cities.' The second came, saying, 'Your mina, master, has made five minas.' And he said to him also, 'And you are to be over five cities.'" (vs. 16-19)

A mina was a unit of weight for either silver or gold, about 1.25 pounds. So these minas were worth somewhere from hundreds to thousands of dollars in silver or gold. but in buying power, a mina was worth over three months' pay, so by today's standard, three or more months of pay would add up to about seventeen thousand dollars on average. Although we don't know how long the noble had been gone, five or tenfold growth is excellent, even if it was years.

Notice that the servants says, "your mina," not, "my mina." The king rewards each faithful steward with the oversight of a corresponding number of cities. That doesn't necessarily mean we will be rewarded with cities. This is a parable, meaning it's a symbolic story. Jesus is imagining what an earthly king would do for a faithful manager. It's the principle of "He who is faithful in a very little thing is faithful also in much" (16:10).

The Wicked Servant

At this point, we meet the main servant of interest in the story.

> "Another came, saying, 'Master, here is your mina, which I kept put away in a handkerchief; for I was afraid of you, because you are an exacting man; you take up what you did not lay down and reap what you did not sow.'" (vs. 20-21)

NLT translates, "You are a hard man to deal with, taking what isn't yours and harvesting crops you didn't plant." The internal contradictions in this statement are immediately evident to the king, who says, "I will judge you by your own words" (v. 22).

First, the bad steward claims the king (who stands for God) was such a hard man to deal with that this steward decided to disobey the king's instructions to "Invest this for me while I am gone" (v. 13) and instead do nothing? That's how you act with an exacting, harsh master? To the contrary, the steward is obviously counting on the king to be soft and weak. His actions suggest he isn't worried at all about punishment for his negligence.

Also, if the master is so mean and fierce, why isn't the bad steward afraid to insult him to his face? He calls him harsh and charges that he's a thief of other people's property and food. That's not how a servant would address a harsh master.

Actually, the master doesn't seem too hard to please, based on his reaction to the previous two stewards. And he later points out that he would have been satisfied if the steward just put the money in the bank (v. 23). That's not harsh.

The bad steward claims the king takes things that don't belong to him, and reaps where he didn't plant. In other words, he's a thief. But in fact, the king does own his estate. He's not stealing harvest from others. He is taking harvest that belongs to him. The same goes for earning a return on his money. He's not stealing, he's doing business.

The bad steward knows that. But he wants to intimidate the master with accusations. This tactic is familiar to students of Scripture. It matches Satan's method of trying to manipulate God. He hurls accusations at God, especially that he's unloving, selfish, and harsh. Then, if God acts in judgment, the accusations are crafted to make it seem like the lies are confirmed. You see this in Satan's accusation in heaven against Job, but also, by implication, against God. No wonder Satan's title, "the devil," actually means "the accuser."

Not Weak

The bad steward was counting on the king being a weakling. To lay that view to rest, Jesus included the fate of those who rebelled against him becoming king. The master, now king, said, "Bring them here and slay them in my presence" (v. 27).

This is a picture of what is going to happen to those who persist in their revolt against God and his Messiah. This picture matches Revelation 20:11-15, where God sits on a great white throne and casts everyone whose name is not in the Book of Life into the lake of fire. God is a God of grace, mercy, and love. But it would be a fatal mistake to take his grace as a sign of weakness. God is a God of justice, and that becomes extremely clear at the cross, where Jesus paid the full price for God's justice.

Other Things to Notice

The Parable of the Minas contains more than one lesson. It's a fairly complex parable. In addition to what has been said, notice the following points:

- At the center of the story is the bad steward. His sin was a sin of omission, not commission. Of course beneath his failure to lift a finger was his low view, even contempt for the king.
- In addition to committing a sin of omission is his effort to shift the blame for doing nothing onto the king. God won't permit that. We are all responsible for our own sin.
- The king makes an intriguing comment in verse 23: "Why did you not put my money in the bank, and having come, I would have collected it with interest?" The way he introduces this option suggests that if the bad steward had done this, it would have been more reasonable. Although we should avoid pushing the symbolism too far, you could argue that putting the money in the bank would stand for simply accepting salvation by faith but never living out the implications of the gospel. That possibility, if not implied here, is specifically taught in other passages, such as the man "saved as though by fire" in 1 Corinthians 3:15. The presence of this option rebuts the apparent salvation by works message.
- In Matthew 25:14-30 Jesus told the very similar Parable of the Talents. In that parable, the man who buried his treasure received this judgment from the master: "Throw out the worthless slave into the outer darkness; in that place there will be weeping and gnashing of teeth" (v. 30). This is an unmistakable reference to being thrown into hell. It shows how Jesus viewed a life of doing nothing with the stewardship we all have from God.
- We also read,

  > "Then the master said to the bystanders, 'Take the mina away from him and give it to the one who has the ten minas.'

> "And they said to him, 'Master, he has ten minas already.'
>
> The master answered, "To everyone who has, more shall be given, but from the one who does not have, even what he does have shall be taken away" (vs. 24-26).

Clearly, the master was rewarding faithfulness. He also reveals that even among those who are faithful, the standard is not equality. Some had multiplied their minas fivefold and some tenfold. They are rewarded accordingly. This matches other discussions of the reward judgment for believers (e.g. 1 Corinthians 3:10-15).

The Big Picture

With Zaccheaus, we see that God is so merciful that he is willing to accept even the most rotten people if they repent and believe. In the parable of the minas, Jesus declared that people will be held fully accountable under the threat of God's wrath. Both pictures are true.

As the multitude with Jesus began climbing the road up to Jerusalem, Jesus was the only one who knew what was coming. Passover was at hand, so the journeying crowd with Jesus had had swollen with thousands of other travelers. Everyone was fascinated by Jesus. Was he really the one? Was this the time he would take over?

According to Mark and Matthew, this is when John, James, and their mother came and brazenly asked Jesus to promise them the top two positions in the coming kingdom (Matthew 20:23). It was an ugly example of the selfishness and spiritual blindness that still afflicted even Jesus' closest followers.

The other disciples were indignant, but only because James and John were trying to make an end run past them. Others were following along for self-serving reasons as well. The multitude was more interested in what the Messiah might mean for their deliverance from Roman domination than in anything concerning their relationship with God.

35

THE FINAL WEEK

LUKE 19:28-48

The Triumphal Entry

> When he approached Bethphage and Bethany, near the mount that is called Olivet, he sent two of the disciples, saying, "Go into that village over there," he told them. "As you enter it, you will see a young donkey tied there that no one has ever ridden. Untie it and bring it here. If anyone asks, 'Why are you untying that colt?' just say, 'The Lord needs it.'"
>
> So those who were sent went away and found it just as he had told them. As they were untying the colt, its owners said to them, "Why are you untying the colt?"
>
> They said, "The Lord has need of it." They brought it to Jesus, and they threw their coats on the colt and put Jesus on it. (Luke 19:29-35)

This lead-in to the story of Jesus' entry has his disciples acting out a sequence that was pre-ordained. We see none of the spontaneity evident earlier in the book—like a woman Jesus doesn't know touching his cloak, or randomly running into a funeral procession. Here Jesus was well aware of the sequence. He knew Passover was a few days away, and he knew he was the true Passover lamb.

He mounted the young donkey and began the short two-mile ride down into the Kidron valley and up into Jerusalem.

> As he was going, they were spreading their coats on the road. As soon as he was approaching, near the descent of the Mount of Olives, the whole crowd of the disciples began to praise God joyfully with a loud voice for all the miracles which they had seen, shouting: "Blessings on the King who comes in the name of the Lord! Peace in heaven, and glory in highest heaven! Peace in heaven and glory in the highest!" (vs. 36-38 quoting Psalm 118:26)

This entry outwardly looked every bit like a Roman triumphal entry known as a *parusia*. These events were typically triggered by a great military victory, or the return of the emperor from a journey. They were like our ticker tape parades after World War II.

But something is wrong. The returning general should be riding on a huge white charger or driving a gilt chariot. He should be wearing gleaming armor, and his troops smartly marching behind him. What is this? Jesus didn't even ride a normal donkey. He rides on a foal of a donkey! His feet were probably almost touching the ground! No gleaming armor . . . no ranks of soldiers marching behind. . . .

It's the king who serves.

The Psalm they were alluding to was a Messianic Psalm. Also, they recognized the well-known prediction in Zechariah 9:9:

> Rejoice greatly, O daughter of Zion!
> Shout in triumph, O daughter of Jerusalem!
> Behold, your king is coming to you;
> He is just and endowed with salvation,
> Humble, and mounted on a donkey,
> Even on a colt, the foal of a donkey.

There it was, right before their eyes! No wonder Jesus needed to retrieve a donkey colt for his ride. And Zechariah goes on to predict:

> I will cut off the chariot from Ephraim

And the horse from Jerusalem;
And the bow of war will be cut off.
And He will speak peace to the nations;
And His dominion will be from sea to sea,
And from the River to the ends of the earth. (Zechariah 9:10)

This is the worldwide reign of King Messiah predicted in so many Old Testament passages. You can see it includes international disarmament, the end of war, and that the kingdom spans "from sea to sea" and "to the ends of the earth." None of this came to pass in Jesus' day, but it will all be fulfilled later, at Jesus' second coming. The crowd, of course, had no way to know that.[1]

The Pharisees and other leaders were horrified. Here was a large crowd proclaiming Jesus to be King Messiah. This was exactly the kind of thing that could result in a Roman legion attacking an uprising. They called on him, "Teacher, rebuke your disciples" (v. 39). So often up until now we have seen Jesus hushing his followers. He kept insisting that his hour had not come. But this day, something has changed. "Jesus answered, 'I tell you, if these become silent, the stones will cry out!'" (v. 40). Apparently his hour was now at hand.

The Time of Your Visitation

Jesus knew this was his final week. This was the fatal crossroad where many in this very crowd proclaiming him as Messiah would decide finally what to do with him. That's why "When He approached Jerusalem, He saw the city and wept over it" (v. 41). He knew the adulation was superficial. The crowd expected power and freedom from the Romans. He knew if they didn't get that, they would soon cry "Crucify! Crucify!"

As tears rolled down his cheeks, Jesus cried out to Jerusalem,

> "If you had known in this day, even you, the things which make for peace! But now they have been hidden from your eyes. For the days will come upon you when your enemies will throw up a barricade against you, and surround you and hem

1. This passage in Zechariah is another example of a "prophetic gap." A prophetic gap happens when a prophet skips from one time period to another without notice. You see in this passage the prophet moved from Jesus' first coming to his second coming, but nothing in the passage signals that. Only later do we realize the passage refers to two different comings of Messiah. Clearly, God deliberately set this up for reasons that become clear later.

> you in on every side, and they will level you to the ground and your children within you, and they will not leave in you one stone upon another, because you did not recognize the time of your visitation." (vs. 42-44)

Jesus loved Jerusalem and the people who lived there. He had argued his case before them on many occasions, backing his words with miracles and Scripture. And he would do so again this week, but he knew so many of them wouldn't listen. Of course some of them were listening. We later read that the common people "hung on his words" (v. 48).

The Coming Judgment

We've seen cases earlier where Jesus didn't know the future or even current events. This isn't one of them. Jesus had known this week was coming and had repeatedly warned his followers about it. He knew Judas would betray him. He knew he was going to suffer torture and death.

Jesus also felt sorrow because he knew the future of Jerusalem. He described the siege and destruction of the city. He even added the detail that the attackers would "not leave in you one stone upon another."

This prediction was fulfilled less than forty years later, in AD 70, when the Romans utterly destroyed Jerusalem and the temple.

All this was coming, according to Jesus, "because you did not recognize the time of your visitation." The visitation refers to Jesus' coming. They had seen enough supernatural validation through Jesus' miracles to know he was from God. Even years earlier, a leading Pharisee, Nicodemus admitted, "We know that you have come from God as a teacher; for no one can do these signs that you do unless God is with him" (John 3:2). Yet, Jesus was more than a teacher, and the leadership had rejected the truth—that he was God's son and Messiah.

The people in Jerusalem were accountable to know the time of his visitation for another reason. One of their scholars, a historian, Flavius Josephus, explained the importance of the Old Testament prophet, Daniel. We saw earlier that Josephus said,

> "We are convinced by [his book] that Daniel spoke with God, for he was not only wont to prophesy future things, as did the

> other prophets, *but he also fixed the time at which these would come to pass.*[2]

He is correct that other prophets tell what will happen, but they never predict the date. Only Daniel names the date for the fulfillment of one of his most important prophecies. It's a prophecy about the coming and the death of the Messiah written hundreds of years before Jesus.

The prophecy is in Daniel 9:24-26. There, an angel told Daniel that 476 Hebrew years after a decree to rebuild Jerusalem, the Messiah would come and die. The decree was issued in 444 BC, and after correcting for the "0" year, the math comes out to AD 33—the very year of this story and Jesus' death![3]

The Jews knew this prophecy, and expected it to be fulfilled soon, although they didn't have exact records (like we do today). They only knew the general time was at hand.[4] That was enough to make people watchful for the coming one, and according to Jesus, they were accountable for believing what they read.

Agitation

No sooner did Jesus arrive in Jerusalem than he began agitating the leadership. He launched an attack at the sellers in the temple courtyard:

> Then Jesus entered the Temple and began to drive out the people selling animals for sacrifices. He said to them, "The Scriptures declare, 'My Temple will be a house of prayer,' but you have turned it into a den of thieves." (vs. 45-46 NLT)

Why would Jesus attack these sellers? Why does he call them thieves? My childhood Sunday school teacher said this event shows that you

2. Josephus, *Antiquities*, 10.266-67, emphasis added. Amazingly, Roman historian Gaius Tacitus also appears to have heard of Daniel's prophecy. He wrote, "The majority [of the Jews] firmly believed that their ancient priestly writings contained the prophecy that this was the very time when the East should grow strong and that men starting from Judea should possess the world." Gaius Tacitus, *Histories*, V. 13. It's a muddled recounting, but likely refers to the Messiah and other visions of world takeover in Daniel.
3. I give a full explanation of this prophecy with documentation and context in Dennis McCallum, *Discovering God: Exploring the Possibilities of Faith* (Columbus, OH: New Paradigm Publishing, 2011), 61ff.
4. Josephus, *Wars of the Jews* 6.312-313. He called it "an ambiguous oracle that was found in their sacred writings." Josephus thought Daniel was predicting Emperor Vespasian, but that's almost 40 years off. We know the exact year for events in this period because of solunar tables that tie ancient events to specific dates because they mention solar or lunar eclipses.

shouldn't have church bazaars or anything involved with selling inside a church. That's wrong.

Jesus was attacking a corrupt system. Historical records from this time reveal that the priests and their co-conspirators, the sellers, were engaged in a scam that was making hundreds of millions, much of it taken from the poor.

How It Worked

People who wanted to offer a sacrifice at the temple needed to have their animals inspected by priests to make sure they weren't flawed. Many animals turned out to be flawed. Then, the priests would direct the worshipers to the tables where the animal sellers had pre-approved animals for sale at a significant markup. The sellers also had to pay a kickback to the priests for the privilege of having a space in the temple court.

Likewise, all Jewish males were obligated to pay a "temple tax" once in their lives. But most coins had a picture of Caesar or some other ruler that people believed to be divine. That meant they were graven images of another god, unacceptable for the temple treasury. But one Syrian Shekel had no face, just a picture of a boat. These were considered untainted and suitable for the tax. So again, worshipers had to exchange their Roman or Greek coins for a shekel. These are the money changers that Mark says Jesus also drove out (Mark 11:15). They, too, kept a profit and had to pay a kickback to the Sadducees and Levitical priests.

The inflow of gold and silver had reached incredible levels. Jewish historian, Josephus says,

> And let no one wonder that there was so much wealth in our temple, since all the Jews throughout the habitable earth, and those that worshiped God, nay, even those of Asia and Europe, sent their contributions to it, and this from very ancient times.[5]

As an example, he says that during Crassus' campaign in 53 BC,

> He came into Judea, and carried off the money that was in the temple, which Pompey had left, being two thousand talents,

5. Josephus, *Antiquities*, 14.7.2.

> and was disposed to spoil it of all the gold belonging to it, which was eight thousand talents.[6]

A Roman talent was just over 71 pounds. Eight thousand talents would be 568,000 pounds of gold and silver! Even if it was all silver, today, that would cost over $260 million! While most historians believe Josephus was prone to exaggeration, other sources back up his claim that the temple contained great wealth. And Josephus had sources that were in a position to know, including his friend, Titus Flavius, who sacked the temple in AD 70.[7] Records from the time also describe polished solid gold plates, hung along the front of the temple where they would reflect the sun like mirrors.[8]

Jesus' Verdict

While this gold belonged to the temple, the leadership could easily have designated some of it to programs for the poor. This was a time and place in history where most people were poor. Roman oppression kept poor people poor. Only a small elite were wealthy. But instead of helping the poor, the Sadducees and priests were milking the poor for yet more money. Their large profit margins were clear indications of corruption. Just like in Jeremiah's day, they were a "den of thieves" (v. 46, quoting Jeremiah 7:11).

We saw earlier how angry it made Jesus when he saw people profiteering using religion while leading people astray (17:2). He also knew he was signing his own death warrant by agitating the bosses of this corrupt system.

Jesus was fulfilling another prophecy: "Behold, I send my messenger, and he shall prepare the way before me: and the Lord, whom you seek, shall suddenly come to his temple" (Malachi 3:1). Jesus knew that in a

6. Josephus, *Antiquities*, 14.7.1. *Mishnah* Middot 3 and 4 describe the temple and the impressive massive gold grapevine at the doorway—a description that accords well with that of Josephus. A full history of the temple treasure is given by Lambert Dolphin, "The Treasures of the House of the Lord," *Temple Mount*, July 16, 2021, https://www.templemount.org/TMTRS.html.

7. None of this treasure was from the Old Testament period when David and Solomon gave vast quantities of gold and silver to the temple. Those treasures were all taken by Nebuchadnezzar in the sixth century BC (1st temple). More treasure was looted by the Selucid king, Antiochus in 170 BC (2nd temple) (2 Chronicles 36:18-19; 1 Maccabees 1:20ff).

8. Leen Ritmeyer, "The Gold of the Jerusalem Temple," *Ritmeyer Archaeological Design* (blog), December 14, 2015, https://www.ritmeyer.com/2015/12/14/the-gold-of-the -jerusalem-temple/.

few days, this temple would be the scene of the most amazing drama, as the veil would be torn in two.

Fury

The leaders had been scheming to kill Jesus for years at this point. But they were frustrated in their efforts, as Luke explains:

> After that, he taught daily in the Temple, but the leading priests, the teachers of religious law, and the other leaders of the people began planning how to kill him. But they could think of nothing, because all the people hung on every word he said. (vs. 47-48 NLT)

The Romans absolutely would not tolerate public disturbances or riots, and the Jewish leadership knew that. The risk was too great to grab Jesus right while he was preaching.

The Big Picture

During the triumphal entry and the cleansing of the temple, Jesus publicly announced himself as the promised King. That gave the people their chance to finally take sides for or against him.[9] He knew the leaders wanted him dead, but he was getting up into their faces during this final week, driving their hatred to the point where they would act. One thing was missing—how to apprehend him in secret. Judas would soon supply that piece.

How was Jesus able to tear through the sellers and money changers? Why didn't a group of men close in on him and subdue him? Was he wielding a whip like he did in John 2:15? Was he a large, intimidating man? He probably was strong, being a carpenter in a day with no power tools. Maybe his twelve or more disciples were following close by—maybe even some of the multitude? Or was it that Jesus had a spiritual gravitas that frightened the sellers?

He apparently cleansed the temple at the end, but also at the beginning of his ministry, recorded in John 2. On that occasion, he made the cryptic comment, "Destroy this temple, and in three days I will raise it up"

9. Geldenhuys, *Luke*, 480.

(John 2:19). The crowd was baffled and scoffed at that comment. But John explains, "He was speaking of the temple of His body" (John 2:21).

Jesus linked the temple with his body, forecasting the doctrine of the body of Christ, so important in the writings of Paul. The Old Testament temple stood for the "house of God" even though he didn't literally live there (1 Kings 8:27). Rather, it was symbolic of God's house and provided a place where the people of God could meet him and make atonement.

Jesus was the actual, real dwelling place of God. And through what theologians call the "mystical union," we, his people, become joined with him to form the "body of Christ" (Romans 12:5; 1 Corinthians 6:17; 12:1-31). All of this was in the future as Jesus strode through the temple court.

36

Building Hostility

Luke 20:1-21:4

The leaders must have discussed Jesus' attack on the sellers and arrived at a plan. They would try to trap him by getting him to say something incriminating; something that would hold up in court and might even be persuasive to the crowd. They came walking up as a group in the presence of the crowd.

> One day as Jesus was teaching the people and preaching the Good News in the Temple, the leading priests, the teachers of religious law, and the elders came up to him. They demanded, "By what authority are you doing all these things? Who gave you the right?" (Luke 20:1-2 NLT)

These men were the local government. The leading priests, the scribes, and elders (probably referring to members of the Sanhedrin) constitute the governing power, especially over the temple mount. They had the power to arrest, imprison, beat, or torture Jesus. They sound like they're curious and seeking an answer to a reasonable question. But that's not the case. Again, they are hunting Jesus. They were no doubt furious after Jesus' cleansing of the temple. Jesus knew exactly what they were up to. Instead of answering their question, he said,

> "Let me ask you a question first," he replied. "Did John's

> authority to baptize come from heaven, or was it merely human?" (vs. 3-4 NLT)

With a single question, Jesus laid bare their duplicity and sin. They had earlier rejected John the Baptist, but the crowd knew John came from God. Jesus now impaled them on the so-called horns of a dilemma. Instead of giving a plain, honest answer, they huddled up to prepare a statement.

> They talked it over among themselves. "If we say it was from heaven, he will ask why we didn't believe John. But if we say it was merely human, the people will stone us because they are convinced John was a prophet." (vs. 5-6)

At this point they broke the huddle and strode back toward Jesus with their answer: "We don't know where it was from." (v. 7)

Their carefully manicured reply was a lie. How would Jesus respond? A fierce denunciation? No. He simply said what they didn't expect: "Neither will I tell you by what authority I do these things" (v. 8). The leaders are left looking at each other with frowns. Did the crowd laugh?

These leaders were pseudo-seekers. Pseudo-seekers already know what they believe, and have no openness to a different view. In this account, we get an example of how Jesus responds to pseudo-seekers: Silence! Once God knows that further speaking will do no good, he simply stops speaking. We saw the same point earlier in Jesus' explanation for why he taught in parables in chapter 8.

It's also laughable to see how easily Jesus dismantled his enemies' carefully constructed trap. He would do this repeatedly during this last week.

The Evil Vine Growers

Instead of answering the leaders' dishonest question, he addressed the crowd and gave another parable that mirrored the current situation. It's clear that the leaders are still standing right there because later we read, "They realized he was telling the story against them" (v. 19).

He begins, "A man planted a vineyard" (v. 9). Mark adds the details that "He built a wall around it, dug a pit for pressing out the grape juice, and built a lookout tower" (Mark 12:1). The wall is to keep out thieves and animals that feed on grapes. The pit is a winepress, built into the vineyard, not the shared press used by the village. The tower meant the vineyard was well guarded. This is a top-quality vineyard. The owner created the vineyard, and therefore owned it and had control over it, just like God has control over his high-quality creation. Ownership conveys authority over what is owned.

> "[The owner] rented it out to vine-growers, and went on a journey for a long time. At the harvest time he sent a servant to the vine-growers, so that they would give him some of the produce of the vineyard; but the vine-growers beat him and sent him away empty-handed. And he proceeded to send another servant; and they beat him also and treated him shamefully and sent him away empty-handed. And he proceeded to send a third; and this one also they wounded and cast out." (vs. 9-12)

So far, this is a story of incredible lenience, or more likely, weakness. What's wrong with this landowner? Why would he allow his emissaries to be treated this way? Maybe he's unable to do otherwise. And the vine-growers—what's wrong with them? When someone rents a field out to sharecroppers, they pay their rent as a portion of their crop. They had agreed to this. The owner wasn't *giving* them the land, he was *renting* it to them, so they owed this rent.

Instead, the vintners act like they own the field. They view these emissaries as intruders trying to steal from them. It's a picture of the unbelieving leaders of Israel, and their treatment of the prophets God sent them. By rejecting his messengers, they were acting like God was out of line for being God.

Mark's version of this parable adds, "And so with many others, beating some and killing others" (Mark 12:5). It's a sad description of the treatment of God's messengers throughout the Old Testament. And Jesus had earlier argued that when the leaders in his own day sought his death, they were in complete harmony with their murderous ancestors (6:23, 26; 11:47-50; 13:34). He continued:

> "The owner of the vineyard said, 'What shall I do? I will send my beloved son; perhaps they will respect him.'" (v. 13)

Oh no! What a terrible idea!

> "But when the vine-growers saw him, they reasoned with one

> another, saying, 'This is the heir; let us kill him so that the inheritance will be ours.' So they threw him out of the vineyard and killed him." (vs. 14-15)

With this crew, nothing good could come from sending the son. And sure enough, they killed him and flipped his body over the wall. How ironic that the leaders standing right there as Jesus spoke were planning his death! And in telling this parable, he clearly signaled to them that he knew all about their plans to kill him.

At this point, Jesus asked the key question, "What, then, will the owner of the vineyard do to them?" (v. 15). He may well have stopped and stared at various people—the crowd, the leaders—then he went on, answering his own question:

> "He will come and destroy these vine-growers and will give the vineyard to others." (v. 16)

The idea that this landowner might be weak was a big mistake. There will be a day of reckoning after all. Rather than being weak, the owner was being merciful. The repeated chances he gave the evil vine-growers to change their minds was a picture of God's patience and reluctance to judge people. He could have destroyed them at any time.

Their assumption that they could gain ownership of the vineyard was absurd. The only thing they were going to receive was justice at the hands of the landowner.

"When, [the crowd] heard it, they said, 'May it never be!'" (v. 16). This expression is similar to our expression, "No way!" Jesus ended the story suggesting a grim future for the leadership. The leaders knew it was about them; did the crowd understand that? We can't be sure.

The Cornerstone

Jesus gave the leaders a warning from the Old Testament:

> But Jesus looked at them and said, "What then is this that is written: 'The stone that the builders rejected has now become the cornerstone.' everyone who falls on that stone will be broken to pieces; but on whomever it falls, it will scatter him like dust.'" (vs. 17-18 citing Psalm 118:22)

In ancient building, a key step was the selection and placement of the cornerstone. They used the cornerstone to set the angles, height, and width of the other stones. In government buildings or temples, the stones could be very large—as tall as a man and just as wide. Architects would often come down to the quarry to pick out a choice stone to be the cornerstone, And they would also oversee the shaping of the stone to fit their specifications.

So it is very unexpected that a stone already rejected by the builders would end up being the cornerstone. This expression from Psalm 118 is a picture of Jesus being rejected by the builders (symbolically, the temple rulers), but ending up being God's choice after all.

In fact, the rejected cornerstone becomes the standard for all else. Anyone stumbling on the cornerstone will be broken. And anyone on whom the stone falls will be scattered like dust.

It's an interesting parallel to a key Old Testament passage in Daniel 2:34-35, where he saw a stone destroying all human empires but then growing and filling the earth. It's the kingdom of the Messiah.

The two passages in Psalms and Daniel fit together perfectly.

The leaders were infuriated.

> The teachers of religious law and the leading priests wanted to arrest Jesus immediately because they realized he was telling the story against them—they were the wicked farmers. But they were afraid of the people's reaction. So they watched him, and sent spies who pretended to be righteous, in order that they might catch him in some statement, so that they could deliver him to the rule and the authority of the governor. (vs. 19-20 NLT)

These "spies" take turns trying to stump Jesus by getting him to say something incriminating.

Paying Caesar

Their first attempt shows they had conspired and carefully structured their attack.

> They questioned him, saying, "Teacher, we know that you

> speak and teach correctly, and you are not partial to any, but teach the way of God in truth." (v. 21)

You need hip boots to wade through this pseudo reverent opening. It's always a bad sign when someone comes in with extreme flattery intended to manipulate. They went on, "Is it lawful for us to pay taxes to Caesar, or not?" (v. 22)

Their trap was well-planned. The Romans were not in Israel for any legal or fair reason. They were invaders and conquerors. Only their naked power and brutal enforcement of that power enabled them to rule. Their taxes were unfair and capricious. The money, mostly taken from poor people, only went to pad the lives of rich Roman patricians and to further build and equip the oppressing Roman army. Jewish victims of this system hated the Romans. If Jesus were to say that people should pay Roman taxes, he would forfeit his favor with the crowd, and validate Roman corruption.

If he said not to pay taxes, even once, he would be subject to prison or death. The Romans didn't mess around with anyone questioning their taxes. Would Jesus stammer, or stall?

> Detecting their trickery he said to them, "Show me a denarius." (vs. 23-24 NLT)

He must have held it up in front of them, and asked,

> "Whose picture and title are stamped on it?"
>
> They said, "Caesar's."
>
> And he said to them, "Then render to Caesar the things that are Caesar's, and to God the things that are God's."
>
> And they were unable to catch him in a saying in the presence of the people; and being amazed at his answer, they became silent. (vs. 24-26 NLT)

His answer was so unexpected that they had no response ready. The logic of the answer was irrefutable. How effortlessly he replied. It wasn't hard for Jesus because he had God's perspective. His enemies looked at each other and shook their heads in confusion.

Jesus also called on people to "render unto God the things that are God's."

The coin had Caesar's image stamped on it, but what has God's image stamped on it? We do! Humans were created "in the image of God" (Genesis 1:26). God isn't interested in coins. He could create any number imaginable. He is concerned about humans in their lostness and desperate need for reconciliation.

Attack on the Afterlife

Next another group advanced—the Sadducees. We don't have much historical material about them. The main sources are the New Testament and a few passages from Josephus.[1] Some priests were Sadducees, and they apparently had some cooperative arrangement with the Romans. They seem to have been in charge of the temple grounds. Josephus agrees with the New Testament that they didn't believe in the afterlife. They became implacable enemies of Jesus along with the Pharisees (e.g. Acts 5:17).

> Then Jesus was approached by some Sadducees—religious leaders who say there is no resurrection from the dead. They posed this question: "Teacher, Moses gave us a law that if a man dies, leaving a wife but no children, his brother should marry the widow and have a child who will carry on the brother's name." (vs. 27-28)

This is the ancient kinsman redeemer law, designed to protect women from losing the family farm (Deuteronomy 25:5-6). Widows needed a male offspring to legally inherit property at that time, and the brother of the deceased was expected to marry her and have the male child. The law had been ignored by most Jews for centuries. The Sadducees went on:

> "Well, suppose there were seven brothers. The oldest one married and then died without children. So the second brother married the widow, but he also died. Then the third brother married her. This continued with all seven of them, who died without children. Finally, the woman also died. So tell us, whose wife will she be in the resurrection? For all seven were married to her!" (vs. 29-33)

In Matthew's account, Jesus rebuked them: "You are mistaken, not understanding the Scriptures nor the power of God" (Matthew 22:29).

1. Josephus, *Wars*, 2.119, 164–166; *Antiquities*, 13.171–173, 293–298, 18.11, 16–17, 20.199; *Life*, 10–11.

Their little scenario amounted to an insult to God. Did they actually think this would be a difficult quandary for God? If so, they didn't understand who they were dealing with.

Jesus effortlessly dismissed their tricky ruse:

> "The sons of this age marry and are given in marriage, but those who are considered worthy to attain to that age and the resurrection from the dead, neither marry nor are given in marriage; for they cannot even die anymore, because they are like angels, and are sons of God, being sons of the resurrection."' (vs. 34-36)

While he was at it, he went on and rebutted their deistic view of God and disbelief in the afterlife. Their excuse for not accepting the afterlife was their claim that it wasn't taught in the Pentateuch—the first five books of Moses. So Jesus went straight to the Pentateuch.

> "But now, as to whether the dead will be raised—even Moses proved this when he wrote about the burning bush. Long after Abraham, Isaac, and Jacob had died, he referred to the Lord as 'the God of Abraham, the God of Isaac, and the God of Jacob.' So he is the God of the living, not the dead, for they are all alive to him." (vs. 37-38 NLT)

The essence of his argument has to do with the tense of the verb. God didn't say, "I was the God of Abraham . . ." but, "I am the God of Abraham." Abraham was a living soul as God spoke, even though he had he had been dead for six hundred years.

> Some of the scribes answered and said, "Teacher, You have spoken well." And then no one dared to ask him any more questions. (vs. 39-40)

Counterattack

Since his opponents lost nerve and were sullenly listening, Jesus came at them:

> Then Jesus presented them with a question. "Why is it," he asked, "that the Messiah is said to be the son of David? For David himself wrote in the book of Psalms:

> 'The Lord says to my Lord,
> "Sit in the place of honor at my right hand
> until I humble your enemies,
> making them a footstool under your feet."'
>
> Since David called the Messiah 'Lord,' how can the Messiah be his son?" (vs. 41-44 quoting Psalm 110:1)

No reply is recorded. They were stumped.

The rabbis of Jesus' day knew that this was a Messianic Psalm.[2] Their problem arose from their picture of the Messiah, whom they saw as a strictly human king. That's not an adequate reading, as Jesus explained. Why would David—an absolute monarch—write, "The Lord (Yahweh) says to my Lord (Adonai)?" Who would he refer to as "my lord"? Only King Messiah.

But even then, if the Messiah was to be nothing but a human descendant of David, such a Messiah would need to show respect for his elder ancestor, David. Instead, it's David calling him "My Lord." It's an internal contradiction in their understanding of this admittedly Messianic Psalm. They had no category for the incarnation.

They also had no adequate explanation for how the Messiah from the line of David could be a priest in the order of Melchizedek (Psalm 110:4). Jesus didn't get into that part here, but we have a full explanation later in Hebrews 5-7.

Denunciation

Jesus' exposure of this hole in their theology no doubt further enraged the scribes, but he wasn't done. His anger extended to their character even more than to their theology. His earlier denunciation in 11:37–52 was in a private home. Here, he was in the temple courtyard with a crowd listening:

> Then, with the crowds listening, he turned to his disciples and said, "Beware of these teachers of religious law! For they like to parade around in flowing robes and love to receive respectful greetings as they walk in the marketplaces. And how they love the seats of honor in the synagogues and the

2. *Midrash Rabbah* Genesis 85.9. Although this is from later, it reflects earlier interpretation.

> head table at banquets. Yet they shamelessly cheat widows out of their property and then pretend to be pious by making long prayers in public. Because of this, they will be severely punished." (vs. 45-47 NLT)

He describes a group using religion to garner undeserved respect and money for themselves. Meanwhile they were willing to roll over anyone who got in their way—even the most helpless people in society, like widows.

Widows were in a bad position at this time and place in history. Ancient Israel was patriarchal and had a low view of women. Women could own property at this time, but they could easily lose it too. A widow only had to fall slightly behind on payments of a debt and her home could be immediately foreclosed and seized. A scribe could shrug that he was only following the law. But he also could have shown mercy. There was no law against that. What a jarring collision between the holy man image and the cruel, self-serving, wealthy exploiter. To see that man standing and offering long prayers in their flowing robes made Jesus' flesh crawl in disgust.

The Widow's Mite

The unknown friar who added the chapter breaks and verses to our Bible clearly missed the correct chapter break after Luke 21:4, not before.

> And he looked up and saw the rich putting their gifts into the treasury. And he saw a poor widow putting in two small copper coins. And he said, "Truly I say to you, this poor widow put in more than all of them; for they all out of their surplus put into the offering; but she out of her poverty put in all that she had to live on." (21:1-4).

The tiny copper or bronze coins called *lepta* were the least valuable coin in circulation. It took 128 of them to equal one denarius. Jesus drew the contrast between the rich flashing their large gifts and this humble widow giving her tiny pittance. The contrast is not between the value of the gifts, but between the givers' heart attitudes. The widow was sacrificial. The rich were giving what was convenient, and they were showing off, which was self-serving (c.f. Matthew 6:1-2).

The Big Picture

Jesus strode into the temple courts and initiated a rumble. Those profiting from the selling and money changing would never accept the cleansing of the temple. That act alone was like a declaration of war.

His parable of the evil vintners publicly portrayed the leadership as vicious, corrupt, selfish, and violent. He continued to drive their hostility with a public denunciation right in front of a crowd of their followers.

When they came at him with tricky hypothetical problems, he deftly dismissed their shallow arguments in a way that must have been quite embarrassing.

The stage was set for his execution. At this point, he withdrew with his disciples to discuss the future, and have Passover dinner. He would remain with them until the authorities came for him.

37

When Will These Things Be?

Luke 21:5-38

Admiring the Stones

The next scene unfolds as they are leaving the temple courtyard. We read that

> Some were talking about the temple, that it was adorned with beautiful stones. But Jesus said, "The time is coming when all these things will be completely demolished. Not one stone will be left on top of another!" (Luke 21:5-6)

You can view some of these stones today where the Romans pushed them off of the temple mount onto a street a hundred feet below.[1]

1. A persistent story claims that when the Romans burned the wooden members in the temple, they believed that temple gold had melted and lodged between the

These massive building stones were the ones Jesus' disciples were admiring; now lying where the Romans left them in AD 70. The wall to the left is Herod's retaining wall, built to greatly expand the size of the temple mount.

Jesus' prediction that the temple would be destroyed led his disciples to ask, "When will all this happen? What sign will show us that these things are about to take place?" (v. 7).

The Olivet Discourse

In answer, Jesus gave the Olivet Discourse, so-called because he was on the Mount of Olives when he gave it. This discourse is also recounted in Matthew and Mark, so faithful interpretation under a high view of Scripture requires us to harmonize all three passages. That's not easy. Each account includes or drops details—exactly what you would expect from multiple eye-witness accounts.

One problem comes immediately when we compare the disciples' questions here in Luke to Matthew's version. Here in Luke, they seem to be asking the same question twice. "When therefore will these things happen? And what will be the sign when these things are about to take place?" (v. 7). But in Matthew's wording they clearly asked two distinct questions: "Tell us, when will these things happen, and what will be the sign of your coming, and of the end of the age?" (Matthew 24:3).

You can see they were asking both about the near-term future ("these things" associated with the destruction of the temple) and the distant future ("the sign of your coming at the end of the age").

Today we realize these two events are separated by thousands of years.

---

stones. That's why they tore every stone down, looking for the gold, and fulfilling Jesus' prediction that not one stone would lie atop another. In fact, this story is unsupported by the historical sources from that time. Josephus does briefly mention that the Roman soldiers believed the rooms around the temple were full of money, and that they attacked the temple for that reason, setting it on fire: "But as the flame had not as yet reached to its [the temple's] inward parts, but was still consuming the rooms that were about the holy house, and Titus supposing what the fact was, that the house itself might yet be saved, he came in haste and endeavored to persuade the soldiers to quench the fire . . . yet were their passions too hard . . . as was their hatred of the Jews. . . . Moreover, the hope of plunder induced many to go on, as *having this opinion, that all the places within were full of money*, and as seeing that all round *about it was made of gold* . . . the commanders retired, and Caesar with them . . . and thus the holy house burnt down, without Caesar's approbation." Josephus, *Wars*, 7.7 (emphasis added). So they believed there were riches in the temple, but we have nothing saying they were looking for gold between the stones. Israeli scholars today believe the Romans threw the stones over the retaining wall to discourage rebuilding the temple.

But at that time, they probably viewed the two events as one and the same, or that one would immediately follow the other. When interpreting Jesus' discourse, the reader has to carefully discern which part refers to the destruction of the temple and which part refers to the end of history as we know it. We will focus mainly on Luke's version, but also compare it with the others.

Jesus starts out,

> "Don't let anyone mislead you, for many will come in my name, claiming, 'I am the Messiah,' and saying, 'The time has come!' But don't believe them. And when you hear of wars and insurrections, don't panic. Yes, these things must take place first, but the end won't follow immediately." (vs. 8-9 NLT)

Jesus' main point here is about when the end is *not* coming. Jesus seems to be well-aware that future crackpots and con artists would use the end of history as a tool to manipulate gullible people. We already saw in chapter 17 that Jesus will return like lightning across the sky.

Jesus went on:

> "Nation will rise against nation and kingdom against kingdom, and there will be great earthquakes, and in various places plagues and famines; and there will be terrors and great signs from heaven." (vs. 10-11)

Nobody in this group would have guessed that two thousand years or more would pass before the end would come. Jesus is teaching that believers should resist the urge to think wars or natural disasters signal that the end is at hand. He is recounting the things that will be typical of the ages ahead.

All are commonplace except for "terrors and great signs from heaven." That sounds rather extraordinary. The word here for heaven doesn't necessarily mean heaven where God is. It often refers to the atmosphere, or the sky. It could be talking about storms or comets, which frightened ancient people.

Birth Pangs?

Matthew has the same list, but adds an intriguing comment, "But all these things are merely the beginning of birth pangs" (Matthew 24:8).

Clearly, birth pangs signal a birth. But how far should we push the comparison?

Not all birth pangs signal an imminent birth. Pangs, or contractions, can begin weeks or even months before the actual birth. To distinguish between these "false labor" contractions and actual labor, the parents have to watch for contractions that steadily increase in frequency and intensity. When the contractions are both frequent and intense, it's time to go to the hospital.

If Jesus intended this part in the comparison to birth pangs, it would suggest that things like earthquakes, famines, plagues, and terrors from the sky will increase in frequency and intensity as the birth [the end] draws near. Birth pangs must mean something, and Jesus' choice of words here does suggest the interplay of true and false labor. Notice Matthew's phrase "the beginning of birth pangs." Jesus is pointing to the beginning, more than to the end of birth pangs. These negatives will probably increase as we near the end of history.

But . . .

Suddenly, Jesus interjected, "But before all these things. . . ." Here, he breaks away from talking about the distant future back to his own day and the events in the immediate future. It's a warning of tough times ahead for the people of God.

> "They will lay their hands on you and will persecute you, delivering you to the synagogues and prisons, bringing you before kings and governors for my name's sake. It will lead to an opportunity for your testimony. So make up your minds not to prepare beforehand to defend yourselves; for I will give you utterance and wisdom which none of your opponents will be able to resist or refute. But you will be betrayed even by parents and brothers and relatives and friends, and they will put some of you to death, and you will be hated by all because of my name. Yet not a hair of your head will perish. By your endurance you will gain your lives." (vs. 12-19)

This part is not discussing end-times persecution. It's the persecution like that in the book of Acts and following decades. The early church was born and grew in the face of constant persecution. Most of the worst persecutions lay in the future at the time of Luke's writing. Persecutors like Nero and Domitian would slaughter tens of thousands of believers in the most gruesome manner. A dozen other emperors launched persecutions, some empire-wide, until the fourth century.

He says, "not a hair of your head will perish," but he just said some of them would be killed. He must mean they won't perish in the ultimate sense—in hell. It's a reassurance that even if we face pain and death, it's only momentary. Heaven awaits.

He also says, "by your endurance you will gain your lives," or "souls" (*pseuchas*). It's a reflection of his often-taught principle of losing your life in order to save your life.

Jerusalem

Next, continuing to talk about near-term predictions, Jesus unpacked the demise of Jerusalem:

> "But when you see Jerusalem surrounded by armies, then recognize that her desolation is near. Then those who are in Judea must flee to the mountains, and those who are in the midst of the city must leave, and those who are in the country must not enter the city; because these are days of vengeance, so that all things which are written will be fulfilled." (vs. 20-22)[2]

Flowing with the previous train of thought, this refers to the destruction of Jerusalem in the first century. There was a short period before Titus' siege when Jerusalem was surrounded by armies. The Roman governor of Syria, Cestius Gallus, tried to put down the Jewish revolt in AD 66. He managed to surround the inner city of Jerusalem for nine days, but gave up and withdrew.

So this is what Jesus refers to in his warning about the city being

2. What is Jesus referring to when he says this event must happen "so that all things which are written will be fulfilled?" (v. 22). Where does the Old Testament predict the destruction of Jerusalem by the Romans? One clear prediction comes from Daniel, again in chapter 9:26b. "The people of the prince who is to come will destroy the city and the sanctuary." The time setting for this prediction is shortly after the coming and death of Messiah (v. 26a). The perpetrator of the destruction is not "the prince who is to come," but "the people of the prince who is to come." In Daniel, the Beast is consistently associated with Rome, so under that logic, the people of the prince would be the Romans.

"surrounded by armies." Gallus' withdrawal gave people three years to leave before the final surrounding, from which there was no escape.[3]

Later, Roman general, and eventually emperor, Titus Flavius fulfilled the rest of Jesus' prediction. He surrounded the city again in a ruthless siege that culminated in the complete destruction of Jerusalem.

Josephus recounts that many Jews were actually approaching Jerusalem during the siege because the Passover was at hand, and they wanted to offer sacrifice. They apparently didn't realize that a siege was going on. The Romans let them go into the city, but wouldn't let them come back out. This greatly increased the population of the city, at the same time it increased their need for food and water.[4]

In light of this event, Jesus' warning "Those who are in the country must not enter the city" (v. 21) suddenly makes perfect sense. No wonder unbelieving scholars insist Luke was written after the destruction of Jerusalem. How would he know such details about the future?

True to Jesus' earlier statement about the stones being taken down until not one stone was left on another, Josephus says that the city and wall "was so thoroughly laid even with the ground, by those that dug it up to the foundation, that there was left nothing to make those that came thither believe it had ever been inhabited."[5]

Of the inhabitants of Jerusalem, Jesus said,

> "Woe to those who are pregnant and to those who are nursing babies in those days; for there will be great distress upon the land and wrath to this people; and they will fall by the edge of the sword, and will be led captive into all the nations." (vs. 23-24)

The "wrath" here doesn't refer to God's wrath, but to the wrath of the Romans. They were furious after suffering many losses and wasting months of hard work to put down this revolution.

True to this prediction, Josephus talks about how the Roman soldiers stabbed everyone they found until the second day after overcoming the

3. See the full story in S. G. F. Brandon, "The Defeat of Cestius Gallus, A.D. 66," *History Today* 20, 1 January 1970.
4. Kate Lohnes, "The Siege of Jerusalem," in *Encyclopedia Brittanica*, August 29, 2018, https://www.britannica.com/event/Siege-of-Jerusalem-70.
5. Josephus, *Jewish Wars*, 7.1.1.

walls. Only then did Titus command that no more Jews be killed but captured instead. Many thousands were captured and given as gifts to several cities where they were slaughtered in their amphitheaters for entertainment.

Thousands more were made slaves. The Romans transported 60,000-100,000 Jewish slaves to Rome, where they built the Roman Colosseum. Today in Titus' arch outside the Colosseum you can see engravings depicting the sacking of Jerusalem. They show a Jewish menorah, a table for show bread, and sacred trumpets taken from the temple.

The Jewish Christian community largely escaped this gruesome event according to early church historian, Eusebius. He says the Christians had been warned to escape Jerusalem and flee to the east, ending up in Perea.[6]

Until . . .

Then Jesus adds one more surprising prediction: "And Jerusalem will be trampled underfoot by the Gentiles [non-Jews] until the times of the Gentiles are fulfilled" (v. 24). Not only were the Jews defeated in the revolt in AD 70, but also in another revolt in AD 132-136 called the Bar Kokhba revolt. This time the Romans stripped Judea of Jews, and the Jewish nation ceased to exist. For the next two millennia Jerusalem was trampled under the feet of Gentiles, just as Jesus predicted.

But notice the key phrase, "until the times of the Gentiles are fulfilled." The word "until" implies that the Gentile ownership of Jerusalem would be only temporary. This points to the often-repeated Old Testament prediction that the Jews would one day be exiled to all nations and later regathered from the exile to reinhabit their ancient homeland.[7]

---

6. He says in part, "The people of the church in Jerusalem had been commanded by a revelation, vouchsafed to approved men there before the war, to leave the city and to dwell in a certain town of Perea called Pella. And when those that believed in Christ had come there from Jerusalem . . . the judgment of God at length overtook those who had committed such outrages against Christ and his apostles." Eusebius, *Church History*, 3.5.3.

7. Although some passages are disputed because they could refer to a different regathering, those that talk about Jews coming from all sides, from many nations, and from the ends of the earth are clearly not talking about the return from Babylon. These are some of the clearest predictions: Deuteronomy 4:27-30, 28:64, 30:1-5; Isaiah 10:20-23, 11:11–16, 27:12-13, 43:5-7, 66:19-20; Jeremiah 3:14-18, 16:14-15, 23:3-8, 30:3, 10-11, 32:37-44; Ezekiel 11:16-20, 20:41-42, 28:25, 34:12-14, 37:1-14, 21-22, 25, 38:8, 39:25-29; Hosea 1:11, 3:4-5, 11:10-11; Micah 2:12-13, 4:6, 5:2-4, 7:9-13; Zephaniah 3:18-20; Zechariah 8:3, 7, 20-22, 10:9-12. Notice that in the Ezekiel 37 prediction it is clear that the Jewish people will be gathered first in unbelief. It took another, later prophecy to

The Gentiles' ownership of Jerusalem would be during the "times of the Gentiles." What does that refer to? It's not defined in the Old Testament. God does predict through Isaiah that the Suffering Servant "will bring light to the nations" (e.g. Isaiah 42:6-7). This and other passages predict the worldwide spread of the gospel. But it doesn't use the term in question.

"The times of the Gentiles" probably refers to the period in history when God is focusing more on Gentiles and spreading the gospel worldwide. The apostle Paul talks about it in Romans:

> I say then, [the Jews] did not stumble so as to fall, did they? May it never be! But by their transgression salvation has come to the Gentiles, to make them jealous. . . . A partial hardening has happened to Israel until the fullness of the Gentiles has come in. (Romans 11:11, 25)

This was Paul's explanation for what God was doing during a time when most Jews were refusing Jesus. But he agreed with Jesus that it was only temporary. He goes on to say, "All Israel will be saved . . . for the gifts and the calling of God are irrevocable" (Romans 11:26, 29).

So Jesus' statement in verse 24 covers many years. The expression "the times of the Gentiles" sounds like it could be a long time. This is, in fact, another prophetic time gap. With only the hint about the times of the Gentiles, he moves from talking about the destruction of Jerusalem in the first century to the second coming and their question: "What will be the sign of your coming, and of the end of the age?" (Matthew 24:3)

Signs of the Times

We move to the apocalypse:

> "There will be signs in sun and moon and stars, and on the earth dismay among nations, in perplexity at the roaring of the sea and the waves, men fainting from fear and the expectation of the things which are coming upon the world; for the powers of the heavens will be shaken." (vs. 25-26)

Readers of Old Testament apocalyptic passages immediately recognize the signs in the sun, moon, and stars. Most passages see these things

---

summon the Spirit to indwell them.

happening in the context of war (e.g. Isaiah 13:6-16; 24:19-23; 34:4; Ezekiel 32:7; Zechariah 14:6-7; 12:7-8; Joel 2:30-3:17; Haggai 2:6; also later in Revelation 16:18-21). Descriptions of the end of history consistently see it as a time of terrible warfare. Descriptions of these signs make it seem like the luminaries are darkened. Perhaps the atmosphere is so full of smoke and dust that it dims the sky?

One theory is that the prophets, or in this case, Jesus, had to speak in language people understood when describing modern warfare. None of them have ever seen flying machines, missiles, bombs falling from the sky, explosions, etc. So the author uses "perspectival language"—language from the perspective of the reader.

So, for instance, is it that the stars shake, or is it the earth shaking, which makes the stars look like they're shaking from the perspective of someone on the ground? That's far more plausible.

What about the roaring of the sea and waves? Only Luke included this. Is it the culmination of climate change leading to huge storms? Or is it a natural disaster like an asteroid producing immense tsunamis? What about massive earthquakes? Or is it more metaphorical like Isaiah 17:12: "Alas, the uproar of many peoples who roar like the roaring of the seas, and the rumbling of nations who rush on like the rumbling of mighty waters?" We don't know.

In Daniel 12 the prophet asked for more information on the vision he had just seen, but could not understand. A mighty angel answered, "Go your way, Daniel, for these words are concealed and sealed up until the end time" (v. 9). In other words, end time prophecies are sometimes beyond understanding until their fulfillment draws near.

The Coming of the Son of Man

Jesus continued,

> "Then they will see the Son of Man coming in a cloud with power and great glory. But when these things begin to take place, straighten up and lift up your heads, because your redemption is drawing near." (vs. 27-28)

See Daniel 7:13 where "With the clouds of heaven one like a Son of Man was coming." Jews would have immediately thought of this passage. This is also where Jesus got the title he so often used, "Son of Man."

It's very clear by now that Jesus is no longer talking about the destruction of Jerusalem in AD 70.[8] That means we have another prophetic time gap in this chapter. Jesus' picture of the second coming is consistent with other descriptions (e.g. Acts 1:11; Revelation 1:7; 19:11).

NASB reads "When these things begin to take place . . ." which could be misleading. It sounds like it could be just one or two signs showing up. But the NLT captures the wording better here by translating "When all these things begin to happen. . . ." The pronoun reference is to all the signs, not just a couple.

The Fig Tree

> Then he gave them this illustration: "Notice the fig tree, or any other tree. When the leaves come out, you know without being told that summer is near. In the same way, when you see all these things taking place, you can know that the Kingdom of God is near." (vs. 29-31 NLT)

Teachers who dislike studying predictive prophecy (like some amillennial theologians) love to quote Mark 13:32, "But of that day or hour no one knows." But you can see from this illustration of the fig tree that Jesus did expect people to recognize the general approach of the second coming. As we saw earlier, trying to name dates or other specifics leads to error. But believers should recognize when summer is near.

This Generation

Next comes ground zero for the "Preterist" view that the whole discourse has already been fulfilled. Right after describing how the signs point to the time of his coming in the parable of the fig tree, Jesus said,

> "Truly I say to you, this generation will not pass away until all these things take place." (v. 32)

8. Again, the strict "Preterist" school of interpretation is the exception. They believe even the second coming has already happened! Read a good explanation in James M. Rochford, "A Critique of Preterism," Evidence Unseen (website), https://www.evidenceunseen.com/theology/eschatology/a-critique-of-preterism/ and in Fred Zaspel, "Preterism: Has All Prophecy Been Fulfilled?" The Gospel Coalition (website), https://www.thegospelcoalition.org/essay/preterism-prophecy-fulfilled/.

To the Preterists, this means that everything in the Olivet Discourse happened in the first century. As noted earlier, we will not engage in a lengthy rebuttal of this view, but others have. We will simply note that in context, Jesus just gave the illustration of the fig tree, followed by, "So you also, when you see these things happening, recognize that the kingdom of God is near" (v. 31). Then, "This generation will not pass away until all these things take place." The question is, who is "this generation?" The answer, in context, is, "the generation that sees 'all these things.'"

Jesus was explaining that the future scenario he was explaining will not stretch out for a hundred years. Rather, it's going to happen in a relatively short time—less than a generation.

Another alternative is that the term *genea* for "generation" can mean "a people." In that case, it would be a promise that the Jewish people will not pass away before the end.[9] I think this suggestion is far less likely than the previous one, but at least it's not as far out as the full Preterist view. The Preterist view puts entirely too much weight on a particular reading of this single verse.

My Words

Jesus capped the illustration by saying, "Heaven and earth will disappear, but my words will never disappear" (v. 33). It's an important statement, showing that Jesus ranked his own words on the same level as the rest of Scripture. The last time he used this expression about heaven and earth passing away, it referred to the Old Testament (Matthew 5:18). Here it has the same effect as God's saying, "I, the Lord, have spoken" (e.g. Numbers 14:35; Jeremiah 39:18).

Be Ready

Jesus concluded,

> "Watch out! Don't let your hearts be dulled by carousing and drunkenness, and by the worries of this life. Don't let that day catch you unaware, like a trap. For that day will come upon everyone living on the earth.[10] Keep alert at all times. And

9. Liefeld, *Luke*, 1023.
10. When Jesus says, "That day will come upon everyone living on the earth," he makes it clear that he is not referring to the revolt in AD 70, as Preterists claim.

> pray that you might be strong enough to escape these coming horrors and stand before the Son of Man." (vs. 34-36 NLT)

His curious reference to drunkenness and carousing could be an echo of the parable Matthew recorded at this point in the discourse. There, it was an evil slave left in charge of the household, who begins "to beat his fellow slaves and eat and drink with drunkards" (Matthew 24:49). But the point in both accounts is clear: drunkenness, carousing, and the worries of this life "dull" people's hearts. The result is that they become oblivious to what's going on.

One of the main reasons believers should avoid drunkenness, drugs, or materialistic worry is that any of these inhibits our sharpness and awareness of spiritual issues. We face a brilliant enemy, and we can't afford to be staggering around in a stupor.

The main imperative here is "Keep alert at all times." The mentality that lives in readiness for the coming of the Son of Man should characterize all followers of Jesus. Throughout the rest of the New Testament we see authors talking about how Jesus' coming could be soon. We now know they were wrong on that, but wrong in a way that is right. Believers should live in the mindset that Jesus could come sooner than people think.

Added Statements from Matthew

Matthew's account is longer and it includes some key statements not found in Luke. We don't know who Luke's source was, but he has some items not found in Mark or Matthew, like the comment about the roaring of the waves. The differences are enough to suggest Luke had a different source. Matthew's source was no doubt Matthew himself. He wrote the book and was there in person when Jesus spoke.

Another factor for Luke is that he already covered some of Jesus' end-times teaching earlier in chapter 17. He may have omitted some of those points because they would be redundant.

Love Grows Cold

In the discussion about birth pangs, we read another of Jesus' statements not found in Luke.

> "Because lawlessness is increased, most people's love will grow cold." (Matthew 24:12)

It's an intriguing proposition. The word *anomos* means "no law" or "without law." It can mean disobeying the law. But if that's the case, it's hard to imagine which age in human history is more disobedient than any other. But if Jesus meant that we take the term literally, it could refer to the loss of any knowledge of moral categories. Large swathes of people might come to doubt whether there is such a thing as objective moral good and evil. If so, it begins to look more like our own postmodern culture.

And what is the connection between loss of moral categories and people's love growing cold? Our culture knows something about that as well. Before our eyes, we in the postmodern west are seeing the wholesale loss of people's ability to form deep or lasting relationships. In place of real relationships, people stare at screens full of videos, letters, and memes. Will the electronic mode of relating become a type of prison house? Is this the love growing cold Jesus predicted? And how will it develop going forward?

A lawless landscape where anything goes is frightening. People begin to sense that opening up too much or growing too close is dangerous. So they insert a persona online, a false but useful version of themselves more acceptable to the public.

Beginning in childhood, people are learning to substitute online stimulation for the far more difficult project of learning how to relate deeply in person. Sociologists and psychologists are warning that the trend is highly damaging to people's mental health, especially young people.[11]

Matthew also includes this statement from Jesus:

> "But the one who endures to the end, he will be saved." (Matthew 24:13)

The plain sense reading sounds like salvation is by works. But Jesus is

---

11. Good analyses to read include: Nicholas Kardaras, *Glow Kids: How Screen Addiction Is Hijacking Our Kids - and How to Break the Trance* (New York: St. Martin's Press, 2016); Aric Sigman, "Screen Dependency Disorders: a new challenge for child neurology," *Journal of the International Child Neurology Association* 1, no. 1 (April 19, 2017); Jeanne Twenge, *iGen: Why Today's Super-Connected Kids Are Growing Up Less Rebellious, More Tolerant, Less Happy—and Completely Unprepared for Adulthood—and What That Means for the Rest of Us* (New York: Atria Books, 2017); Aviv Weinstein and Michel Lejoyeux, "New developments on the neurobiological and pharmaco-genetic mechanisms underlying internet and videogame addiction," *The American Journal on Addictions* 24, no. 2 (March 2015): 117-25.

not talking about eternal salvation in this context. The verb *sozo* can mean rescue from any threat. Here Jesus is talking about persecution and other harsh conditions during the great tribulation. It is from these that people can be rescued through perseverance. This statement in Matthew is probably just a different wording for the saying in Luke that "you will save your lives" (v. 19).

Gospel Spread

Matthew included another important condition in verse 14: "This gospel of the kingdom shall be preached in the whole world as a testimony to all the nations, and then the end will come." This is one of the most amazing predictions Jesus ever uttered. That this small band of ancient disciples would end up spreading the gospel to the whole world and every nation in it.

If the word "nations" means nation states, this sign is already fulfilled. Every nation on earth has witnessing churches today. But the word for nations, *ethne*, more likely refers to ethnic-linguistic subcultures who need to be reached with the gospel in their own language. Missions experts call them "people groups."

The number of remaining unreached people groups is inching downward. Joshua Project says there are still seven thousand unreached groups. When I was in college, they taught us that over 20,000 groups were unreached. Also, Jesus only said the gospel would be preached in all nations. He didn't say they had to accept it to any given degree. Clearly, we are close to fulfilling this condition.[12]

The Great Tribulation

Another segment found in Matthew but not in Luke is Jesus' warning concerning the so-called "abomination of desolation." We briefly mentioned this earlier in connection with Jesus' teaching in chapter 17. Jesus

12. The definition of a people group is somewhat subjective. For instance, Joshua Project shows 545 people groups in China, with 441 of those groups considered unreached. This is in spite of the fact that China has seen more growth in conversions than any other country during the past several decades. The definition of "unreached" also changes from group to group. The most common definition is that if a people group has less than 2% of its members as walking Bible-believing Christians, it's unreached. Some of the unreached groups are quite small. They may have their own language, but may also know a trade language that is shared throughout many groups. For all these reasons, we don't know if this sign has been completely fulfilled, but it's coming close.

warned that when people see the abomination of desolation spoken of by the prophet Daniel, they should flee because, "Then there will be a great tribulation, such as has not occurred since the beginning of the world until now, nor ever will" (Matthew 24:21).

That is certainly a poor description of the fighting in AD 70! That war was a mere footnote in the history of warfare. In fact, this "great tribulation" still lies in the future today. And his follow up comment hasn't happened either: "Unless those days had been cut short, no life would have been saved; but for the sake of the elect those days will be cut short" (Matthew 24:22). This is referring to a war that threatens to destroy all life on earth. No conventional war could come close to that description. But in our day, such a war is literally possible because of thermonuclear weapons.

Another passage in association with the final war mentions a third of mankind dying (Revelation 9:15). Isaiah speaks of a war that leaves "mortal man scarcer than pure gold" (Isaiah 13:12).

All of these and others fall in line with what Jesus said about the tribulation endangering all life on earth. At that point, Jesus intervenes with the second coming and prevents the annihilation of the human race. Jesus said, "For the sake of the elect those days will be cut short" (Matthew 24:22).

The Big Picture

Students of the history of religion find that most religions hold to a "cyclical" view of history. That is, a view that history is repeating itself. Most scholars agree that this cyclical view takes its inspiration from nature. Day and night, winter and summer, cycles of the moon, nature moved in cycles because of our planet orbiting the sun while revolving. The moon also orbits the earth, creating another cycle. These cycles can be linked up with biological cycles, such as birth, rites of passage, reproduction, and death.

In the Olivet Discourse, Jesus revealed that this cyclical view of history is false. He declared instead that history had a beginning at creation, and it will reach its culmination in his second coming. Before his coming will be the great tribulation. Science now confirms that the history we see in our day is unique. None of this has happened before, and the nature cycles underlying the cyclical view have now been explained apart from any spiritual cause.

Moving forward, science is again warning us that the human race is completely out of control and headed for disaster in the not-too-distant future—a view they also share with biblical teaching. The explosive growth of human population, now past eight billion and growing, poses an unprecedented threat to the entire earth.

Dangerous technologies are multiplying as the climate heats up, fisheries are depleted, and formerly fertile land becomes desert. Smoke rises from our burning forests. The rapid travel options in the modern world allowed the covid pandemic to blanket the earth in a matter of weeks!

Instead of modernity delivering a humanistic utopia, we stand helplessly watching negative trend lines converging toward something ominous. Jesus described "men fainting from fear and the expectation of the things which are coming upon the world" (v. 26).

These are the pressure points that will make people willing to do anything to escape—anything including giving up their freedom. The great power of the end times is an authoritarian anti-Christian empire headed by the beast. At the end comes something so terrible Jesus warned it could destroy all life on earth—Armageddon.

Fortunately, we have Jesus' promise that he won't allow it to get to that point. He pulls out his whistle and blows it hard (actually a trumpet), ending the autonomy of the world. It's time for God to take over.

At that point, Jesus sets up the thousand-year reign according to Revelation 20 and parallels. Other interpreters think the new heaven and new earth follow immediately after Jesus' second coming. That seems wrong, but either way, Jesus takes over. Finally, comes an end to war, to suffering, to death, along with a new wonderful direct access to God and to the people of God. Joy and love will replace gloom and fear.

38

Passover

Luke 21:38-22:23

Chapter 22 should clearly begin here, instead of the current awkward placement at the end of chapter 21. All week Jesus taught in the temple court. Luke says, "The crowds gathered at the Temple early each morning to hear him" (Luke 21:38).

So not everyone was against Jesus. The common people were attracted to his teaching. That only increased the leaders' hatred, and meant that they needed one more thing—where was he staying at night? Luke says, "Now during the day he was teaching in the temple, but at evening he would go out and spend the night on the mount that is called Olivet" (v. 37).

It later turns out they were staying either in, or next to, the garden of Gethsemane. This olive grove is at the base of the Mount of Olives, and it's still there today. In fact, archeologists believe that some of the ancient olive trees there (some with twenty-foot diameter trunks) may have been alive in Jesus' day!

The gnarly, slow growing olive trees grow and die back over and over, sometimes from fire, sometimes from disease. This is one of the authentic sites in the Holy Land from the time of Jesus. The Orthodox shrine next to it is not. The grove is within eyesight of the temple mount.

Betrayal

Judas had seen enough. By now it was clear that Jesus was doing nothing but alienating the Jewish leadership. He was making no move to improve relations. The coronation of Jesus as king was clearly not going to happen. Judas decided to cash in. He probably was bitter at Jesus for wasting three years of his life. Was he also angry because Jesus rebuked him when the woman washed his feet? (John 12:4-7). Bitterness is known to be a key entry point for Satan.

> Now the Feast of Unleavened Bread, which is called the Passover, was approaching. The chief priests and the scribes were seeking how they might put him to death; for they were afraid of the people. And Satan entered into Judas who was called Iscariot, belonging to the number of the twelve. And he went away and discussed with the chief priests and officers how he might betray him to them. They were glad and agreed to give him money. So he consented, and began seeking a good opportunity to betray him to them apart from the crowd. (22:1-6)

Satan was engineering Jesus' death, working both sides toward the middle. He was motivating the Pharisees, Sadducees, and scribes, using their hatred of Jesus. Now the Evil One had an inside man apparently possessed by Satan himself. Jesus must have revealed this to the disciples after his resurrection (see also John 13:2).

Why?

But how odd that Satan would conspire to put Jesus on the cross! Didn't he realize the cross would free the human race from God's sentence of death? Didn't he know that Jesus was intending to go to the cross? Jesus had announced that often enough to his disciples. Hadn't he read the Old Testament prophecies of Jesus' death? Didn't he know what Jesus was soon to say: "Now judgment is upon this world; now the ruler of this world will be cast out. And I, if I am lifted up from the earth, will draw all men to Myself?" (John 12:31-32).

The answer to all these questions is no, he didn't know. Satan is an incredibly smart being. Even God called him "full of wisdom and perfect in beauty" (Ezekiel 28:12). But all his smarts didn't keep him from walking into a carefully laid trap. Only too late would he realize what was going on, and that he had mistakenly played a key role in bringing it to pass. Satan is a freewill being, but he is only finite. He's nothing like God.

Satan suffered from the same tendency to engage in paradigmatic thinking—where it's hard to comprehend new information that contradicts your current paradigm or thought conclusion. Satan was like everyone else, expecting that Jesus was about to seize power and be King Messiah. That's what the Old Testament taught about the Messiah.

It also taught about a suffering servant of the Lord, but it never linked that picture with the picture of the reigning king. Crucially, the Old Testament never said that the Messiah would come twice. Without that critical piece, it became almost impossible to see the Suffering Servant and King Messiah as one and the same person. How could they be the same, when the king is said to reign forever, but the servant dies a horrible death? (Compare Isaiah 9:6-7 and Isaiah 53:7-9).

What about Jesus' multiple warnings that he was going to be put to death? Satan would have understood those warnings, wouldn't he? The most likely answer is that Jesus only gave these warnings when he knew Satan wasn't around to hear them. Satan is not omnipresent, even through his many demonic followers.

Jesus implied this in the upper room when he said, "I will not speak much more with you, for the ruler of the world is coming, and he has nothing in me" (John 14:30). He didn't want to speak about in-house truths when the enemy could hear.[1] Jesus clearly implied that he could only talk openly when Satan was not there to hear.

The Last Supper

The Passover was at hand.[2]

1. For a full explanation of the messianic secret, see Dennis McCallum, *Satan and His Kingdom: What the Bible Says and How It Matters to You* (Minneapolis MN: Bethany House Publishers, 2009), chap. 4 and 5 with appendices. Or see the shorter article, Dennis McCallum, "The Mystery Hidden for Ages Past," Dwell Community Church (website), https://www.dwellcc.org/essays/mystery-hidden-aeons-past.
2. The synoptic Gospels have the last supper as a Passover meal on the day of Passover. The gospel of John seems to say that the last supper and arrest of Jesus happened the day *before* Passover (John 19:14). This is the so-called Passover problem. Bible scholar, Harold Hoehner says that the Mishnah indicates that worshippers from Galilee counted their days from dawn to dawn. Worshipers from Judea counted their day from sundown to sundown. This was to alleviate crowding at the temple. Hoehner, *Chronological Aspects*, 86. This conclusion is based on comparing *Mishnah* Pesachim 10:9 and *Mishnah* Zebahim 5:8. Josephus, who was a contemporary and lived in Judea as a practicing

> Then came the first day of Unleavened Bread on which the Passover lamb had to be sacrificed. And Jesus sent Peter and John, saying, "Go and prepare the Passover for us, so that we may eat it." They said to Him, "Where do You want us to prepare it?" And he said to them, "When you have entered the city, a man will meet you carrying a pitcher of water; follow him into the house that he enters. And you shall say to the owner of the house, 'The teacher says to you, "Where is the guest room in which I may eat the Passover with my disciples?"' And he will show you a large, furnished upper room; prepare it there." (vs. 7-12)

Again, you see the script they follow had been arranged by God. This "large, furnished upper room" probably was the same upper room the believers used as their meeting place in Acts 1 and 2. It must have been quite large to hold 120 people (Acts 1:13-15).

They had to go to the temple to get their lamb offered and roasted, then brought the carcass to the room. There were bitter herbs and matzo crackers to pass out, and four cups of wine. When Jesus arrived with the other disciples,

> He said to them, "I have earnestly desired to eat this Passover with you before I suffer; for I say to you, I shall never again eat it until it is fulfilled in the kingdom of God." (vs. 15-16)

Jesus knew he was the Passover lamb. He knew he was about to fulfill Passover's original meaning. As the thirteen men reclined on their mats, Jesus was the only one who knew what was really going on.

The New Passover

The Old Testament covenant under Moses was rich in ritual. Unlike pagan worship that was often believed to affect nature, Old Testament rituals were meant to teach. The Children of Israel weren't stupid, but they were illiterate. They were a slave population that had just escaped from Egypt. Very few of them could read or write. So the rituals were divine dramas, acting out theological truth in a visual way.

Pharisee, seems to reckon his days from morning to morning. Josephus, *Antiquities*, 3.10. So some Jews reckoned their days different than others. Or it's possible that Jesus decided to have the dinner a day early because he knew what was coming on Passover.

When you add up all the festivals and other sacrifices they observed, it came to scores of different ritual acts each year. In Jesus' New Covenant, the number of rituals would be dramatically reduced—from scores down to two. And one of those is baptism, which you only do once. That leaves only one to be observed in an ongoing way. This one—the last supper.

The First Communion Dinner

> When the hour had come, he reclined at the table, and the apostles with him… And when he had taken a cup and given thanks, he said, "Take this and share it among yourselves; for I say to you, I will not drink of the fruit of the vine from now on until the kingdom of God comes." (vs. 14-18)

When I was in college, I was leading a high school group that was growing rapidly. One day one of the students was down at our house on campus, and asked if I was coming to the meeting with the Mormons. My ears perked up. He went on to explain that some members in the group had been talking to some Mormons students and decided to have a meeting where they could come together and be unified at the high school. Two Mormon elders were also expected.

I frowned and said I thought there was something wrong with Mormonism, but I didn't know what. I said I would definitely be at the meeting. That afternoon, I went to the campus bookstore and picked up a small book that the Mormons put out. I read it and learned how Jesus had come over to the new world during the time after the cross. That intrigued me, because I always wondered what the first peoples in America were supposed to do to come to God.

At the end of the book, they suggested a prayer you could pray to the effect that if this story is true, God would show you. That made sense to me, so I briefly prayed that God would show me whether to believe this account.

Instantly, a verse I had read earlier that week came to mind. It was Jesus saying, "I will not drink of the fruit of the vine from now on until the kingdom of God comes" (v. 18). I had my answer, because the Book of Mormon said he came over and had communion with people here in America. A direct contradiction! That night I confronted the Mormon elders with my experience. They didn't know what to say at first, but eventually argued that the Bible was a lot older than the Book of Mormon, so it had more mistakes.

Later, I learned this discrepancy was the least of their problems. But the way the verse so instantly came to mind, I'm sure it was the Holy Spirit using God's word to speak. Our group did not merge with the Mormons.

The Cup

Luke doesn't have Jesus' statement recorded in Matthew:

> "Drink from it, all of you; for this is my blood of the covenant, which is poured out for many for forgiveness of sins." (Matthew 26:27-28)

Covenant is a central concept in Scripture from the earliest times. God enacted a covenant with Noah, then he made additional covenants with Abraham, Moses, and David. Finally comes the New Covenant.

A covenant is a promise or pledge, like a contract today. Covenants typically spell out the expectations and commitments from both parties in a relationship. That avoids misunderstandings and allows the parties to relate in harmony. Covenants were often executed between a greater and a lesser people, in order to avoid war. The Old Testament covenants are quite unique, because unlike other ancient covenants, these obligated the greater Lord, not just the lesser party. That was unheard of.

This is the first mention of the New Covenant in the New Testament. Jeremiah predicted that a new covenant was coming (Jeremiah 31:31-34), but only part of that promise came to pass. It's another case of an unforeseen, partial fulfillment.

The New Covenant centers on the blood of Jesus. Just like the Mosaic Covenant was initiated with blood, when Moses sprinkled blood on the people (Exodus 24:7-8). They were also given Passover, with the picture of the blood of the lamb smeared on the doorposts and lintels. Both \\ would be fulfilled, as God counted Jesus' blood to forgive sins.

In the Old Testament, blood stood for life in the sacrificial system. Farmers knew that when an animal's blood was shed, it died. God declared to Moses,

> "For the life of the flesh is in the blood, and I have given it to

> you on the altar to make atonement for your souls; for it is the blood by reason of the life that makes atonement." (Leviticus 17:11)

This giving of a life fulfills God's decree to Adam, that in the day he ate of the forbidden fruit "you will surely die" (Genesis 2:17). Paul says simply, "The wages of sin is death" (Romans 6:23).

On the original Passover, when the Jews were escaping Egypt, they spread the blood of a lamb on each family's doorposts and lintels. Then, when the angel of death came to punish sin, it passed over any house with this blood display, as if to say, "Death has already occurred here." Jesus was the true Passover lamb (1 Corinthians 5:7). His blood showed that the price for sin had been paid, this time for real, not symbolically.[3]

The connection between blood and forming a covenant also matches the formalization of the covenant of Moses described in Exodus 24. He sprinkled the people with blood when they agreed to the terms of the Mosaic Covenant.

The Disciples

Once again, the disciples didn't understand what Jesus was saying. This is when Jesus said, "These things I have spoken to you, so that when their hour comes, you may remember that I told you of them. These things I did not say to you at the beginning, because I was with you" (John 16:4).

He also said, "These things I have spoken to you in figurative language; an hour is coming when I will no longer speak to you in figurative language, but will tell you plainly of the Father" (John 16:25). Why couldn't he speak plainly on this night? Jesus knew it was better for them to fully comprehend later. They may not have been capable of comprehension at this point in time.

By comparing John, Matthew, and Mark, it's clear that Judas left during the meal, but before the bread and wine. It would have been inappropriate for him to take communion, because he wasn't a true believer.

3. Jesus mentions the cup before and after the bread. That could be because the traditional Jewish Passover meal had four different cups that stood for different things.

His Body

> And when he had taken some bread and given thanks, he broke it and gave it to them, saying, "This is my body which is given for you; do this in remembrance of me." (v. 19)

Jesus broke the bread and would soon see his own body being broken. And here is the grand reason for taking communion: "Do this in remembrance of me." As fallen people, even believers can slip into taking Jesus' death for granted. No wonder he gave us a tangible way to focus our attention and appreciation on who he is and what he did.

You can see from the text of all three synoptic Gospels that Jesus gave no other reason to take communion than as a remembrance of him. It doesn't forgive sin or restore one's closeness to God.

The apostle Paul later explained another symbolic meaning for the bread. In 1 Corinthians 10:16-17:

> Is not the cup of blessing which we bless a sharing in the blood of Christ? Is not the bread which we break a sharing in the body of Christ? Since there is one loaf, we who are many are one body; for we all partake of the one bread.

The early Christians passed a loaf around and each person pulled a piece off, unlike most churches today that have little individual crackers or chips on a plate. Under the first century practice, Paul explains that it's a picture of the unity of all believers as the body of Christ makes sense.

Later Developments

The changes brought in centuries later made communion into a religious work mediated by priests, instead of a simple act of remembrance. The church insisted that God's grace was mediated through the church and the sacraments.

This picture clashes sharply with the picture we have in the New Testament, where communion was completely informal. They practiced communion as part of a communal dinner, without priests or liturgies. It is a *eucharist*, a thanksgiving—that part is true. But all the added claims that exceed anything taught in Scripture are unauthorized and invalid.

The formalized approach of later centuries had priests holding the bread and wine up and offering them to God as a sacrifice. Then, when members receive it, communion conveyed actual forgiveness. This suggests that forgiveness must be secured week by week, and that the work Jesus did remains unfinished, rather than "once for all time" (Hebrews 10:12).

The Bible teaches that "By one offering he has perfected for all time those who are set apart" (Hebrews 10:14). We do not obtain forgiveness week by week, but all at once. That's why, "There is now no condemnation for those who are in Christ Jesus" (Romans 8:1).

Judas

At this point, Jesus revealed that he knew which of them would betray him.

> "Behold, the hand of the one betraying me is with mine on the table. For indeed, the Son of Man is going as it has been determined; but woe to that man by whom he is betrayed!" (vs. 21-22)

His expression "Woe to that man . . ." is an expression of sorrow as we saw earlier, not a threat.

How bizarre that Judas was sitting right there in this intimate scene! He even had the money for the betrayal already in his pocket. Careful reading shows that he actually had Jesus wash his feet! We know he was still there because Jesus used the present tense when he said, "You are all clean, but not every one of you" (John 13:10). And only after that did Jesus say to Judas, "What you do, do quickly" (John 13:27). Even then, the disciples thought he was being sent on an errand (John 13:28-29).

What pathos must Jesus' have felt as he washed Judas' feet? Did Judas avert his gaze? Was his head thumping in fear and guilt? He must have sensed that Jesus knew his little secret. Jesus had in fact known all along that Judas was a fake. That's why, more than a year earlier he said, "Did I myself not choose you, the twelve, and yet one of you is a devil?" (John 6:70). John also said that Judas was stealing money from the common purse, so he had been on the take for some time (John 12:6). Jesus must have filled the disciples in on that little detail after the resurrection.

When Jesus said the betrayer was present at the table, amazingly, nobody rotated his head toward Judas. Nobody said, "I know, it's Judas, right?"

Instead, they doubted themselves more than Judas. That means Judas was a good deceiver. He knew how to play the part and he kept his doubts to himself.

Finally to keep from sticking out, Judas himself asked, "Surely it is not I, Rabbi?" Jesus said to him, "You have said it yourself" (Matthew 26:25). We have similar figures of speech—"No kidding!" or "You said it."

Some modern portrayals of Judas suggest that he was compelled to do what he did . . . maybe even by God . . . that he didn't really have anything against Jesus, but wanted to pressure him to step forward and make his move. In other words, perhaps Judas was doing what he thought was right.

One thing doesn't fit that picture: the money. Why would he say he wouldn't do it unless he got paid? Thirty pieces of silver (Matthew 26:15) was a month's wage. A month's wage today in America is maybe four or five thousand dollars. It was a significant sum in that culture.

Jesus' words also don't fit the altruistic Judas picture. Here he observes, "Woe to that man by whom he is betrayed!" (v. 22). And Matthew adds that Jesus went on, "It would have been good for that man if he had not been born" (Matthew 26:24). That implies that Judas ended up in hell.

Again, when praying to the Father, Jesus spoke of his disciples, saying, "not one of them perished but the son of perdition." So it's quite implausible that Jesus would speak this way if there was any redeeming aspect in the betrayal. And beneath the betrayal was Judas' unbelief.

Earlier, the leaders had decided to kill Jesus, but they said, "Not during the festival, otherwise there might be a riot of the people" (Mark 14:2). But when one of Jesus' own followers came with an offer to give him up discretely, it was an immediate change of plans. They decided to get it done right away.

The Big Picture

Jesus said he had been longing to share this Passover with his disciples (v. 15). He knew it was his last night with them. His heart was heavy "to the point of death" (Matthew 26:38). The traitor was sitting there at the table with the money in his pocket. So was the one who would deny him with cursing later that night. The rest of his men are arguing about which one of them was the greatest. What a disheartening landscape! That night, it would only get worse.

39

AFTER DINNER
LUKE 22:24-38

Who Is the Greatest?

Then, as they were discussing who would betray Jesus, the topic drifted into another argument about which of them was the greatest! They might not have described the argument in those words. But analyzed objectively, many arguments involving self-defense or the legitimacy of one's actions really boil down to "Who is the greatest?" You're defending your own greatness.

Luke's language points the finger at their problem. He says they were arguing about "which one of them was regarded to be greatest" (Luke 22:24). The word "regarded" means regarded by other people. Striving for recognition and impressiveness has to do with playing to the human audience. Overcoming such self-aggrandizement comes from a focus on God as our only audience.

This is almost certainly the point at which Jesus washed the disciples' feet. In a perfect rebuttal without words, Jesus again demonstrated what humble, serving love is. But he added some words as well:

> And he said to them, "The kings of the Gentiles lord it over them; and those who have authority over them are called

> 'Benefactors.' But it is not this way with you, but the one who is the greatest among you must become like the youngest, and the leader like the servant. For who is greater, the one who reclines at the table or the one who serves? Is it not the one who reclines at the table? But I am among you as the one who serves." (vs. 25-27)

These words are so similar to what John has Jesus saying after washing their feet, they are really the same message in different words.[1] Jesus was literally acting as a servant washing the guests' feet. His reference to becoming "like the youngest" came from the ancient middle eastern reverence and respect for older people. The youngest had the lowest status.

Jesus made it clear that he was modeling the servant attitude for them, not seeking to put them to shame. Jesus was not the kind of leader for whom nothing is ever good enough. He appreciated the sacrifices his disciples had withstood:

> "You are those who have stood by me in my trials; and just as my Father has granted me a kingdom, I grant you that you may eat and drink at my table in my kingdom, and you will sit on thrones judging the twelve tribes of Israel." (vs. 28-30)

They need not (and we need not) worry about securing our own glorious future. Jesus will take care of that. How awesome will it be to eat and drink at Jesus' table! We have no reason to spiritualize this scene, as though it's metaphorical. It's a plain, literal promise Jesus made to his followers. So were his warnings about losing reward in heaven when we play to people to get glory from them (e.g. Matthew 6:1-6).

His reference to the twelve tribes of Israel shows that the Jewish people are not disbanded or rejected, as some teach. They will be front and center in the coming kingdom. Judging here means leading or governing like the judges of old, not judging people for their eternal destiny.

---

1. How could Luke, Matthew, and Mark fail to tell the awesome story of Jesus washing the disciples' feet? In answer to this, remember that John wrote his Gospel well after the other three. He was aware of previous Gospels. When writing yet a fourth gospel, it would be natural for John to focus on things the earlier gospels had passed over. John himself says he was very selective in choosing what to recount, "And there are also many other things which Jesus did, which if they were written in detail, I suppose that even the world itself would not contain the books that would be written" (John 21:25). No doubt the other authors felt the same way.

The Helper

This was the occasion for the "Upper Room Discourse" also recounted in the Gospel of John. In this talk he gave them as much as he could on the coming Helper, the Holy Spirit. They were trying to imagine something they didn't know by experience.

He described the indwelling of the Holy Spirit: "If anyone loves me, he will keep my word; and my Father will love him, and we will come to him and make our abode with him" (John 14:23). Blank stares must have been their response. What did it mean?

Why go over future matters that were beyond their comprehension? He explained: "From now on I am telling you before it comes to pass, so that when it does occur, you may believe that I am he" (John 13:19).

They were definitely confused: "Judas (not Iscariot) said to Him, 'Lord, what then has happened that you are going to disclose yourself to us and not to the world?'" (John 14:22). Jesus was talking about leaving and how they couldn't follow, but Judas Alpheus' question, "What has happened?" shows that their current paradigm had no place for this. They were baffled.

Jesus gave an important promise that became one of the key bases for the inerrancy of the New Testament. "But the Helper, the Holy Spirit, whom the Father will send in my name, He will teach you all things, and bring to your remembrance all that I said to you" (John 14:26). So he pre-authenticated the apostles' writings, not only the Gospels, but also new material, like the doctrines concerning the body of Christ and spiritual gifts. Such apostolic teachings were possible because the Spirit would "teach you all things."

He left them with the great assurance, "If I go and prepare a place for you, I will come again and receive you to myself, that where I am, there you may be also" (John 14:3).

Sifting Like Wheat

Jesus then turned to Peter:

> "Simon, Simon, behold, Satan has demanded permission to sift you like wheat; but I have prayed for you, that your faith

> may not fail; and you, when once you have turned again, strengthen your brothers." (vs. 31-32)

How can Satan demand anything from God? We have the example in Job, where Satan was granted permission to inflict suffering. In that case, the Evil One launched accusations against both Job (that he was in it for the money) and against God (that he was buying love). God was apparently unwilling to let those accusations stand, but he also had plans to use the suffering as a positive force in Job's life, not to mention creating an important book in the Bible.

We don't know what Satan said to God in this case, but it does seem that God has a similar plan in mind to use the disciples' suffering and failure to build them up. Peter would lead the way. When sifting wheat, the intent is to remove undesirable pieces of the plant.

Something important in this passage fails to come through in most English translations. When Jesus says, "to sift you like wheat," the "you" is plural. In Greek the plural "you" is spelled differently than the singular "you." So Jesus isn't just saying Peter will be sifted, but that "you all" will be sifted.

But in verse 32 he says, "I have prayed for you, that your faith may not fail; and you, when once you have turned again, strengthen your brothers." Here he uses the singular. So it means they all will be sifted, but Peter will play a special role, strengthening his brothers.

It happened as predicted. The other disciples all fled when the leaders arrested Jesus (Matthew 26:56). Perhaps Peter would break through to true repentance sooner than the others? He would certainly experience significant needed breaking, as seen in his prideful attitude:

> But Peter said to him, "Lord, with you I am ready to go both to prison and to death!"
>
> And Jesus said, "I say to you, Peter, the rooster will not crow today until you have denied three times that you know me." (vs. 33-34)

Peter must have been astonished. Was it really possible? Surely he shook his head in disbelief.

Jesus knew even the details of what was coming. That and their boasting to each other on the very night when Jesus was in such pain paint a grim picture. Jesus' response? A stinging rebuke? No. He took off his clothes, wrapped his waist in a towel and knelt down and washed their feet. He promised them they would eat at his table and sit on thrones. Even Peter's denial, which would prove to be especially ghastly, receives nothing more than a sad recitation of the coming events, and a ray of light—that he would strengthen his brothers.

Jesus loved his men when they did well, but also when they were doing poorly. It's an important example for people engaged in ministry. Working closely with people entails a lot of disappointment; also abandonment and betrayal. The hurt can be severe, easily bad enough to bring tears to your eyes. But even worse, it can be bad enough to make you want to protect your heart from further pain. Just a bit of self-protection seems so reasonable when you have been let down so completely—just a bit of distancing yourself from others who might do the same.

But that's the wrong way to go as Jesus showed us here. That little bit of self-protection and distance can ruin your ministry. First, it can easily tip the scales against success in influencing people. When people are kept at arm's length, you have far less influence than you would with close, warm relationships. Self-protection involves less than a full giving your heart over in love. That's not good enough.

Second, it's self-confirming. Putting some distance in and avoiding hurt has a certain reward. But it's hard to see why, if a little self-protection works, a little more might work even better. This becomes a negative spiral downward. It ends with superficial, disengaged relationships and a lot of time staring at a screen.

Preparing for Their Mission

Here in the upper room we get our first clear glimpse of the new supernatural lifestyle available through the indwelling Holy Spirit. One aspect of that lifestyle was learning how to trust God to meet the costs of ministry.

> And he said to them, "When I sent you out without money belt and bag and sandals, you did not lack anything, did you?" They said, "No, nothing." (v. 35)

But that was only a lesson, not the norm. He went on to characterize preparing for a mission in the future:

> And He said to them, "But now, whoever has a money belt is to take it along, likewise also a bag, and whoever has no sword is to sell his coat and buy one." (v. 36)

They were being sent out into a difficult and dangerous field. The norm in the future would be that people going out to a field of ministry would need to plan ahead and pack well. But what about the sword? Probably the sword was for self-defense on roads that might harbor bandits. Just the sight of a band of men wearing swords would deter attack.

Taking him quite literally, they said, "Lord, look, here are two swords." And He said to them, "It is enough" (v. 38). This reply is probably like our expression, "Yeah, whatever."

Jesus' Prayer

This was Jesus' last full night with his disciples. He could now pray to the Father, "The words which you gave me I have given to them; and they received them and truly understood that I came forth from you, and they believed that you sent me" (John 17:8). Looking forward, he also said, "I do not pray on behalf of these alone, but for those also who believe in me through their word" (John 17:20). As he said earlier, he knew this small band would spread the gospel to the whole world.

So as Jesus sat praying with his friends, he was looking down the corridor of time to new friends—you and me. He envisioned the mystical union that was coming, as he prayed to the Father: "I in them and you in me, that they may be perfected in unity, so that the world may know that you sent me, and loved them, even as you have loved me" (John 17:23). He knew this new oneness, demonstrated in the community of the people of God, would be compelling evidence that he was truly God's son.

Finally, he prayed "That the love with which you loved me may be in them, and I in them" (John 17:26). It's a short word, and easily missed. He meant that the same love with which God the Father loved Jesus is now ours for the asking. Paul would later explain, "The love of God has been poured out within our hearts through the Holy Spirit who was given to us" (Romans 5:5). This perfect love is his gift to us. Only what Jesus did the next day would make that possible.

Mark adds that they sang a hymn before going out to the Mount of Olives. It was the Jewish custom to sing Psalm 118 after the Passover (Mark 14:26). What did Jesus feel as he sang verse 6: "The Lord is for me, so I will have no fear. What can mere people do to me?" He knew he would soon be answering the question through experience. But this is also the Psalm that declares, "The stone that the builders rejected has now become the cornerstone" (Psalm 118:22). Jesus knew that was about him.

The Big Picture

Jesus was in agony. Just minutes after this account, he said, "My soul is deeply grieved to the point of death" (Mark 14:34). This would be the perfect situation to call for some "me time." He did move away from the crowds at times, as we read, "He went away and hid Himself from them" (John 12:36). But the crowds never understood him anyway. Surely on this night he had a right to call for some understanding from his closest friends. Instead, they were self-absorbed, competing for glory, oblivious to what was really going on, and even betraying him for money!

What's a savior to do?

Instead of blasting them, he stripped down and knelt before each one, washing his feet! Jesus' life contained many jarring and ironic events, but none more so than this one. The rest of the night he continued to move toward them in love, instruction, and reassurance. He didn't see his men as they were that night, but as they would be when filled with the Holy Spirit and matured through suffering. He knew these were the men who would spark the Jesus movement and press it through until their own deaths.

Jesus' example contains a powerful lesson for today. Are you feeling grieved? in pain? lonely? disappointed? anxious? depressed? If so, remember what Jesus said of his washing their feet: "I gave you an example that you also should do as I did to you."

In other words, get up off the couch, turn off the screen, and go out into fellowship or the world to find a way to serve. Invest in relationships.

You will be surprised how quickly you experience what Jesus promised that night: “If you know these things, you are blessed if you do them” (John 13:17). To be blessed means to be happy.

40

Capture
Luke 22:39-62

In Gethsemane

When Judas left the upper room, we read ominously, "It was night" (John 13:30). Sometime later we read,

> Then, accompanied by the disciples, Jesus left the upstairs room and went as usual to the Mount of Olives. There he told them, "Pray that you will not give in to temptation." (Luke 22:39-40 NLT)

After leaving the upper room they took the thirty-minute walk to Gethsemane. For the next few hours Jesus and his disciples were in this grove of Olive trees.[1] John points out that "Judas, the betrayer, knew this place, because Jesus had often gone there with his disciples" (John 18:2).

Matthew clarifies that Jesus left most of the disciples in one place and took Peter, James, and John further on. He left them and went further by himself (Matthew 26:36-39). Then,

1. Matthew and Mark say he was in Gethsemane, while Luke just says the Mount of Olives. Gethsemane is on the Mount of Olives. How long was he there? In Matthew he finds the disciples asleep and says "So, you men could not keep watch with Me for one hour?" (Matthew 26:40). Then, the same thing happened two more times! So the hours are not exact, but he was probably praying for at least two and maybe four hours.

> He withdrew from them about a stone's throw, and he knelt down and began to pray, saying, "Father, if you are willing, remove this cup from me; yet not my will, but yours be done." Now an angel from heaven appeared to him, strengthening him. And being in agony he was praying very fervently; and his sweat became like drops of blood, falling down upon the ground. (vs. 41-44)

Almost all of our best manuscripts are missing verses 43 and 44. they should be omitted, as most modern translations affirm using brackets and a marginal note.

Jesus certainly must have been convulsing in incredible misery and soul-shredding fear, as other Gospels affirm (Mark 14:33). After kneeling here, he threw himself face down on the ground (Matthew 26:39).

He pleaded that his cup might be removed. Drinking a cup full of the wrath of God was an often-used Old Testament image. He must have looked at it like a cup full of raw sewage that he was expected to drink down. No wonder he asked for a way out! But he knew that wasn't going to happen. He was just expressing his feelings.

Jesus knew what torture and agony he would soon experience in his flogging and crucifixion. But he also knew something no one else knew—the true nature of the wrath of God. To have the wrath of God for all sin rain down upon him—this is what made Jesus' blood run cold with terror. Peter later explained,

> He himself bore our sins in his body on the cross, so that we might die to sin and live to righteousness; for by his wounds you were healed. (1 Peter 2:24)

Like when the priest laid his hands on the animal and confessed the nation's sins, those sins were symbolically passing through his hands onto the innocent animal (Leviticus 1:4). Here with Jesus, it wasn't symbolic. It was real. Exactly what it means to have the sin of all humanity transferred into your body, we can only guess.

Then came the slaying of the substitute. This is why Jesus needed to have a divine nature, an infinite nature. Only an infinite person could absorb infinite wrath. What naked horror! His willing acceptance of this ultimate sentence of death is the bravest deed ever done in history.

As he writhed in the agony of anticipation, his disciples were blissfully unaware.

> When he rose from prayer, he came to the disciples and found them sleeping from sorrow, and said to them, "Why are you sleeping? Get up and pray that you may not enter into temptation." (vs. 45-46)

Amazingly, this same thing happened again, as he went off to pray and returned to find them asleep. Then, it happened a third time! (Matthew 26:40-45). How disappointing! How pathetic! Was Jesus furious? No. He mercifully said, "Go ahead and sleep. Have your rest." But it was too late. Looking up he said, "But look—the time has come. The Son of Man is betrayed into the hands of sinners!" (Matthew 26:45).

Betrayal with a Kiss

> While he was still speaking, behold, a crowd came, and the one called Judas, one of the twelve, was preceding them; and he approached Jesus to kiss him. But Jesus said to him, "Judas, are you betraying the Son of Man with a kiss?" (vs. 47-48)

Betrayal with a kiss—what an unnatural, twisted act! And a cowardly act. He must have been trying to obscure the fact that he was the one giving Jesus up. What other reason would he have? He had earlier arranged the signal: "You will know which one to arrest when I greet him with a kiss" (Mark 14:44). Even Jesus seemed to be horrified by the extreme hypocrisy. And it's not easy to shock the Son of God. Why not just point at him and say, "That's him?" Maybe the soldiers were far enough behind him so he could pretend he wasn't part of the group.

Jesus stood forward and confronted the priests and soldiers.

> Then Jesus spoke to the leading priests, the captains of the Temple guard, and the elders who had come for him. "Am I some dangerous revolutionary," he asked, "that you come with swords and clubs to arrest me? Why didn't you arrest me in the Temple? I was there every day. But this is your moment, the time when the power of darkness reigns." (vs. 52-53 NLT)

When Jesus first identified himself, "they drew back and fell to the ground" (John 18:6). These men knew that Jesus had supernatural powers. His miracle-working was well known even by his enemies. Some of them had earlier suggested he was wielding the power of Beelzebub, as we saw. They were afraid of him. Why else would they have sent both a Roman squad and a squad of temple guards? Even knowing Jesus had some disciples, this was overkill. Matthew says it was "a large crowd" (Matthew 26:47).

Luke mercifully doesn't say it was Peter who struck the ridiculous sword blow on one of the high priest's slaves, but John names him (John 18:10). That was going to turn this situation around? He was lucky he didn't get speared on the spot. Jesus called him down and healed the servant (vs. 50-51). At this point, "all his disciples deserted him and ran away" (Mark 14:50). So much for any heroism. And it wasn't over.

They bound Jesus and led him away.

Denial with a Curse

Even though it was still dark, they didn't wait until the next day to proceed. They wanted to handle his case quickly and in secret, before the public could rise up in his favor.

> Having arrested him, they led him away and brought him to the house of the high priest; but Peter was following at a distance. After they had kindled a fire in the middle of the courtyard and had sat down together, Peter was sitting among them. (vs. 54-55)

Peter must have realized they didn't know who he was. He slipped in quietly, acting like he belonged there. But a young lady blew his cover:

> A servant-girl, seeing him as he sat in the firelight and looking intently at him, said, "This man was with him too."
>
> But he denied it, saying, "Woman, I do not know Him."
>
> A little later, another saw him and said, "You are one of them too!" But Peter said, "Man, I am not!" (vs. 56-58)

Matthew adds that this time "he denied it with an oath" (Matthew 26:72). So he was saying something like, "May God strike me down if I ever knew him!" Or, "I swear to God!" Later it happened again.

> After about an hour had passed, another man began to insist,

> saying, "Certainly this man also was with Him, for he is a Galilean too."
>
> But Peter said, "Man, I do not know what you are talking about." Immediately, while he was still speaking, a rooster crowed. (vs. 59-60)

They recognized Peter's hillbilly accent and knew he must be from Galilee (Matthew 26:73). Again, Matthew gives us the fuller version: "Then he began to curse and swear, 'I do not know the man!'" (Matthew 26:74). Swearing by God and throwing in some intense cuss words suggests he was really blowing up in the hope his language would throw them off the trail. Did he pronounce a curse on Jesus?

Next comes the most shocking part of the account: "The Lord turned and looked at Peter" (v. 61).

What?! He was right there! He at least heard the last and worst denial. This must have been during one of the times they took Jesus out of the meeting place while they deliberated. Imagine the electricity when Jesus' eyes met Peter's. What did Jesus' eyes say? Where I work, they would say a soft descending "Dude. . . ."

> And Peter remembered the word of the Lord, how he had told him, "Before a rooster crows today, you will deny me three times." And he went out and wept bitterly. (vs. 61-62)

So Peter "went out" into the dark streets of Jerusalem staggering along, weeping bitterly. His failure was so complete, that's all he could do.[2]

Peter and Judas

Judas' sin was horrific, but so was Peter's sin. Judas' was worse, because it was premeditated. On the other hand, Peter committed his sin three times! At least Peter felt sorry for what he did—he wept bitterly. But wait, Judas also felt sorry:

> When Judas, who had betrayed him, realized that Jesus had

2. We saw evidence earlier that Acts (also written by Luke) includes a lengthy section that comes exclusively from Peter's perspective. It includes material nobody but Peter would have had access to. This section about his denial must also come from Peter. Although both Matthew and Mark have the account, here in Luke is the only place we learn that Jesus was actually there for the third denial—a detail loaded with pathos. Not to mention his wandering through the streets weeping, presumably by himself.

> been condemned to die, he was filled with remorse. So he took the thirty pieces of silver back to the leading priests and the elders. "I have sinned," he declared, "for I have betrayed an innocent man." (Matthew 27:3-4)

In fact, Judas felt so remorseful that he refused to keep the money and threw the thirty coins into the temple.[3] Then he went out and hanged himself! (Matthew 27:5). That's remorse! I've felt sorry enough to cry for bad things I've done, but never sorry enough to kill myself!

So these two sins have a lot in common. The difference is not the severity of the sins, but how differently they affect the two men. Peter went on to become the leader of the early church and a hero of the faith. Judas ended up hanging from a rope, and ultimately in hell. Why such different outcomes?

One clue comes from the King James' mistranslation of Matthew 27:3: "When he saw that [Jesus] was condemned, he repented himself." But that's wrong. The word for repentance is *metanoeo* from *nous*, the mind. It means a change of mind or a change of heart. This word in Matthew is *metamelomai*. It means a change of feeling such as regret or remorse. To feel regret or remorse may have little spiritual value in God's eyes. Most criminals feel regret when they get caught. But God isn't interested in people feeling regret. He wants us to repent, to change our hearts.

Paul explains that there are different kinds of sorrow:

> For the sorrow that is according to the will of God produces a repentance [*metanoeo*] without regret [*metamelomai*], leading to salvation, but the sorrow of the world produces death. (2 Corinthians 7:10)

When experiencing repentance a person doesn't feel weighed down with guilt and sorrow. Instead, repentance is an opening of the eyes that enables us to come to God in humility. It actually feels good to come clean and repent. But remorse like Judas felt is a proud sorrow. Why

3. Although Judas didn't realize it, he fulfilled the prophecy in Zechariah where the prophet had been acting out a role depicting Christ in a spiritual drama. As the shepherd of a doomed flock, Zechariah asks for his wages and receives 30 shekels of silver. God calls it "that magnificent price at which I was valued by them" (Zechariah 11:12-13). Then Zechariah gives the money to a potter by throwing it into the temple, just like Judas threw the thirty pieces of silver into the temple. Then, in Judas' day, when the priests didn't want to put the money into the treasury because it was blood money, they used it to buy a potter's field (Matthew 27:6-7). So the thirty pieces went to a potter by throwing them into the temple.

didn't Judas turn to God for forgiveness? Because he wanted to pay for his sin himself. He couldn't comprehend grace. It led to death.

Peter, on the other hand, didn't just weep bitterly. He also repented—a humble presentation of oneself to God in helplessness and openness. In true repentance you feel a joy that comes from returning to the father. Repentance opened the door for God to transform Peter into a man almost unrecognizable compared to the old Peter.

The Big Picture

Throughout this night the behavior of Jesus' followers was incredibly disappointing. From sitting at the last supper squabbling over who was the greatest, to sleeping on the job, to betrayal with a kiss, to pointlessly wounding a servant, to abandonment, Jesus saw nothing but failure, weakness, greed, deception, and self-serving. Then, as though that wasn't enough, he got to watch his lead disciple shouting curses and oaths while denying he even knew who Jesus was.

How did he handle that?

For one thing, as John had earlier explained, "Jesus, on his part, was not entrusting himself to people, for he knew all men, and because he did not need anyone to testify concerning man, for he himself knew what was in man" (John 2:24-25). The depravity within each of us is truly total. Any romanticism about human nature only leads to heart crushing disappointment. Jesus didn't harbor any illusions about humans. But he never took the next step of self-protection. He stayed heavily engaged.

This is an important point to remember for those attempting to serve God. We sometimes see even leaders abandoning their post and giving up on serving because they can't handle the betrayal and selfishness from fellow humans. But they should have known all about that before they ever went in. Being stabbed in the back even by fellow believers is hardly surprising, although you never get used to it.

Jesus' disciples didn't have the indwelling Holy Spirit, so their failures are even less surprising. But even with the Spirit, substantial failure is inevitable.

Jesus had already braced himself for abandonment. He said at dinner, "All of you will desert me" (Mark 14:27). But knowing something is coming sometimes hardly helps. Jesus' consolation was the same one we need to depend on. He said, "You will be scattered, each one going his own way, leaving me alone. Yet I am not alone because the Father is with me" (John 16:32). Unfortunately, Jesus faced a future when even the Father would turn his back.

41

Jesus' Suffering
Luke 22:63-23:31

At the High Priest's Home

Jesus' physical and psychological suffering rose to a new level at the high priest's house.

> Now the men who were holding Jesus in custody were mocking Him and beating him, and they blindfolded him and were asking him, saying, "Prophesy, who is the one who hit you?" And they were saying many other things against Him, blaspheming. (Luke 22:63-65)

Matthew and Mark add that they "spat in his face and beat him with their fists; and others slapped him" (Matthew 26:67). The phrase "beating him" should probably read that they smote him with rods or walking sticks.[1] The spitting and beating had been predicted for the Servant of the Lord in Isaiah 50:6.

> "I gave my back to those who strike me, and my cheeks to those who pluck out the beard; I did not cover my face from humiliation and spitting."

1. The word *dero* used here means to skin, or to rip one's skin, often with rods or canes.

This was a brutal beating. It shows their fierce hatred for Jesus and the sadistic delight they took in his pain.

At the Sanhedrin

Now the scene changes. They've gone from the chief priest's home to their official chamber next to the temple mount.

> When it was day, the council of elders of the people assembled, both chief priests and scribes, and they led him away to their council chamber, saying, "If you are the Christ, tell us."
>
> But he said to them, "If I tell you, you will not believe; and if I ask a question, you will not answer. (vs. 66-68)

He was reminding them of their refusal to answer his question about John the Baptist the last time they were demanding to know by what authority he acted (20:1-8). He said at that time that he refused to answer their question because they wouldn't answer his. He went on,

> "But from now on the Son of Man will be seated in the place of power at God's right hand."
>
> And they all said, "Are you the Son of God, then?"
>
> And he said to them, "Yes, I am."
>
> Then they said, "What further need do we have of testimony? For we have heard it ourselves from his own mouth." (vs. 69-71)

When he said in verse 70, "Yes, I am," he used an idiom. He literally said, "You say that I am" (NLT). To us, that sounds like he's saying, "You said that; I didn't say that." But Jesus is not being evasive. The NASB translation, "I am," is correct. It's an idiom along the lines "Yeah, you said it."

We can confirm this translation by cross-referencing Mark's account. It's the same setting in the council room and the same question put to Jesus—whether he was the Christ. He answered, not in the idiom, but a straight, "I am." So Luke and Matthew gave the idiom, and Mark gave what the idiom meant. That answer was yes.

His statement that they would see him "seated at the right hand of God" was probably an allusion to Psalm 110:1, a well-known Messianic Psalm. Likewise, in Mark's version he alludes to Daniel 7:13-14:

"And behold, with the clouds of heaven
One like a Son of Man was coming,
And he came up to the Ancient of Days
And was presented before him.
And to him was given dominion,
Glory and a kingdom,
That all the peoples, nations and men of every language
might serve him."

At this point, they felt they had enough to go to the Romans for permission to execute Jesus. But claiming to be the Messiah probably would not draw a death sentence from the Romans. They would need more.

Before Pilate

Very early, before the streets were full of people, they scurried to Pilate's palace. They must have warned Pilate that they had a high priority prisoner who would need immediate judgment. It's clear they were talking to Pilate before the arrest because a squadron of Roman troops accompanied the arresting party. Everything to this point was done in secret. Most think this trial happened at the Antonia Fortress, just a short walk from the Sanhedrin's chamber.

> Then the entire council took Jesus to Pilate, the Roman governor. They began to state their case: "This man has been leading our people astray by telling them not to pay their taxes to the Roman government and by claiming he is the Messiah, a king."
>
> So Pilate asked him, "Are you the king of the Jews?"
>
> Jesus replied, "You have said it." (23:1-3 NLT)

They padded their charges with a lie—that Jesus told people not to pay their taxes. We already saw that he said, "Render unto Caesar what is Caesar's" (20:20–26). Jesus replied to Pilate with the same idiom, "You have said it," meaning yes. They must have spoken longer, because "Pilate turned to the leading priests and to the crowd and said, 'I find nothing wrong with this man!'" (v. 4).

The apostle John recorded part of the discussion between Jesus and Pilate that led to this conclusion:

> Jesus answered, "My kingdom is not of this world. If my kingdom were of this world, then my servants would be fighting so that I would not be handed over to the Jews; but as it is, my kingdom is not of this realm." (John 18:36)

That meant he was no threat to Rome. But the leaders weren't going to be denied so easily.

> Then they became insistent. "But he is causing riots by his teaching wherever he goes—all over Judea, from Galilee to Jerusalem!" (v. 5 NLT)

They added another lying charge concerning nonexistent riots. Upon hearing that Jesus was a Galilean, Pilate was delighted to send him over to Herod Antipas who happened to be in town.

Before Herod

Herod was idly curious about Jesus, and he challenged him to perform a miracle. He asked him multiple questions, but Jesus just stood in silence. He knew Herod had no interest in believing. God is not our court jester, putting on a show until we dismiss him. He sees the heart, and he knows when someone is merely toying with him. His response then, and still today is silence. The interview ended poorly. It became more disorderly as the priests and scribes shouted accusations. Eventually Herod and his soldiers were "mocking and ridiculing Jesus" (v. 11).

The Robe

Herod "dressed him in a gorgeous robe and sent him back to Pilate" (v. 11) It sounds like the robe went with him. In Matthew, it's Pilate's soldiers who "stripped him and put a scarlet robe on him" (Matthew 27:28). But then Matthew adds, "When they were finally tired of mocking him, they took off the robe and put his own clothes on him again. Then they led him away to be crucified" (Matthew 27:31).

Matthew didn't say where they got the robe or what they did with it. It could have been the same one Herod sent over earlier. A large, beautiful robe would have been extremely expensive at that time, and well beyond Jesus' budget.

Before taking the robe off, Pilate brought him out to the crowd still wearing it and the crown of thorns according to John. "Then Jesus came out wearing the crown of thorns and the purple robe. And Pilate said, "Look, here is the man!'" (John 19:5).

The crown of thorns was a contribution from Pilate's soldiers. They put it on him and then beat his head with a reed driving the thorns into his scalp (Matthew 27:29-30). It would have bled profusely. Like an artist displaying his work, torturers exhibited Jesus' bleeding and bruised body to the crowd in a robe and crown of thorns.

This is probably the same robe that led the soldiers to casting lots: "They also took his robe, but it was seamless, woven in one piece from top to bottom. So they said, 'Rather than tearing it apart, let's throw dice for it'" (John 19:23-24).

Then John adds, "This fulfilled the Scripture that says, 'They divided my garments among themselves and threw dice for my clothing.'" He was referring to the amazing Psalm 22, which describes multiple aspects of the crucifixion hundreds of years before crucifixion even existed! The soldiers probably wouldn't have been casting lots if it wasn't for the robe.

Luke's Sources

Luke gives us an aside: "(Herod and Pilate, who had been enemies before, became friends that day)" (v. 12). It's a curious statement, in part because we wonder where Luke would have obtained this information. Did the believers of his day include an insider from this earlier time? We already saw that one of Jesus' followers was from Herod's household. She was "Joanna the wife of Chuza, Herod's steward" (8:3). They could easily have heard palace gossip about Pilate and Herod.[2]

The same could be true in Pilate's household. Mark writes that even Pilate knew the shady motives in Jesus' accusers: "For he was aware that the chief priests had handed him over because of envy" (Mark 15:10).

That information could come from an insider, or it could be translated as in NLT: "For he realized by now that the leading priests had arrested Jesus out of envy." This reading suggests he was realizing this in real time,

2. Neither Matthew nor Mark have this whole part of the story. But Luke also mentions Herod Antipas several other places where the other gospel authors don't (3:1; 9:7–9; 13:31). Perhaps Luke had access to the Herod source (Joanna?) and the other synoptic authors didn't.

not something he knew from earlier. That's a plausible reading and it fits the imperfect tense used here.

Pilate's Verdict

Pilate gave out his verdict on Jesus:

> Pilate summoned the chief priests and the rulers and the people, and said to them, "You brought this man to me as one who incites the people to rebellion, and behold, having examined him before you, I have found no guilt in this man regarding the charges which you make against Him. No, nor has Herod, for he sent him back to us; and behold, nothing deserving death has been done by Him. Therefore I will punish Him and release Him." (vs. 13-16)

Pilate's verdict on Jesus was "not guilty." It was important to Luke that Pilate saw Jesus as innocent, and that he allowed him to be executed only because of the angry crowd, not because of Roman law.

Pilate probably hoped that seeing Jesus beaten up by the torturers would satisfy the people's blood lust. But the accusers fought on.

> But they cried out all together, saying, "Away with this man, and release for us Barabbas!" (He was one who had been thrown into prison for an insurrection made in the city, and for murder.) (vs. 18-19)

Where does this Barabbas come from? A later copyist anticipated that question and supplied the answer in verse 17: "Now he was obliged to release to them at the feast one prisoner." The copyist got his information from either Mark or Matthew's account (Matthew 27:15; Mark 15:6), but it is not in our early manuscripts of Luke. A common source of copyist errors comes when copyists harmonize different gospels, trying to enhance the reading experience. These are usually easy to recognize with the manuscripts we have.

The Crowd

Although Luke earlier portrayed the masses as hanging on Jesus' words, this crowd is hostile.

> Then a mighty roar rose from the crowd, and with one voice they shouted, "Kill him, and release Barabbas to us!" (Barabbas was in prison for taking part in an insurrection in Jerusalem against the government, and for murder.) Pilate argued with them, because he wanted to release Jesus. But they kept shouting, "Crucify him! Crucify him!" For the third time he demanded, "Why? What crime has he committed? I have found no reason to sentence him to death. So I will have him flogged, and then I will release him." (vs. 18-22 NLT)

What accounts for the difference in crowd attitude? Was the mob so fickle that they changed their view from a few days earlier when they were singing messianic psalms to him? Or did the scribes and Pharisees take the precaution of recruiting a crowd from their synagogues that would shout out against Jesus? Yes. Mark says, "The chief priests stirred up the crowd to ask him to release Barabbas for them instead" (Mark 15:11). So the shouting was a planned conspiracy. Also, now that the leaders were clearly going for capital punishment, yelling in favor of Jesus would be quite dangerous.

> The mob shouted louder and louder, demanding that Jesus be crucified, and their voices prevailed. So Pilate sentenced Jesus to die as they demanded. As they had requested, he released Barabbas, the man in prison for insurrection and murder. But he turned Jesus over to them to do as they wished. (vs. 23-25 NLT)

This picture of the crowd intimidating Pilate into doing something he didn't want to do doesn't fit what we know of Pilate from history. Pilate was a brutal tyrant who wouldn't hesitate to launch armed attacks on any civilian crowd that protested his actions. For example, Josephus describes massacres perpetrated against the Jews who protested his introduction of idols into Jerusalem.[3]

How then, do we explain his apparent weakness in the face of this crowd? John adds the detail that right before he finally turned Jesus over for execution, "the Jews cried out saying, 'If you release this man, you are no friend of Caesar; everyone who makes himself out to be a king opposes Caesar'" (John 19:12). That bothered Pilate so much that he relented.

3. Josephus, *Antiquities*, 18.3.1ff.

But again, why would he back off so easily and execute Jesus contrary to his own "not guilty" verdict?

The answer is another case of the biblical account crossing paths with secular history and confirming the accuracy of the biblical text.

It begins with a Roman official named Sejanus. He was Emperor Tiberius' main executive; basically running the empire while Tiberius frolicked about on an island enjoying feasting and perverted sex. At some point in the 20s AD, Sejanus decided to try to take over the empire with the help of other officials and governors that he had appointed. The conspiracy spread to much of the empire. But right before Sejanus made his move he was betrayed. Tiberius stormed into Rome with an armed force and summarily killed Sejanus.

There followed a bloody purge of officials appointed by Sejanus. Some of them were guilty, and others were not, but Tiberius wasn't taking any chances. He relentlessly attacked anyone who might have been involved in Sejanus' conspiracy. The year of Sejanus' execution was AD 31. The purge following his death was in full swing as Jesus was crucified. And Pilate? He had been installed as governor under the sponsorship of Sejanus![4]

This fully explains why Pilate would fear the cry that he was no friend of Caesar's if he let Jesus go. If any charge of disloyalty got back to Rome, it could mean Pilate's life. It also shows that the AD 33 date for Jesus' death is correct, rather than the only other possible date, AD 30.[5]

Matthew adds another detail that may account in some measure for Pilate's reluctance to condemn Jesus. His wife sent him a message saying, "Have nothing to do with that righteous man; for last night I suffered greatly in a dream because of him" (Matthew 27:19). How did Matthew learn this story? The most likely witness was Jesus. Pilate may have discussed the dream in his presence. Or, he may have told any of the Jewish leaders there, some of whom later came to faith (e.g. Acts 15:5).

4. For full documentation, see Gary DeLashmutt, "Sejanus and the Chronology of Christ's Death," Dwell Community Church (website), https://www.dwellcc.org/essays/sejanus-and-chronology-christs-death.
5. For a comparison of the 30 and 33 date, see Dennis McCallum, "Chronological Study of the Life of Christ," Dwell Community Church (website), https://www.dwellcc.org/essays/chronological-study-life-christ.

Flogging

Luke says Pilate handed Jesus over for execution, but Matthew adds that "after having Jesus scourged, he handed him over to be crucified." (Matthew 27:26). So he received another beating, this time at the hands of the Romans.

This flogging was at least the third one (1. at the Sanhedrin 2. at Herod's house 3. here). The Roman flogging was an incredibly brutal torture session.[6] These floggings frequently resulted in death. Jesus' short time on the cross before death (six hours[7]) was probably because of the trauma and loss of blood from his floggings. Or, maybe he just chose to give up his spirit at that time.

When imagining the searing pain Jesus felt as his back and legs were lacerated and torn, it's important to remember what he earlier stated—that if he asked, the Father would send twelve legions of angels to strike down his opposition (Matthew 26:53).

Everything that happened to Jesus was voluntary. He had earlier declared, "No one has taken [my life] away from Me, but I lay it down on My own initiative. I have authority to lay it down, and I have authority to take it up again" (John 10:18). At any moment he could snap his fingers and the ordeal would be over.

How did Jesus feel toward that laughing, jeering group of soldiers? The irony is that he was doing this for them! Paul points out that, "While we were enemies we were reconciled to God through the death of His Son" (Romans 5:10). So it wasn't only for his friends that he died, but also for his enemies. Some of these very men may have come to faith later. We know that one of them saw the light later that day at the cross (Matthew 27:54).

Luke omits the scene where Pilate pointlessly washed his hands, declaring he was not to blame. But he was actually the only man who could decide either way on Jesus' fate.

---

6. For a detailed explanation of Roman flogging and crucifixion, see William D. Edwards et al., "On the Physical Death of Jesus Christ," *JAMA* 21 (April 1986): 1455-63.

7. Mark 15:25 says he was nailed to the cross at the third hour (9 A.M.). Mark 15:33 describes the darkness from the sixth hour to the ninth hour (Noon until 3 P.M.) followed by death. Luke agrees that he died about the sixth hour (23:44) but doesn't give a time for the beginning of the crucifixion.

On the Way

> As they led Jesus away, a man named Simon, who was from Cyrene, happened to be coming in from the countryside. The soldiers seized him and put the cross on him and made him carry it behind Jesus (v. 26 NLT)

Probably, the beating left Jesus so weak he couldn't continue carrying his own cross beam. They snatched this man and made him carry it. The soldiers may have feared Jesus would die before they got him onto the cross.

Mark adds the curious comment that Simon was "the father of Alexander and Rufus" (Mark 15:21). He clearly expected his readers to know who Alexander and Rufus were. The apostle Paul later greeted "Rufus, a choice man in the Lord" (Romans 16:13). Many believe it's the same man mentioned here and that he had become well-known to the early church as a missionary.[8] Another Jewish Christian worker appears in Ephesus named Alexander, but that was a very popular name, unlike Rufus (Acts 19:33).

Luke continued:

> A large crowd trailed behind, including many grief-stricken women. But Jesus turned and said to them, "Daughters of Jerusalem, don't weep for me, but weep for yourselves and for your children. For the days are coming when they will say, 'Fortunate indeed are the women who are childless, the wombs that have not borne a child and the breasts that have never nursed.' (vs. 27-29)

People viewed not having children as a great misfortune for women at this time. But in view of what Jesus knew was coming in the destruction of Jerusalem, having children would lead to increased agony as a mother might have to watch her children killed or taken away as slaves. The same goes for the mountains falling on them—probably a picture of wishing they could hide from the coming disaster.

The Big Picture

As they led Jesus out Luke says, "A large crowd trailed behind" (v. 27).

8. Bauckham, *Jesus and the Eyewitnesses*, 52. Rufus was in Rome, where Mark composed his Gospel.

The crowd following Jesus and the two thieves out of town was a mixed group. We know his enemies were there, blissful, excited, taunting, and gloating. They were eager to see him suffer and die.

But many others were probably stunned and baffled. How was this possible? He certainly had demonstrated supernatural power before. Why was this happening? Maybe he was about to turn the tables on his enemies? How could they all have been so taken in, to believe this was the Messiah?

In the whole multitude, only one person knew what was really happening. He silently struggled forward to the place of his death.

42

The Cross
Luke 23:32-56

They nailed Jesus to the cross using the coarse seven inch long spikes archeologists have found. The nails for the heels were shorter, about four or five inches. The heels were nailed astride the cross, one on each side. Then they lifted his cross up until it locked into either a hole, or a peg previously installed in the ground for this purpose. Sometimes they had poles permanently in place and the crossbeam or *patibulum* was fastened on top. We can't be sure how Jesus' cross worked.

The crowd stood around probably at some distance, including at least one of his disciples (John 19:26). His mother was there along with other women followers. What shock and unbelief they must have felt! Could this really be happening? Tears were running down their faces.

Mary was there, watching her son being tormented by the vicious soldiers and mockers. The baby she had so often bathed . . . the one promised by a majestic angel. Could this possibly be part of the plan? Or had something gone terribly wrong? We know she and her friends didn't anticipate the resurrection. They went to the tomb to anoint a dead body. It's important to see that even now, nobody understood what was happening.

When "two others also, who were criminals, were being led away to be put to death with him" (Luke 23:32), he fulfilled Isaiah 53:12: "He was numbered with the transgressors." Soon he would fulfill the rest of the verse: "yet he himself bore the sin of many, and interceded for the transgressors." Then,

> When they came to the place called The Skull, there they crucified him and the criminals, one on the right and the other on the left. (v. 33)

The Romans used crucifixion for crimes committed by non-Roman citizens. It was designed to horrify onlookers with raw cruelty. The victim was stripped naked—no modest loin cloth like in modern movies. The whole object was to expose the victim to ultimate shame and agony. It was more violent and savage than anything any of us has ever seen. It was so horrifying and ghastly that it would definitely be banned from any TV broadcast and even from most internet platforms. The message was, "This could be you if you mess with Rome."

Most popular portrayals of the crucifixion show Jesus at the top of a fifteen or twenty-foot cross. Research indicates that trees of that size rarely grew anywhere near Jerusalem in the first century. And if they did find some longer timbers, they wouldn't use them for crucifixion. Most trees in this area were short, like olive and mulberry trees. The post for Jesus' cross was probably only about six or at most seven feet tall. In other words, he was right in the face of onlookers with his feet just off the ground.

None of the Gospels gives all of Jesus' sayings on the cross. Each probably reported what his source heard, or, in Matthew and John's case, what they heard themselves. He may have said other things we don't have. Only Luke reports that, "Jesus was saying, 'Father, forgive them; for they do not know what they are doing'" (v. 34). That perfectly fits with Luke's emphasis on Jesus' love for sinful people. He genuinely wanted even his torturers to get another chance to repent.

Mocking

> And the people stood by, looking on. And even the rulers were sneering at him, saying, "He saved others; let him save himself if this is the Christ of God, his Chosen One." The soldiers also mocked him, coming up to him, offering him sour wine, and saying, "If you are the King of the Jews, save yourself!" (vs. 35-37)

To these people, the fact that Jesus was publicly humiliated and crucified proved that he was not the Messiah, not a king, not even a man of God. Their view fulfilled prophecy as they spoke. Isaiah had warned centuries earlier that the prevailing view of the dying Servant of the Lord would be "We ourselves esteemed him stricken, smitten of God, and afflicted" (Isaiah 53:4). Their perception was that God was against Jesus, and he was receiving what he deserved.

The psychological pain from watching his enemies baiting him must have been awful for Jesus. The irony is that while they mocked him as a man who thought he was a king, he really was the king! He just didn't look like it. He didn't have to, but he continued in agony, allowing himself to be abused. It's even more ironic that he was enduring this for the benefit of the mockers.

Jesus' Certificate of Debt

Above Jesus' head hung a sign, possibly personally inscribed by Pilate himself. Luke reports it as saying, "This is the king of the Jews" (v. 38). A more complete description comes from John: "Jesus of Nazareth, the King of the Jews" (John 19:19). It was clearly an insult hurled less at Jesus, and more at the Jews. Pilate didn't appreciate being pressured and manipulated, so he used this placard to get the last mocking word.

John explains that it was written in Hebrew (probably meaning Aramaic), Latin, and Greek.[1] So Pilate was turning the sign into a sarcastic slam that everyone could read. The leaders were incensed. They went to Pilate and objected, saying, "Change it from 'The King of the Jews' to 'He said, I am King of the Jews.'"

Pilate was firm, and probably grinning: "What I have written, I have written" (John 19:22).

Posting such a sign was not unusual. The sign over Jesus' head should have listed his crimes. But instead we have this further irony. He was guilty of nothing worse than being the king of the Jews. Meanwhile, Paul explains that we all have a certificate of debt that lists our sins.[2] It wasn't for his own sin, but ours that Jesus died, as Paul explains:

1. The Latin version reads Iesus Nazarenus Rex Ieudaeorum. The first letters being INRI, a symbol that later became important in the traditional church. It's often seen on the front of church altars.
2. "Certificate of debt" was not a technical term. The phrase here literally means "hand writing against us." It's referring to a decree, like one over Jesus' head. In Colossians it meant that God has

> . . . having canceled out the certificate of debt consisting of decrees against us, which was hostile to us; and he has taken it out of the way, having nailed it to the cross. (Colossians 2:14)

These certificates of debt were in use widely, either for a private debt, unpaid taxes, or crime. The certificate was like an IOU.

Just before Jesus gave up his spirit, he cried out with a loud voice, "It is finished!"[3] It's the Greek word, *tetelestai*. That word is found written on ancient certificates of debt. When the debtor, prisoner, or in this case, a victim of capital punishment served their term or paid the debt, this word was the equivalent of writing "paid in full." Jesus had fully paid our debt of judgment from God.[4]

The Thieves

Not only Jesus' enemies, but even one of the crucifixion victims attacked him.

> One of the criminals who were hanged there was hurling abuse at him, saying, "Are you not the Christ? Save yourself and us!"
>
> But the other answered, and rebuking him said, "Do you not even fear God, since you are under the same sentence of condemnation? And we indeed are suffering justly, for we are receiving what we deserve for our deeds; but this man has done nothing wrong." And he was saying, "Jesus, remember me when you come in your kingdom!" And [Jesus] said to him, "Truly I say to you, today you shall be with me in Paradise." (vs. 39-43)

This conversation goes well beyond what Matthew or Mark record. It suggests Luke had a different source. We know Mary was standing there, close enough to hear Jesus' weakening voice. So was the disciple John.

---

a record of our sins that he nailed to the cross. It's a good way to illustrate substitution.

3. Compare John 19:30, "Therefore when Jesus had received the sour wine, He said, "It is finished!" And He bowed His head and gave up His spirit," and Matthew 27:50, "And Jesus cried out again with a loud voice, and yielded up His spirit." Scholars debate whether crucifixion victims died of suffocation, but Jesus clearly did not. We see Jesus crying out on the cross—something a suffocating person could not do. Jesus apparently died of congestive heart failure.

4. Greek readers can read a discussion of papyri fragments of Roman tax receipts with *tetelestai* written in the sense of "it is paid," or "paid in full" in Bernard Grenfell and Arthur Hunt, eds., *New Classical Fragments and Other Greek and Latin Papyri* (Oxford: Clarendon Press, 1897), 78ff, https://archive.org/details/newclassicalfrag00gren/page/n7/mode/2up.

Of course, Jesus was there also, and may have discussed the scene after his resurrection.

This narrative is important for several reasons. First, the believing thief is a clear case of pure salvation by faith apart from works. He never had any opportunity to perform a single good work. This flies in the face of those who claim good works are necessary for personal salvation.

Jesus also specified the date when he would see the believing thief in paradise—today. That refutes the belief that Jesus descended into hell, or Hades, for three days before ascending to heaven. This belief, enshrined in the Apostles' Creed, assumes that Jesus was tormented in hell for the punishment of human sin.[5] Instead, he was in paradise the same day he died.

Jesus completed the payment for human sin while still on the cross. It didn't take three days or three hours, but probably was accomplished in one blinding moment of infinite wrath that only an infinite being could absorb. It happened right before he cried out, "It is finished!" The best Scripture in favor of this view is this passage on the believing thief and the following one on the veil.

If Jesus descended at all, it must have been very brief. Perhaps he went to visit dead believers from previous ages to announced what he had done on the cross, as Peter suggests: "For the gospel has for this purpose been preached even to those who are dead, that though they are judged in the flesh as men, they may live in the spirit according to the will of God" (1 Peter 4:6). He then immediately went on to paradise, where he met up with the believing thief.

Death

The most dramatic moment was at hand.

> It was now about the sixth hour, and darkness fell over the whole land until the ninth hour, because the sun was obscured; and the veil of the temple was torn in two. And Jesus, crying out with a loud voice, said, "Father, Into your hands I commit my spirit." Having said this, he breathed his last. (vs. 44-46)

5. This isn't exactly stated, but it is implied by the words "He descended into hell. On the third day he rose again from the dead; he ascended into heaven, and is seated at the right hand of God the Father."

The sixth hour was about noon, so the ninth hour was 3:00 pm. This darkness must have been supernaturally supplied by God as a statement. It wasn't an eclipse. There was no solar eclipse at this time and place. It could have been heavy clouds.

The Veil

During this darkness "the veil of the temple was torn in two" (v. 45). This veil was the dividing curtain symbolizing the separation between God and humans. On one side was the "holy of holies." It stood for the actual throne room of God. On the other side were humans—unable to enter past the veil; separated from God by their sin. It was a visual picture of Isaiah's declaration in Isaiah 59:2:

> "Your iniquities have made a separation between you and your God, and your sins have hidden his face from you so that he does not hear."

The whole architecture and procedure of the temple (and earlier, the tabernacle) cry out "separation!" The stress is on the "holiness of God," which means the differentness or distinctiveness of God. Profane, sinful humans cannot stride into God's presence. He's too holy for that.

Even the priests couldn't enter into the holy of holies. Only the high priest entered past this veil. Even the high priest only entered once a year on the day of atonement. He brought with him a bowl of blood from an innocent animal, which he sprinkled on the top of the Ark of Testimony. It was a picture of how substitutionary death worked.

As Jesus hung dying, suddenly, *Ripppp*! That veil of separation was torn open and people were left, as it were, staring right into the presence of God! (vs. 45). And he is a welcoming God.

Pointing to this event, the author of Hebrews declared,

> The Holy Spirit is signifying this, that the way into the holy place has not yet been disclosed while the outer tabernacle is still standing . . . and not through the blood of goats and calves, but through his own blood, he entered the holy place once for all, having obtained eternal redemption. (Hebrews 9:8, 12)

It turned out that Jesus is the ultimate high priest. He's also the blood offering. The final outcome is stellar:

> We have confidence to enter the holy place by the blood of Jesus, by a new and living way which he inaugurated for us through the veil, that is, his flesh. (Hebrews 10:19-20)

When God tore the veil he signified that the Old Covenant was at an end, and that the separation between God and his people could now be removed. There would be a gap in time (only days) between the tearing and the actual enactment of the New Covenant on the day of Pentecost. Jesus spent part of this time preparing his disciples for what was coming, as we will see.

Believing Romans

Next Luke says, "Now when the centurion saw what had happened, he began praising God, saying, 'Certainly this man was innocent'" (v. 47). But it was more than the centurion. Matthew says,

> Now the centurion, and those who were with him keeping guard over Jesus, when they saw the earthquake and the things that were happening, became very frightened and said, "Truly this was the Son of God!" (Matthew 27:54)

Did these soldiers become followers of Jesus? We don't know, because people confronted with a miracle will often affirm God in the moment. But before long the miracle fades in their memory and they end up hardening their hearts. The Old Testament story of the exodus from Egypt illustrates this powerfully.

The Crowd

Luke ends his account of the cross by saying,

> All the crowds who came together for this spectacle, when they observed what had happened, began to return, beating their breasts. And all his acquaintances and the women who accompanied him from Galilee were standing at a distance, seeing these things. (vs. 48-49)

It sounds like most of the crowd were sympathetic to Jesus and agonized that he was dead. Beating one's breast stands for mourning.

Luke mentions the women standing at a distance, and we again have to wonder if one of them might be his special source. Matthew calls the group "many women" (Matthew 27:55).

Luke omits Jesus calling on John to take care of his mother who was also standing there (John 19:25-26). John, who recounts the story, was clearly in a position to hear what Jesus said, while other witnesses might not have been close enough to the cross to hear. Mary, of course, was right next to John.

Comparing the four accounts, we find numerous differences as the result of authors omitting different details. That's exactly what you would expect from eye-witness testimony. Each witness sees things from a different angle, each remembers some things but not others. Nobody's memory is perfect, but they can still report true events.

Accounts coming from different locations (for instance positions around the cross, or distance from the cross) saw and heard different things. If the accounts all lined up perfectly it would suggest that they colluded with each other and were not independent.

John, who has the most different details, was in a position to purposely tell stories the other authors missed. John knew about the other three gospels and he wrote much later than they. John was written in the 90s, decades after the other three gospel books. Rather than write another gospel that was no different than the existing ones, it would be natural for him to fill in gaps that he knew about. This is why John is so different from the synoptic gospels, even though it sits on the same broad outline.

The Burial

Jesus' body was dead.

> And a man named Joseph, who was a member of the Council, a good and righteous man (he had not consented to their plan and action), a man from Arimathea, a city of the Jews, who was waiting for the kingdom of God; this man went to Pilate and asked for the body of Jesus. And he took it down and wrapped it in a linen cloth, and laid him in a tomb cut into the rock, where no one had ever lain. (vs. 50-53)

Joseph was unknowingly fulfilling Isaiah's prophecy that the Servant of the Lord's grave "was assigned with wicked men, yet he was with a rich man in his death" (Isaiah 53:9). Only the rich could afford a hand-hewn grave.

It was important to Luke that people see how Jesus had followers among the educated and respected Sanhedrin (here called "the Council"). That would garner respect in a Roman court. The detail in the account suggests Luke's witness was right there, and indeed, we read,

> It was the preparation day, and the Sabbath was about to begin. Now the women who had come with him out of Galilee followed, and saw the tomb and how His body was laid. Then they returned and prepared spices and perfumes. And on the Sabbath they rested according to the commandment. (vs. 54-56)

Only Luke describes the women marking the place of burial, making preparations, and avoiding working on the Sabbath. Again, the level of detail suggests that one of these women was his source, perhaps Mary.

The Big Picture

As darkness fell, Jesus' followers and his mother quietly wept and mourned. Eventually, their tears ran dry. There was nothing to say—only an occasional expression of unbelief that it could all end this way. Were they calling out to God for an explanation? Were they reviewing the past three plus years, and trying to figure out how it fit with what happened that day?

Surely they would have at last remembered some of the things he said? That he would die, that he would rise, that Mary was anointing his body for burial? No. Not a single one connected the dots.

Nobody was waiting at the tomb for him to come walking out. The only thing we see on Sunday is shock, astonishment, and unbelief. As far as these believers were concerned, this was the end of the road.

The eleven regathered as some point, because Sunday morning the women find them together. Were they struggling with where to go from here? Were they crying out to God in prayer? Probably they slept in the upper room.

The biggest shock was just ahead.

43

He Is Risen!

Luke 24

A day passed because it was Sabbath. They couldn't work or walk beyond about one kilometer. You can see here the Jewish tendency to count any part of a day as a whole day. That's why Jesus could say he would be dead three days—that is, parts of three days.

> But on the first day of the week, at early dawn, they came to the tomb bringing the spices which they had prepared. And they found the stone rolled away from the tomb, but when they entered, they did not find the body of the Lord Jesus. While they were perplexed about this, behold, two men suddenly stood near them in dazzling clothing; and as the women were terrified and bowed their faces to the ground, the men said to them, "Why do you seek the living among the dead? He is not here, but he has risen." (Luke 24:1-6)

The women looking up, unable to comprehend what they were seeing. Were they talking? Or were they too dumbfounded to speak?

The angel went on,

> "Remember how he spoke to you while he was still in Galilee, saying that the Son of Man must be delivered into the hands

> of sinful men, and be crucified, and the third day rise again." (vs. 6-7)

The women look at each other. Yes, he *did* say that! Why hadn't they taken it literally? These angels were using the prepared prophecies Jesus uttered earlier. He knew they didn't understand what he was saying at the time, but he also knew that they would remember him saying it. And it worked! They suddenly "remembered his words" (v. 8), and now, finally, they began to understand what he meant.

The fact that all the gospels have women being the first to discover the empty tomb is a clear sign of authenticity. Women were considered untrustworthy at this time. That's why they couldn't testify in court. You see the same distrust when the women reported what they had seen. The eleven thought it was "crazy talk" (v. 11). If Luke and the others were crafting a fictional work, they never would have had women as the first witness to the resurrection. That women were first points to Luke and the other Gospel writers being faithful to an account that actually happened.

Word Spreads

Luke names some of the women scurrying back to the eleven, but also mentions "the other women with them" (v. 10). We don't know how many women were in the area on this morning. That explains why different names come up in different accounts.

They excitedly told the eleven what they had seen and heard, but Luke adds that they told "all the rest" (v. 9). So there was a gathering of more than eleven men. We saw earlier their reaction: "But these words appeared to them as nonsense, and they would not believe them" (v 11).

Luke only mentions Peter running to the tomb, but John also ran with him (John 20:3-4). John also explains that it wasn't until they both entered the empty tomb that they finally believed, "For as yet they did not understand the Scripture, that He must rise again from the dead" (John 20:9).

In fact, even after this event, they *still* didn't understand. But for the moment they had the data of their own eyes to go on. This slowness to comprehend what was happening becomes important evidence for the resurrection. It's clear from all the accounts that the disciples were not expecting any resurrection. That lays to rest secular claims that the resurrection was dream fulfillment or hallucination.

Mary Magdalene didn't understand, even after all she had seen. After everyone had gone home, she stayed at the tomb, and the two angels appeared again and asked why she was crying. She answered, "Because they have taken away my Lord, and I do not know where they have laid Him" (John 20:13). It's clear she is clueless as to the real reason his body was missing. Jesus eventually showed up in person to set her straight.

On the Way to Emmaus

Luke gives us another story found nowhere else. It starts with two men walking to the village of Emmaus, near Jerusalem. Suddenly Jesus came up and began walking with them. As they talk, Luke says, "their eyes were prevented from recognizing Him" (v. 16). This could be a veiling from God, or maybe they didn't know him that well. Maybe they had only listened to him from a distance. Or, Jesus' appearance might have been altered a bit in his resurrection, because a number of people don't recognized him at first.

Jesus questioned them on what they had been discussing:

> One of them, named Cleopas,[1] answered and said to Him, "Are you the only one visiting Jerusalem and unaware of the things which have happened here in these days?"
>
> And he said to them, "What things?"
>
> And they said to him, "The things about Jesus the Nazarene, who was a prophet mighty in deed and word in the sight of God and all the people, and how the chief priests and our rulers delivered him to the sentence of death, and crucified him. But we were hoping that it was he who was going to redeem Israel. Indeed, besides all this, it is the third day since these things happened. But also some women among us amazed us. When they were at the tomb early in the morning, and did not find

1. Cleopas is named in this text, but the other man is not. Early church historian Eusebius says that according to Hegesippus (another earlier historian), Symeon became the lead elder in Jerusalem after James was killed. He was the son of Clopas, an alternative spelling of Cleopas. Cleopas, in turn was a brother of Joseph (Jesus' stepfather). If so, Cleopas was "a cousin of the Saviour." Eusebius, Church History, 3.11. Bauckham plausibly thinks Cleopas is named because he was Luke's source for the story. Richard Bauckham, *Jesus and the Eyewitnesses*, 39ff.

> his body, they came, saying that they had also seen a vision of angels who said that he was alive. Some of those who were with us went to the tomb and found it just exactly as the women also had said; but him they did not see." (vs. 18-24)

Their description of Jesus as "a prophet mighty in deed and word" was deficient. They must have been companions of the eleven, because they had heard the report from earlier that same day. But why hadn't they followed up with what they heard? Why were they walking away from Jerusalem as though giving up?

Jesus was frustrated:

> And He said to them, "O foolish men and slow of heart to believe in all that the prophets have spoken! Was it not necessary for the Christ to suffer these things and to enter into his glory?" Then beginning with Moses and with all the prophets, he explained to them the things concerning himself in all the Scriptures. (vs. 25-27)

This seems to fly in the face of our earlier arguments that Jesus knew people didn't understand his mission or Bible prophecy, and he accepted that. Here he clearly expected them to comprehend. The difference is the resurrection report they had already described. After the resurrection he expected people to connect the dots and comprehend the whole picture. In particular, he no doubt expected them to remember what he said.

Again we see the centrality of the role of predictive prophecy in validating Jesus' life, nature, and mission. No good explanation exists for how these passages predicted the future apart from divine inspiration. The documents are all provably written long before Jesus' life. In his post-resurrection appearances Jesus consistently challenged people to go to the word to understand God's great plan of the ages and his unmistakable verification of the whole package.

He agreed to stay with them when they arrived at the village. Then:

> When he had reclined at the table with them, he took the bread and blessed it, and breaking it, he began giving it to them. Then their eyes were opened and they recognized him; and he vanished from their sight. (vs. 30-31)

What an astonishing ending to the story! He was corporeal enough to break bread and hand it out, but then . . . a poof and he's gone! So was he a ghost? He refutes that idea later. Yet, Jesus' resurrection body did have unusual properties. He walked through walls. He appeared out of nowhere and disappeared. He ate food. We don't know the details of what a spiritual body is, but we know we are going to be given one when Jesus returns.

The two men were left gasping with amazement:

> They said to one another, "Were not our hearts burning within us while he was speaking to us on the road, while he was explaining the Scriptures to us?" (v. 32)

It's that burning excitement we can still feel today when God is speaking to us, usually through his word. When the Holy Spirit is opening your eyes to comprehend what God is saying, it's one of the rare pleasures known only to walking believers.

In their zeal,

> They got up that very hour and returned to Jerusalem, and found gathered together the eleven and those who were with them. (v. 33)

Back to Jerusalem

They said earlier that it was getting dark and the day was at an end, so by now it was dark. Ancient people didn't travel at night. There were no lights like today, and it was just dangerous. But these men felt compelled to find someone they could tell what just happened.

The eleven uttered their news first. "The Lord has really risen and has appeared to Simon" (v. 34).

The men from Emmaus told their story.

> And just as they were telling about it, Jesus himself was suddenly standing there among them. "Peace be with you," he said. But the whole group was startled and frightened, thinking they were seeing a ghost! (vs. 36-37)

Jesus must have had a keen eye for the dramatic, to show up at this very moment when the two men were finishing their story. And from nowhere, he pops into view. "Shalom!"

A spontaneous cry must have arisen from the group. Jesus tried to reassure them.

> "Why are you frightened?" he asked. "Why are your hearts filled with doubt? Look at my hands. Look at my feet. You can see that it's really me. Touch me and make sure that I am not a ghost, because ghosts don't have bodies, as you see that I do." As he spoke, he showed them his hands and his feet. (vs. 38-40)

Luke says, "Still they stood there in disbelief, filled with joy and wonder" (v. 41). They must have stood in silence, their eyes wide, their minds choking as they confronted the unbelievable. Something this far out would simply be hard to accept. It defies every law of physics and rationality. We, who know all about the resurrection, must imagine what this was like to those who never heard of such a thing. They were, as Jesus had said a few hours earlier, "slow of heart to believe."

> Then he asked them, "Do you have anything here to eat?" They gave him a piece of broiled fish, and he ate it as they watched. (vs. 41-43).

Opening Their Minds

That must have done it. Luke's narrative passes over to a time of Bible study. They probably spent plenty of time in the book of Isaiah. That's where God says,

> "I am the Lord; that is my name! I will not give my glory to anyone else, nor share my praise with carved idols. Everything I prophesied has come true, and now I will prophesy again. I will tell you the future before it happens." (Isaiah 42:8-9)

Then he follows with the amazing anonymous servant songs (Isaiah 42:1-9; 49:1-13; 50:4-11; and 52:13-53:12). They culminate in Isaiah 53. There Isaiah says of the Servant of the Lord,

> He was pierced through for our transgressions,
> He was crushed for our iniquities;
> The chastening for our well-being fell upon Him,
> And by His scourging we are healed. (v. 5)

And then he is killed:

> Unjustly condemned,
> he was led away.
> No one cared that he died without descendants,
> that his life was cut short in midstream. (v. 8)

After his unfair death, he was buried:

> He had done no wrong
> and had never deceived anyone.
> But he was buried like a criminal;
> he was put in a rich man's grave. (v. 9)

But the story isn't over:

> If he would render himself as a guilt offering,
> He [God] will see his offspring,
> He will prolong his days. (v. 10)

It's right there in black and white. After dying and being buried in verse 9, the servant's life is prolonged. It's resurrection! And the servant gets the last word:

> And the good pleasure of the Lord will prosper in his hand.
> As a result of the anguish of His soul,
> He will see it and be satisfied;
> By his knowledge the Righteous One,
> My Servant, will justify the many,
> As he will bear their iniquities. (vs. 10-11)

Here is the point all along. Jesus must have explained the substitution aspect of his death. That's what enabled him to "justify" the many. To justify means to declare innocent, or declare righteous. Here Jesus lead his followers into true, New Testament faith. And not just them.

> Therefore I will give him a portion among the great,
> and he will divide the spoils with the strong,
> because he poured out his life unto death,
> and was numbered with the transgressors.
> For he bore the sin of many,
> and made intercession for the transgressors. (v. 12)

Jesus concluded,

> "Thus it is written, that the Christ would suffer and rise again from the dead the third day. and that repentance for forgiveness of sins would be proclaimed in his name to all the nations, beginning from Jerusalem. You are witnesses of these things." (vs. 46-48)

Really? This little band of confused followers is going to proclaim this message "to all the nations?" How likely is that? Especially when you consider that the expression "to all the nations" (*panta ta ethne*) should read "to all the peoples." It's not referring to nation states, but to ethnicities. As we saw earlier, this amazing prediction is nearly fulfilled in our day.

At this point, or possibly at verse 44, Luke passes over about forty days. During that time, Jesus appeared to various people, including his half-brother James (1 Corinthians 15:7). He probably appeared to his other brothers and sisters as well, not to mention his mother.

John's account of the encounter with the disciples in Galilee happened during these days (John 21). So too, the confrontation with Thomas' unbelief (John 20:24-29). It seems likely that Jesus met with the disciples periodically, and to five hundred others (1 Corinthians 15:6).

Other Things

John reminds us,

> And there are also many other things which Jesus did, which if they were written in detail, I suppose that even the world itself would not contain the books that would be written. (John 21:25)

So we're left to imagine what all Jesus did during these days. Our knowledge is partial. In his companion volume, Luke summarizes his activities this way:

> To these [his followers] he also presented himself alive after his suffering, by many convincing proofs, appearing to them over a period of forty days and speaking of the things concerning the kingdom of God. (Acts 1:3)

And Then It Happened

In the final scene in Luke, Jesus is walking with a group of his followers a mile or two east of Jerusalem. We don't know who all was in this group. It could have been his disciples, or the approximately 120 followers we see in the next scene in Acts—the upper room.

We know from the book of Acts that Jesus "commanded them not to leave Jerusalem, but to wait for what the Father had promised" (Acts 1:4), The Holy Spirit was still not given, and ministry would be impossible until that happened.

Then,

> He lifted up his hands and blessed them. While he was blessing them, he parted from them and was carried up into heaven. (vs. 50-51)

Conclusion

Luke's first and second book overlap at this point. In Acts, Luke included the appearance of the "two men"—angels who promised he would return just like they saw him go.

With the ending of Luke, we still have only a hint of what is about to happen. It's essential that you study Acts after finishing Luke to get the rest of the story. Of course, I could only recommend my own work, *Experiencing the Book of Acts.*

At this stage in God's plan, Jesus had secured the victory. But it remained for the people of God to go forth and enforce the victory, taking back Satan's slaves to the freedom found in following Jesus. As the Gospel spread, thousands and then tens of thousands of people came to eternal life.

Curious what happened after Jesus' Resurrection?

Also By Dennis McCallum

Discovering God: Exploring the Possibilities of Faith-
Have you ever wished you had a short simple book you could hand to a non-Christian friend who is willing to explore the claims of Christ? This is the book. In easy to read prose, McCallum lays out the case for Jesus' and the Bible's authenticity.

Lessons from Genesis Vol. 1 and 2 –
No book in the Bible is more important than Genesis. In this two volume study, McCallum takes you through the story while addressing problem passages in a way suitable for general readers.

Organic Discipleship: Mentoring Others into Spiritual Maturity and Leadership-
McCallum and Jessica Lowery, wrote this text based on their combined 60 years' experience in fostering a disciple making church.

Walking in Victory: Why God's Love Can Change Your Life Like Legalism Never Could-
is a study on spiritual growth as taught in Romans 5 through 8. This passage is easily the Apostle Paul's most complete discussion on the subject. Easy to read and highly practical, this title breathes God's grace.

What should a real Christian community look like? What should its ethos be, and how should it function? If you are interested in these kind of questions, then Dennis McCallum's *Members of One Another* is the book for you!

- Dr. Ben Witherington

Spiritual Love: How to Build Deep Friendships and Marriages –
McCallum and his co-author, Gary DeLashmutt combine biblical insight with practical application in this study of relationships.

Also By Dennis McCallum

Christian Parenting: A Relational Approach - What does Scripture teach about parenting? What insights can we gain from science? McCallum has taught multiple courses on parenting over his fifty years in ministry. Here, McCallum offers the crux of his courses on the subject.	
Satan and his Kingdom: What the Bible Says and How It Matters to You – Balanced, biblical, and practical. Learn everything the Bible teaches and how you can respond.	
Liberation: Follow the Book of Hebrews Into a Life of Radical Grace- The lynchpin book of Hebrews is an indispensable guide to the relationship between the Old and New Testaments.